Meditative Reason

Revisioning Philosophy

David Appelbaum
General Editor

Vol. 14

PETER LANG
New York • San Francisco • Bern • Baltimore
Frankfurt am Main • Berlin • Wien • Paris

Ashok K. Gangadean

Meditative Reason

Toward Universal Grammar

PETER LANG
New York • San Francisco • Bern • Baltimore
Frankfurt am Main • Berlin • Wien • Paris

Library of Congress Cataloging-in-Publication Data

Gangadean, Ashok K.
 Meditative reason : toward universal grammar / Ashok K.
Gangadean.
  p. cm. — (Revisioning philosophy : vol. 14)
  Includes bibliographical references.
  1. First philosophy. 2. Reason. 3. Meditation. 4. East and
West. I. Title: Universal grammar. II. Series.
BD331.G274   1993   128'.3—dc20   92-26731
ISBN 0-8204-1991-5   CIP
ISSN 0899-9937

Die Deutsche Bibliothek-CIP-Einheitsaufnahme

Gangadean, Ashok K.:
Meditative reason : towards universal grammar / Ashok K. Gangadean.
—New York; Berlin; Bern; Frankfurt/M.; Paris; Wien: Lang, 1993
  (Revisioning philosophy ; Vol. 14)
  ISBN 0-8204-1991-5
NE: GT

The paper in this book meets the guidelines for permanence and
durability of the Committee on Production Guidelines for
Book Longevity of the Council on Library Resources.

Printed in the United States of America.

To my Teachers and Students

ACKNOWLEDGMENT

Certain portions of the essays of this book have appeared in whole or in part or in modified form in prior publications. The author is grateful to the following publishers and editors for their kind permission to publish these portions in the present volume:

1) Chapter 5 - "Universal Theology: Beyond Absolutism and Relativism" was originally published in *Religious Issues and Interreligious Dialogues: An Analysis and Sourcebook of Developments since 1945*, C.W. Fu and G.E. Spiegler, eds. (Greenwood Press, Westport. CT 1989. Copyright (c) 1989 by Charles Wei-hsun Fu and Gerhard E. Spiegler. Reprinted with permission.

2) Chapter 6 - "Meditative Reason and the Logic of Communication," with the exception of Part 2, was originally published in *Rationality in Thought and Action,* Martin Tamny and K.D. Irani, eds. (Greenwood Press, Westport, CT 1986). Copyright (c) 1986 by Martin Tamny and K.D. Irani. Reprinted with permission.

3) Chapter 7 - was originally published under the title "A Hermeneutic for Inter-Cultural Religious Life" in the *Journal of Religious Studies*, Punjab University, Patiala, India, (Autumn, 1984), Wazir Singh, Editor. Reprinted with permission.

4) Portions of Chapter 8 and Section 3 of Chapter 3 were originally published under the title, "Universal Relativity and the Holistic Mind" in *"Man's Search for Meaning in a Fragmented Universe: A Buddhist Dialogue with Contemporary Thinkers,"* Padmasiri De Silva and Henry O. Thompson, eds. (Unification Theological Seminary, Barrytown, New York, 1988). Reprinted with permission.

5) Chapter 9 was originally published under the title "Madhyamkia Dialectic and Holistic Psychotherapy" in the *Journal of Buddhist Philosophy,* Vol. 1 (1983) edited by Richard S.Y. Chi and Kenneth K. Inada. Reprinted with permission.

6) Chapter 10, "Meditation, Metaphor and Meaning" was originally published in *Indian Philosophical Quarterly* (University of Poona, Poona, India), Vol. 15, No. 4, October 1988. Reprinted with permission.

CONTENTS

Page

Preface · ix

Overview of the Essays · xi

Chapter 1: General Introduction— Meditative Reason: Toward Universal Grammar · 1

Chapter 2: Explorations Toward Meditative Reason · 45

Chapter 3: Meditation, Rationality and Universal Relativity (Introduction to Meditative Reason) · 77

Chapter 4: Universal Relativity: Meditation, Mind and Matter · 121

Chapter 5: Universal Theology: Beyond Absolutism and Relativism · 165

Chapter 6: Meditative Reason and The Logic of Communication · 207

Chapter 7: Meditative Reason: Foundations For Inter-Cultural Discourse · 245

Chapter 8: Meditative Critique of Pathology in the Human Condition · 275

Chapter 9: Meditative Dialectic and Holistic Psychotherapy · 297

Chapter 10: Meditation, Metaphor and Meaning · 341

Postscript: Universal Grammar, Natural Reason and Religious Discourse · 361

PREFACE

The following experiments in Meditative Reason attempt to show that the birthing of Universal Law and its expression as Universal Grammar has been a primary generative principle or moving force in the global evolution of cultural life. The very idea of Meditative Reason as the practice and articulation of Universal Grammar is itself an expression of this global evolution of Universal Law. Our philosophical investigations suggest that the presiding history in the evolution of thought in the global context is the emergence of Universal Grammar as the Universal Logic of natural reason. Our experimental findings show that this is equally true of the evolution of meditative thinking in "eastern" cultures and traditions as it is true of the centuries of evolution of the rational enterprise in the European or "western" traditions.

It is found that Meditative Reason and Universal Grammar are common universal explanatory and dynamic forces in the evolution of global discourse, in the evolution of human reason and of the human condition itself. Our findings suggest that there is a common origin and principle at the heart of eastern and western thought and cultural evolution— that in the practice of philosophy, in the development of religious life, in the emergence of the sciences and arts, and in the evolution of moral-political life— the historical birthing of the Universal Law is a presiding moving force.

Our experiments over the past thirty years suggest that a primary concern in the evolution of the human condition focuses on how we humans conduct our mind and discourse; and when our conduct of mind conforms to Universal Law and lives the practice of Universal Grammar, the universal force of natural reason, the powers of mind and language, the nature of truth and reality, are revealed in a universal light. Thus, our explorations suggest that there is a Universal Ethics for the conduct of mind— for right reason— and our clarification of Meditative Reason calls for a radical rethinking and revisioning of the evolution of global thought in the light of the emergence of Universal Grammar.

A.K.G.
Haverford, 1992

OVERVIEW OF THE ESSAYS

Background

If there is a perennial and universal theme in the global evolution of cultures it is the intuition and realization that there is and must be a Primordial Origin that is the vital foundation and source of all that exists. This intuition has played out recurrently in a range of classical cultures with remarkable diversity. It is deep in the Judaic Biblical origins in the revelation of the Infinitely Unitive nature of the Living God in whom and from whom all reality flows. It resonates profoundly in the Biblical religions of Christianity and Islam which build upon the disclosure of Divine Unity and Living Presence in the Living Infinite Word or Spirit. An analogous intuition emerges at the core of classical Greek cultural life and surfaces in philosophical reflections of pre-Socratic thinkers and becomes central in the Platonic-Socratic vision of the world of forms and essences presided by the Universal Form of Goodness, the form of all forms. It is clear that this Supreme Form is the Absolute Foundation of Reality and is a generative and unitive force that brings order, regularity, being and truth to all that exists. This Unitive Force of Goodness is the very light of Reason that illumines the mind and makes things intelligible. In Aristotle's modifications of this intuition we find a magnificent opening up of the formal sciences of logic and ontology which gravitate to the articulation of the First Principles of Thought and Being, and in the articulation of the Universal First Cause or Unmoved Mover of all that exists. And with Aristotle we witness a birthing of the science of Reason and the early articulation of First Philosophy— the scientific articulation of What is First.

This intuition of What is First, of the Infinitely Unitive Force or Origin of all life and existence resonates at the core of Asian classical cultures as it does in African origins and among Native American classical cultures, and other classical cultures across the spectrum of the global evolution of cultural life. In the Indian cultural origin this Intuition is the very essence of Vedic Scriptures and Upanisadic texts. Here we see in Hindu origins the revelation of the Primordial Sacred Symbol, AUM, the foundation and origin of all names and forms, of all that exists, of all life and intelligence and discourse. In these scriptures we see both the wealth of Diversity and Unity of disclosures of this Original Principle which is the very life and light of mind, discourse and world. This intuition into the Infinitely Unitive Powers of What is First reveals that there must be a profound Unity between the true nature of Consciousness or Self (Atman) and the Infinite Original foundation or cause of all that exists— the Absolute Infinite Brahman. So deep is this Original Living Unitive Force or

Presence that it cannot be thought or objectified in the conventional methods of everyday mind.

Similarly, in contrast to the Hindu discourse of What is First we find in the teachings of Buddha a remarkable breakthrough into the disclosure and direct encounter of What is First. The Buddha's strategy for the emancipation of human life from the bondage and suffering of conventional modes of human existence is radically to let go of all forms of objectification of What is First and come to the direct existential encounter of Absolute Emptiness— Sunyata. It is remarkable that the Buddha's enlightenment concerning What is First would stand in such apparent stark contrast to the revelations of the Absolute Infinite Presence of the Universal Self or Divine Being. Nevertheless, it is apparent that the articulation of What is First has played out in a magnificent diversity of narrative forms across the range of global cultures.

Thus, in classical Chinese origins we find profound disclosures of What is First in the teachings of Confucius in his articulation of the Mandate or Way of Heaven— the revelation of the Universal Moral Law at the core of his Humanism. Again, in a remarkable contrast we find profound revelations of What is First in the meditations of Lao Tzu concerning the *Tao,* the Absolute Unitive Nameless Field which is the foundation and source of all that exists. And as we scan a wider range of classical cultures it becomes evident that the diversity of articulations of What is First proliferates. In a range of African cultures we see diverse strategies for articulating and honoring What is First. For example, in the cosmology of Bantu religion and philosophy we see the focus on the Original *Vital Force* that rules the Universe. And so on.

Despite the wide variety of cultural modes of recognizing, articulating and celebrating What is First it becomes apparent upon deeper analysis that in one way or another diverse cultural forms of life gravitate to and focus upon the profoundly *Unitive* Powers of What is First. It appears that there is a latent consensus that this Origin of life and existence must be Absolutely and Infinitely Unitive, Universal and All-encompassing, First and Original, the presiding and Organizing Principle that generates and orders the Universe and thus makes things intelligible and lights up experience and existence with meaning and truth. And whether this Absolute unitive Origin is called *God, Universal Form, Absolute Presence, The Nameless, Universal Law, Infinite Spirit, First Principle, First Cause, Absolute Emptiness, Universal Consciousness, Nature, Divine Being,* and so on, it is clear that this Origin *functions pragmatically* and *existentially* as the presiding moving force that brings order, regularity, coherence, unity, diversity and relationality to the universe or universal field of reality. And it becomes apparent that these diverse alternative strategies, methods and narrative attempts in the evolution of cultures to make sense of things in virtue of the Unitive powers of What is First are attempts to express *Natural Reason* and its *Universal Law*. In this light it may be said that in one way or another diverse cultural experiments in the evolution of cultures are expressions of Natural Reason.

Nevertheless, for various reasons, the universal themes of Natural Reason and Universal Law have remained suppressed or eclipsed in the global evolution of thought. Despite the recurring Universal and Unitive theme at the heart of diverse cultural forms of life, the provincial, parochial and localizing ethnic forces in cultural practices work pragmatically to discourage, undermine or abort the full flourishing of the Universal Force of Natural Reason that lives in the heart of diverse cultural worlds. This, together with the failure to have an adequate Universal Language or Grammar for Natural Reason has been a real barrier to the clear vision and articulation of the latent consensus and common existential ground between and amongst diverse cultural worlds in the global context. For whenever we begin to think and speak across cultures and between worlds, to reflect and generalize universal patterns or features across cultures or religions we immediately hit the walls of localized languages and particular grammars of culture and experience which tend to displace, resist and eclipse the real universal common ground between forms of life. So it is both exciting and dangerous to venture into the uncharted space of inter-cultural universality and alleged unity or common ground. And of course this makes all the more vital and urgent the need to develop adequate technology of Universal Grammar or Language for the effective negotiation of Natural Reason across cultural worlds and language forms.

In this context of developing more adequate technology of mind for negotiating the space of Universal Grammar it becomes more apparent how the Unitive Origin of Natural Reason functions in everyday life and cultural practices. For the clarification of Universal Grammar or Language makes it clear precisely how and why the Infinitely deep and powerful Forces of Unity work to make language, thought, experience, existence and cultural life possible. It becomes clear why there must be a transcendental and operative Unifying Force or Field pervading all aspects of experience and reality; it becomes clear why there is and must be a Universal Common Ground between and across cultural worlds and forms of life; it emerges in deeper clarity how the Unitive force is the existential power of Natural Reason and Universal Law. For the clarification of Universal Grammar releases the latent universal and unitive powers inherent in all aspects of human life. And it becomes evident that it is the Unitive Force that existentially and pragmatically makes the Self possible, makes mind and language and thought work, that makes it possible for there to be a world of things, events, individuals and laws. It is the Unitive Force that grounds the local unities of all things— all names and forms, all words and concepts, and makes unity and diversity possible. Were it not for the operative presence of the Unitive Force nothing could be, nothing could work.

So the clarification of Universal Grammar and its Natural Reason opens the horizon all the way and it becomes apparent that it is not just in classical or modern cultural narratives of reality that we find the operative presence of the Unitive Force of What is First, but throughout all possible experience and in all forms of life, in all fields and disciplines and art forms. The Universal Law of Natural Reason operates and presides when the form of life in question has no concern whatsoever with thinking about or attending to What is First. In any form of life or cultural practice the Unitive Force of Universal Law makes that form of life or practice possible. Thus, in the cultural enterprise of doing "science," for example, even if it proceeds in a method of thinking or ideology that pays no attention to or even denies the presiding presence of the Unitive Force of Natural Reason it nevertheless existentially operates and makes that form of life possible. Thus, wherever Natural Reason operates, wherever mind and language and experience are found, the vital Unitive Force of Universal Law is pragmatically operative. In this way the Unitive Force of the Origin or Foundation of What is First is existentially functioning and presiding in every life form, in every life-world, even in one which insists that there is nothing First, Original, Universal or Unitive. For it must engage in Natural Reason and Universal Law to articulate its denial, declare its protest and vent its resentment.

In this connection we may now see that it makes all the difference for the existential quality of life how we stand pragmatically regarding What is First— how we live and conduct our mind regarding Universal Law, the Unitive Force-Field that operates in Natural Reason and its Universal Grammar. And this has been stressed in diverse classical cultures and world religions through the ages: as widely variant as the diverse cultural expressions of What is First may be, there remains a common intuition that human life works best when we are rightly aligned and in harmony with What is First, be it God, Universal Law, Nature, and so on.

There is a perennial recognition that this Foundation of Reality is fully active and somehow directly presides in the everyday workings of existence and the human condition, and that things make sense and life works in the highest way when the conduct of our life is in harmony with the Unitive Law expressed in Natural Reason. Our rational life thrives, we are in deeper touch with Reality, the moral quality and meaning of our life flourishes, our existential well being and health is augmented, the depth and authenticity of our religious life blossoms, the inner integrity and psychic life of the individual finds fulfillment, freedom and happiness, and there is moral and political well being in the polis when a community lives in true Unity with the Law.

On the other hand, one of the great lessons from the global evolution of cultures is that when our existential relation with What is First, with the Unified Field of Universal Law, is broken or severed this has devastating consequences for human life and the human condition. When humans live and conduct their minds in breach of Law and Natural Reason, all that is desirable in life becomes deformed and perishes— reason falls into fragmentation, incoherence and irrationality; we lose the higher powers of knowledge and lose touch with Reality; understanding and judgment become pathological; we lose touch with the true Self and the Community of Others; human relations become compromised and lodged in disorder and strife; our inner psychic life fragments and there is a fall from authentic meaning and truth; the quality of our moral and religious life is damaged and there are grave consequences for the human and natural environment. So the most urgent pragmatic concern in everyday human life is how we stand regarding What is First and our existential relation with Universal Law and Natural Reason. When we conduct our life in accord with Natural Reason life flows in a healthy and life-promoting way. But when we are existentially in breach of Law the opposite result follows and there is eclipse of God, Reason, Law, Language, Self, Mind, Reality, Truth, Meaning and Environment. In such a breach the conduct of mind becomes shrouded in darkness and existential pathologies of life result.

However, with the articulation and clarification of Universal Grammar certain fundamental and vital lessons already available in the global evolution of discourse come into focus and explicit clarity. It becomes apparent that it is our very conduct of mind— our technology and methods of minding— that is all important and decisive in determining how we stand existentially regarding Universal Law. It becomes more apparent that perhaps the greatest lesson in the evolution of thought is that the profound Unitive nature of Universal Law and Universal Grammar implies a great *paradigm shift* in our technology of mind. For the tools and innovations of Universal Grammar make clear in a way not hitherto possible that the Unitive power of Universal Law implies that Reality is a Holistic Continuum or Unified Field, that the Unitive and Unifying Power of What is First plays out into an infinitely deep Universal Domain or Unitive Force-Field comprising the Universe. Diverse classical cultures have insisted as their deepest and most treasured insight into What is First that it must be a Living Form, a Living Presence, the origin of Intelligence and Conscious Life. And this classical perennial insight is vindicated and brought into its more universal formulation in the space of Universal Grammar.

Here it becomes clear that human reason— the power and practice of mind and consciousness— stands existentially in an immediate Continuum relation with this Living Unitive Field of Reality; human natural reason is a consummate expression of the Living Continuum of Universal Form and this means that the conduct of mind, the method of minding, is Law-like and Law-ful when it flows harmoniously in Unison with the Unitive Powers of the Law. This is what it means for the conduct of mind to conform to Law: it means that it is Mind-ful when it thinks and judges and lives this Unitive Force-Field. For this is the very Light of Reason, the living form of Truth and Meaning.

The technology of Universal Grammar, as a method of minding in accord with the dynamics of the Unitive Force of Law clarifies the nature of natural reason and shows how and why a deeper understanding of the methods of meditative minding are the key to natural reason, for it is in the technology of meditative methods that minding rises to its Unitive and Law-like consummation. Characteristic of meditative minding— meditative reason— is conduct of mind that flows in unison with the Holistic nature of the Unified Field or Living Continuum of Existence.

This vital disclosure of Universal Grammar becomes more evident in the light of another fundamental lesson from the evolution of thought— namely, that the paradigms of minding which are centered in practices of ego-thinking inherently eclipse and violate the Unitive dynamics of Universal Law. This theme has echoed through the ages in diverse cultural traditions and the universal form of this insight comes into sharper relief in the light of Universal Grammar: the methods and dynamics of egological minding violate the space of natural reason by severing, eclipsing and *objectifying* itself, its world, its experience, its existential condition. By its nature it severs itself from the Unitive Force-Field and engages in a pernicious technology of mind which alienates it from the Continuum of existence.

It is impossible to exaggerate the pervasiveness, depth and persistence of the egological practices of mind in the evolution of the human condition. The habits of mind of the egological paradigms run deep in the human condition and it would take a more powerful, effective and superior technology of mind to truly root out and leave behind this deeply entrenched obsolete and dysfunctional ego-technology. In a sense it may be said that every important cultural advance in religious, moral, philosophical, scientific and political life has been a step away from the pernicious effects to human life of the practices of egological minding, and a step in the direction of the technology of Natural Reason and Universal Law. And in this respect it may be said that the global evolution of cultural life may well be seen as an ongoing confrontation and battle between the Unitive Forces of Natural Reason and the inherently divisive and fragmenting counter-forces of egological practices.

It is in this dialectical interplay of the technology of meditative reason and the methods of egological thinking that we may best see why the Unitive ways of natural reason promote and augment the higher flow of Life, while the habits of ego-minding work to the opposite effect. Indeed, it is apparent that the egological paradigms are always situated in the higher space of Universal Law and must essentially trade on the presiding forces of Unity and Relationality to even sustain the appearance of making sense and being rational. It is in this dialectical context that Universal Grammar clarifies another important classical insight in the evolution of thought— that it is the conduct of mind that is all important in shaping our experience. our world, our very existential condition. The egological ways of minding inherently eclipse the Universal Law and the Living Continuum of the Unified Field; it constitutively breaks from What is First in its very methods of objectification and severance of holistic or living form.

For this reason it is inherently skeptical about Universal Law, the Living Continuum of Reality, and all that this implies. For ego-reason constantly trades on the Unitive forces of Universal Law and benefits from its natural reason even as it turns away and denies the Living Law. And to the degree that an individual or culture is dominated by the egological methods of minding it will naturally be deeply skeptical about Universal Law, Foundations, Universal Form and meditative reason. Here it should be noted that much of the skepticism and negativism we have seen through the ages, and stronger than ever in our contemporary time, regarding Universal Law and Foundations and Living Form is due more to the limits and bondage to egological paradigms of reason than to any truly open and objective inquiry into alternative paradigms of natural or meditative reason.

In the light of Universal Grammar we see more readily that egological minding by its nature generates boundaries, artificial limits, walls and barriers to open healthy inquiry and communication. It tends to reduce living dynamic Grammar to fixated, closed ideology and dogma. While the technology of meditative reason opens the mind in dynamic and dialogical growth and inquiry, the egological methods of minding bring closure, blinders and bind the mind in dogmatic ways, and place the open mind in bondage. Thus, it is not just the "content" of ideology and dogma that entraps the natural mind in fetters, it is the method and practice of ego minding that generates the bounds of mind.

Thus, it is in this historic contrast between the ways of meditative reason and the counter-forces of egological minding that we may appreciate how much is at stake for the well being of humanity. To say that we are rational beings may be well and good, but it makes all the difference to our being human whether we conduct our mind in the ways of ego practices or in the ways of natural reason. We have suggested in this preliminary background sketch that meditative reason is the highest expression of natural reason, for it is the method of minding that allows mind to proceed in unison with the Universal Law— it is the Unitive practice of minding that honors and promotes the Living Unitive Form of the Continuum of Existence. It is in the meditative technology of natural reason that the life of reason is enhanced; it is here that Universal Ethics or Right Reason expresses itself. It is here that we can directly encounter the Living Foundations of cultural life wherein the universal form of religious, moral, philosophical, scientific and political life truly meet and find mutual expression. And it is in this context that the devastating effects of egological practices become manifested. This is the general context for the following essays which are experiments and explorations in the clarification of Universal Grammar and Natural Reason.

The Essays

The essays of this book were composed over the past twelve years. They build upon an earlier series of essays which shall appear soon in a companion collection entitled, *Between Worlds: Alterity, Meaning and Truth*. The present essays were composed for different contexts and occasions, but they all have a central concern with the experimental articulation of Universal Grammar and natural or meditative reason. While the earlier essays of *Between Worlds* struggle with the difficult passage to the higher paradigm of meditative reason, the present essays are performative explorations within the paradigm of meditative reason and Universal Grammar. This paradigm of natural reason, deeply rooted in the classical religious and philosophical traditions, and under ongoing evolution and emergence through the centuries, must be engaged in a first person performative spirit. Meditative reason, by its very nature, cannot be externally thematized or objectified in the ways of egological practice. Rather, meditative or natural reason calls for direct first person encounter— the participant is invited to experiment in the direct enactment and performance of the paradigm and its methods of conducting mind. Accordingly, the reader is invited to attempt to set aside egological habits of thinking, or to be self consciously and self critically watchful and sensitive to the habits and methods of minding and attempt where possible to engage directly the paradigm of meditative reason which is being experimentally articulated and tested throughout the essays.

Chapter 1 is a general introduction opening up the theme of the perennial quest for Universal Grammar and the Universal Logic of Natural Reason and language. It is suggested that there is a Universal Law inherent in Reality— in consciousness, language, experience, nature, and in the human condition— that presides over all cultural life. This Universal Form or Principle is found to be a generative Force which expresses itself as a Universal Unitive Field or Continuum— the foundation of all life and existence. This chapter opens the diverse themes of meditative reason showing that the quest for Universal Grammar or Law has been a presiding existential and pragmatic force shaping cultural evolution. This is illustrated by focusing on the exemplars of Greek and Indian philosophical origins of meditative reason. Here it becomes apparent that the generic understanding of meditative reason centers on the conduct of mind in its direct unitive encounter with the Universal Law or Continuum of Reality. What marks off meditative or natural reason is precisely this original unitive conduct of mind beyond the naive and uncritical egological paradigms of minding. In this context the mutual terms "reason" and "meditative" are expanded to their more formal and generic senses and we see that the dynamics of meditative reason are being opened up in different and related ways in the Greek and Indian philosophical origins.

One pressing concern in the evolution of thought has been the need to excavate the deep structure or universal logic of rational consciousness, of thought, language, experience and world. Through the ages there has been an ongoing attempt to articulate Universal Form as a way to decode and decipher the grammar of life, experience and existence. And we have seen in the modern period of Anglo-american analytical philosophy as well as in the continental post-Cartesian phenomenology gallant attempts to clarify the universal formal logic of discourse and the grammar of thought. We have also witnessed the deep polarizations within the modern analytic traditions alone to get at the logic of natural language. *Chapter 2* is a more specific introductory essay which focuses on our earlier philosophical experiments in articulating Universal Grammar and the Logic of natural reason and natural language.

In particular we focus on our personal philosophical journey beginning with our earlier research in the context of contemporary analytic philosophy of logic and language, recounting the struggle to find the common ground between the classical Greek paradigm of logical or philosophical grammar with that of the contemporary grammars of thought opened by Frege, Russell, Wittgenstein, Sommers and others. One main focus in this struggle is our coming to realize that to the degree that egological paradigms of logic and reason dominate, logical form itself appears to be polarized between the great paradigms of philosophical grammar. And this brings into sharp relief the question of the nature of thought and the logic of Natural Reason. For if logical form itself turns out to be polarized and equivocal across diverse paradigms of grammar, then this raises troubling concerns for the rational enterprise. It is here that the turn to meditative reason and the unitive powers of Universal Form— the Unified Continuum of discourse— becomes vital in opening more deeply the foundations of Universal Grammar and the Universal Logic of natural reason and language. We suggest that as long as our thinking remains lodged within the egological paradigms of minding, logical form itself will be inherently self divided and polarized. It is through the meditative turn to natural reason that we open the horizon of the Universal Logic of natural language.

When Descartes attempted in his meditative experiments to probe more rigorously and deeply the foundations of mind, knowledge and experience he performed a magnificent breakthrough in the evolution of European thought. When he entered dramatically into the meditative voice of the *Cogito* a new era in the evolution of natural reason was inaugurated. However, in his own struggles with the pre-meditative technology of egological mind the rigorous clarity rightly sought for became sometimes garbled and confused. For the opening of the meditative voice enters a higher order to rational unitivity that calls for more powerful tools of thought— it calls for the clarification of the methods of Universal Grammar and a paradigm shift to meditative reason. The philosophical experiments of Husserl, Heidegger and Sartre made significant strides towards the horizon of Universal Grammar, and it is no accident that in the full maturity of his career Heidegger arrived at this horizon of meditative thinking. So it is apparent that the advance of Natural Reason calls for a more rigorous meditative analytic which can make accessible the powerfully unitive space of the meditative voice.

In *Chapter 3*— "Meditation, Rationality and Universal Relativity" we attempt to explore and articulate the logical space of the meditative voice incorporating the valuable technological advances in meditative reason opened in certain eastern traditions of meditative philosophy. This chapter begins with the meditative voice and attempts to perform the paradigm of Universal Grammar and introduces certain fundamental features of meditative reason. The meditative narrative begins with the formulation of the Universal Law or Form governing all life and discourse and attempts a meditative articulation of the Unitive and explicative and analytic powers of Universal Form. It is found that the Universal Law of Natural Reason— the Principle of Universal Relativity— plays out in a primordial Unitive Continuum or Unified Field wherein all things mutually constitute each other and co-arise. The narrative explores the structure of this non-dual Unitive Field of Reality which grounds and generates all aspects of reality— nature, culture, evolution, discourse— and is the pragmatic foundations of experience. The emergence of the paradigm of Universal Grammar places the paradigms of egological mind under critique, and it is suggested that such paradigms of reason, discourse, experience, existence inherently fail to qualify as the Logic of Natural Reason. And in our meditative explication of the Continuum of discourse we begin to see more clearly the conceptual or categorial structure of the Unified Field of Universal Grammar. With certain innovations of meditative reason we are able analytically to open up the inner non-dual continuum structure of the universal categories and concepts of experience and world.

Perhaps one of the most urgent and enduring concerns in the evolution of cultures is the quest to uncover and articulate the Unified Field of Reality. This perennial quest, we now see, is not a casual option for rational inquiry— for scientific, religious, moral inquiry, but the very essence of the quest for knowledge and understanding— the life pulse of Natural Reason itself. *Chapter 4*, "Universal Relativity: Meditation Mind and Matter" builds on the previous chapters and attempts to develop a Universal Grammatology as a general hermeneutical method for all discourse. It is in the unitive force of the Universal Law of Relativity that we find the universal hermeneutical code for decoding the structure of rational life, the origin of experience and cultural formation, the grammatical code for world formation and for unlocking the deep structure of the Unified Field of Nature and Existence. For all fields are constitutively situated in the Unified Field of Universal Grammar which is the active and pragmatic foundation of all fields, disciplines and hermeneutical forms of life.

The narrative attempts to perform the paradigm shift from egological ontology to meditative Grammatology of Natural Reason. And in opening the deep structure of the Unified Field we find the universal hermeneutical code for the understanding and interpretation of diverse texts, signs, narrative fields, disciplines, hermeneutical forms of life. It is in this practice of Grammatology that the universal structure of Language and Discourse is found and this illumines the nature of inter-cultural discourse, inter-grammatical transformations, opens the common ground between Philosophy, Religion, the Sciences, the Arts and Cultural life in general. In this respect we explore the foundations of inter-disciplinary transformations and discover the universal common ground for a higher educational practice of the diverse liberal arts.

More specifically, it has been one of the persistent philosophical problems through the ages to decipher and understand the secret connection between mind and matter. And in the exploration of the grammatical Continuum or Unified Field of Nature— in understanding how the basic ontological categories of discourse and existence mutually arise in a Continuum we are able to get closer to understanding the Mind-Matter Continuum of Nature. It is here that we can situate the contemporary urgency in Physics to articulate and conceptualize the "grand Unified Field" in its theoretical discourse. The longstanding concern to uncover the unity of the sciences and the grand unified field of nature is right minded and vindicated by Grammatology, for this inevitable expansion of Natural Reason is essential for the substantive advance of scientific knowledge. Here we see that insofar as the sciences are lodged in the obsolete technology of egological minding, the open access to the Unified Field of Nature is self-eclipsed by this very conduct of mind. And egological habits of mind distort and impede the healthy evolution of scientific method— the methods of Natural Reason— to their full blossoming in Universal Grammar.

In thus opening up the foundations of the Unified Field of Nature the ground of the diverse sciences becomes accessible. With the clarification of the Mind-Matter Continuum in Universal Relativity we see more clearly why Nature exhibits a Living Form and why the "ultimate stuff" of the Universe is originally psycho-physical. This opens a higher horizon for conceptual and categorial advances in the theoretical and grammatical practice of the sciences of Nature. Thus, it is of the utmost importance in the advancement of scientific knowledge that the diverse sciences become more grammatically sensitive, become more in touch with the foundations of the Unified Field of Nature and become keenly aware of the ways in which the outmoded technology of egological minding materially blocks the open inquiry into Reality.

Perhaps it is in the foundations of religious life and Theology that these themes reach their consummate form. For one of the deepest concerns in the global evolution of cultures is the articulation of Divine Presence, Divine Nature, Divine Being. And although on the one hand it would appear that Divine Being, as Absolute, Universal and Unitive, as the Infinite Living Word, *must be* the universal foundation for all religious worlds and all forms of life, the religious and ideological battles have persisted through the ages and continue to rage in the contemporary world. And the localizing ethnic and provincial forces of diverse religions appear to compromise the Universal Revelation of Divine Presence. So we find another deep polarization in the human condition that calls for the creative mediation of Universal Grammar— the Grammatology of Universal Theology. *Chapter 5*, "Universal Theology: Beyond Absolutism and Relativism" carries the meditative narrative further in the exploration of the Universal nature of Divine Form or Divine Presence. In this context we see that the ideological idiosyncrasies of egological religious practice by their nature reduce and violate Divine Form. It becomes apparent that The Living Infinite Unitive Word requires the minding of Universal Grammar and inherently condemns the violent and pathological ways and means of egological religious practice. The meditative narrative of Universal Theology attempts to clarify the universal foundation of religious life and to make clear why Divine Form *must be* Univocal and Universal for all religious forms of life. In this way the common ground between diverse religious forms of life becomes more accessible and the creative grounds for true dialogue and conversation between diverse religions become pragmatically operative.

This narrative focuses on the inherent rational and religious pathologies that inevitably arise with the egological practice of minding. It is seen that in its constitutive eclipse of Divine Form (Universal Law, Natural Reason) the ego voice falls into deep indeterminacy, incoherence and incommensurability. In this context it is seen that the ego mind is lodged in alienation and a pernicious dynamic of self-splitting, existential fragmentation and rational pathologies of polarization. It becomes clear why the egological mind has repeated its pattern throughout history in fluctuating between the oppositional poles of absolutism and relativism without the possibility of true resolution in its own terms. We see that absolutism and relativism are two sides of the same egological coin, generated from the egological practice of objectification of its life and world and God. In the objectification of God or Divine Presence, the ego mind enters a form of religious life which constitutively violates the holistic, unitive, living presence of Divine Form. And so the explorations of Meditative Theology show that the pathological religious practices of egological life must reform and self-transform in performing the paradigm shift to Universal Grammar and Natural Reason. Divine Being— the Infinite Living Word, Divine Presence— reveals its Living Presence in the Unified Field or Continuum of Reality. It is in this non-dual structure of Holistic Divine Form that the depth of Divine Infinite Unity keeps its integrity. Here we find the Absolute foundations of all life and existence beyond the pathologies of egological absolutism and relativism. And it is in this profound Unitive structure of Divine Presence, beyond all egological objectification, that we see the Continuum between the Infinite and the Finite.

Still another perennial and enduring concern in the evolution of thought focuses on existential and pragmatic problems of human communication. Our natural reason rightly works on the intuition that in genuine and real communication we humans are able to truly meet in the unity of the conversational space of discourse and achieve a certain real consensus and communion in our existential condition. We have the intuition, if not the hope, that we can truly come to a meeting of minds and reach common ground and truly touch one another. But history has taught how difficult it is to truly communicate. Indeed, the human condition often seems to be a hostile place in which all sorts of divisions and barriers preempt communication and promote the opposite effects of conflict, strife, breakdown in human relations and violence.

Chapter 6, "Meditative Reason and the Logic of Communication" attempts to continue the meditative exploration of Natural Reason by investigating the universal grounds and foundations of communication. This experiment in meditative reason shows that it is the egological conduct of mind that generates the fragmentation of rational and personal space which leads to incommensurability, polarities, paradox, skepticism and the failure of discourse and communication. The narrative examines how the ego mind entraps itself in ideological pathologies which eclipse and preempt the possibility of true communication. In particular it is found that ego practice, in breaking from the Unified Field of Natural Reason and Universal Grammar reverses the existential priorities of discourse and falls into a pernicious practice of the objectification of meaning and discourse which fixates and literalizes the vital power of signs. By contrast, the meditative narrative shows that primary discourse and meaning are profoundly metaphoric, and it is in the unitive Continuum of natural language with its Universal Grammar that we find the foundation of communication. For Natural Reason and its Principle of Universal Relativity are inherently dialogical and show the higher rational space in which true unity and diversity can work. The full power of metaphoric meaning becomes accessible in meditative reason and here we find that natural language is inherently violated by the literalist egological practices, and works essentially in the metaphoric forces of Natural Reason. It is in the Unified Field of original language that the true meeting and common ground of communication is realized.

These themes are explored in greater depth in *Chapter 7*, "Meditative Reason and the Foundations for Inter-cultural Discourse." Here we find another pressing concern in the human condition— the nature of transformations and discourse between diverse cultures and life-worlds. And again we find the intuition of Natural Reason that we humans, as diverse as our cultural worlds may be nevertheless live in a common world and share a common reality. This chapter continues the meditative exploration of the nature of discourse between diverse cultural worlds and attempts to clarify the dynamics of inter-cultural discourse and communication and transformations. And here the tools and technology of Grammatology become vital, for it is essential to get clear on the nature of how life-worlds, cultural worlds, are formed and transformed. It is critical to appreciate the depth of real differences between cultural worlds in order to understand the foundation of inter-cultural relations and common ground.

In contemporary discussions much attention has been paid to the nature of conceptual revolutions, to radical and dramatic paradigm shifts in cultural life, etc. But these discussions have not had the grammatical tools of Universal Grammar that are essential for clarifying the origin of world-formation and transformation. In exploring the foundations of inter-cultural reason we see how the Continuum of Universal Relativity opens the common ground between diverse cultures and shows how transformations between diverse cultures can work. The pragmatic implications of this exploration for dealing effectively with violence and strife and breakdown of relations between cultures come to the fore. It is in the Unitive Space of the foundations of all cultural forms of life that we find the mediation between the honoring and preserving of a healthy and open ethnic and cultural diversity in the very midst of celebrating the unities and common ground between diverse peoples and life-worlds. It is in the space of Universal Grammar that we can see that with all the diversity of cultural worlds we still exist and live in the common world of the Unified Field.

In this connection we see another enduring and urgent concern in the human condition. It is the recognition that human life faces deep pathologies and forms of existential alienation that profoundly play out into all aspects of cultural life and infects the quality of life in the human condition. *Chapter 8*, "Meditative Critique of Pathology in the Human Condition" continues the meditative narrative and attempts to move more deeply to the foundations of diverse pathologies in human life. The analytical and hermeneutical tools of Grammatology help us to probe more deeply into the ontological and hermeneutical origins of pathology in the existential dynamics of egological life. The narrative attempts to uncover the deep structure and generic origin of existential disorders in the conduct of life. And here we see that a diverse range of pathologies— rational, religious, moral, hermeneutical, psycho-social, political, etc. have their roots in the malpractice of the egological mind. The narrative shows precisely how and why the egological malpractice of minding generates fragmentation, existential indeterminacy, incoherence and inner disintegration, and the breakdown of human relations in the polis. It is in this very conduct of ego voice that we find the roots of violence to self and others— the origin of diverse forms of human violence (ethnic, racial, religious, personal, ideological, etc.). Thus, the tools of Universal Grammar help to open a more generic diagnosis of the origin of human existential disorders and indicate the direction for the therapeutic overcoming of these pathologies.

This theme is explored in greater depth in *Chapter 9,* "Meditative Dialectic and Holistic Psychotherapy." This narrative builds on the findings of the previous chapters and strives to open the foundations of Psychology and meditative or holistic psychotherapy. The narrative goes in greater depth into the inner dialectics of the meditative analysis of the psyche and the origins of egological malpractice. We focus on important innovations in meditative dialectics in the teaching of the Buddhist dialectician, Nagarjuna, who made unprecedented contributions to the development of meditative reason. Here we see that meditative reason is inherently transformative, performative and existentially therapeutic. The central focus of the Buddhist dialectic shows how the conduct of the egological mind is the source of existential disorders and suffering, and how the therapy of meditative reason can overcome this pathological form of life. This insight is developed and applied to a range of existential and psychological disorders that have been explored in great depth in contemporary psychotherapy and psychoanalysis. Here it becomes clear that to cultivate the life of natural or meditative reason is to enter into a profound dialectic of therapeutic self-transformation that focuses on overcoming egological ways. To become rational is to engage in such radical self-transformation.

It is in this therapeutic self-awakening of the mind and voice of natural reason that the prejudices and pathologies of egological practices are overcome, and with the emergence of this meditative voice a powerful inversion and transvaluation in experience and discourse takes place. In actually performing the paradigm shift to the meditative voice the true origins of common sense, everyday experience, natural language and the ways of natural reason come to clarity. *Chapter 10,* "Meditation, Metaphor and Meaning," attempts further to perform this paradigm shift in the voice of reason and thus to make clear that the question of voice becomes all-important for philosophical reflection on the nature of discourse and on the human condition in general. This narrative builds on the previous findings and attempts to demonstrate performatively that there is no getting around the question of voice and the conduct of mind. The narrative shows why the conduct of voice or mind makes all the difference for meaning, truth and experience in everyday discourse.

It becomes clear that the Principle of Universal Relativity is the operative force in natural language and the functional and pragmatic principle that makes common sense work. The narrative performs the meditative phenomenology and hermeneutic in which natural language is found to be originally metaphoric in its powers, and in which it is found that the literalist discourse of ego practice is always abstracted or constructed or derived meaning, always trading on the inexhaustible metaphoric powers of natural language which make common sense work. In this meditative experiment it is seen that there can be no severance of the voice of the thinker-speaker from the Unitive Field of Grammar; it is found that the voice of the thinker always co-arises in grammar, and that the grammar or life-world of the thinker co-arises in the conduct of voice. This Chapter specifically picks up the themes of metaphoric meaning already opened in Chapter 6 and proceeds to show why natural consciousness and everyday common sense cannot work on the egological practice of naive identity, and can and does work on the Principle of Relativity— the dynamic principle of natural reason. It is in this "rough ground" of everyday natural language and natural meaning that we find the original continuum between the voice of the thinker-speaker and the Unified Field of Natural Reason or Universal Grammar. It is in the natural logic of meditative reason that we can see that the logic of everyday language is already in perfect order. Once the distortions and literalist pathologies of the egological mind are left behind the natural perfection of Universal Grammar which is always at work in everyday language is revealed. And so it is in actually performing the paradigm shift to the existential encounter of the Unified Field of natural language that the full powers of metaphoric meaning is experienced and the logic of natural language becomes manifest.

Finally, the *Postscript* attempts to bring the diverse themes explored in the essays together in a higher order unitive performance of the paradigm of Universal Grammar. In summing up the main findings of our meditative explorations we see that perhaps the greatest lesson in the global evolution of cultures is that how we conduct our mind is the most important factor in the quality of our rational life. Our very *being* as human beings turns on whether we conduct our mind in accordance with the Universal Law of natural reason, or whether the conduct of mind becomes deformed and falls into the malpractice and fragmentation of egological habits. If there is one presiding lesson that we may glean from the vast pool of experiments in the evolution of thought it is that the ways of ego minding have failed to give any adequate account of the workings of natural reason, and by its very nature entrap human life in pernicious and pathological patterns that diminish life, eclipse the Universal Law and undermine our very humanity. The other side of this historic lesson is that we humans rise to a higher form of life and realize our common humanity to the degree that we individually and corporately overcome the pathological technology of ego minding and enter into the ways of natural reason which flow in harmony with Universal Law.

In performing the meditative turn to natural reason the human mind blossoms to its full natural holistic form and an astounding transformation in the experience and conduct of life emerges. When we situate our thinking in the fragmented and fragmenting ways of egological mind we find ourselves in divided domains in which we cannot see and experience the profound unity of religious, moral, scientific, political and artistic life. But when we proceed in a well-formed conduct of mind in the Unified Field of Universal Grammar we directly experience through this universal method of minding the existential meeting and communion of diverse fields of experience. In the living practice of Holistic Form we can encounter the Universal Law and directly experience the holistic nature of Self, Knowledge, Ethics, Science, Natural Reason and Religious life. It becomes apparent that it is in the universal *method* of minding that the meeting point of scientific, moral, political, psychic and religious life is realized. In entering the paradigm of Universal Grammar we see that the single most important step in the material advancement of knowledge comes with this dramatic turn to the universal method of minding rightly in the Law. And it becomes evident that this direct encounter with the Universal Ethics of natural reason essentially turns on the right conduct of mind: without this moral life degenerates into the pathological forms of absolutism and relativism; religious life becomes distorted and deformed; scientific life and method become compromised and undermined by egological malpractice; and cultural life in general suffers. So moral, religious, philosophical and scientific life all turn essentially on the right methods and technology of minding.

In this context of the right conduct of natural reason we see how the Universal Foundation of experience works in everyday common sense. While the egological methods of minding deform the Law and eclipse the Foundations of natural reason, the right conduct of mind which refuses to reify, fixate and objectify the Living Law *lives foundationally* in a way that avoids the now well documented egological pathologies of foundationalism. For the foundational power of the Unified Field of Universal Grammar is not "transcendent" or far away from everyday common sense; rather, it is the very life-pulse of everyday natural reason. And in this foundational method of minding in the Universal Law we can clarify the nature of Truth between diverse worlds. The Universal Standards and Criteria of Truth and Right Conduct for any form of life come to clarity and we encounter the true source of Objectivity in the conduct of Ethics, Scientific Method and Religious Life. It begins to emerge that the form of life which is conducive to the higher realization of Unitivity moves in the direction of Truth; and that form of life which, through egological malpractice, produces greater fragmentation, divisiveness, incoherence and strife moves in falsity and against the practice of Universal Law.

Thus, how we conduct our mind is the most vital and urgent issue facing the human condition. *We are as we conduct our mind*, and the egological conduct of mind deforms our very *being*. Here it may be said that the right conduct of mind is our ultimate concern, a matter of Life and death, the very essence of what it means to be human. And we realize our true *human potential* when we advance to the higher individual and corporate practice of natural reason and live in the paradigm of Universal Grammar. We humans are holistic beings and we become more fully human in entering the Universal Ethics of Right Reason. For being human is the consummate moral and rational art— the right conduct of mind, of our very being, according to Universal Law. It becomes apparent that Right Reason *is* Universal Ethics— and it is in this moral fulfillment of natural reason that we consummate our human form and enter into the highest practice of religious, scientific, moral and political life. And so this paradigm shift to the living practice of Universal Grammar is vital to our human well being, perhaps the most pressing existential priority in the evolution and advancement of our human condition. In this healthy blossoming of natural reason we come closer to realizing how it is possible authentically to honor true diversity in human forms of life without undermining the vital unity and common ground that is the essence of our humanity.

Meditative Reason

CHAPTER I

MEDITATIVE REASON: TOWARD UNIVERSAL GRAMMAR

PREFACE

The Current State of East-West Discourse

East-West discourse has developed remarkably over the past twenty years and perhaps it is timely to stand back a bit and try to get a self conscious reading on the current state of the evolving discourse. On this occasion it would be good to see if we could measure the progress already made and formulate the presiding concerns that would contribute to a deepening of this evolving conversation.

On the one hand, from the sheer volume of texts that have emerged in this area of discourse in recent years we might get the impression that we have come quite far, and that this fledgling field has come of age and gained respectability in academic discourse. We have seen a flood of important translations of classical texts in a range of eastern traditions ranging from India to China and Japan. The Kyoto School has become fairly well known on the international scene through the writing of Nishida, Nishitani and Abe. A rich diversity of texts in the various Indian traditions have become available to the English speaking world. Western classical and modern texts have been carefully studied by eastern philosophers. And a range of interesting and challenging comparative studies have been produced over a wide variety of topics and authors in the eastern and western traditions. We have seen interesting comparative discussions of such topics as "Derrida and Nagarjuna," "Heidegger and Shankara," "Wittgenstein and Buddhism," to mention only a few.

On the other hand, as we pause to take a hard critical look at the current state of the dialogue it is timely to wonder how much progress we have made on the deepest challenges facing the enterprise of philosophy east and west. One obvious challenge is the need to understand and explain how discourse between such apparently variant universes of discourse is possible. We seem to take for granted that we can make effective and intelligible comparative judgments between the discourse of Derrida and Nagarjuna, or between Heidegger and forms of Zen, etc. And indeed, it seems quite legitimate and illuminating to do so. But this apparent fact highlights the need to come to terms with the obvious hermeneutical concern: how is intelligible discourse between profoundly diverse philosophical worlds, narrative forms of life, possible? Is there a common ground or shared universal field between diverse philosophical narrative worlds?

It would seem that this is the most intriguing question we might ask in the context of east-west discourse. For if there is, indeed, a universal common ground out of which eastern and western thought has emerged, and which grounds our ongoing dialogue and comparative inquiry, it would be of paramount importance directly to thematize this issue and try more self-consciously to come to terms with it. And so we propose to inquire into this question in the following essay: Is there a universal grammar of thought - east and west? Is there a Universal Unified Field for human thought? Is it possible directly to investigate, articulate, formulate, explicate this Unified Field of discourse? To what extent have the diverse philosophical narratives of east and west already attempted to make this alleged Universal Field manifest? How can texts situated in eastern modes of meditative thought which purport to be beyond conventional forms of discursive reason enter into rational transformations and intelligible comparisons with texts which *are* situated in such discursive reason? Is there a higher Dialectic of Reason that is being played out in the evolution of global philosophy? Is there a Universal Grammar that is powerful enough not only to embrace the rich diversity of texts within the eastern meditative traditions, and the diversity of texts within the evolution of Greco-european thought, but which also presides over the global evolution of thought east and west? Even if we take the position that there is no pre-given "common ground" or "unified field", for this is precisely what is yet to be negotiated in an open ended conversation, the very same issues are raised, and call for priority attention. The following essay is an attempt to explore these and related questions. We suggest that there is such a Universal Grammar of Thought.

PART 1: INTRODUCTION

Meditative Reason and the Perennial Quest for Universal Grammar

The deepest drive in human thought, east, west or other, has been to bring to articulate clarity the primal condition, principle, form, law or presence that universally presides over all life, existence, discourse. For it appears that there is a latent consensus among the diverse philosophical traditions and narratives that natural reason is constitutively a quest for the full expression and realization of Unity. It appears that inherent in Reason or consciousness or Intelligence is a supremely powerful Unitive presence or force that rules over experience and discourse. In this context no philosophical or cultural narrative or world-view can escape having to come to terms in one way or another with this Original Presence. And global history has shown again and again that every attempt to deny, reject, eclipse or dis-confirm this Presiding Original Presence can only dialectically confirm in the end that there is something higher that is given, and which makes it possible to think, experience and engage in discourse in the first place. It would be helpful in our global context to call this perennial quest for What is First, "First Philosophy" or "Formal Philosophy". We call it "formal philosophy" because the diverse range of philosophical traditions which have attempted to disclose What is First have often seen this Original Condition as Universal Form, Law, or First Principle.

The global history and evolution of Formal or First Philosophy encompasses a vast range of traditions, texts, philosophical or religious strategies, and forms of thinking and writing. In the Indian traditions, for example, it encompasses such diverse narrative forms as the *Upanisads,* the *Bhaguvudgitu,* Shankara's great *Commentary on the Brahma-sutras,* texts in the Buddhist traditions such as the *Dhamapada* or the *Karikas* of Nagarjuna, and so on. In the Chinese or Japanese traditions it would encompass the teachings of Confucius, Lao Tzu, Mencius, and of Dogen, and Nishida. And in the Greco-european traditions it would encompass texts and authors as diverse as Plato, Aristotle, Descartes, Kant, Hegel Husserl, Frege, Wittgenstein, and Heidegger.

The suggestion that these widely variant thinkers, texts and traditions share a deep common concern, are situated in a universal common ground and even gravitate to a latent common consensus, strains our philosophical imagination, to say the least. For within the evolving Indian traditions alone, there appears to be such deep and perhaps incommensurable differences between the Hindu meditative texts and the Buddhist meditative methods, as epitomized in the diverse hermeneutical methods of Shankara and Nagarjuna, for example, that there does not appear to be a common universal "logic" of meditative thinking. The meditative methods of Shankara, for example, approach What is First as the realization of Brahman, the Absolute, the realization of Atman or the true Universal Self. Whereas the meditative dialectic of Nagarjuna, in purporting to clarify the true teaching of Buddha, attempts to realize What is First as the realization of Sunyata or Absolute Emptiness. So it is already a radical challenge to demonstrate that there is a Universal Logic of meditative thinking being played out in these contrasting approaches to What is First.

Our attempt to discern a universal rational space for Global First Philosophy appears even more strained if we look at the patterns of thought that have characteristically recurred in the evolution of the Greco-european traditions. For example, we see at an early stage such a deep polarization between the narratives of Parmenides and Heraclitus, the former stressing the absolute universality of Being and the latter stressing the absolute universality of Becoming, that Rational Space itself seems to be polarized into incommensurable alterity. And here Plato's great attempt to save Absolute Reason by finding a creative synthesis between these polar narratives appears to raise more questions than it purports to solve. Plato inaugurates the European tradition of rationality in playing out the paradigm of discursive and dialectical thinking, reasoning and argumentation, dialogue and conversation. Here we find a movement of transcendental thinking, as contrasted with meditative thinking, which moves upwards in ever higher universality to the presumed Universal Form.   So we find in Plato a paradigm of First Philosophy which approaches What is First— The Absolute Universal form of Goodness— through the methods of dialectical, discursive and transcendental Reason. Thus, through the methods of Reason Plato confirms that there is a Universal Principle or Form which is Absolutely First and which makes existence, thought, experience, discourse possible.

We may well wonder whether this paradigm of Formal Philosophy through the rational methods of dialectical and transcendental thinking shares any common ground with the methods of meditative thinking we find in the paradigms of Formal Philosophy, for example, in Shankara or Nagarjuna. For the term "reason" is often taken to be synonymous with discursive reasoning, predicative or propositional thinking, and with dialectical and transcendental movements of thought. And "meditative thinking" is often taken to indicate an "extra-rational" radical form of thought which purports to be pre-predicative and beyond discursive forms of reason. Typically, the meditative mind sees itself as performing a radical deconstruction of the ego-centered voice together with its discursive methods of "rational thinking". The meditative narratives characteristically present themselves as moving beyond the space of ordinary conventional thought and discourse to a higher space where "reason" is silenced.

Nevertheless, upon deeper critical reflection it begins to become apparent that there are important analogies and common interests between transcendental reason and meditative dialectics. Both forms of thought are concerned with dialectical movement of thought and transformations of understanding to higher truth. Both attempt to open a path to what is Absolutely First— to original conditions or foundations, to Universal Law. Both forms of critique involve a certain deconstruction and distantiation from conventional mind, conventional "reason" and the ways of "common sense". Indeed, one may well wonder whether the radical expansion to primal Rational Intuition of Goodness in Plato's thought is not profoundly analogous to meditative transformations we find to Original Consciousness in such texts as the *Upanisads* or *Bhagavadgita*. Plato insists, in approaching the Universal Form of Goodness, that it is beyond "truth" and "being" and far nobler. And this has deep resonances with the meditative disclosures that AUM, Atman, Brahman is beyond conventional predication and discursive thought.

These common interests between the highest telos of discursive reason and meditative dialectic suggests that there is a higher Universal Reason at work in both forms of thinking. It stands to Reason that What is First, Absolutely Original, whether we call it "Goodness", AUM, "Atman", "Sunyata" or "Tao"... should preside over all forms of thought and discourse, whether meditative or discursive. It would seem that when we truly begin with the Beginning, with What is First, all possible forms of thought, experience, culture, are found necessarily to be under its presiding universal jurisdiction. If discursive reason self-transforms dialectically in transcendental thinking to a higher form of mind in encountering What is First, or meditative methods radically deconstruct the dualistic structures of ego-centered mind to come into Presence of What is First, these alternative forms of critical thinking follow the same Universal Law. It is this Universal Law or Original Form that opens the space of Universal Reason— the universal common ground of all possible forms of thinking and discourse. And we use the term "Meditative Reason" as a synonym for this Universal Reason.

We suggest then, that Meditative Reason is the universal form of reason which finds expression in meditative thinking and in various forms of discursive thinking including dialectical and transcendental movements of thought. Meditative Reason is the universal space of all forms of thinking and thus presides in the workings of everyday thought or common sense. The Universal Space of Meditative Reason is the original common ground in which all possible narratives and philosophical universes of discourse are situated. We suggest that the disclosure of Meditative Reason as the expression of Universal Law or What is First is the highest telos in all forms of inquiry, especially in the dialogical inquiry of east-west explorations, indeed of all philosophical inquiry. For what is Absolutely First, in whichever avenue of thought it is approached, discloses itself as a beginningless and endless Unitive Force which is the Continuum of all possible narrative forms of life. So Meditative Reason proceeds in an Original Continuum or Unified Field which is the space of Universal Grammar. It is this Universal Grammar of Thought which is essentially played out in diverse forms of thinking— meditative, discursive, transcendental or in everyday common sense. Here it may be said that First Philosophy or Global Formal Philosophy, is the exploration of Meditative Reason, the Unified Field or Universal Continuum of all narratives, the articulation of the Universal Grammar of Thought.

Let us reflect on this theme further. We are suggesting that there is a Universal Logic to meditative thinking, indeed to all forms of thinking, and the various methods, styles, approaches, dynamics employed by diverse teachers in meditative praxis are special expressions of Meditative Reason. This means, for example, that despite ethnic differences and ideological alterity between diverse meditative texts, there are universal dynamics and features to meditative thinking. It is this presiding presence of Meditative Reason with its Universal Grammar that would allow us to find common ground and rational transformations between, for example, the discourse of Shankara and the dialectics of Nagarjuna, or between the *Bhagavadgita* and the *Dhamapada*.

But Meditative Reason is the highest fulfillment of meditative thinking in another sense as well. For we have suggested that one characteristic feature of meditative thinking, whether Hindu, Buddhist, Zen or other is that it radically questions and deconstructs the ego-centered voice with its constitutively dualistic narrative forms. The meditative narratives typically speak in a mediative voice which purports a profound non-dual unity and which inherently deconstructs the egological mind which is centered in self-identity and its perniciously polarizing duality. Indeed, in its diverse strategies, meditative narratives attempt to teach that the egological life is a life of suffering and bondage and that true liberation comes with a radical overcoming of this condition in one way or another. In stressing this distantiation from ego-existence (which is always found to be fixated in reification, objectification, self-splitting, and a certain understanding of existential particularity) the meditative narratives stress that true consciousness, the right conduct of mind, involves rising to a higher form of life in which the objectification and particularity of the situated finite ego is deconstructed.

This deconstructive tendency of meditative thinking can lead to another form of dualism that makes it difficult to see how the liberated mind, in its profound unitive, non-dual phenomenology, can think and move and act in the practical everyday world. This has been the perennial challenge to the meditative narratives. They all rightly purport that liberated intelligence can truly live in the here and now, and they all involve a deeper understanding of moral praxis in the real world. They equally stress that the ego-centered mind is cut off from the here and now and is in a primal ignorance and unable to negotiate the real practical world. But this full meditative dialectical cycle from egological malpractice, to liberated consciousness, to effective moral practice in the here and now of everyday life (rightly encountered) has been a characteristic problem for the diverse meditative narratives. Nagarjuna was brilliant in insisting that in truly liberated awareness, there cannot be the slightest difference between *nirvana* and *samsara*. But a more developed meditative narrative is needed to make lucid the phenomenology of the everyday world rightly seen and negotiated.

This is precisely where Meditative Reason is most powerful and effective. For it combines the highest virtues of meditative thinking and discursive reason in a unitive narrative. It preserves the deepest existential immediacy of phenomena with the highest unitive, non-dual force of the Universal Form— it is the meeting point of the highest universal signification and the most abysmal existential presence and particularity of what is immediately given, here and now. Meditative Reason, as the unitive force of the Universal Unified Field, brings out the full holistic import of things in their mutual co-implication and co-arising. Thus, while at a lower level of discourse a line is drawn between the egological realm which is lodged in identity, polarization and duality, on the one hand, and the higher non-dual realm of higher liberated consciousness which achieves universality and transcendence from ego existence and particularity, on the other; in the higher narrative of Universal Grammar or Meditative Reason this dual distinction is itself deconstructed, as Nagarjuna has rightly taught, and the highest truth is revealed in the immediacy of the existential here and now. This holistic completeness of Meditative Reason, which is of course already implied in meditative thinking, is the full consummation of meditative thought.

Thus, Meditative Reason combines in higher form the virtues of meditative thinking with its powerful non-dual hermeneutic together with the virtues of discursive reason in its capacity to encounter and negotiate the existential immediacy of the here and now, once egological pathologies of reification, objectification, polarization and pernicious dualization of experience are deconstructed. This suggests that the full development of Meditative Reason is the deepest realization of the narratives of discursive reason and transcendental thinking. And of course this is a most radical suggestion since it implies a dramatic re-reading of the Greco-european philosophical tradition. For it suggests that the Universal Grammar of Meditative Reason has been actively presiding all along in the development of the diverse philosophical narratives in the evolution of European thought. This critical reading of the evolving tradition in the light of Meditative Reason would revise the more standard cannonical traditions of self-interpretation that have settled over the centuries and re-situate the classical texts in a more universal context. Such a re-visioning of the tradition would open up new evidence not hitherto given sufficient weight or perhaps even eclipsed by hermeneutical biases.

In this spirit let us quickly scan and anticipate how Global Formal Philosophy or Universal Grammar has been a motive force in the evolution of philosophical grammars over the centuries. We have already suggested in the paradigm of Plato that his transcendental experiment opens the way to a direct Intuition into Goodness as the Absolute Universal Form. We suggest that this was a classic opening to Universal Grammar and implies a profound Unitive Field for existence, thought and discourse. If we give full appropriate weight to this consumate breakthrough in Socratic-Platonic thought it would be seen that this was an opening to Meditative Reason. Furthermore, to place the polar narratives of Parmenides and Heraclitus in the space of Meditative Reason, would show how their apparently contradictory and incommensurable narratives may find their Univocal common ground and meeting point. For Meditative Reason, which is the narrative of the Primal Unified Field, precisely discloses that the meditative reading of Parmenides and Heraclitus mutually co-arise and confirm each other. What appears to be contradictory and incommensurable in discursive egological reason may be found to be mutually constitutive and co-confirming in the space of Universal Grammar.

In this context, we may discern a powerful unitive narrative in Aristotle's paradigm shift and revision of Platonic discourse. While Plato struggled with a deep dualism at the heart of his discourse between the world of forms, universal, essence, soul, on the one hand, and the existential particulars situated in the world of body, time, becoming, on the other, Aristotle attempted to move to a more primitive disclosure of Primary Being in his First Philosophy— one which showed that these two world-fields which were lodged in dualism in Platonic discourse were in fact inseparable existentially in his unitive paradigm: the form and the matter mutually constituted one another in a primitive individual or primary being. This innovation and revision may be seen as a classic move towards Meditative Reason, one which more coherently fulfilled Plato's important opening to Goodness as the Presiding Principle in all discourse. Aristotle's brilliant analysis of the primitive individual, if seen in the light of Meditative Reason, can contribute importantly to the expansion of narratives of meditative thinking.

Furthermore, it is well known that Aristotle made remarkable contributions to the development of Formal Philosophy in his articulation of an early version of the logistic thesis. In his *Organon* (Logical Writings) he began to make clear that human reason— thinking, inference, argument, discursive thought— is governed by formal laws or first principles. And this gives to Logic or Formal Philosophy a certain universal jurisdiction over all areas of thought or experience. For any particular form of thinking— whatever the subject matter or field may be— is taken to be under the normative or prescriptive force of the formal laws of predication.

The laws of thought in this respect purport to be a formal or universal grammar of discourse. And a general understanding of the "logistic thesis" is that the field of formal logic or rational form presides over all particular forms of thought and language and presumably has jurisdiction over diverse fields of human experience and of reality itself. In this way the formal laws of reason constitute a universal formal grammar of thought, language, world. Another way to state this classical logistic thesis is that the universal grammar of thought is a primitive and unifying domain of discourse— which is one opening to the presence of the Unitive force of Meditative Reason. This early local formulation of the logistic thesis presumes the presence of Universal Grammar and the Continuum of a Unified Field.

The evolution of this tradition reaches a certain breakthrough into Meditative Reason with the meditative experiment of Descartes. If we read Descartes' meditative voice in the light of Meditative Reason we find that he performed an unparalleled advance in the opening up of the unitive field of Universal Grammar. If we grant for the moment that Descartes, in the crucial transformation into the space of Cogito, left behind the egological voice and entered into the non-dual unitive field of meditative thinking, we get a powerfully coherent reading of the Cartesian project as it unfolds in the subsequent meditations. For in Meditative Reason, the "I am" is a pre-predicative meditative utterance which is inherently non-dual in its logical force. There can be no dual space between the very pronouncement "I am" and the higher form of existential presence disclosed in this primal utterance. We are suggesting that when Descartes experimentally crossed over into the Voice of Cogito he entered the powerful existential space in which thinking, existing, acting, speaking, meet in a primitive non-dual univocity. And of course his subsequent experiment in realizing that "God Is" follows the classical course of Meditative Reason as well.

In any case we are not suggesting that Descartes was always clear headed in his meditative experiment in being fully aware that he had ventured into a higher space of reason and discourse. For it is clear that he was struggling with the scholastic tools and predicative habits to express insights that call for a higher pre-predicative form of speech. What we are suggesting is that if we grant Descartes the benefit of the doubt, and take him at his word in reaching a more powerful and primitive existential self encounter and form of thinking, then we discover a Descartes that has not been sufficiently appreciated. When read in the light of Meditative Reason, we suggest that the deeper importance of Descartes' research begins to emerge more clearly. And we may find that much of the bad press he has received in recent years as the culprit obsessed with "foundations" is misdirected. On the contrary, we find something heroic in the Cartesian experiment— a brilliant breakthrough to true foundations in the Unified Field of Universal Grammar.

To continue our scan through the tradition, we find that Kant is another good exemplar who advances the unfolding dialectic closer to the full turn to Universal Grammar. For once the transcendental field of the Cogito was opened up by Descartes, subsequent thinkers had to come to terms with this voice of reason in the human condition. And if we place the Kantian experiment in the light of the evolution of Meditative Reason, we find classical moves inaugurated by Kant. His recognition that the person was a citizen of two worlds, the phenomenal and the noumenal; the insight that "knowledge" was restricted to appearances and not to "things-in-themselves;" that the space of freedom of will was in our noumenality where the Law of Freedom presides in pure practical reason; that the categories of judgment/predication must be restricted to the realm of appearance or phenomena; that every presentation to awareness is accompanied by "I am" (transcendental unity of apperception); these are important preliminary steps towards Universal Grammar. The horizon of the noumenal self may be seen as the opening to the meditative voice of the Cogito— the opening to the Unified Field of Universal Grammar or Pure Reason which is pre-predicative and beyond the scope of egological thought. This may be seen as an important correction of the Cartesian experiment in that it at least sees clearly that the noumenal space of presence— the meditative voice— cannot be approached naively in the discourse of discursive egological predication, which of course is a classic insight of meditative thinking.

Of course the Hegelian experiment may be seen as another brilliant advance towards the explication of Meditative Reason and Universal Grammar. His powerfully Unitive narrative of the unfolding of history under Absolute Geist (Spirit) is an anticipation in the material mode of the narrative force of the Unified Field presiding over all history, experience, culture, life. To achieve this dynamic dialectic Hegel rightly pressed the static and reified form of Identity to its dynamic and dialectical form which brings it closer to the dynamic law of Meditative Reason. This expansion to higher form of the principle of Identity in Hegel's narrative parallels the classical move in meditative thinking to deconstruct the pernicious forms of egological identity. And of course Hegel's powerful dialectical play of opposites in his phenomenology of mind comes closer to the Universal Law of Meditative Reason which reveals the profound co-arising and mutual constitution of polar opposites in one another— the feature of alterity in the Principle of Relativity.

Another important exemplar where we find a relentless dialectical movement toward Universal Grammar comes with the careful and systematic work of Husserl, which was later developed by one of his prominent students, Heidegger. Husserl took up the theme of the Cartesian Meditations and looked more closely at the new opportunity opened up by Descartes in arriving at the space of the Cogito. Clearly Husserl did not make the full move to meditative voice with its non-dual narrative form, but his deep intuition that it should be possible to reach a pure form of awareness which is free of bias and presuppositions— a pure phenomenology— is clearly an ideal and reality for Meditative Reason. It appears that Husserl instinctively moves to the right horizon where major progress could have been made, but he hit the walls of egological praxis and discourse, even in the alleged higher voice of the transcendental ego. It appears that his heart was in the right place, but his mind was still lodged in the dualizing ways of identity and discursive reason. Apparently it takes expertise and training in meditative methods satisfactorily to negotiate the meditative space of the Cogito. It appears that Husserl clarified Descartes' paradigm shift somewhat but still lacked certain essential tools of meditative thinking to bring out the full impact of Descartes' revolutionary advance.

In this connection we find the evolution of Heidegger's thought to the horizon of meditative thinking in his later career most revealing. Heidegger carried forth Husserl's experiments in phenomenology in new directions and attempted a radical reformulation of presiding first questions and concerns in the analysis of Dasein. And it is well known that he encountered certain deep barriers in following through on his earlier attempts, and in his later career made a significant turn to meditative thinking. It appears that the opening to the space of meditative thinking performed by Descartes continued to be played out in the evolving dialectic of European thought and haunted the tradition in one way or another until it emerged more explicitly in the radical turn performed by Heidegger towards the end of his career. We suggest that such an evolution is called for by the presiding dialectics of Meditative Reason and that this horizon opened up by Heidegger is one of the frontiers that must now be rigorously explored on the way to Universal Grammar.

To resume the central theme of the evolution of Universal Grammar in the conversation of discourse east and west, we suggested earlier that Meditative Reason (or Universal Grammar) at once consumates the ultimate telos of the non-duality of meditative thinking and the deepest strivings of discursive reason and transcendental thinking in its relentless attempt to articulate the existential presence of primary beings in their abysmal individuation. Let us now clarify this further. It may be said that the presiding principle of discursive reason is the Principle of Identity— the principle that a given name, form or thing has self-identity, self-existence. In Aristotle's clarification of the "laws of thought" or "first principles" it was shown that this first principle of Identity governs all predication and was also expressed as the laws of non-contradiction and excluded middle. In his transcendental argument for the absolute status of this first principle Aristotle stressed that without this principle of determinacy predication could not work: it is allegedly the condition that makes all thought possible. This principle is also the primary ontological principle that warrants the individuation of primary beings: to be is to be one, to be individual. So the principle of Identity is formally tied to the very being of individuation.

On the other hand, it might be suggested that the presiding principle of meditative thinking is the Principle of Relativity— the principle of radical and absolute Unity which implies that all possible names, forms, things must co-arise in a unitive mutual co-implicature. This principle of meditative thinking— whether articulated in the form of the unitive force of the Aumic field, or in the form of the principle of dependent co-arising that we see in the discourse of Nagarjuna— implies that no "thing" can have independent self-existence, and that all things are mutually constitutive and co-arise in a non-dual unitive field. In this respect it appears that Identity, as the principle of discursive reason, and Relativity, as the principle of meditative thinking, could not be more opposed and farther apart. It appears that meditative thinking inherently deconstructs the alleged individuated self-identical being and moves to a higher non-dual unitive field of co-relationality and co-arising; whereas discursive thinking with its principle of Identity gives a central place to the existential, individuated presence of determinate things. So given this apparent deep polar opposition between Identity and Relativity it is natural to wonder how Meditative Reason can purport to fulfill and univocate the deepest virtues of Identity and Relativity. We suggest that this is precisely the challenge that Meditative Reason must face. It is the challenge issued to us by Nagarjuna when he suggests at a mature state of his dialectic that there cannot be the slightest difference between "Nirvana" and "Samsara". And it is precisely the challenge taken up by Nishida in his attempt to develop a universal logic of Basho— a universal logic of absolute nothingness in which the deepest integrity of the historical individual is preserved. We shall call the Universal Principle of Meditative Reason which expresses Universal Grammar— "The Principle of Universal Relativity."

Let us focus for a moment on the origins of Universal Grammar in the Indian philosophical tradition. Our interest in Meditative Reason resonates deeply in certain classical traditions of Indian formal philosophy. In the Hindu tradition of formal philosophy, for example, the highest fulfillment of rationality is found in the realization of Original Unity or Universal Form. Here too it is presumed that there must be an original Universal and Unifying Form or Principle that has jurisdiction over all possible forms, over all existence, experience, discourse. In the case of the Hindu sage, Shankara (Seventh Century, A.D.) the classical Hindu teachings of the *Upanisads* are clarified in a systematic formal philosophy of Advaita Vedanta. In this philosophy of Advaita (Non-dual) Vedanta we find an insistence that the Original Presiding Form cannot be objectified or reified in any way, but must be approached through the method of meditative thinking. The Aumic Principle— that all things, all names and forms, derive from AUM— is clarified by Shankara in his grammar of Advaita. The Universal Principle that governs Reason, Mind, Experience, Discourse entails a non-dual Unified Field— the Universal Field of Brahman (AUM) - which is the universal context of all intelligibility. The phenomenology and hermeneutics of Shankara demonstrate how this Aumic formula renders language, thought and experience intelligible. We have suggested that this supposed Original Principle, Form or Presence is in striking ways analogous to Plato's original principle of Goodness, which is the form of all forms. It is helpful here to see Shankara's formal philosophy as a phenomenology of pure reason or meditative thinking which insists that rational form may not be objectified in any way. And this early version of Universal Grammar and genealogy of form attempts to explicate how all forms must derive from the Universal Unified Field of AUM.

In the Buddhist tradition of formal philosophy we find analogous but interestingly different explications of Universal Grammar. The Buddhist dialectician, Nagarjuna (Second Century A. D.), founder of the Madhyamika School, attempts to systematize the analytical insights of the Buddha by stressing that the only coherent account of discourse must recognize the original principle as Sunyata (Absolute Emptiness). This early attempt at Universal Grammar agrees with the Hindu narrative that the Original Principle must be accessed through the methods of meditative thinking and is beyond all objectification, representation or reification. This original principle of "Radical Emptiness" is also called the Principle of Relativity or Dependent Co-arising, and is discerned as an original unifying field for all names, forms, terms. Relativity or Co-arising implies a presiding unitive field wherein all possible things are constitutively co-relational. Here we see that the Aumic Principle and Relativity share a generic formal commitment to a profound original Unitive Field— the Unitive Field of Universal Grammar.

In the next two sections we shall continue our preliminary exploration of Universal Grammar by focusing first on Greek origins in the paradigm of Plato, and then on Indian origins in the Hindu tradition.

SECTION 1

Greek Origins of Universal Grammar

That there is an Original Principle or Universal Form that presides over all reality is a powerful intuition that has persisted in the evolution of thought in the European tradition. This intuition appears to be equally prominent in both the Greek and Judaic classical origins of discourse. And despite varying formulations of the intuition of the presiding Absolute Principle it is nevertheless evident that there is a common universal intuition generating the diverse narratives. Thus, in the Biblical tradition the Absolute First Principle is disclosed as an Absolute and Infinite Presence, as Divine Being, as the Original Word which is the source of all reality and out of which all names and forms are generated. Similarly, in the Pre-Socratic origins of Greek thought we find alternative narratives of the Absolute First Principle which appear to be not only at odds but even directly contradictory. For example, Parmenides presents the Absolute as the One, as Absolute Being, so profound in its Unity that it renders change, becoming and plurality to be illusory appearance. On the other hand Heraclitus presents a radical narrative of the First Principle as Change itself; as radical Flux, Becoming, Process, which renders any appearance of substantial Identity or Unity or Being to be illusory. So we find polar narratives of Reality which disclose the Absolute on the one hand as One, Identity, Being, beyond the possibility of becoming, and on the other as Difference, Multiplicity, radical perpetual Becoming, beyond the possibility of self-identity or being.

This primitive polarity in the disclosure of Reality inaugurated a crisis at the core of rationality and set the agenda for the evolution of the European tradition through the centuries and into contemporary times. Socrates and Plato confronted this perceived crisis directly and it may be said that on a certain reading of the Platonic dialogues the Socratic revolution in philosophy was precisely designed to find a creative synthesis out of the polar crisis and vindicate reason from the growing threat of misology and sophistry. The portrait of Socrates we get in the dialogues is of a passionate lover of wisdom who saw the crisis of rationality as a moral crisis and who attempted to re-center philosophical inquiry from the focus on nature to the focus on self-understanding and analysis. One standard reading of the Socratic challenge is that the apparently irresolvable contradiction between the persuasive polar narratives of Parmenides and Heraclitus undermined the credibility of the Absolute and opened the way for skepticism and certain forms of relativism and sophistry. For one intuition of reason appears to be that a contradiction cannot be real, and if the polar narratives of reality presented by Parmenides and Heraclitus *both* appear to be rationally compelling and irrefutable, then one may draw the conclusion that reason itself is incoherent and groundless. And this skepticism concerning the foundation of reason may well suggest that there is no absolute truth, no Absolute Form or First Principle, no objective science, but at best only subjective opinions and personal judgment. This scenario, it is sometimes suggested, naturally opens the way for an attitude that truth is a matter of personal taste guided by subjective interests and needs. And in cases of conflicts of interest and opposition in judgment the question of truth reduces to the question of marshalling superior force or persuasive power. Indeed, one characterization of "sophistry" is that it is committed to certain forms of relativism or subjectivism and rejects any suggestion of objective truth, universal standards or Absolute form. And Socrates is often characterized as the moral hero who challenged "sophistry" and attempted to reinstate a true rationality grounded in Absolute forms and principles and values. The very possibility of knowledge and science and objectivity were seen to be at stake and

Socrates, in the ultimate act of self-sacrifice for truth and principle, is taken to be the champion of Absolute Form, of Truth and Reason.

In this reading of the Platonic Socrates we find that Plato may be credited with performing a creative synthesis of the highest order and with clarifying the agenda of rationality that is still being played out today. In this respect it may be said that Plato is the founder of Formal Philosophy and Socrates is the embodiment of rational inquiry, truth and moral integrity. In Plato's vision of the highest Form, the Form of Goodness, we find the seeds of formal philosophy and the inauguration of holistic reason. This vision of the presiding Universal Form and the holistic or teleological nature of reason is presented in his *Republic* in a climax of the inquiry in which the blueprint of discourse is revealed. Here, in the summary presentation of the "divided line" model of the structure and stages of rational awareness, we find certain key ingredients of formal philosophy. Most remarkable in this paradigm is the revelation of a supreme universal form— the Form of Goodness— which is taken to be the form of all possible forms— the absolute foundation and source of all intelligibility, the Light of Reason itself. Plato stresses in this vision that the supreme universal Form is beyond Being and Truth and even more noble and worthy than these. It is clear that this ultimate Form cannot be known or thought or objectified as other forms perhaps may be, for as the very Light of Reason it is the source that makes all things intelligible and visible to the understanding. And of course it is no accident that Plato names this nameless Form "Goodness"— the supreme value— since as the Absolute, it is the source and cause of the existence of all things, of all names and forms. Nothing can be or be conceived which does not ultimately derive from this Original Cause and hence which in some way refers to, indicates or expresses the Absolute in its innermost being. It is the Good of all things, that which orders Reality, holds it as a profound Unity and Coherence and hence is the source of all meaning. The Absolute Form is thus the supreme Telos of the universe that places all things in Order and organizes Reality into a coherent rational unified whole. As the organic principle that Unifies the universal field the first principle of rationality and existence is disclosed as holistic. The Absolute Form is holistic in the sense that whatever exists is essentially a function of its relation to the Absolute and of its place in the unified ordered field of reality as a whole. Nothing can exist apart from its *relation* to the First Principle, and thus to the ordered unified field of Reality as a whole. Thus Plato's paradigm is essentially holistic and presents reality, mind, reason, meaning as holistic in nature. And so Formal Philosophy is initiated as the discipline which explores the power of Universal Form and its unitive or holistic force in organizing reality.

This holistic nature of Plato's paradigm needs to be stressed because it is all-important and sometimes slips by without being given sufficient prominence in certain platonistic traditions. It is especially important because the holistic paradigm of mind and reason has been deeply formative of European culture through the centuries, and when it has not emerged to explicit awareness as it did in Platonic discourse, it nevertheless presides pre-consciously in the conscience of reason. It is the primitive intuition we spoke of earlier that there is an Absolute Principle which generates all reality and holds all things together in a unitive universal field. This presiding Universal Form or Presence orders the universe and is the source of intelligibility and coherence. In the blueprint of the "divided line" we see that reason is successful to the degree that it achieves systematic unity in rising to ever higher coherence under a unifying principle. Similarly, we see that knowledge is accomplished to the degree that it follows the path to the Universal Unitive Form. The higher the realization of inner unity the higher the order of knowledge, until knowledge is consummated in wisdom, which is the direct revelation or intuition of Goodness itself, which is beyond any objectification of knowledge, truth or being. This vision of mind, reason, knowledge, has in one way or another, consciously or pre-consciously influenced the evolution of the culture.

The genius of Plato in articulating an early version of the holistic paradigm is that it opened a higher horizon in Reason for coping with the appearance of incommensurable opposition, polarity, contradiction in the disclosure of reality. In facing the crisis in rationality precipitated by the appearance of irresolvable contradiction in the polar narratives of Parmenides and Heraclitus, Plato attempted to vindicate Reason by showing that the Absolute First Principle is untouched by contradiction and can cope with contradictory opposition, duality or polarity. Plato, in the blueprint of the "divided line" model, attempted to mediate and find a creative synthesis between the polar visions of Being vs. Becoming, Unity vs. Plurality, Rest vs. Motion, Identity vs. Difference, etc. This attempt at reconciliation of the apparent polarization of reality had limitations because it seemed to privilege one side of the polarity over the other; it appears that Plato sided with the Parmenidean narrative over the Heraclitean one, and valorized Being over Becoming. In this attempt at creative mediation Plato conjectured that the narrative of Being more accurately expressed reality, while the narrative of Becoming was lodged in appearance and thus participated in some degree of ignorance and perhaps even illusion. The realm of Becoming, in its involvement with particularity, change, flux, contingency, matter, the senses, etc. was designated as a world of appearance with some participation in un-reality. On the other hand, the realm of Being, the domain of intelligible form, of mind and reason, of changeless eternal beings or essences, of universals, was taken to be the real world— the domain in which there can be absolute standards, objectivity and genuine knowledge of timeless truth. So this distinction between "appearance" and "reality" seemed to open a resolution of the incommensurability between the polar narratives of reality, but it did so at the price of a possible ontological dualism or pernicious split at the heart of Plato's discourse.

So Plato's more youthful attempt to vindicate Reason left something to be desired. And ironically Plato himself was acutely aware of the dialectical difficulties in his model and was perhaps the keenest critic of the problems in his later dialogues, especially the *Sophist* and *Parmenides*. As his thought matured Plato apparently saw that the deep dualism at the core of his discourse— the tension between two domains or worlds which appeared to be fundamentally different, of different natures and alienated from one another— had to be redressed. His valorization of one domain over the other— treating the world of Being as ontologically superior to the world of Becoming— did not satisfactorily resolve the polarization in the ontological narratives of Parmenides and Heraclitus, but only relocated it in internal dualism between the polar domains. Plato, being the superior philosopher that he was, revised his earlier conjecture and sought a more dynamic and dialectical model for understanding how Reality can unify the profound polarity between Being and Becoming, Permanence and Change, Universal and Particular, Soul and Body, Identity and Difference, without *either* privileging one pole over the other, *or* falling into incoherent dualism. His holistic faith that the Absolute Principle of Goodness could cope with the primitive polarity and alterity and reconcile polar opposition in a unitive coherence spurred on his research program. Thus we see that in some primary way any account of Reason or Reality must come to terms with the theme of mediating between worlds, between polar narratives of existence, and give some satisfactory account of the apparent primitive polarity, duality, alterity or opposition in the discourse of Reality.

Plato's revision of his earlier work in the *Sophist* presented a vision of a science of dialectic— a philosophical grammar— which he took to be the essence of the discipline of philosophy. In this dialogue, in the voice of the Eleatic Stranger, the paradigm of formal philosophy takes another step. In attempting to define the sophist, one who ostensibly trades in appearances and falsity, the dialogue makes an "unexpected" turn to the characterization of the philosopher, the lover of wisdom. And here we get a pregnant sketch of the need for a science of dialectic which will explain the grammar of discourse, which will make clear the basic categories and kinds and primitive forms which constitute Reality and discourse, and which will explain how these basic forms relate or dis-relate in the weaving together of meaningful discourse. This science of dialectic or philosophical grammar, the free man's knowledge, is anticipated to be the essential mark of the philosopher, "now or in the future". In this sketch of formal philosophy or philosophical grammar it is suggested that there must be some deep structure which explains why some forms "blend" to make sense, while others do not, and why there must be some unifying form which gives coherence and unity to discourse and orders the basic forms and kinds into rational intelligibility. This would be a remarkable science which excavated the intelligible structure of reality and thus explain how discourse is possible— how language, thought and reality could successfully reflect one another in meaning and truth.

This more mature vision of dialectics proved to be prophetic and it becomes quite clear that reason is intrinsically *dialectical,* involving primitive polarity, duality, alterity, or otherness primitively synthesized in a unifying principle. In the vision of dialectic sketched in the *Sophist* we can see a certain continuity and mediation between Plato's earlier and later understanding of dialectical science or formal philosophy. Here we see a dynamic and dialectical sense of Being and an exploration of how it is possible that Being could at once blend with both Rest and Motion— in other words, how both the Parmenidean and Heraclitean polar narratives of reality could both simultaneously hold— how could Being Become? This line of inquiry seems to accord more equal status to the basic domains of Rest (Permanence, timeless reality) and Motion (Becoming, Process, Change, the reality of space and time). Presumably the presiding Universal Form of Goodness— the unitive and intelligible light of reason— is still at the source of dialectic and is playing the role of the unitive force which holds Being, Rest and Motion together in intelligible order. It appears that dialectic can work because of the unifying field or force of the presiding presence of Goodness, which is beyond Being and Truth.

In any case, although the holistic paradigm of formal philosophy opened up by Plato is seen to be incomplete and facing challenging problems, the general direction and agenda for future research on rationality were brilliantly laid out. In this context we may appreciate how ingenious it was to connect the art-form of dialogue and dialectic as a preferred rhetorical mode of philosophical discourse and inquiry. For Plato's innovative research on rationality made it clear that reason is constitutively dialogical and dialectical: in the dynamic drama of two or more voices or narratives creatively confronting one another in the mediating space of living conversation we find a deep insight into the nature of discourse. Indeed, it appears that the creative conversational space of dialogue is a perfect analogue for dialectic— for it displays in its form what it purports to be about— the creative mediation in a unified field of polarity, duality, diversity and alterity. Dialogical form, understood dialectically, pictures the form of Reason and Reality.

SECTION 2

Indian Origins of Meditative Reason and Universal Grammar
A general feature of Hindu and Buddhist formal philosophy is the shared radical thesis that the human existential condition is constitutively due to a primal ignorance and original Self alienation. The primary objective of philosophical analysis is Self clarification— meaning and existence become clarified only with the radical transformation and clarification of Consciousness or Self. Both traditions agree that the primary purpose of philosophical discourse is liberatory— the existential self is seen to be in a real bondage and the objective of philosophical reflection is to liberate life or consciousness from alienation, suffering and bondage. Their hermeneutical methods are accordingly designed to transform mind from a pathological condition to rational health and freedom. Both traditions teach that all forms of duality are symptoms of the pathological existential condition and are to be overcome. Indeed, they find that duality is the very form of rational disorder and inherent in the existential condition. Both traditions develop a radical form of rational critique based on meditative thinking. They claim to show that all attempts at rational coherence by the mind centered in the existential condition are doomed to failure and frustration. All thinking from the existential condition is conceived in duality and necessarily ends in duality and failure of true unity. The Meditative hermeneutic insists that true rational unity arises only when the dualized mind is deconstructed and a profound "non-dual" Unity is realized. The essential rational transformation, then, is the deconstruction of dual thinking and the expansion of mind to its non-dual rational form. In effect both traditions teach that true rational consciousness must be non-dual in form— that logical form is non-dual Unity.

However, it is not at all evident that there is a general form of meditative reason operative in the hermeneutical methods of Advaita Vedanta or Madhyamika Buddhism. It needs to be established that there is a general formal logic for meditative thinking operative in the diverse meditative traditions. Indeed, the two traditions of meditative reason under consideration have evolved over the centuries with a sense of mutual tension and hermeneutical incompatibility. This alone is *prima facie* evidence that they have not seen or acknowledged a common hermeneutical method in their modes of formal analysis. Accordingly, in what follows we shall pick out certain themes in each of these two traditions and bring them into mutual critical mediation to show that there is a common formal logic of meditative thinking governing their respective hermeneutical styles and rhetorical modes.

One striking feature in the evolution of Indian formal hermeneutics is the dialectical struggle with the deep tendency of the conventional mind to reify itself, its world, its discourse. And in this context it is appropriate to say that the methods of meditative thinking are designed to resist and overcome the fatal error of reification in all its forms. Of course it remains to be seen whether there is a generic formal logic of meditative thinking which embraces the diverse teachings, schools, traditions of meditative hermeneutics. Nevertheless at this preliminary stage it is fair to say that diverse forms of meditative reason are characteristically concerned with a relentless and radical critique or deconstruction of the mentality which is given to the vice of reification.

A dramatic evolution towards formal philosophy is already apparent in the movement from the early Vedic texts to the later *Upanisads* where Vedantic Philosophy begins to blossom. Throughout the *Upanisads* one encounters highly potent formulae which must be rigorously meditated upon to release their semantic force. It is evident that conventional forms of rational thought cannot decode the formulas which purport to disclose Absolute or Universal Form. The sacred formulas reveal that there is an all-encompassing Universal Form which is the form of all possible forms. This Absolute Universal is symbolized as "AUM" or "Brahman". But the remarkable disclosure is that the true Self ("Atman") is another name for this Universal Form. It may be said that the essential teaching of the formulas of Vendanta is that all possible names and forms derive from AUM, that Brahman is the original cause of the Universe, the First Principle from which all beings derive, and that Atman or Self is one with (or non-different from) Brahman or AUM. These three Universal Symbols are fully one, equally symbolizing Universal Form or the Form of Unity.

The formulas or verses of the *Upanisads* offer instruction or advice to the listener reminding him or her that Truth, Reality, Self cannot be objectified, cannot be discerned by ordinary means of perception, cannot be known by ordinary ways of cognition, cannot be referred to or described by conventional modes of discourse. One is reminded repeatedly that Universal Form or Self must be approached through a profound discipline of meditative practice wherein Self is realized and the conventional existential condition which is lodged in deep ignorance is overcome. The theme of liberation and bondage recurs throughout the text. It is disclosed that the existential condition, called "samsara", is a form of bondage and suffering and is constituted in primal ignorance. And liberation from this existential bondage comes only with a profound transformation of Self awakening which comes through disciplined meditation on AUM or Brahman.

The initial impression one gets from a serious encounter with this teaching is that Reality, AUM or Atman is some mysterious transcendent state which is radically different from the range of everyday experience. One gets the impression that one must somehow deny or overcome all that is familiar in everyday life and escape from human existence to this alleged higher transcendent Being. Since the processes of "natural reason" or thought are declared to be totally inadequate for approaching one's true Universal Self the listener typically feels that meditative thinking must be some extra-rational mysterious process that is beyond the reach of ordinary mortals. The purported Presence of Universal Form in everyday life and thought seems too remote a possibility to be taken with rational seriousness or commitment.

Indeed, the self which is situated in time and space, situated firmly in history, in particularity, in existence naturally has a strong reaction and resistance to this Aumic discourse. In a real sense this apparently transcendent teaching is life-threatening to the very existentiality of the self— for it purports to reveal that the individuated self is mere appearance due to profound ignorance. It teaches that the form of life of this self is irrational, incoherent, confused and pathological. It claims to reveal that Truth, Cognition, Wisdom, Rationality, Sanity, Happiness can be realized only when the Universal Form of the Self is realized. And this Self-Realization requires nothing less than a radical detachment from the illusory existential self. So it is quite clear that this is a matter of life and death for the self.

It is to be expected that the situated self will fight back for all it is worth. For it is more certain than anything that it exists, that it is particular, individual, self-existent, finite, historical, and it has a certain natural confidence in its own judgment. Its deepest faith is precisely in its existentiality and unique specificity. It therefore experiences the Aumic narrative as artificial and abstract and making claims upon it which go counter to its deepest felt instincts and natural reason. How can it be required to deny and reject its own existence? How can its clear and distinct particularity and finitude and historicity be questioned, much less dissolved? How could it live, act, breathe, speak, if this self is somehow let go? The alleged Universality and Unity of the Aumic Self appears to be completely out of this world and beyond all life and action. This Self appears to be infinite, to be indistinguishable from God or Divine Form itself. And this goes beyond the sound common sense of the situated self. The Aumic narrative strains the rational faith of the existential self.

So the lines are firmly drawn. On the one side we hear the Aumic Voice which purports to be the Voice of Pure Reason, Pure Consciousness, Universal Truth, Absolute Cognition, of Self Unity. This Absolute Self appears to deny all individuation, all specificity, plurality and existentiality. It appears to present itself as a Universal Presence that is beyond all determination, determinacy, definition and conceptualization. From a conventional logical point of view, it appears to be in a realm of silence, beyond predication, reference, description, or ordinary discourse. On the other hand, the existential self is absolutely certain about its specificity and situatedness in space and time, and is fully confident in its ability to refer to, describe, conceptualize itself. It has a robust sense that it can distinguish between right and wrong, between reality and illusion, between knowledge and ignorance. It understands how to differentiate itself from others, how to deliberate and make informed choices in guiding its conduct. And so on. It appears that we are here faced with two deeply opposed voices which express narratives that are diametrically opposed and could not be farther removed from each other. The Aumic Voice presents Universal Form that it takes to be Absolute Unity beyond all limitations and determinacy. The existential voice presents its self as absolutely self existent, particular, situated, specified and differentiated. Each presents itself as speaking absolute truth and as being rational and intelligible. We seem to be faced with a deadlock or stalemate between these polar voices.

Some effective form of hermeneutical mediation or negotiation seems to be needed to bring these two apparently contradictory narratives into meaningful conversation. And this is what we find in a text like the *Bhagavadgita*. This text is a dialogue between Lord Krishna, the incarnation of the Aumic Voice, and Arjuna, the embodiment of the existential voice.

Through the rich symbolism and metaphoric layers of this intense drama on the battlefield it is immediately apparent that Arjuna represents the ego-centric voice situated in the existential condition and Krishna as his guide and charioteer leads him step by step from his despair and bondage to higher consciousness. It is apparent that this external encounter on the battlefield in a life and death situation represents the inner struggle and conversation between a lower and higher voice in human rational consciousness. Arjuna's identity as a warrior on the battlefield of existence has collapsed and he sinks into confusion and despair. His world has collapsed and he finds himself in a self contradictory predicament which apparently has no resolution. Of course his ontological-moral crisis represents the inevitable breakdown that must come for the existential self. When he drops his weapon, totally demoralized, refusing to proceed in the imminent battle of good versus evil this is a symbolic act of a kind of ontological suicide. Thus, it is only when the ego-centric self has awakened sufficiently to a heightened rationality and directly encounters the deep incoherence of its living narrative that the stage is prepared for the presence of the higher Voice and for rational therapy to proceed.

At the same time, the Aumic voice cannot appear to stand aloof of the existential condition issuing injunctions from afar. It must incarnate itself in a Voice that speaks the language of the existential condition form within without compromising the Rational Integrity of the Aumic Principle. This Incarnated Voice must be rationally potent enough to Univocate the two apparently estranged voice fields. It must open up a Unified Voice field between the Universal Aumic Form and the finite existential voice. The incarnation of the Aumic Principle in the voice of Krishna creates a dialogical space wherein a rational therapeutic conversation with the existential voice may proceed.

I shall not here attempt to recreate the dialectics of this dialogue. Instead I shall focus on certain main themes which are relevant to our interest in understanding Hindu formal hermeneutics and its elaboration of rational form in the context of meditative reason. First, it is clear that the dialogue is a dialectical journey in which the voice of Arjuna is progressively expanded until he is prepared to have a direct intuition of Universal Form or Krishna Consciousness. It is equally clear throughout this dialectical process that Krishna's speech is primarily for the rational awakening or liberation of Arjuna and not intended for description or conceptualization of Reality. Here it may be said that the rational force or Krishna's speech is not descriptive but therapeutic or transformative. It is not only the existential narrative of Arjuna that is being deconstructed but the existential voice or self itself. Since Arjuna's life-world and narrative or grammar has collapsed in an existential crisis he is ready for self expansion to higher forms of rationality. So it is meaning, grammar, voice, discourse and rational form that are under self-transformation. In this respect Krishna's speech makes powerful use of metaphoric meaning and keeps shifting and moving in a dialectical dance as Arjuna's consciousness expands. The incarnation of the Aumic Principle remains unfixable and defies reification. Its discourse is disposable and self-deconstructs precisely when it succeeds in expanding the rationality of the existential voice.

For example, in Chapter 2 Krishna initiates the therapy by instructing Arjuna on the hermeneutical incoherence of his despair. He provisionally speaks in the grammar of ontological dualism, distinguishing between

Being and Becoming and showing that the Self is categorially beyond Becoming and cannot be slain. Krishna presents considerations reminiscent of the ontological arguments developed by Socrates in the *Phaedo* to show that the soul is of a different nature from the body and cannot die. This first phase of instruction in basic ontology is designed to awaken Arjuna to grammatical differences between the kind of thing that can be born and die and kind of thing that is the Self. But this is only the beginning of the dialectical journey and Krishna soon lets go of this grammatical voice as soon as Arjuna gets the point. It would be a mistake to reify Krishna's speech at this point and attribute a categorial dualism to Krishna. For it is immediately apparent that Krishna is preparing to take Arjuna through the dialectics of dualism to a higher form of rational consciousness and Self Unity.

Krishna is masterful in playing with grammars and shows his fluency in the grammar of Being and the grammar of Becoming. He shows Arjuna that both grammars entail that grieving over slaying his kin in battle is not only false but nonsense. For if the self is something that /Becomes/ it is constantly in a state of becoming and the cycle of birth and death will continue. And Krishna ends the first movement by reminding Arjuna of his duty and enjoins him to pick up his weapon and enter the battle of good against evil. It is noteworthy that Krishna repeatedly insists that the rationally awakened person must engage in Action.

To help Arjuna understand this higher form of Ethics Krishna begins to take him through a higher phenomenology of the Mind which has passed beyond the egocentric voice and has been liberated from the existential condition which is self-divided in duality. Krishna introduces Arjuna to the Yoga of Understanding— to the higher Rational Consciousness which has detached itself from the grammar of conventional existence and has recentered itself in Universal Form. Krishna shows how the oppositional forces of conventional existence which split and disturb everyday consciousness is overcome in the higher phenomenology. It is clear that the liberated mind does perceive, and live and act, but it's rationality and world are apparently of a higher order which overcomes the strife and incoherence of everyday life. Of course Krishna, being the incarnation of Universal Rational Form, is an expert Logician and knows a thing or two about formal logic. He reveals to Arjuna the inherent self-dualizing that arises with conventional existence and the unsatisfiable /desire/ that comes with self-reification. In the higher phenomenology or rationality the liberated person is not attached to objects of the senses or motivated by /desire/ nor attached to the fruits of /action/. The net effect of the therapy is a radical deconstruction of the ego-centric self and it's incoherent hermeneutical form of life.

This systematic and disciplined ego-deconstruction unfolds in stages. And at every stage the Grammaticality of Krishna self-expands towards higher Self-Unity. It is the hermeneutical friction between the voice fields of Krishna and Arjuna that both provokes and invokes the movement of the dialectic. Obviously Arjuna is of superior intelligence and as a brilliant student of Krishna he presses the appropriate questions and voices the sceptical doubts at every stage of the journey. It is this healthy rational skepticism and honesty that permits the rational therapy to advance. It is through the dialogue that the cause of Rationality is advanced. So in subsequent chapters as Arjuna is introduced to higher Grammar his capacity for Rationality, for apprehension of Universal Form, advances.

By way of conclusion of this preliminary exploration of the origins of Universal Grammar in the early Hindu tradition it would be timely to summarize some of the main advances clarified by Shankara in his development of Advaita discourse. These include the following:

That there is an Absolute Universal Presence (Brahman, AUM) that is the origin of all possible names, forms, things

That this Absolute has universal jurisdiction and presides over all discourse, existence, experience, reason

That this Absolute Original Presence is Infinitely Unitive and hence cannot be objectified or reified in any way

That this unitive Presence must be non-dual (Advaita) and approached in the rigorous methods of meditative mind

That all objectification, duality, arises from a primordial eclipse of this Absolute Presence, which is the Self (Atman)

That all thought, experience, phenomena arising from egological mind is lodged in primal ignorance arising from Identity

That all egological thought is predicative and inherently dualistic and self-reifying and objectifying

That Asolute Presence cannot be approached in egological mind, and cannot be predicated in any way

That all egological thought and predication must be radically deconstructed and brought to silence through meditative discipline

That none of the categories constitutive of egological mind can truly apply to Absolute Presence

That the Self-Realization of this Absolute Presence is the Self-Revelation of Pure Consciousness or Self

That this Self, when egological self is deconstructed, is non-different from Absolute Presence

That Samsara, the egological constituted world, is the space of appearance and not Reality

We suggest that these are classical themes in the clarification of Meditative Reason, and that Shankara made monumental contributions to the clarification of Universal Grammar.

Conclusion

Of course these are preliminary explorations. We have suggested that there is a higher Dialectical Reason presiding over the evolution of global discourse and in the evolving conversation of east-west philosophical dialogue and inquiry. We find that east-west dialogical inquiry is in a unique position to make unprecedented contributions to the future clarification of this space of Meditative Reason and Universal Grammar. And we have suggested that this articulation of Universal Grammar is of paramount importance in global formal philosophy, indeed the perennial presiding concern for all philosophical inquiry.

PART II: INTRODUCTION

The Perennial Quest for Universal Grammar

One perennial concern in the evolution of global philosophy is the quest for Universal Grammar. This quest has taken an interesting variety of approaches and strategies, so much so in fact that it is often quite difficult to see that there are deep common interests and affinities in these variations. One focal point is the interest in understanding the nature of discourse in the widest sense of the term. This includes the nature of human reason, the logic of natural language, the grammar of thought, experience and existence. Any account which attempts to explain the workings of discourse may be taken to be a philosophical grammar, and since such accounts typically purport to give a universal account of discourse, we may speak of the quest for universal grammar. The classical Greek proposals for human reason and philosophical grammar have affinities and differences with certain developments in modem analytic philosophical grammar since Frege, Russell and Wittgenstein. And developments in philosophical grammar in the continental traditions in the work of Husserl, Heidegger, Derrida and others have interesting affinities and differences with both the classical Greek paradigms and the more recent post-Fregean paradigms of the grammar of thought. Again, in a wider global context of philosophical discourse, we find fascinating affinities in approaches to philosophical grammar in the meditative traditions, such as in Hindu Upanisadic discourse or in Buddhist dialectics, such as the discourse of Nagarjuna. The diverse dialectical paradigms of philosophical grammar all purport to be universal and comprehensive of discourse in general. Thus, when we bring these variant paradigms of philosophical grammars into conversation we find new horizons open up in the quest for Universal Grammar.

The Idea of Universal Grammar

What is a "grammar of thought"? The idea of a "grammar" in the philosophical sense arises from diverse contexts. In the traditions of logic it has long been the ideal of the science of logic to articulate the logical structure of reason and articulate the laws of thought. These traditions claim that the formal laws of thought have a certain universal jurisdiction over all modes of thought, whatever the particular subject matter, and in this respect the science of logic has claimed a certain universal jurisdiction in the conduct of rationality. Presumably the laws of reason would elucidate not only right reasoning, but also the dynamics of right thinking or thought formation. And any philosophical logic that develops a narrative of the right conduct of reason would provide a grammar of thought. So in this sense a narrative of logic in making clear the dynamics and laws of right thinking may be considered a grammar of thought.

In a closely allied context of philosophical inquiry, the science of Being, or ontology, the idea of philosophical grammar also emerges. While philosophical logics focus on reason and thought, philosophical ontologies focus on Being and the strictures of existence. Here, too, the idea of a philosophical grammar emerges in the attempt to give an account of the primal categories of existence and the structure and configurations of the primal categories which make up a world. An ontological grammar presents the primitive categories which make up a world and which are expressed in an ontological language or grammar of existence. In this respect, any philosophical ontology that presents a language of existence—a grammar of being— which elucidates the form and structure of the language-world, expresses a philosophical grammar.

Again, in the closely related inquiry into the nature of discourse and language, the narratives which give an account of the origin of meaning and structure of a given language are also explorations in philosophical grammar.

Here we find a variety of approaches in the philosophy of language. The attempts in Wittgenstein's *Tractatus* may be seen as one attempt at philosophical grammar which combines logic, ontology and philosophy of language. But his later attempt to present an account of the nature of natural language in his *Investigations* is also a grammatical investigation, as he himself makes explicit. Here, to understand the diverse language-games that constitute natural language, to understand the rules of use which give rise to meaning in a particular language-game or form of life, to actually explore how certain concepts of a given language-game are mutually deployed, their affinities and differences in their "logics"— this would be one exemplar of philosophical grammar. Similarly, the phenomenological researches of Husserl in his *Logical Investigations* and *Formal and Transcendental Logic* are paradigm cases of philosophical grammar. In another context, the explorations of Sommers in developing the categorial logic in the classical Greek paradigm of predication— the discovery of the "ordinary language tree" and the formal rules for category formation in the sense structure of a language— is another exemplar of philosophical grammar. Again, the research of Frege in his *Begriffschrift* in developing a formal language of concept-writing is a powerful model of philosophical grammar.

But a philosophical grammar need not explicitly be an account of logic, or ontology or language. It may be a lived grammar. And here the hermeneutical tradition developed by Heidegger and Gadamer and others shows that human life is always situated in interpretation. In this respect we humans are grammatical beings— to be is to be grammatical, to exist is to be situated in a grammar of experience that structures the sense of the world.

In this context we see that all cultural life is grammatical— and this is the hermeneutical sense of a lived grammar or life-world. A form of life is a lived grammar which structures a system of sense. So in a generic sense, any narrative which involves making sense of things— whether it is a lived grammar or form of life which makes sense of the world or of life would be exemplars of grammar. Thus, in this generic sense, wherever there is an attempt to make sense of things the activity of grammar is involved. So it may be said in this philosophical context that grammar is the art of making sense. And any form of common sense, any lived cultural world, any particular disciplinary form of life, like the activity of science, directly involves the grammatical art. In this generic sense, where there is a form of life, participation in discourse, the activity of interpretation, indeed, of the conduct of experience itself, grammar is at work.

This generic sense of grammar and the hermeneutical activity of making sense helps to open the way to the idea of universal grammar. Here we see that the ongoing conversation of diverse grammatical forms in their variety of expressions is the open space of Universal Grammar. We find a continuum between the varied contexts and activities of philosophical grammar whether a theory of sense or a praxis of making sense. If we consider a diversity of cultural grammars, religious worlds, philosophical ontologies, the question of Universal Grammar would open up issues of universal features or common ground between such diverse grammars. If we consider a multiplicity of philosophical grammars concerning the nature of discourse, reason, thought— the question of Universal Grammar would focus on common ground, consensus and conversation between such grammars of thought, and so on. The question of Universal Grammar opens up the considerations of there being a universal ground of grammars. And the quest for Universal Grammar is the ongoing conversation of the community of diverse grammatical forms of life.

The universal quest for Natural Reason and rationality in the human condition has been alive in world cultures throughout global history. This is quite evident in the range of ancient and classical civilizations, and we could begin our exploration in any number of cultural contexts. We could open up our topic, for example, by investigating the early evolution of human understanding in world views of ancient Chinese culture, or in a diversity of world views in early Indian culture, or in Greek culture or African cultures, and so on. We shall begin by reflecting on certain intuitions into Natural Reason in classical Greek thought and trace a dialectical line of evolution into the development of modern contemporary discourse.

An Experimental Inquiry Into The Paradigm of Universal Grammar

1) Alterity and Polarization in Reason

The power of Natural Reason to disclose itself in a primitive polarity or alterity— a primordial unitive force which manifests itself in alterity or otherness— is evident in early Greek origins of philosophical grammar. This is clear in the alter-narratives of Parmenides and Heraclitus, which focus and prioritize one side or the other of the Unitive Alterity of Reason or Logos. Parmenides focuses on one face of Reason— Identity, Sameness,

Rest— and develops one side of a polar narrative of Absolute Being— Eternal, At Rest, non-Becoming, Unity, Substance, Self-Identity. This Absolute Being is taken to discredit process, change, becoming, potentiality, multiplicity, temporality, duality. And so the appearance of change or becoming was discredited and reduced to mere "appearance", and the not-Real. The other face of Reason is focused on by Heraclitus and prioritized as Absolute Becoming, Change, Difference, Multiplicity, Process, Potentiality, Indeterminacy, Non-Identity. This alter-narrative of Reason is taken to be primitive and absolute, and to displace and exclude the Parmenidean Narrative, which is seen as mere appearance and the not-Real. In this early stage of accounting for Logos or Reason the rational tools needed to show that these polar alter-narratives were unified in Reason in a Unitive Dialectic or Unified Field were not yet fashioned. Instead of seeing that these alter-narratives entailed one another and mutually co-arise and constitute one another in a dialectical continuum, they polarized into separate domains, into presumed independent mutually exclusive narrative worlds or universes of discourse. In this way they appeared to be worlds apart and lodged in a certain incommensurability. Each polar narrative took itself to be absolute, universal in scope and jurisdiction, and hence drew a distinction in what Appeared between Reality and mere "appearance". What conformed to the philosophical grammar was taken to be Real, and what was incompatible with it was dismissed as mere "appearance". Thus, at an early stage, Reason or Logos, which purported to be Absolutely Unitive, appeared to be self divided, polarized and multiple.

This apparent antinomy or self-contradiction in the heart of Reason set the agenda for subsequent experimental inquiry into the nature of Reason which has played out over the centuries and into our contemporary times. The challenges inherited from "ancient" times are perhaps more alive and raging today than ever in the evolving history of Reason. In a certain sense the dialectical evolution of Reason over the past twenty-five hundred years constitutes one continuous moment in global discourse.

Socrates and Plato took up the challenge to vindicate Reason from the appearance of polarization and incoherence. Plato portrayed Socrates as the living teacher who embodied the living conversational dialectic of Reason and dramatized this effectively in dialogical inquiry. In his earlier work culminating in the *Republic* Plato attempted to present a Unitive narrative of Reason which purported to disarm the apparent split in world views bequeathed by Parmenides and Heraclitus. This vision is summed up in his "divided line" model which placed the two world-views in a certain continuous relation, but also divided them into two worlds or universes of discourse. However, the two philosophical grammars did not have equal ontological status— the Parmenidean world of Being was accorded privileged status of being Reality in itself, while the Heraclitean world of Becoming was the under-world of mere appearance. And the line dividing these two worlds symbolized a profound division of the two grammars into two ontological types of being. In this way an ontological dualism severed any continuum between the two domains.

As Plato's thought matured and found expression in the later dialogues, specifically the *Sophist* and the *Parmenides,* we find brilliant advances in his attempt to overcome the earlier naive dualism and present a deeper unitive dialectic of Reason. In the *Sophist* we find presented in the voice of the Eleatic Stranger a dynamic dialectic of Being and Becoming which is more faithful to the Unitive Alterity of "Reason. In this dialogue we get a vision of discourse as the blending of primitive forms or kinds or categories which constitute the structure of Reason and discourse. Such primitive forms as Being, Rest, Motion, Identity and Difference are found to be most basic in the dynamics of discourse, and the dialogue speculates about possible models for the appropriate "blending" of the basic kinds or categories which constitute rational discourse. The discussion settles on a preliminary vision of a "science of dialectic" or grammar which governs discourse and which would show how the basic forms of reason configure to produce intelligible discourse. This science of grammar was envisioned as the essence of the philosophical enterprise and so the science of Reason at this early stage focused on clarifying the laws and dynamics of the predictability of basic forms or categories which constituted discourse. In this context Plato's mature thought situated philosophical grammar in a dynamic, dialectical, dialogical and categorial model of Reason. And if Plato did not himself resolve the antinomies and paradoxes in the center of reason which ripened in his investigations, he left to future inquiry a clarified more articulate sense of the aporias that had to be addressed.

What emerged more clearly in the evolution of Plato's grammar is that Reason presents a network of fundamental polarities which needed to be sorted out and mediated: Unity/Multiplicity; Identity/Difference; Rest/Motion; Being/Becoming; Universal/Particular; Form/Matter; Intelligible/Sensible; Eternal/Temporal; Soul/Body; and so on. We suggested earlier that Plato tended to privilege one side of these polarities over the other, and thus appeared to valorize Unity, Being, Universal, Form, Eternal, Essence, Intelligible, Soul... over Multiplicity, Becoming, Particular, Matter, Temporal, Existence, Sensible, Body...

Aristotle, Plato's distinguished disciple, inherited the challenge and brilliantly advanced the dialectics of reason to a more powerful unitive narrative or philosophical grammar. Aristotle made ingenious innovations in the grammar of discourse which attempted to bring the two worlds into existential and primitive unity. Aristotle's genius was in seeing more clearly the primitive alterity in Natural Reason— that Being and Becoming mutually constituted one another, so that *Being is Becoming*; that the Universal and the Particular are existentially united so that one could not exist without the other; that Form and Matter were meant for each other and could not be apart from one another; that the Intelligible (essence) and the Sensible (existent) co-exist as a unit; that soul and body exist for each other, and so on. This dynamic ontology or philosophical grammar stressed that the individual entity, existing in space and time as the primary subject of process and becoming is the primary reality. Such individual primary beings embodied a specific intelligible form or essence which defined its being. These individual substances which appeared to common sense were specific, particular and determinate. This means that primary beings were constituted in certain attributes or properties which made them what they are. And Aristotle brilliantly opened a space for real becoming by clarifying the nature of potentiality: showing that for a real being to become it must be-and-not-be at the same time— as an acorn is-and-isn't an oak at the same time. This was a powerful innovation since it opened a way to mediate between Being and Becoming in a way that did not place one above the other: this was one recognition of the Alterity structure of Reason and Reality.

In order to bring about this meeting and unity of the two worlds, Aristotle had to revise and expand the grammars of Parmenides and Heraclitus, and of course of Plato as well. While Plato favored a Unitive narrative in which Being was One and well-ordered under the Absolute Universal Form of Goodness, Aristotle stressed a diversity of Being, many senses of "being", a multiplicity of primary beings making up Reality, and a world of common sense divided into fundamental categories or attributes and fundamental types or kinds of beings. Where Plato stressed Unity, and Sameness and Univocity, Aristotle counter-stressed Multiplicity, and Difference and Equivocity. Where Plato stressed a certain deep synthetic Unity to Reality, we find Aristotle stressing analytical divisions and existential distinctions in what exists. And in this way we find a certain polarity and complementarity between their philosophical grammars. In stressing the presiding Unity of Being, Plato did not give a compelling account of the appearance of multiplicity and differentiation and specification in the world. On the other hand, in insisting on the primary importance of distinctions, particularity and categorial differences Aristotle sometimes appeared somewhat arbitrary and stipulative in positing primitive Unity. For example, in his powerful ontological analysis of primary substances or individuals, he rightly insisted that beings are *constituted* in the unity of form and matter. He found upon analysis that the primary beings making up the world always had "form" (a rational or intelligible essence making it what it is) and "matter"(an immediately given existential thisness or potentiality) which embodies the form. Neither could exist without the other, and yet they were different. Aristotle's intuition here is that primary beings are *individual*— a primitive ontological unity— hence not composed. It is here that the deep Alterity in Reason is somehow being recognized. But we are left with the sense that it is being posited or stipulated and not adequately explained. How can "form" and "matter" which are so fundamentally different from each other, alien and in a certain sense incommensurable, be a true primitive or existential unity?

Or take another related example. Aristotle lay the foundations for the science of ontology by breaking new ground with the inner categorial structure of primary beings. He showed that beings are constituted in basic attributes— that Reality presented itself in fundamental apparently irreducible categories— like being located in Space, being situated in Time, being a Quality, being a Quantity, being a Relation, being a Substance, and so on. These primary categories are features of Reality or modes of Being, and since they were fundamentally *different* Aristotle conjectured that there must be different senses of "being" or modes of "existence". And yet the alterintuition of Unity and Identity was also stressed in the indivisible unity of primary substances— Aristotle insisted that these ultimately diverse categories were united in some way in having a central reference to substances in which they all inhere. The basic attributes or features of Being all inhered in the primary beings and this is how they found their existential meeting and relationality. But if we press here and inquire precisely how can these ultimately diverse fields or categories meet and "blend" in the being of individual entities— we find no real explanation and get no satisfaction. When we press to understand how there can be ultimate differences and diversity in the domain of Reality on the one hand, and how these diverse fields or features can find true meeting and unity and common ground, on the other, we find no better answer than we get when we press Plato to explain how the two worlds can meet and intelligibly interact.

Thus, the advance in the grammar of Reason in Aristotle's discourse is the clearer recognition of the primitive alterity in Natural Reason— that somehow Reason is Unitive, and yet discloses itself in diversity, multiplicity, difference and particularity. *That* this is so is seen by Aristotle, but *how* this is possible, how to account for this Alterity is not satisfactorily explained. It is not acceptable simply to posit Unity-in-Multiplicy or to stipulate Identity-in-Difference. If "space" and "time' and "quality" and "quantity" are ultimately distinct, how do they existentially come together in a true meeting in the individual substance? The term "individual" means "primitively one, undivided" and so the unitive nature of the individual being must somehow unify the diversity and multiplicity of the fundamental categories or features that constitute it. But there is no individual substance apart from the attributes, nor are there attributes apart from the substances. So right at the very heart of the alleged "individual substance" lurks the dialectical tensions and paradoxes that we have seen plaguing Plato's grammar of two worlds, and indeed Reason, Experience and discourse in general.

Furthermore, there is a problem with the posit of "individual substance or primary beings" itself. If the world divides into basic attributes or categories on the one hand, and types or kinds of entities on the other, what is the alleged unity of a kind? If, for example, humans constitute a kind of being or ontological type of entity, how do the uniquely particular existing individuals, each existentially specific, constitute a unified kind of being? More generally, if "the world" divides into types of entities, how do the basic types of entities stand in existential relations to constitute the unity of a world?

We begin to see a recurring pattern of the same generic problem of Unity-in-Diversity and Identity-in-Difference. And the primitive Alterity in Natural Reason will always show itself in one way or another in any philosophical grammar. In Aristotle's narrative we see the polar forces at work in every direction. There appears to be one alter-voice in his narrative which is committed to ultimate difference, multiplicity, plurality— that the world consists of a plurality of self-existent individual beings— and we may call this the "atomic voice", since the postulate of "self-existent individual beings" presumes a certain autonomous independent existential status to such beings. this is why they are primary substances. The other complementary alter-voice is the "anatomic" or "holistic" voice which posits that the unit of being is the systematic whole— Reality as a whole, or the well-ordered world-field as a whole.

The anatomic or holistic voice insists that "things" do not exist alone or in atomic isolation, but are profoundly situated in relationality to each other and to the whole, and could not exist apart from this Unitive Whole. In this respect the true essence of any entity would be a function of its place and role in the organic unity of the world as a whole. And indeed, we see it is clear that Aristotle inherits from Plato and shares in the intuition that Reality, Nature, World is teleological and forms a certain well-ordered systematic or organic Unity. To be is to have a function, a telos, in the Unitive field of Reality. So in these two functional voices or agendas in Aristotle's narrative we see in macroscopic form a generic version of the polar force of Alterity in Reason and Reality. And it is natural to ask here:

how can these polar voices— the atomic and the holistic— both be operative and cooperative at the same time? They appear to be polarized, opposite, mutually contradictory in claiming primacy, and hence incompatible— the same sort of incompatibility we feel between the universal narratives of Parmenides and Heraclitus, or between the two worlds of Plato's grammar.

This recurrent self-polarity or alterity pervading all areas of the microscopic level of analysis and the macroscopic level of Aristotle's narrative naturally leads us to wonder whether Aristotle's philosophical grammar is self divided and in a sense incoherent and split, or whether it is truly a unitive narrative as a whole. We have raised this concern regarding Plato's grammar already. But now in placing Plato's discourse and Aristotle's discourse together we also find an interesting polarity or alterity that leads us to the same consideration *between* their philosophical worlds: just as we have seen polar voices operative *within* each grammar, could it be that these two grammars complement one another and thus form a certain continuum or continuity in yielding jointly a more adequate disclosure of Reason and Reality?

We have suggested that in Plato's grammar the anatomic or holistic voice dominates in privileging Unity over Diversity. We see the inner tension in Plato's discourse between his presiding intuition that there is a unitive Absolute and all-pervasive Form— Goodness— that is the absolute ground of all forms, of all that could be or be conceived, on the one hand, and his intuition that there are many differentiated forms, on the other. When the holistic intuition is privileged, the challenge is to give an account of how this Absolute One may be diversified and differentiated into many. And we have suggested that Aristotle's grammar favored the atomic or pluralistic in privileging the multiplicity of primary individual beings over the Unitivity of Being. We saw the inner tension in his grammar between the intuition into the plurality of individual differentiated beings, and the polar intuition that there is a teleological or organic order and unitivity to the world as a whole. Here the challenge is to give an account of how the primacy of the Many, the diversified and plural, can be held together in a primitive existential Unitivity. If Unity is Primary, then how are we to account for true Diversity or Plurality. If Plurality is Primary, then how are we to account for true Unity or Univocity? We wonder whether there is a creative way to find inner coherence or unity *within* the respective grammars of Plato and Aristotle, and *between* their philosophical worlds. Could it be that there is a dialectical unity and continuity and complementarity between their grammars which can disclose a more adequate account of Natural Reason? Could it be that Plato's intuitions capture insights into Reason that are eclipsed by Aristotle's grammar; and could it be that Aristotle's intuitions capture insights into Reason that are eclipsed in Plato's discourse? We shall see in what follows that this theme of dialogical or dialectical Unity *within* a given grammar and *between* grammars recurs in the evolution of Natural Reason.

2) The Emergence of Reason and First Philosophy

In preparing now to explore the evolution of the paradigms of Natural Reason that culminated in the grammars of Plato and Aristotle it would be timely to elaborate further on fundamental advances in the disclosure of Natural Reason which emerged in the grammars of Plato and Aristotle and which profoundly shaped the subsequent evolution of grammars through the centuries. One such advance is the opening up of the foundations of Universal Grammar in the birth of the sciences of logic and ontology. We have seen that Plato opened up the vision of a science of dialectic which would clarify the basic forms, kinds, categories which constituted discourse, and explicate the grammar of how the basic forms "blended" to yield intelligible discourse. This preliminary vision of a science of grammar was developed in remarkable ways by Aristotle who attempted for the first time to give a systematic account of the basic categories of being and discourse, and to formalize and formulate the dynamics of predication and predictability. It began to become clear that there is a deep isomorphism between the space of discourse (thought, reason, intelligibility) and the space of being. If reality consisted in primary individuated beings which divided into diverse ontological types or kinds, and which were constituted by basic primary attributes or properties, then thought and its expression in language reflected this structure and mirrored this order of reality: thought consists of logical subjects and predicates being joined in a way to replicate the way things were in existence. So on the one hand we have the ontological order of existence or world consisting of primary substances constituted by their basic attributes or properties, and on the other we have the order of logic which disclosed logical subjects characterized by logical predicates. One major advance in the co-development of ontology and logic as sciences is the clarification of the space of *predication* — the space of Natural Reason. It began to emerge in the discourse of Plato and Aristotle that Reason is a unitive power that pervaded Reality, Mind, Thought, Language, Experience; and the common space of Reason that structured these domains is the space of predication — the space in which rational and intelligible life and discourse proceeds.

Aristotle opened the foundations of ontology — the science of Being — by exploring the formal structure of how beings show themselves in the space of predication — the space of Reason. To be is to be a logical subject of discourse, and if we can understand the form and features of the primary logical subject we would have insight into the being of beings. And so in beginning the explication of the basic categories of being and the dynamics of how these operate and co-operate the origins of ontology and logic opened up. Since reality presents itself in the form of substances and attributes, thought manifested itself predicatively as the blending of subjects and predicates. And the science of grammar envisioned by Plato would make clear the formal laws governing how the basic terms of predication blended to yield meaning and truth. In this way the laws of sense or intelligibility immediately reflected the order of things— namely which categories or predicates ontologically blended with which primary subjects. So meaning and truth arose in this space of predication and immediately reflected the union of the order of thought and the order of Reality.

In thus formulating and civilizing the space of predication Aristotle carried Plato's program forward in founding the science of Logic. What is remarkable is that this science is found to be a *formal* science having universal jurisdiction. Aristotle discovered that the correctness of thought— thinking and reasoning— turned on the formal laws that govern predicability and the play of predication in the art of reasoning or inference making. A thought is well-formed if it follows the grammar of thought— the structure, pattern, regularities— which is grounded in the way things are. And here we find that Reason is *categorial*— a predicate may be significantly predicated of a given subject if it is the *kind* of thing to which the category applies. Non-sense arises if a predicate is applied to a subject which is in breach of the categorial order of the world. What is especially remarkable is Aristotle's formulation of the laws and dynamics governing the patterns of correct reasoning in drawing inferences and expressing arguments. This is the development of Aristotle's logistic or syllogistic logic which formalized certain laws of reasoning in the space of predication. Here he found that the correctness or validity of a syllogistic inference depended on the *formal* configuration of terms in the space of predication, and not on the particular content of the terms themselves.

Thus the birthing of formal logic and ontology arose together in the grammar of predication. Formal ontology focused on articulating the formal or generic features of any being in general— clarifying what it means to be a being as such. And in this joint development of ontology and logic Aristotle sought to formulate the first principles— the formal principles of Thought and Being. This was an important step in the articulation of First Philosophy or Universal Grammar. For Plato and Aristotle saw that Philosophy— the love of Wisdom— was peculiarly concerned with the articulation of What is First, what has universal scope and jurisdiction, with what presides in discourse. There is a potent intuition here that Natural Reason presents a profound Order which is the origin of intelligibility and truth. And so it is of the utmost importance to rational life to come to articulate clarity on the First Principles that shape all other principles, laws and phenomena.

Perhaps it is timely as we now prepare to take a quick glance at some of the major recurring patterns in the evolution of Reason and Grammar to stand back a bit and reflect on the importance of the breakthrough to First Philosophy and the birth of Formal Science. One presiding theme that begins to become clear in the shared vision of Reason is that the domains of Consciousness, Language, Experience, World are somehow held together in the power of Reason. It is clear that Reason pervades Reality, and in some important sense they are one: what is real exhibits the presence of Reason, and Reason discloses what is real. And since Reality incorporates the diverse domains of consciousness, thought, discourse, language, experience, phenomena, world, life, action, etc., it becomes clear that somehow Reason is a unitive force or power that holds these diverse domains together. Or rather that Reason is a primitive and unitive force out of which the diverse domains of discourse co-emerge in a certain order and coherence.

In treating the philosophical grammars of Plato and Aristotle as alter-paradigms taken jointly and constituting a certain dialectical unity and conversational continuum we see the alterity in Reason. Plato opened the horizon of First Philosophy in his intuition that there must be a primal form— a Universal Form of Forms— which is First and which presides over all other forms, essences, names, things, fields. He calls this Origin of the universe of discourse "Goodness" and it is clear that this is the source of Reason— the origin of intelligibility, of Being and Truth. It is clear that Goodness is the Absolute presiding presence that orders the universe and thus holds things together in coherence. This intuition into the origin of Reason is of the utmost importance in the emergence of Universal Grammar. It is the postulate that all things are situated in a unitive field or force which places them in inter-relationality. If all that appears— all forms, categories, kinds, phenomena, etc. have a universal common origin, and if the essence of what they are derives from this origin, then this implies a common ground of inter-relationality and kinship between all that exists. This intuition into Goodness as the unitive power of Reality is the original insight into Reason itself— it is the insight into the *teleological* nature of existence and discourse— that all things are situated and oriented in unity. This is the origin of the primal features of Reason: of Essence, Form, Order, Law, Universality, Individuation, Coherence, Relation, Origin, Cause, Substance, etc. This is the origin of intelligibility— things make sense insofar as their place in Unitivity is seen, and so the very idea of "science" becomes possible. The Unitive Force gives rise to all possible relations and to relationality itself. There could not be Thought in the first place if Relationality were not possible and real. Understanding becomes possible within the Unitive Field which generates Order and Regularity and Organization. The opening of Space for Space and Time originates in this ordering dynamics of Unity. So the very ideas of Science and Knowledge and Truth constitutively emerge with the original intuition into the presence of Unity. So Goodness is the Presence of Reason that spawns all of the original building blocks of rational life and existence. The very idea of Form emerges in this Unitive Intuition and thus all the primitive names and forms are found to co-arise, co-originate and constitute one another in relationality. Because of the original co-implicature of all the basic names, forms, concepts, categories, fields, etc. that are disclosed in experience, to focus on any one will inherently implicate the others.

This is the Alterity at the heart of Reason: the Unitive nature of Reason is Relationality— co-implication, mutuality— and this is the origin of polarity, identity/difference, sameness/otherness, of dialogue and dialectic— the conversational nature of discourse and existence. This means that Consciousness, Thought, Language, Experience, Existence, World, Phenomena ... constitute a Continuum or Unitive Field of coexistence and co-implication. Thought is implicated in Language and World from the start, and they are so implicated in one another that to truly explore any one will inherently involve the other. Thus, in the context of the Universal Continuum, the *unity* of any name or field or thing will always immediately involve its other, and to have others— plurality, multiplicity, diversity— will always immediately involve relationality and unitivity.

We are suggesting that the seeds of Universal Grammar are already encoded or implicit in Plato's intuition into Goodness as the Absolute Foundation of Reason and Reality. This intuition is profoundly rich and encodes the blueprint for the evolution of Natural Reason, and indeed for the centuries of evolution in European cultures. Plato helped to open a door to the Unitive Continuum of discourse and began to tap important formulas in the excavation of Reason. He saw that Truth and Knowledge gravitate to Form, Essence, Universal— which are mutually grounded in Unitive Force. He saw that Thought and Action are co-implicated in such a way that *to know* the Good is *to do* the Good. He saw that the reason or telos of human life is to achieve highest knowledge in the pursuit of Wisdom. He saw that philosophy— the love of Wisdom— plays out in the life of open inquiry which is best dramatized in the play of dialogue. And so the quest for What is First, indeed, the recognition that there is something First and Original— a Unitive Force or Unifying Presence— opened the way to First Philosophy or the Science of Reason.

We are also suggesting that Plato only *began* the work of First Philosophy. It would take centuries of intensive experimentation in the ways of Natural Reason to play out more adequately the depth and power of the Universal Space of Goodness that is Reason itself. Plato assumed and presumed that all forms and fields and names and essences derive from this Unitive Space or Universal Continuum, but he did not explicate how the basic categories and domains of experience or existence derive from What is First, or mutually implicate one another. This is the enterprise of Universal Grammar: Reason as the Unitive Force of the Original Word, Form, Name plays itself forth in all its diversity in the grammar of discourse; if all fields, narratives, forms of life...are inherently the play of the Original Word, then Universal Grammar is the expression of Natural Reason.

This is why First Philosophy is so vital for human interests and well being. If human forms of life are situated in the Space of Universal Grammar— in the Unitive Field of the Original Word— then the clarification of What is First, Formal Science, the articulation of First Principles becomes an ultimate concern in the conduct of thought and discourse. We humans, as rational being, have an immediate vital interest in the clarification of First Principles, for our everyday existence in the world, our form of life, is a function of our conduct of mind and management of discourse. In this context, to be human is to be grammatical— to live a competent and grammatically well-formed life. And so it becomes apparent that the deepest inquiry into What is First, into Universal Grammar, into First Principles— the inquiry into the grammar of thought, logic and ontology— are integral to ethics and politics. Aristotle had the genius to see that the theoretical sciences and the practical sciences had to find existential connection in the moral life— the life of virtue. He struggled to clarify the continuum between the highest expression of theoretical wisdom and the deepest expression of practical wisdom in a well-formed life of virtue. But this did not emerge clearly in Aristotle's discourse. In his privileging of Difference and Differentiation and Diversity over the Unitive force of the Unitive Field, the life of theory and the life of practical virtue appeared not to come together in full force. The profound investigations into Logic and Ontology as "theoretical" did not find full coherence with his recognition of Politics as the "Master Science." Where Aristotle was brilliant in discerning differences and divisions between domains or categories or field of experience, he appeared to fall short (by Plato's standards) in discerning the Unitivity of the Continuum of What is First. But where Plato was exemplary in stressing the Unitivity of Reason and the Continuum of all forms and fields, he did not sufficiently explicate the differentiation and derivation and deployment of fundamental categories and fields of discourse. Thus, in a sense, the complementary grammars of Plato and Aristotle bring to more explicit form the Unitive

Alterity of Natural Reason— the dialectical nature of discourse— and set the parameters, aporias and agenda for the subsequent evolution of discourse.

3) Grammar, Culture, Reason: The Evolution of Discourse

Natural Reason expresses itself in Grammar, and Reason pervades life. This means that everyday life— the life of common sense— is the interpretation and expression of Natural Reason. Every form of life is situated in the Space of Universal Grammar and is in this sense an expression of form. In this respect there is a continuum and alterity between philosophical grammars and grammars of common sense: philosophical accounts of grammar are reflections and refinements of common sense grammatical forms, and common sense life is a practical philosophy— a living enactment and embodiment of philosophical grammars. It is evident in the evolutions of discourse that philosophical grammars have deeply influenced the evolution of cultures, and equally that living grammars of common sense have influenced the evolution of philosophical grammars. So common sense, in all its cultural varieties of expression, participate in the art of sense-making, the art of world-making, the making of grammar and discourse. Thus, to say that we humans are "rational beings" is to say that we are grammatical beings— to live is to participate in the enterprise of making sense, a form of life, a shared grammatical enterprise. To exist is to inhabit a life-world which is always some corporate interpretation of Natural Reason, Natural Grammar. In this respect rational life is always both theoretical and practical: every cultural form of life is implicitly an interpretation or "theory" of the space of Natural Reason and at the same time a practical embodiment of a living grammar— a "praxis." Thus, there is an unbreachable continuum between Natural Reason, Culture and Grammar. And all human discourse, all thinking, all experience is constitutively situated in some mode of interpretation— is hermeneutical. So whether we look at a philosophical grammar or a living cultural form of life— a lived grammar— the activity of sense-making or rational interpretation is involved.

This obvious point— that all forms of life are forms of grammar, interpretations of Natural Reason— helps to bring into relief the hermeneutical nature of the human condition. And this accentuates a certain ambiguity or paradoxical appearance of rational life: all cultural life is the interpretation and expression of Natural Reason, and Natural Reason is a presiding influence in shaping the evolution of cultural life. Another way to express this is that all cultural grammars are situated in the space of Universal Grammar and under the constraints and dynamics of Natural Reason, but all narrative accounts of Reason are situated in some cultural mode of interpretation and constrained by the powers and limits of that particular cultural grammar. This is another encounter with the Alterity of Natural Reason which we shall have to work through. For the history and evolution of cultures show that at any given time a culture is already an intersection of diverse grammatical forms of life or modes of interpretation or "ideologies." So cultural life appears to be inter-grammatical and the ongoing play of both shared and differing grammatical interpretations.

Since cultural life is the play and inter-play of grammatical forms of life exploration of the origin, formation and transformations of grammar is essential for an adequate understanding of culture and natural discourse. And to the degree that we fail to have an adequate knowledge and competence in the enterprise of grammar— the rational enterprise— to that extent we are likely to blunder and grope in the dark and remain the victim to blind forces that reign in the malpractice of reason. Thus, to the extent that we are in touch with the laws and dynamics of Natural Reason to that extent our grammatical life is well-formed. When there are splits and polarizations and fragmentation in the life of reason this naturally plays out into the quality of everyday life, in the fragmentation of experience, in the polarization of inner and outer life, in the collision of different alienated ideologies or world-views, in the grammatical violence of moral-political life.

However, an adequate understanding of the formation and transformation of grammars has not been achieved. The early development of the Science of Reason in the philosophical grammars of Plato and Aristotle pointed the direction in which research had to be done and left this area in a rough, preliminary and programmatic form for future research. We pointed out that in the *Sophist* Plato presents a preliminary vision of the importance for philosophy of a "science of dialectic" which would explain the basic kinds or categories and account for how these kinds "blended" in the weaving together of discourse. And we pointed out that Aristotle made some progress in beginning a systematic exploration of categories and how they structure the world and the space of being and predication. Aristotle's remarkable advances in founding the science of logic focused more on the account of the dynamics of inference and argument in his syllogistic theory. And his brilliant insights in founding the discipline of Ontology focused on the nature of primary beings as they are disclosed as logical subjects in the space of predication. But the area of Natural Reason that governed category formation and the mutual deployment of basic categories in shaping conceptual space, in structuring a grammatical form of life into a system of sense, remained in the background and unformulated. It was not understood how cultural grammars of sense developed, how sense or meaning or predicability altered in alternative categorial structures to yield different forms of sense, and hence different worldviews. Because the categorial tools for understanding the nature of world-making or sense-making were not developed it remained unclear when there was a shift in sense formation that signalled the emergence of a different grammar of experience or worldview. Thus, it was not clear in natural discourse when different grammars of sense, different worlds, were attempting dialogue or whether discussion or debate was proceeding in the common ground of a shared conceptual space. And since sense or meaning can shift dramatically in different categorial contexts, in the space of different worlds, the conduct of discourse remained vulnerable to all sorts of ambiguities and equivocations in sense and failure of communication as diverse grammars of experience encountered or confronted one another.

In the next chapter we shall present some main findings in our experiments into the origins of Natural Reason and the logic of Natural Language. In these explorations of First Philosophy we begin to see the emergence of Universal Grammar and the excavation of Meditative Reason. These themes are further elaborated in the following essays.

CHAPTER 2

EXPLORATIONS TOWARD MEDITATIVE REASON

THE EVOLUTION OF UNIVERSAL GRAMMAR

The clarification of Meditative Reason is essentially a development from research in the logic of language which began over twenty-five years ago. I was drawn to research in logical theory in part due to the influence of founders of the modern analytical revolution in philosophy such as Russell, Wittgenstein and Frege. Russell rightly saw that logic is the essence of philosophy. This intuition was classical and continued the long tradition which went back to Greek thought, especially to the teachings of Plato and Aristotle. Aristotle is considered to be the founder of the science of logic— a universal formal science which explores the nature of thought itself. It was already clear to Aristotle that logic is the science of all science precisely because it explores the formal laws of thought which necessarily govern all forms of rational thinking. So logic is a science which claims a certain priority and jurisdiction over all particular forms of rational thinking. And it was equally clear that the depth of the presumed universality of logic involved an intuition of unity as the essence of rationality. The principles of logic were not only the most universal of all principles, but precisely because they were in a deep sense *first principles* they were thereby unifying principles— subsuming the vast diversity of thought under universal formal law. Indeed, the unifying function of first principles is synonymous with rationality itself since they are the organizing principles which create order, system, coherence, consistency and meaning. In this respect it may be said that the logistic thesis in its most generic form was already implicit in the early Greek intuitions of rationality. We shall suggest that the articulation of Universal Grammar is a fulfillment of the classical logistic thesis with its intuitions of formal universality and unity as the essence of rationality.

However, it is most difficult to discern a continuum in the classical and modern versions of the logistic thesis, for the modern paradigm of the grammar of thought sees itself as making a sharp break with classical logic. The birth of modern mathematical logic came largely with the publication of Frege's important work in 1879 which was recognized and developed by Russell. The development of the new paradigm for logic sparked the revolution called "analytical philosophy" in this century and appeared to reject the Aristotelian model of logical grammar which shaped Greco-european culture for over two thousand years. Thinkers like Frege and Russell believed that Leibniz's dream of finding a universal calculus or grammar of thought could not be realized within the Aristotelian paradigm. Rather, they believed that they were now well on the way to realizing this universal deep structure of thought precisely with the innovations of Frege and the break with the "limited and outmoded" classical logic.

I shall not attempt here to present the specifics of the contrasts between the Aristotelian and Fregean models of logic. It is more appropriate to stress that Frege rejected what was at the heart of the Aristotelian model as misguided— the model of all thought as predicative in logical form. For Aristotle, to think is to predicate— to affirm or deny a logical predicate of a logical subject. Both singular and general statements are equally predicative in form, and Aristotle's remarkable presentation of syllogistic theory— the logic of general statements— was essentially a formal theory of general predication. But this is precisely what Frege rejected, insisting that general statements, that is, statements involving all or some or none of a given class or general term, were *not* predicative in form, but involved quantifiers and propositional functions and *in effect involved a radically new model of predication*. Frege's new grammar of thought rejected the classical view that the term (subject or predicate) was the unit of meaning, and introduced the view that there are atomic propositions which are the units of meaning. The logic of propositions was taken to be the new foundation of theory of language replacing the classical view that the term or concept was the unit of thought or logical grammar.

Of course this radical shift in the paradigm of logic required an across-the-board renovation of all of the concepts of logic. The concepts of predication, negation, affirmation and denial, contrariety, logical subject and predicate, implication, etc. all required radical revision in the Fregean model. And with the remarkable success in apparently resolving long standing problems in logic that persisted for centuries, it was natural for thinkers like Russell to announce the death of the Aristotelian paradigm. The Fregean innovations immediately led to the formalization and apparent simplification of areas of thought that had not been adequately explained before, like the logic of relations, the nature of quantifiers, truth-functions and so on. And the discovery of powerful formal calculi, like the propositional calculus, made it seem undeniable that finally the science of logic was born. Frege, who was deeply interested in the foundations of mathematics, initiated the "logistic thesis" showing that arithmetic was reducible to pure logic, and later Russell and Whitehead in their monumental work— *Principia Mathematica*, attempted to demonstrate that all mathematics was reducible to logic in its newly discovered general form. It was natural to think that Leibniz's dream of a universal calculus of thought had been discovered especially because it was now thought that mathematical logic finally made possible a general and universal formal logic or grammar of thought. The enthusiasm, optimism and energy released by this possibility fueled the early stages of the analytical revolution in philosophy.

But the classical paradigm of logic would not allow itself to be buried so easily. After all, precisely because logic was so deep and formative of thought it stands to reason that to reject classical logic would be tantamount to dismissing the whole tradition of thought that was governed by this paradigm. It is no exaggeration to say that the Aristotelian paradigm of logical form set the agenda for the philosophical tradition. All through the centuries it was primarily the classical Subject-Predicate model that framed metaphysical thinking and thereby influenced all thinking that flows from a given ontology. One finds, for example, that the subject-predicate form of thought reflects the substance-attribute model of reality, and one of the primary concerns of classical metaphysics was to articulate Being in terms of describing the primary substances that comprised reality. All of science was focused on discovering the essential attributes that made a given thing what it is; so epistemology (the theory of knowledge) was oriented around the subject-predicate model which maintained that the world consisted of things of different types. It is not surprising then to find the great thinkers of the tradition from Plato and Aristotle through Thomas Aquinas, Descartes, Spinoza, Leibniz, Locke, Hume, Kant and Hegel and beyond centering their thinking in one way or another on the classical model of rational form. Kant went so far as to praise Aristotle for the remarkable feat of single handedly developing the science of logic in its final form; Aristotle's theory of syllogistic logic remained affirmed as the heart of logic through the centuries. Kant's magnificient attempt to derive the pure *a priori* categories of thought from the logical form of judgment turned on the Aristotelian model of logical form. Certainly Leibniz's dream of discovering a universal calculus of thought was dreamt in the subject-predicate grammar of Aristotle.

And it does not take much imagination to see that Descartes' meditations unfolded in the logical space of substance/attribute, as did the monistic thinking of Spinoza. So it should be apparent that to reject the Aristotelian grammar of thought would be in effect to draw the curtains on the evolution of thought prior to the Fregean innovations. Of course we could reconstruct a post-Fregean Plato or Aristotle and use the modern grammar of thought to discern what Descartes, Spinoza, Leibniz and Kant "really meant". But it should be evident that such reconstruction is bound to be invention and not remain faithful to the tradition.

This is the philosophical context that situated my early research problems and preoccupations. My doctoral research was essentially an attempt to master the two paradigms of logical form, the two grammars of thought, and attempt to understand their similarities and differences and to mediate them with reference to the truth about rationality and the logic of language.

I was most fortunate at an early stage to learn about the exciting research of Professor Fred Sommers of Brandeis University. I had learnt of his recent discovery and publication (1959) of a theory of natural language which was based on the Aristotelian Subject-Predicate logic and which argued that language is governed by a hierarchical order of categories which configured in a "tree" or "pyramid" structure. This discovery of the "tree theory" was exciting for many reasons. For one, it was a direct development of the Aristotelian paradigm which indicated that this model still had creative life in it. It was developed with all the rigor and clarity of the "analytical movement" and spoke to interests and objectives of this movement. It was a powerful theory of categories which promised to be a significant alternative to the then current trends in theorizing about meaning in natural language. This category "tree theory" of natural language had its roots in Plato's thought and according to Sommers it was the shaping paradigm of philosophical languages through the centuries. A leading English philosopher in the 1950's, Gilbert Ryle, came to the conclusion that philosophical analysis was especially concerned with categories and he recognized the potential value of Sommers' discovery and published it in journal *Mind*.

I had the opportunity to work closely with Professor Sommers as a doctoral student at Brandeis University from 1965-68. By this time he had already published several innovative papers further developing the categorial logic for ordinary language. This was a period in the analytical movement when the earlier exhuberance of the analytical revolution had played itself out and philosophers were more ready to see that the Fregean logic had its theoretical limitations when it came to accounting for certain features of natural language.

The analytical movement was polarized into at least two camps. On one side were the formalists who pressed on with the attempt to reform natural language in terms of certain ideal formal logical grammars which they took to be the deep structure of language. On the other side were the informalists who believed that natural language was rich in its logical powers and governed by complex and informal logical forms which could not and should not conform to the contrived formal models of logicians. The career of Wittgenstein is often taken to be a good example of this polarization. For in his earlier career he helped launch the formalist program of ideal language philosophy, but in his later career he was a leader in the counter-movement called "ordinary language philosophy" which was an informalist rebellion against the domination of the formalist program.

I mention this because Sommers saw himself as cutting through both alternatives: he believed that this polarization in philosophy of logic and language was due to the abandonment of the more powerful Aristotelian logical model in favor of the Fregean paradigm. It was because philosophers now only had the Fregean and post Fregean logics that they were forced into the unwelcome conclusion that the logic of natural language must be "informal" since the formal logics could not account for the richness and power and diversity of ordinary language. By contrast, Sommers was a formalist in his approach to natural language, but he was centered in the logical forms of the Aristotelian paradigm. He critiqued the contemporary informalists by arguing that there are formal predicative laws governing conceptual formation and meaning in ordinary language. He argued that the "tree structure" was the appropriate depiction of the formal predicative law governing all thought— it was shown to be derived from the formal features of the Aristotelian predicative paradigm.

It was this dialectic between the Fregean grammar of thought on the one hand and Sommers' revival of the classical grammar of thought that framed the agenda for my earlier research and teaching, and in what follows I shall attempt to sketch the highlights in my explorations over the past twenty years which grappled with problems and issues that were already raised in the early stage of my journey. I shall try to show that the seeds of Mediative Reason are already implicit in developments of logical theory and philosophy of language arising out of the deeper mediation between the classical and Fregean grammars of thought.

My doctoral dissertation *Time, Truth and Logical Determinism* was essentially an attempt to demonstrate the theoretical powers of the Aristotelian model of predication in accounting for certain fundamental features of thought, meaning and language. I focused on a rich classical problem in Aristotle's thought which held fascination for philosophers through the centuries and which at the time of my doctoral research had seen an intense revival of interest amongst post-Fregean logicians. It is the problem of "logical determinism" or "future contingent statements" which gained infamy under the name — "the sea battle tomorrow". I shall not of course explore this problem here. I mention it because this problem of the truth status of statements about future state of affairs naturally opens up many of the basic concepts of logical theory— the nature of predication, the function of the copula, the logical force of affirmation and denial, the place of time and tense in meaning and truth, the nature of assertibility and modality, the referential status of the future *vis a vis* the past and present, etc. This was a perfect place to sort out the dialectics of how the Fregean grammar would handle the problem and how Aristotle handled it. I found that the best logicians on the contemporary scene failed to do justice to Aristotle's analysis. They usually failed because they were re-casting Aristotle's problem formulation in terms of the Fregean paradigm of thought and were missing fundamental points in Aristotle's discussion which of course were a direct expression of the Aristotelian paradigm of predication.

At this early stage of my work I was more sympathetic with Sommers' way of thinking which was to argue for the superiority of the Aristotelian grammar over the contemporary paradigm. My orientation at this time was to try to demonstrate in detail that the Fregean interpreters of Aristotle failed in principle to understand Aristotle's position, and to argue that Aristotle's grammar of thought was superior in theoretical powers in accounting for the logical features of natural thought.

I steeped myself in the contemporary discussions and struggled for over three years on the problem of performing a just and creative mediation of the two paradigms of logic. I assumed that the real facts to be accounted for were "out there" in the nature of language and thought and that the two paradigms were like two competing theories in science— both to be measured in reference to the success in accounting for the objective logical facts of the matter. This hermeneutical posture, I must confess, caused

intense mental cramps. As I attempted to be as sympathetic as possible to
the Fregean logicians I began increasingly to feel the force of their line of
interpretation. And as the lucidity and power of Aristotle's discussion
came into focus I was more convinced than ever that Aristotle's position
was coherent and deeply insightful about fundamental logical phenomena.
I had assumed that the concepts of logical theory were univocal (having one
common meaning) between the two grammars, and that they were
competing with one another directly in presenting the truth about thought.
It was not until some time later that I found that this hermeneutical attitude
on my part was naive and self defeating. For I could already feel the
splitting and polarization of the concepts, "facts," phenomena of language,
as I attempted authentically to live in the two paradigms of thought. All of
my attempts to find the common ground and points of real mediation
between the two paradigms were frustrated. The more effectively I lived
in each paradigm, the less common ground I found between them— the
more I began to feel the systematic equivocation of all concepts and
phenomena spoken of in the two languages of thought.

I think the dissertation retreated somewhat from the ambitious aim of
demonstrating the superiority of the Aristotelian paradigm over the
Fregean model and focused more on stressing the *differences* between
them. The force of my argument was to defend the integrity and ingenuity
of Aristotle's position and to point out the systematic distortions and
inadequacies in the attempts of the Fregean logicians to account for
Aristotle's analysis. The moral of the dissertation was that the Aristotelian
model of logical form and predication had its powers and virtues in the
analysis of logical phenomena and that the Fregean logicians should
exercise more self-conscious care in employing their logical theories. The
effect of this early work was to be quite sensitive to the scope, powers and
limits of a given paradigm, to respect differences between diverse
paradigms, and to recognize the systematic distortions and breakdowns that
arise when one paradigm is misused beyond its legitimate jurisdiction.

With the completion of the dissertation (1969-70) I found myself in a
philosophical limbo on the matter of mediation, truth and common ground
between the two paradigms of thought. It was one thing to discern
important differences and contrasts between two grammars of thought, but
on the question of true dialogue, mediation, negotiation towards the truth, I
found myself groping and frustrated. I had not satisfactorily demonstrated
that the Aristotelian paradigm was *the logic* of natural language and was
the definitive truth about logical phenomena. I grew increasingly uncertain
and shaky about the common ground between the two paradigms. My
dissertation was predicated on the premise that there could be meaningful
communication between the two grammars, but it was not clear that this

was even possible. My very discourse in the dissertation was shaken and I increasingly wondered how the Fregean logicians who live in one paradigm could so confidently believe that they were really arguing against Aristotle's discourse which arose in an alien and even antagonistic paradigm. I took it for granted that legitimate dialogue and discourse was possible between grammars of thought; this was in effect the unfolding story of philosophy itself. But this became increasingly the preoccupation of my research and teaching. It was the very question of truth, meaning and rationality itself.

The polarization of rationality and discourse across the grammars of thought was intensified even further with a remarkable discovery by Sommers between 1967 and 1969. Despite the important results already achieved in the discovery of the "tree principle" and the powerful tool of formal ontology it implied, the research papers published by Sommers between 1959 and the mid-sixties were largely ignored by the Fregean establishment. The importance and creativity of his work was recognized by certain figures but they were exceptions to the general consensus. In fact Sommers encountered outright hostility to his views when he presented them to Fregean logicians. The problem of rational discourse between grammars of thought was not merely a speculative or theoretical issue, but an existential political condition. It was a shock for me when I first began to realize that the question of truth and rationality was ensnared in the politics of meaning and the control of discourse. I began to see that there was a political establishment that attempted to control discourse and this majority presumes the authority to decide what is meaningful and worthy of attention. It was a rude awakening for me to discover this in the philosophical establishment of logicians and analytical philosophers. Those who spoke within the Fregean framework were in, and those who spoke outside of this grammar were out. Sommers realized that if his discoveries in categorial logic were going to be taken seriously it would be necessary to demonstrate beyond doubt that the philosophical grammar within which they were articulated would have to be recognized. Since the predominant attitude among Fregean logicians was that the Aristotelian grammar was obsolete and displaced, any alleged discoveries which came from this "dead" and "invalidated" grammar would be treated in the same way. Sommers was convinced that he could show that the Aristotelian formal logic could be generalized into a powerful formal logic which would be a serious alternative and challenge to the modern formal logics.

This is precisely what he discovered in the late '60's. He discovered a simple "arithmetic" calculus— formal symbolic notation— for Subject-Predicate logic which opened the way for understanding the classical view that all thoughts are logically subject-predicate in form. I shall not get into the specifics of this discovery here. I shall only mention that this notation simplified classically valid argument forms in a perspicuous way showing that reasoning is a kind of calculation or cancellation procedure. The notation made clear the general form of any proposition, elucidated the nature of logical formatives, made clear the functioning of quantifiers and propositional functions, clarified the meaning of the propositional connectives, revealed the logical information in relational terms and provided a universal symbolic language for all forms of propositions and inferences. It was remarkable that the form of this "arithmetic of thought" had striking analogies and similarities to the symbolic notation experimented with by Leibniz. After the initial insights into this new notation were expressed Sommers began to see that he had found the kind of general grammar of thought that Leibniz adumbrated in his logical papers. This generalization of Aristotelian logic was eventually published by Oxford University Press in 1982— *The Logic of Natural Language.*

One would have thought that with the discovery of a clear formal symbolic notation and generalization of Subject-Predicate logic that it would receive a more fair and open hearing from the logicians. For these thinkers traded in formal symbolic notations— that is the language they speak and understand, especially when it is presented in "arithmetic" form. But this was not the case. On the contrary, establishment logicians were even more hostile and closed than ever. I began to encounter this hostility directly in my early attempts to present the new logic to logicians. I began to see more clearly the depth and practical reality of speaking across grammars of thought. So with the discovery of the subject-predicate calculus the Aristotelian paradigm took on even greater life and credibility but the polarization in logic only deepened and the barriers to dialogue and communication between the paradigms grew stronger. Sommers' discovery of the term calculus had the effect of deeper confirmation of the categorial "tree structure" for natural language and it certainly deepened my resolve to continue my explorations in this grammar of thought. I was more determined than ever to try to find an effective way to break through the barriers between the grammars of thought and open a way to dialogue and real conversation.

This set the stage for the next development in my research and teaching. Throughout the '70's I continued to do research in the new subject-predicate calculus and this was reflected in my teaching of the Logic course and the Philosophy of Logic course. These courses attempted to present the two grammars of thought and to explore in a comparative way the powers and limits of each. But my main attention during this period was focused on attempting to think through the implications of the categorial logic, formal ontology and the applications of the "tree principle". As important as the discovery of the new calculus was, I believed that the potential of the categorial logic for ontological analysis and interpretation of the evolution of thought was perhaps greater. It was my sense that the development and application of formal ontological analysis would make clear for the first time precisely how conceptual structures were formed and transformed; it would provide the formal tools to analyse the form of philosophical languages or ontologies as systems of meaning. I began to see the potential of this category theory for exploring the conceptual formation of cultures or world views as well as for the formation of scientific frameworks. It was my judgment that if the theoretical powers of the category logic could be shown (apart from its intrinsic value) it would go a long way towards re-opening the case for a fair hearing of the classical theory of predication and philosophical grammar.

The discovery of the "tree" principle for natural language was in effect the opening up of a new and potent science; the categorial logic needed to be articulated and cultivated to realize its potential. Philosophers from ancient times were characteristically preoccupied with discerning the fundamental categories of reality. And from the start philosophy was born with the intuition that there is a fundamental unity to conceptual space— that there must be a primitive or original all-encompassing concept or category that revealed the nature of reality and unified all other concepts. The pre-Socratic thinkers in particular were deeply concerned with identifying the original principle which explains the vast diversity found in the universe. Such a principle would be a rational principle from which all other names and forms would be derivable and hence explained. This meant that conceptual space was holistic— a unified ordered field— wherein the diverse concepts of thought and language would find their rightful place.

Through the centuries philosophers have been preoccupied with discerning the basic categories of thought and existence, and in particular with trying to understand how the basic categories configure or fail to configure with one another. The tree principle was already anticipated in Plato's *Sophist*, and Aristotle's attempt to discern the fundamental categories of Being formed the heart of his metaphysical thinking. But Aristotle did not succeed in giving a satisfactory explanation of the origin or organization of the categories. He produced a list of about ten categories, but the list appeared somewhat arbitrary and was not presented as a convincing and coherent theory. Kant saw this centuries later and he tried to give a more satisfactory account of the origin of the basic categories of thought and experience. He too attempted to derive the formal categories from the logical form (predicative form) of judgment, but there were problems with his attempts. On the contemporary scene thinkers like Ryle saw that philosophical analysis is especially concerned with categories and categorial relations, but he recognized that this central concern of philosophers lacked the formal tools for performing a linguistic cartography of concepts. Sommers' discovery of the formal "tree" principle for natural language struck a classical cord in opening up categorial logic through deeper formal insights into the predicative form. It explained clearly for the first time the logical structure of a category, it confirmed the classical intuition of the holistic unity of conceptual space (that the sense structure of a given language comprised an ordered unified field) and it provided for the first time a formal tool for carrying out conceptual cartography. To clarify the meaning of a given concept it must be "mapped" or located within the ordered configuration of the categorial structure which defines the language in question. Categorial logic provided a powerful formal method for clarifying meaning and carrying out the aims of the analytical revolution. But these seeds needed to be nurtured and cultivated to bring them to fruition.

This is what I focused on in the 70's. While the Fregean paradigm focused on meaning in terms of truth conditions, reference, and facts, the categorial logic was primarily concerned with the origins of meaning in *sense formation* — it was a formal logic of sense conditions. It became clear that the categorial analysis was striking at a depth of conceptualization and meaning that the Fregean analysis was missing and did not have the tools for tapping. Categorial analysis showed that *sense* is rationally prior to truth or reference as understood in post-Fregean discourse. The logic of truth-condition presupposed the logic of sense-conditions.

The idea is that in natural languages to think is to predicate— to logically join a predicate term to a subject term. And the tree principle is the formal rule governing how we may legitimately predicate terms or meaningfully think in any given language. Any such language has a depth structure of categorial relations which determine which terms may meaningfully configure with other terms. To "predicate" or join two terms which are impredicable is to think nonsense— to fail in sense. This is called a "category mistake." Categorial logic explores the boundaries of sense and non-sense for a given natural language. And sense is logically prior to truth in that a given predication must make sense in order to qualify to be either true or false. A predication which makes sense specifies a state of affairs which is a *possible* fact, so making sense does not *per se* imply actual facticity or existence. Similarly, the specification of a "thing" by the subject term of a senseful predication does not yet imply an actual reference made to a supposedly existent object, only to a categorially possible entity. It is a serious error to confuse the condition of truth of a proposition (predication) with the conditions of sense. Yet post-Fregean strategies of analysis tend to identify meaning with truth-conditions.

Indeed, for Frege logical form is precisely the specification of truth-conditions.

So categorial logic explores the origin of conceptual meaning (sense) for natural languages. But sense does mirror the world (being, reality) as it is categorially determined by the given language. I shall not here attempt to explain how the pyramid structure formally derives from the logical form of predication; it suffices for our present purpose to sketch the tree principle to see how it works:

Since any natural language is predicative, we can discern its sense structure by selecting certain of its categories and mapping their predicative relations as given by the language. Here it is important to notice that the terms of a language depict either types of entities or categories that organize things into types— this reflects the subject-predicate structure of thought. A given world depicted by its language divides into types of things and fundamental attributes or categories which organize diverse things into unified types. So any term in the language is always a specification of a wider term or term of a greater scope that is its origin. This structural feature of conceptualization is reflected in the logic of terms: any term is inherently given with its logical contrary-terms are always given in polar pairs. Thus, if a term "P" is considered, the very meaning of this term is necessarily tied to its polar contrary— "un-P", and the conjoint union of this polar pair specifies a wider universal field whence both "P" and "un-P" derive and take their sense. So we can take any term from ordinary language and pick out its logical contrary, for example wise/un-wise; colored/uncolored; mortal/immortal; married/unmarried and so on. The formal notion of a category (or fundamental predicate) is reached by symbolizing the polar-pairs in one term; and we shall follow Sommers in using slashes to indicate the category-term:

$$/P/ \ = \ \text{the union of "P" and "un-P"}$$

The category term "/P/" specifies a universal class or field that picks out a feature of reality. It exhausts the range of possible application of whatever *could be* either "P" or "un-P". It is precisely this constraint on a term that draws the boundaries of sense or non-sense for this term; if it is used beyond its categorial range a category mistake results.

I shall mention in passing that the type of internal polar opposition in the structure of terms— contrariety— was of fundamental importance in Aristotle's logic, but conspicuously absent in Fregean logic. It is not accidental that post-Fregean logic is not only disinterested in categories in the analysis of meaning, but positively skeptical about the need or legitimacy of categorial analysis or the importance of category mistakes. Nevertheless, it is important to see that in natural thinking both things and attributes are organized and collected into fundamental terms (types and categories). Thus, if we take all the color-terms in ordinary English we find that the full range of such terms, including the term "colorless", are included in the category /Color/; this universal and exhaustive term picks out a fundamental feature of the world which includes all possible color terms including the privation of color— "colorless".

Figure 1

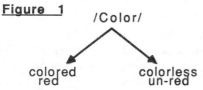

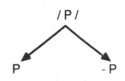

So any property term is always a specification of a more fundamental and logically prior unified and unifying field which is the origin of its meaning. And the same goes for "things" or "objects"— they are always of a given type. Thus, "Socrates" is a type of being, in this case a /Person/— a type term that unifies and encompasses all possible persons. Again, this "stone" is a type of entity— a /material/ body, a /physical/ entity, something /extended/ in space, and so on. And the point being stressed is that in categorial analysis, we understand the nature of a given thing or property when we apprehend the type or category it specifies; its meaning and being are intrinsically tied to its categorial form.

But it is equally crucial to see that the types and categories which comprise a given language are themselves collected and organized into a universal unified categorial field which defines the sense of the language. We may depict the general form of the predicative (categorial) structure of a given language in the following figure: If we use capital letters for the categories and common letters for the types of a given language, its categorial structure, according to the "tree" principle will take the following form.

Figure 2

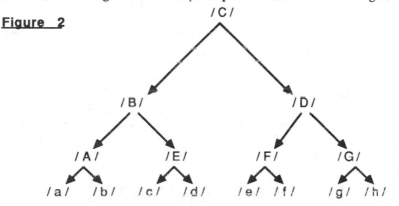

This unified pyramid of terms shows how the terms of a given language may or may not configure intelligibly. It may be intelligibly said of /a/ type things that they are /B/ or /C/ but it would be a category mistake to say that they are /D/ or /F/ or /G/. Only categories which are on a continuous line may be predicated of a type of thing, and this type collects and instantiates the categories which apply to it. These categories constitute the thing and give its essence or nature.

This categorial structure depicts an ordered unified field. The conceptual form of a given language is ordered and organized by the most inclusive term at the top— the "apex". This is the most universal and all-encompassing term of the language— it is the unifying principle of all terms of the language and organizes the discourse into a continuum of meaning. In this way we see that categorial logic is a conceptual holism— the meaning of any term is a function of its organic location in the conceptual domain. Any term is always a specification of a higher category which reveals its true meaning and essence. No term has independent or auto-logical meaning. Here it is crucial to see that meaning is essentially oriented to a higher principle, which we may call the "telos" of the language. This orientation of conceptual space gives direction to meaning and truth. Inquiry into the nature of any thing involves discerning the deeper categories which comprise it, and ultimately its functional unity under the "apex term". No term or thing has unity independently of the Universal Conceptual Domain— the unity of any thing, its principle of individuation, is shown by its locus in the conceptual continuum. Thus, for example, if in a given language /a/ type things are /persons/ which include the individual "socrates", we understand the nature or meaning of "socrates" by understanding the hierarchy of higher categories which it instantiates— /C/, /B/, /A/.

In exploring the categorial domain of discourse it is useful to think of any term of the language as a "field"— as a specification of the Unified Conceptual Domain. So any /term/, whether logical subject or predicate, whether type or category, is a field within the universal logical space of the categorial unified field. And this immediately implies that the meaning of any term is relative to its field specification or locus in the universal conceptual domain. Any term is a specified extension within the hierarchial order of the conceptual domain. In this light it becomes apparent that the apex term has an intriguing logic— it is the transcendental principle of unity of the language and all terms are under its jurisdiction. This unifying principle holds the discourse together and is the origin of its intelligibility or rational coherence. So rationality and meaning are inherently telic in form— it is always in reference to a transcendental first principle or original field that meaning makes sense.

The apex term is an all encompassing universal field whose presence makes rationality possible. It encodes all discourse within its jurisdiction, and all such discourse may be truly "de-coded" or interpreted in the light of this transcendental presence.

But it is timely to stress that the categorial structure not only governs the sense formation or meaning of a language, it equally expresses a world or existential field, it makes thought and experience possible, it makes the rational activity of mind possible and frames a form of life. This becomes more apparent when it is seen that in categorial logic "meaning" is a unifying field which holds "language", "thought" and "world" together in a mutual co-implication. Although these terms may specify diverse domains or fields in conventional thinking, in categorial analysis they mutually expand and are seen to be in a deep mutual co-extension in logical space. Here it is impossible to separate the domain of thought (mind, experience) from the domain of language (discourse, signs) or from the domain of world (reality, existence). Rather, the sense structure is precisely the mutual intersection of these domains— it is a unifying factor in which each domain inherently shapes and constitutes and mirrors the other.

In this respect the science of sense is at once logic, ontology and phenomenology. It is logic because it reveals the inner workings of rationality as this is expressed in language; it is ontology because it reveals the constitutive grammar of a world— the intelligible shape of reality or existence; it is phenomenology because it shows the grammar of experience in a life-world, and makes clear the origins of phenomena which are made possible by categorial structure. In this categorial sense phenomenology makes clear the transcendental conditions of experience and phenomena in a given life-world. So the investigation of *sense formation* has a peculiar depth and priority. We shall find it helpful to use a generic term to indicate this formal science of sense. Let us call it "Hermeneutics". This special use of the term "hermeneutics" will hopefully justify itself as we proceed. It helps to accentuate that all three of these disciplines are essentially concerned with meaning and interpretation and we need some unifying device to help overcome the tendency artificially to split the domains of language, thought and reality from one another. Since each of these fields claims to be universal and to have a certain formal priority over all other fields it would be natural to think of Hermeneutics in our sense as being Universal Science with formal jurisdiction over other more specific hermeneutical arts. Any form of thought or experience would involve categorial or sense structure, and any inquiry into meaning and truth necessarily involves categorial form. So Hermeneutics is the formal discipline that explicates the sense structure which is presupposed in any form of meaning.

On this note it is relevant to see that field which is specified by "I"— the field of self, mind, voice, thinker, experience— is always situated in some categorial field or grammar. The speech, thought and experience of the self already has categorial shape and situatedness in a world or universal grammatical field. In a sense the mind-field or voice-field of the self is co-extensive with its grammatical or logical space— it is one with its world. In this respect, the experience of this self is made possible and conditioned by its categorial structure— all its experience and conceptualization is pre-consciously or transcendentally shaped by the categorial space which it inhabits. In its lived form, this categorial space or universe is a life-world, and in a shared form of life it is a culture, common sense, a language or world view.

This is one way to accentuate the hermeneutical feature of human experience. Any form of life is structured in categorial grammar and interpreted by it. Since the self or mind-field is always situated in grammar it is accurate to say that to experience is to interpret in the light of the lived grammar. And the very self is interpreted by this grammar and in turn shapes its grammar-world through its hermeneutical activity. This recognition that categorial grammar pervades life and that all human experience is always interpretation lends further support to calling the science of sense "hermeneutics"— for it is a formal semantics of experience.

It is equally important to notice that a categorial grammar is an all-encompassing universal field— a universe of discourse. It was just suggested that the apex-term for any given categorial structure unifies the field into a categorial continuum— a unified field with internal coherence and consistency. It is this universal and unifying feature of a grammar that formally constitutes the unity of a universe of discourse— it defines what is to count as one language.

This helps to make clear that the meaning of any term is inherently a function of its relative position in the categorial field. The term is indigenous to this field and cannot be abstracted from this semantic context. But now it is possible for us to clarify formally that a given natural language encompasses a range of diverse possible categorial worlds or universes of discourse— it is an open ended cluster of diverse grammar-fields each of which has categorial universality and internal integrity and unity. So terms of a natural language have a certain hermeneutical ambiguity until their native grammatical contexts are clarified. What makes sense in one grammar does not make sense in another; indeed, there is a real problem of the univocal identity of any term across categorial grammars. Let us call this the "ambiguity thesis"— that any term in natural language is systematically ambiguous across categorial grammars. And of course this thesis extends to all "things", "facts", "phenomena". What is an intelligible phenomenon in one grammar appears to be nonsense in another. In general, the being or existentiality of any given thing is relative to a certain determinate grammatical field, and it cannot be presumed that things or facts have univocal identity across universes of discourse. This includes the sense and reference of "I"— the self, voice, mind, of the thinker. The very identity and facticity of the self is a function of its native grammatical field. The voice of the thinker/speaker has a certain inherent equivocity and indeterminancy of identity across diverse universes.

By the mid '70's the method of comparative hermeneutics began to become clear. As I experimented in research and teaching with testing categorial analysis I began to realize the universal power and scope of the method. One fruitful laboratory was the history and evolution of western thought itself. Sommers had already used categorial analysis in what he called "formal ontology" to analyse the categorial form of certain philosophical positions. As I systematically thought through the implications of formal ontology for discourse in general I began to see that all human experience, all cultural life, all forms of discourse, were governed by categorial form. In this way the earlier idea of formal ontology expanded and was universalized into what I call "formal comparative hermeneutics". During this period I began to see that all fields, all disciplines, had a categorial deep structure which immediately and actively governed their discourse. This came with the recognition that any form of experience was expressed in language in one form or another, was some kind of meaning, and that where there was meaning there was sense or categorial form. It became clear also that it was not only concepts and percepts that were categorial in origin, but that all phenomena, the facts, existence or reality itself that was shaped by grammar; there was nothing that was not saturated in sense or grammar.

This was an exciting discovery. For the categorial logic now made available in a way that we did not have before a powerful formal instrument to excavate the underlying categorial deep structure of any discourse which in effect decoded its meaning. Thus, for example, I began to see the evolution of the history of thought as a series of categorial grammars— the great thinkers were in effect experimenting with grammar— proposing what they thought were more effective language forms or systems of meaning to make sense of the world and human experience. The vast systems of diverse philosophers or ontologists could now be more effectively decoded by explicating their categorial structures. This helped to show that philosophical arguments were often essentially categorial arguments— arguments purporting to show that a given category was more universal and all encompassing than had been thought, or less universal, or that two fundamental categories which had been confused before needed to be clearly separated and relocated, etc. Until the categorial maneuvers were made explicit the arguments and discourse of philosophers were often not in focus. Certain moves appeared to be arbitrary or lacking a rationale. But with the clarification of the underlying categorial arguments it was as if we found the key to unlock the telic forces which governed the flow of discourse.

As I applied the formal hermeneutical method in the analysis of a variety of philosophical texts and positions, I began to see a range of diverse philosophical grammars being proposed. It became clear in Plato's *Phaedo* that Socrates' argument for the immortality of the soul essentially turned on categorial distinctions between the category of body and the category of soul. Here we see the development of a dualistic grammar of experience which claims to show that the realm of the soul was categorially of a different nature from the realm of the body. The entire dialogue turns on making the categorial argument for this distinction. Indeed, one can see much of Plato's thought as the systematic thinking through of the distinctions and relations between the two categorially distinct realms. By contrast, we find a categorial force shaping Aristotle's thought which was attempting to avoid and correct the categorial dualism found in Plato's discourse. Aristotle brilliantly struggled, in the *De Anima* for example, to bring the category of soul and body back into a primitive unity. In examining the ontology of St. Thomas, or Descartes, Leibniz, Spinoza, Locke, Berekely or Hume, we find their discourse essentially shaped by categorial concerns— they were attempting to introduce grammatical innovations or revisions which they thought created more accurate, comprehensive or coherent discourse. It became clear that the philosophical tradition was an evolution of attempts to forge more effective grammars of experience and reality. And the arguments of the philosophers turned on their categorial innovations. Berkeley's philosophy— all his discourse— turned on seeing that he was attempting to demonstrate that the category of /thought/ or /spirit/ was the most fundamental, that all material or physical things were derived from this categorial field— it was an apex term. Similarly, the movement of Descartes' meditations becomes compelling when the underlying categorial concerns and maneuvers are made manifest. His "conclusion" about the dual nature of the person was a predictable result of his earlier categorial discovery that the category of /thought/ was radically distinct from and independent of the category of /extension/. His categorial grammar echoed that of Socrates' in the *Phaedo* and the ontological dualism that resulted was precisely what preserved the coherence of his discourse, given his discovery of the radical independence of the two fundamental categories. For the formal categorial logic made clear the formal constraint of coherence for any proposed grammar— the tree or pyramid structure depicted the laws of thought, and any arrangement or re-arrangement of basic categories had to conform to this tree rule.

It has been said that Descartes set the agenda for the modern age. This makes sense from a categorial point of view. For researchers in all fields have been affected by the challenge of Descartes' proposed categorial discoveries. We find subsequent thinkers struggling to overcome the clarified categorial dualism in one way or another— to find a more fundamental unified field which mediated the split in the human being. Spinoza's brilliant attempt to develop a monistic categorial field was one classical example. He was following categorial laws in developing the monistic grammar. Leibniz attempted to find a more powerful grammatical resolution in developing his monadology— a spiritual atomism in which the ultimate particles of reality are spiritual atoms. This move is the attempt to show that the apex term must be spiritual energy which encompassed all the features of body and physical existence. By contrast, a materialist like Hobbes makes a counter move in trying to demonstrate that the ultimate category— the apex term— must be /material nature/. This categorial proposal attempts to locate the category of /mind/ and /thought/ within the category of /matter/— a perfectly legitimate and predictable categorial strategy to overcome the cartesian dualism.

As the tradition evolved we find other important thinkers moved by categorial law to develop their grammatical options. From a categorial point of view, the vast system developed by Hegel becomes more convincing, accessible, and lucid. Here is a brilliant attempt to develop a universe of discourse— a unified field— which accounted for diversity and dualism and took the direction of dialectical idealism. And it is not surprising to find the grammatical counter-moves introduced by Marx in his dialectical materialism. The categorial logic provided the formal tools for juxtaposing competing alternative categorial language forms— to compare and evaluate their categorial maneuvers and arguments.

But categorial considerations are present and operative in other fields as well. In contemporary psychology, for example, we find the categorial forces at work in the polarization of theories about human intelligence, learning, behavior and disorders. We find certain grammars of psychology influenced by physiology and tending to explain psyche and behavior in terms of the categories of body, as in versions of behaviorism. And predictably we find the contrary mentalist grammars which give priority to the category of mind— mental powers and operations, etc. It is as if the categorial logic were a pre-conscious constraint on theory formation in these and other disciplines.

Certainly we find categorial considerations at the heart of a discipline like physics— the Newtonian grammar of physics wields "concepts" like "mass" and "force" in a certain way. But categorial analysis makes clear that these basic concepts of the language of physics are lodged in categorial form and constrained by categorial laws. The categorial logic allows us to see readily the underlying categorial revision in Einstein's revolutionary proposals. The discovery of a new relation between the concepts of mass and energy and of space and time are powerful categorial transformations which make sense from a categorial point of view. Einstein was in effect making profound categorial revisions and forging an expanded grammar for the discourse of physics. Typically, this reformed not only the sense of the concepts of physics but at the same time made possible the very existence of phenomena which were not accessible in the earlier grammatical forms. And since conceptualization in any discourse is always governed by categorial grammar, the categorial analysis of Einstein's discourse makes more explicit and lucid the implications of this grammatical revolution.

The categorial logic enables us to anticipate and predict hermeneutical powers and limits of the proposed grammar and the new universe of discourse it opens up. The grammatical analysis could measure whether and where the grammar was coherent and where it would need more work and extension. The conceptual innovations could be experimentally accelerated to test out new possible phenomena in this universe and detect categorial conflicts or incoherencies or constraints in this discourse. We could then experiment with categorial revisions of Einstein's proposal and explore new alternative possible worlds.

These diverse applications of categorial analysis made clear that there was indeed an alternative fruitful method of formal analysis of discourse to the post-Fregean methods. Sommers' earlier intuitions in insisting on natural language being governed by formal logic were borne out. The formal categorial analysis was in effect an alternative to the analytical revolution in philosophy — it made possible a method of philosophical analysis that was hermeneutically richer than the formal tools of post-Fregean analysis, and it provided a convincing alternative to the informalist trends which insisted that there was no general formal logic of natural language. Categorial formal analysis struck at a depth of reason, thought and discourse which the Fregean tools were not designed to reach. The informalist thinkers who were influenced by the later Wittgenstein rightly saw that formal mathematical logic was not adequate for the rich and diversified logic of natural language. But because they failed to recognize the alternative Aristotelian formal logic they prematurely abandoned the hope of there being a general formal logic or deep structure for ordinary language. Sommers opened the way for an alternative model for formal analytic philosophy.

Formal categorial analysis of ordinary language began to make clear that a natural lived language in fact consists of a diversity of categorial grammars, forms of life or systems of meaning— a cluster of universes of discourse. For example, from the categorial point of view, ordinary English as spoken in contemporary American culture, is not one monolithic language but a cluster of complexly juxtaposed grammars. The relative independence and integrity of each grammar had to be respected, for as we have seen, a given grammar defines sense within its universe of discourse. Thus, cultural life in ordinary English comprises the diverse grammars of the sciences, the arts, the humanities and the religious and political forms, all of which shape "common sense". The concepts which are wielded in physics or physiology for example are not the same as the concepts commonly used in the disciplinary grammars of psychology or music, mathematics or religious life. Each of these language forms or grammars has its own "logic" as defined and prescribed by its indigenous grammar. The "ambiguity thesis" mentioned earlier suggests that meaning is systematically ambiguous or equivocal or incommensurable across grammars.

The newly emerging method of formal categorial analysis opened up a logical technology that was not available before. It opened the way to the clarification of certain fundamental problems in human reason. One problem was the issue of what is to count as one language. What counts as "one language" in terms of conventional criteria of a lived culture or continuously evolving "tradition" of "common sense" is found in categorial analysis to comprise a plurality or diversity of grammars or sense structures. While natural consciousness may presume that it lives in a unified linguistic space— a monistic or all encompassing universe of discourse, it turns out that a given natural language may well be comprised of a cluster of diverse grammars or universes of discourse. Wittgenstein had already suggested that a natural language was actually comprised of a plurality of diverse "language games" each having its own rules or logic governing its meaning. Here too it was essential to recognize the plurality of forms of meaning and forms of life involved in diverse language games.

The new categorial technology made it possible to excavate in a systematic way diverse grammars that comprise a "single" linguistic system. It began to be clear precisely how a natural linguistic system was actually comprised of a plurality of language forms from an ontological point of view. A given linguistic system has the capability of generating a diversity of categorial languages, each comprising a universe of discourse. Ordinary English, for example, may be considered one linguistic system from a conventional point of view, but it is found to be comprised of a plurality of universes of discourse. The supposed unified linguistic system appeared to have unlimited powers in generating diverse categorial grammars or systems of meaning. And any genuine investigation of meaning requires that the diversity of grammatical forms be respected, for meaning is now found to be relative to some given determinate grammatical context. The meaning of any term is found to be situated within a grammatical field of sense.

This means of course that to learn a natural language is in part to master the diversity of categorial grammars that comprise the language. And this indicates that we have natural access to the logic and laws of categorial formation. The development of categorial logic now allows us to make explicit the unconscious categorial rules of concept formation that govern meaning. This analytical technology opens the horizons for *disciplinary* studies since it now becomes possible to understand how diverse disciplinary languages are formed and transformed. It provides a grammatology for clarifying and "dis-ambiguating" meaning in a natural linguistic system.

But this advance only deepens the awareness of a possible crisis in rationality. For if meaning is always relative to a determinate grammar or universe of discourse, and if there is an irreducible plurality of grammatical forms of life, then truth, (phenomena, facts, reality) is likewise relative to the life-world of a grammar. If there is a radical pluralism of grammars within a cultural tradition then this seems to raise certain serious problems for the rational enterprise. On the one hand, we saw that rationality involves a deep commitment to unifying principles which hold rational life in coherence and relationality. This suggests that there must be some universal unifying field that holds human experience together in commensurable order and intercourse. It further suggests that the unifying forces of rational life keep open the possibility of univocal meaning, universal truth and a shared objective reality. On the other hand the evidence shows that human life is situated in a plurality of grammatical forms of life, each having a certain autonomy and internal integrity as universal fields. This pluralism of universes of discourse suggests that meaning and truth are relative to each language-world and that these worlds are in some significant sense incommensurable. What is possible and makes sense in one world fails to make sense in another. This relativism and incommensurability that comes with grammatical pluralism seems to entail that rational discourse between grammars is not possible. If the mind itself— the thinker, the interpreter, the sense and reference of "I"— is always situated in some determinate grammatical field, then this appears to preempt the presence of a trans-grammatical or universal "self" or "mind" or unified field wherein inter-grammatical transformations may take place.

The polar forces of rationality— the forces of Unity and the counter-forces of Plurality are evident in all forms of cultural life. For example, in the evolution of the so-called "western tradition" it is evident that a rich diversity of grammars have been articulated from pre-Socratic thought through contemporary times. We find philosophers constructing, inventing, discovering new grammatical forms which rehsape meaning, truth and experience. But often the grammatical revisions and advances and creativity are presented in the voice of a critique of other grammatical forms. When a creative grammarian argues for the superiority of a new grammatical form his or her arguments are often presented in the mode of a comparative critique of other supposedly less effective grammars. This comparative evaluation clearly suggests that inter-grammatical discourse is possible and actual. Rational discourse apparently takes it for granted that there are rational transformations between diverse grammars. And this requires that there be inter-grammatical transformation rules for human reason.

On the other hand, the divisive forces of pluralism are equally evident in the history and evolution of cultural life. It is quite evident throughout the tradition and certainly on the contemporary cultural scene that there are real barriers between grammatical forms of life. When grammars collide hermeneutical strife and war break out. The violent clashes of ideologies in cultural life are grounded in fundamental grammatical differences, and this violence is clear indication that rational due process has broken down, faith in common ground is lost, communication is eclipsed, and the irrational forces of incommensurability dominate. We see this hermeneutical violence and breach of dialogue and conversation in the repeated instances of religious wars, political clashes of ideologies, etc. For example, moral and political collisions over the issue of abortion originate from deeper grammatical differences; the deep ongoing confrontations between "science" and "religion" as seen for example in the collisions over "creation" and "evolution" are rooted in a difference of grammatical faith or commitment. One community of speakers who has faith in the grammar of "evolution" inhabit a universe of discourse that presents phenomena and reality according to its grammaticality. But another community inhabits a different grammatical form of life— the "creationists"— and this involves an alternative organization of experience and world. The confrontation and "arguments" between these diverse grammatical faiths often fail to realize that they live in different worlds; they argue as if they are talking about common brute facts or phenomena. Each takes his or her grammaticality to be universally and definitively true and this usually means that the grammatical life and discourse of the opponent is lodged in falsity, illusion, superstition, bad faith or irrationality. Most often the hermeneutical battles of apparently "competing" life-worlds fail to realize that they are situated in profoundly different universes of discourse and are talking past one another. When it is seen that meaning and truth and experience are relative to language-worlds, and when the profound differences, (perhaps incommensurability) between grammars are respected, this places the focus on the question of inter-grammatical dialogue. The formal methods of categorial hermeneutics provide the tools to clarify when discourse is intra-grammatical and when it is inter-grammatical. And this makes a real difference for rational discourse.

It appears, then, that the forces of commensurability (Unity) and of incommensurability (Pluralism) are *both* real in the rational life of a culture. And this is perhaps even more accentuated in the area of inter-cultural life and inquiry. I have been suggesting that the method of formal categorial hermeneutics is essential in understanding meaning and rationality within the cultural tradition. The evolution of "common sense" of a culture obviously involves a complex interplay of diverse grammatical forms of life. In contemporary American cultural life, for example, "common sense" is that vague and sprawling grammatical domain which is always under ongoing transformation from the impingement of diverse grammatical forms: the evolving discourse of physics and the other sciences, the grammatical innovations from the life-worlds of psychology and psychoanalysis, the deep ongoing influence of Biblical grammaticality, etc. all participate in shaping "common sense". And it remains to be seen, pending systematic grammatical analysis, whether this consists of one coherent universe of discourse or remains an incommensurable juxtaposition of diverse life-worlds. But the generality of the Categorial Hermeneutical Method expanded into more general form as I experimented with the inter-cultural rational transformations.

This experimental testing of categorial analysis in the area of inter-cultural rational life began for me in the early '70s when I began to prepare for systematic first hand encounter with Indian thought and culture. I began the study of Sanskrit and lived in India for one year (1971-72) studying Indian philosophy, music and languages. Despite my background and predisposition I nevertheless went through a profound cultural shock and awakening. As I entered more deeply into Indian cultural life, as I encountered the philosophical texts and tradition I experienced dramatic transformations of life worlds. I experienced first hand how profoundly different Indian cultural life was. And as I attempted to sort out these transformations in the subsequent years the hermeneutical tools of categorial analysis were essential. For example, in the encounter with philosophical texts like the *Bhagavad Gita* or the *Upanisads* or the great commentaries of Sankara, it was clear that I was transformed into life-worlds or categorial configurations that I had not encountered before. Making sense of this encounter only deepened, expanded and confirmed the importance of categorial analysis in inter-cultural transformations. It took several years of systematic experimentation to reconstruct my understanding into the grammaticalities of Indian thought and experience. The tools of formal hermeneutics were essential in moving methodically between the cultural traditions. It was in this research that I began to develop the methodology for inter-cultural comparative rationality. It was clear in approaching such fundamental terms as "karma" and "samsara" and "yoga" that they were lodged in universes of discourse that were differently shaped than dominant grammatical forms in the European tradition.

As this comparative methodology emerged I began to see the dangers of rational malpractice in the violation of other cultural traditions by the imposition of one's own grammatical form of life. Failure to understand the depth of inter-cultural transformations often led to "mis-translations" and "mis-representations" of the grammaticality of the alien cultural form of life under investigation. The comparative methodology helped to recognize and respect the real differences in foreign or alien forms of life, but it also helped to make clear important analogies or similarities across cultural traditions. For example, it became clear that a rich diversity of philosophical grammars had evolved over the centuries in the Indian tradition which shaped certain formal categorial features with certain grammars in the European tradition. For example, we now see that certain categorial forms of ontological dualism in both traditions had more in common than incompatible categorial structures in their own tradition. For formal hermeneutical method made it possible to discern and respect the fundamental differences and authentic analogies in inter-cultural rationality. The method punctured a certain arbitrariness in the conventional criteria of what is to count as one "culture" or "tradition" or "language."

Thus, this extension of formal hermeneutics to cultural and inter-cultural understanding expanded the scope of categorial analysis, and this was further confirmation that all dimensions of human experience were governed by categorial laws. This method now made it possible to explore the inner grammaticality of a given culture or tradition to discern the degree to which that form of life comprised diverse universes of discourse and to what degree it succeeded in a truly coherent and integral grammaticality in its cultural life. For example, in the Indian tradition it is clear that there are profoundly diverse grammars or life worlds that co-exist in the culture and shape its "common sense". It is naive and even irresponsible to speak of "the Indian mind" or "Indian world view" without recognizing the diversity of grammatical life forms. But it is also valid to see that there is a certain deep coherence in the cultural life— the esthetic art forms for example— often reflected the grammaticality of the religious imagination; the classical music, the dance form, sculpture and painting reflected a certain degree of grammatical consistency and mutual implication. In this way, the categorial method provided formal tools for exploring the inner logic of a given culture.

But at the same time it opened the way to exploration of inter-cultural rational discourse in a way that was not possible before. This application of formal hermeneutics was well received by a range of scholars in a variety of fields who were preoccupied with inter-cultural and cultural studies. For example, researchers interested in comparative philosophy, or the investigation of another cultural form of life or with inter-religious dialogue, etc. began to see the value of categorial analysis. It became clear that the deep problems of inter-grammatical translatability called for more powerful rational tools than were known before. In general, how does any researcher investigating an alien culture or grammaticality overcome logocentrism and ontocentrism in the "translation" process? Clearly authentic translatability of this radical sort required that grammatical differences be respected as well as the transformation rules that permitted the restructuring of the understanding as the researcher translated his categorial imagination into the foreign grammaticality. So the comparative methodology was opened up with new insights into categorial translatability between grammars and the logic of inter-cultural discourse.

With these expansions of categorial analysis we saw the emergence of a General Formal Hermeneutics that clarified the deepest perennial problems of human reason. The method of formal analysis had taken on a more universal form in which it applied to all forms of meaning and experience. Since meaning was always centered in grammar it made possible the analysis of the inner logic of world views or life-worlds. This also provided the tools for the rational formation of a disciplinary language— any discipline, as a form of interpretation, expression, representation, discourse, experience, etc., essentially originates with grammar, and the method was in effect a general *formal grammatology* which opened up a way to explore the integrity of any given disciplinary language. It likewise opened the horizon for a rigorous method to negotiate inter-disciplinary reason. In the liberal arts, for example, we can readily discern a range of diverse grammars or disciplinary languages, and it is essential to understand the grammatical forms which shape these modes of experience and interpretation. But it is equally true that there are powerful inter-disciplinary rational transformations and forces which have not been adequately understood. In this respect formal hermeneutics makes possible a way to understand the deep connections between logic, music and mathematics, or between the discourse of biology and physics and chemistry. Indeed, as we have suggested, wherever there is human experience there is categorial interpretation and it is a priority for rational inquiry to explore the grammatical forms that make a given mode of interpretation possible.

As I experimented with this method of grammatology a universal problem for rationality became clarified. The very concept of "rationality" went through extensive expansion as the hermeneutical theme emerged. This theme revealed that any possible form of human experience was governed by grammar, hence in one form or another involved sense and meaning— all life and experience involved interpretation. This expansion in effect revealed that the generic concept of rationality was present in any form of life— in reasoning and inference, in thinking and predicating, in conceptualization and judgment, in conceivability and imagination, in theorizing and interpreting, in communicating and translating, in representing and dreaming, in any form of consciousness. The laws of grammar were somehow present and operative in all states of mind. The hermeneutical theme, then, involves the mutual co-expansion of the domains of /meaning/, /experience/, /thought/, /grammar/, /rationality/ and /interpretation/— these apparently diverse domains were now found to converge and coincide, each inherently involving the other. Wherever there is experience there is meaning, wherever there is meaning there is grammar and where there is grammar the dynamics of rationality are present.

But we have seen that the mind of the thinker or experiencer is always situated in grammar. The domain that is specified by "I"— which we may call the "self" or "mind" or "voice" of the thinker— appears to be lodged in some determinate grammaticality. This very self or voice-field finds itself living in some grammatical mode and this invests it with specificity, sense, reference and existentiality. A given voice-field coincides with its grammar or universe of discourse— its very being is constituted by its situatedness in its grammatical field. The existential or determinate condition of voice raises a problem of the Univocity of Voice across grammars. If thought, experience, meaning are relative to its universe of discourse then Voice is likewise relative as well. The Ambiguity Thesis indicated earlier applies not only to the meaning of concepts or the being of things, it applies as well to voice. Voice appears to be systematically equivocal between grammars; it cannot be presumed that there is a universal and univocal voice-field that is trans-grammatical or inter-grammatical.

Nevertheless, we have seen that the powerful polar forces operative in rationality— the forces of Unity and the forces of Plurality are both present and evident in rational life. We have seen that a given grammar as a universe of discourse has a powerful autonomous, atomic or monadic effect that constitutes its own meaning and reality. This monadic force of a grammar tends to make it self contained as an internally coherent system of meaning and experience. And rational life appears to disclose a range of diverse grammars, each being a universe of discourse. But at the same time we have seen that rationality essentially involves the Unifying forces that hold consciousness and discourse together in inter-grammaticality. These Monistic or Anatomic forces make possible the conceptual self-revision and expansion that is at the heart of all cultural life. In this respect it may be said that rationality is essentially inter-grammatical. The inter-grammatical dynamics of reason are already present and constitutive of any determinate state of grammar.

The generic problem of /rationality/ is this: if mind or voice is situated in grammaticality and systematically equivocal across grammars, then *how is inter-grammatical discourse possible*? If rational consciousness or /interpretation/ is lodged in determinate grammar, how is rational discourse between grammars possible? Inter-grammatical reason necessarily involves some kind of trans-categorial or inter-grammatical Univocity— let us call this the "Univocity Condition". In some sense, the Univocity Condition is the Transcendental condition of meaning, experience and rationality. On the one hand, the Ambiguity Thesis entails that voice is equivocal between grammars. Here we find that the postulate of a "pluralism" would be in question since the situatedness of voice would always lodge it in a monadic universe of discourse. Ironically we see the hypothesis of a pluralism of grammars already involves some recognition of a trans-grammatical presence or rational unified field which holds the multiplicity together as a plurality. On the other hand, the Univocity Condition requires that mind or voice must be Univocal across grammars for there to be inter-grammatical discourse. This rational condition entails the presence of a Unified Voice field which keeps open the possibility of rational coherence and commensurability between grammars. The two formal constraints on rationality appear to polarize rationality into two incompatible features: Either there is Commensurability or

Incommensurability between grammars; Either there is Univocal or Trans-grammatical Voice or Voice is systematically equivocal between grammars. If there is no transgrammatical Voice-field, then incommensurability results, and this destroys rational discourse. But if Voice is Univocal and Inter-grammatical then this preempts the equivocity of voice across grammars. The universal problem of rationality then is to resolve this apparent polarization in rational awareness— Can the forces of rational Unity and Plurality be mediated and reconciled? Is there commensurability or incommensurability between grammars? If meaning and experience are always relative to some determinate grammatical context then how is inter-grammatical discourse possible? If mind or voice is always existentially situated in some determinate grammatical context, how is trans-grammatical mind or voice possible?

The method of categorial logic both clarified the predicament and attempted to resolve it. Its proposal is that the formal tree rule— the formal structure of categorial grammar— accounts for the Univocity and Equivocity requirements of rationality. Its hypothesis is that any grammar has its unique categorial configuration, but that any possible grammar must conform to the tree rule. It attempts to mediate the constraints of Unity and Plurality along the lines of "form" and "matter"— the material content of any grammar is unique, but the form (the tree structure) is universal for any possible grammar. The suggestion is that the tree rule provides the common ground or unifying principle which makes inter-grammatical transformations possible; diverse grammars are commensurable, it suggests, because they all share the same predicative logical form. Ostensibly this explains how it is possible for a thinker situated in one determinate grammatical form of life to go through rational transformations into an alien or foreign grammatical universe of discourse. If the diverse grammars did not share the same categorial deep structure such transformations would not be possible. Supposedly, the open and creative thinker should be able to translate his understanding into the foreign grammaticality.

Of course this proposal has its virtues and limitations. On the one hand it had the distinct advantage of at least acknowledging the Univocity condition as essential to rational discourse and it attempted to provide some explanation as to how inter-grammatical rationality was possible. On the other hand, it suffered the typical formalist plight of sacrificing diversity and difference in favor of unity and universality. The formalist understanding of the metaphor of "form and matter" tends to play down the monadic and atomic forces of plurality in favor of the higher status of form and unity. The formalist strategem of categorial logic did not satisfactorily explain how mind or voice can be at once radically situated and constituted in its grammaticality, and yet be univocal, transcategorial or transgrammatical. The postulate of "common form" does not yet explain how the human mind or voice is a living universal and unified field for all possible grammars. To postulate common form is one thing, to show that voice is a transcategorial unified field is another.

Furthermore, despite the universalization of categorial hermeneutics as a general method of formal philosophical analysis it is clear that a range of post-Fregean analytical philosophers, both formalists and informalists, would have trouble with categorial analysis and its understanding of the "problem of rationality". For example, the Wittgenstein of the *Investigations* rejects any suggestion of an underlying universal logical form for natural language. He insisted on a radical plurality of diverse "language games" for language, each having its own constitutive rules or "logic". He strongly resisted and opposed any formalist attempt to "discern" an essential logical form governing all discourse. Of course in this insistence Wittgenstein eclipsed the Univocity condition of rationality in favor of a radical pluralism and diversity. He apparently did not notice that certain fundamental features of rationality were eclipsed in his informalist approach. Indeed, it is apparent that Wittgenstein's authorial voice must have provided some kind of unified voice field within which his thesis about the diversity of language games could be articulated— i.e., he begged certain essential points about the Univocity condition, placing his own voice at odds with the content of his diversity thesis. It is no wonder that this approach fizzled out in a certain dead end. This is bound to happen for a philosophy of language that makes a special point of rejecting and denying the Univocity features of rationality.

Similarly, in the insightful work of Quine we find this leading analytical philosopher following through on insights from Frege and Russell. Quine would reject all this talk of categorial hermeneutics and the suggestion that there are categories and grammars in the sense in which we have spoken of them. By contrast, in the grammar of post-Fregean logic we get a very different narrative about the workings of language and thought. There is skepticism about talk of different "worlds". The tree rule and its alleged categorial logic would not be countenanced; the talk of categories and types and predicability would not be taken seriously. Instead, we find such a radically different account of language and meaning that it is hardly recognizable that the two narratives about discourse are talking about the same thing. While Quine and Kuhn both recognize that meaning, truth and phenomena are relative to a given "conceptual framework" as a whole, their understanding of conceptualization and the formation of a conceptual framework appears almost incommensurably different from the understanding of concept formation and categorial structure in the narrative of categorial logic. And since Quine insists that even the laws of logic are revisable in radical conceptual revision, certain troubling problems about rationality arise in his scenario. The Univocity condition is either eclipsed or becomes mysterious.

Thus, the earlier impasse in mediating between the narratives of classical logic and modern post-Fregean logical theory only deepened. The development of formal categorial hermeneutics helped to uncover the deeper chasm between the two forms of discourse as well as to disclose its own limitations. It became more apparent that the logical grammar operative in Sommers' discourse was dramatically different from the logical grammar shaping the speech of Quine. The model and method of categorial grammatology made it more evident that there were two diverse universes of discourse here with all the expected systematic ambiguity between them. It became clear that the fundamental terms of logical theory were equivocal between the two grammars of thought: sense, reference, predication, logical subject, predicate, truth, affirmation, denial, negation, generality, and so on. In the light of this radical ambiguity it was natural to wonder whether these opposed narratives of logical form, meaning, thought and language were talking about the same subject matter. The phenomena of one were paralogical and foreign or recalcitrant for the other. It was now clearer that each discourse was speaking from a different voice-field and countenanced diverse logical or rational phenomena. This recognition challenged the generality of categorial hermeneutics and its grammatology because the grammar of Fregean discourse appeared to be beyond the grammaticality of categorial logic. So even the concept of "grammar" had to be revised and expanded to encompass the two models of logical form and grammar.

In this respect the problem that was posed ten years earlier in the doctoral dissertation reached a deeper and even more troubling form. If we accept the provisional validity of the two complementary grammars of rationality and logical form then it seems that rationality itself is self divided in the deepest way. After all, the telos of formal philosophy is to discern the universal deep structure of human reason; the discourse of logical form is precisely designed to reveal the deepest unifying principles of thought. But if we now face two opposed and competing grammars of logical form, each having a certain validity and irreducibility, then this appears to destroy the hope of uncovering a unified logical space with univocal formal laws for human thought. Is there univocal, universal and unified logical form governing human reason and discourse? Or are we left in the end with an irreducible pluralism and equivocity in logical form and rationality? If logical form is self-divided then the human voice will reflect this equivocity— meaning, discourse, rationality and experience would be lodged in deep equivocation. This apparent polarization in rationality and logical form seems to take us back to the analogous deep impasse in rationality brought to a head in the ontological mode in the voices of Parmenides and Heraclitus. Is the univocity condition of human reason impossible or unrealizable? Is it a necessary condition for rationality? Is there a universal unifying and univocal voice-field for human consciousness? Must formal philosophy inevitably end in self-division and equivocation? Is univocal meaning for human discourse possible? These and similar questions set the agenda for the next phase in the clarification of Universal Grammar.

It became increasingly obvious that a more radical approach was needed to address the challenge of formal analytical philosophy and the question of univocity of voice. And through the 1970's as the discovery of the polarization of logical form emerged my hermeneutical experiments in Indian models of formal philosophy intensified. Here I focused primarily on the Hindu hermeneutical tradition as clarified by the teachings of Sankara (8th Century A.D.), and on the Buddhist dialectical tradition which was founded by Nagarjuna (2nd Century A.D.). He initiated the Madhyamika tradition of radical formal analysis. At first my research in the European logical tradition was seen as one project, and my experiments in Indian paradigms of formal analysis were seen as a different project. Of course I did develop and apply the formal categorial hermeneutics in a comparative way to grammars in the Indian tradition, but it only dawned on me later that the powerful models of formal analysis found in Sankara and Nagarjuna had an immediate and direct bearing on the problems of rationality and logical form which I had been struggling with. Thus, what was at first approached as two independent research and teaching concerns came into deeper dialogue and univocation, and this helped to open the way for the discovery of the Unified Field. The long quest for the Univocity condition of rationality, for the Unified Voice field which disclosed Universal Logical Form and resolved the split in rationality, reached a new horizon. But the expansion of mind to the Unifying Principle required the more radical and rigorous form of thinking called for by the hermeneutics of meditative reason.

CHAPTER 3

MEDITATION, RATIONALITY AND UNIVERSAL RELATIVITY
(Introduction to Meditative Reason)

FOREWORD

Rationality and the Holistic Unity of the Diverse Hermeneutical Arts

Universal Hermeneutics demonstrates the unity of human rational life by discerning the Universal Unified Field of Reality. Holistic Science (HS) begins with the presence of the Holistic Continuum of Reality whence all life, all meaning, all rational intelligence, all experience, all names and forms derive. It makes clear why failure to begin with the Universal Continuum of Nature has led to the fragmentation of human life and the pathology of meaning and rationality. It shows precisely why the life that is centered in self existence and self identity must suffer such pathological fragmentation. And in so doing it makes clear why the radical return of our rational life to its Holistic Origins in the Universal Continuum heals the splits in human life and opens the way to true rational coherence and sanity.

By beginning with the Holistic Unity of the Continuum of Nature or Reality HS shows why all possible forms of human life and experience must be an expression of the Continuum. In this way it avoids the false start of the fragmented mind which begins with the pathological condition of fractured and incoherent life that is broken into separated pieces. The fragmented mind always replicates itself in all its thinking and cannot discern the deeper original unity that is Reality itself. It takes the condition of life in which there are diverse and separate areas as being "normal" and the way things are. It has trouble seeing how and why this condition is artificial and pathological and it cannot in its own terms find its way out of this condition to its holistic origins.

HS revolutionizes human reason by beginning with the Holistic Origin of Life, Reason and Reality and can thereby discern the true unification of all life. It is here that HS makes clear that all life is hermeneutical— the expression of rational energy of the Continuum, and in this Unified Field we may perceive the holistic unity of all the diverse hermeneutical arts which make up human life and culture. Universal Hermeneutics explicates the holistic unity of philosophy, religion, the sciences and the arts by placing these in the context of the Continuum of Nature. But it begins with the deepest challenge of all; it requires the calling forth of the holistic mind which alone can discern the Universal Continuum of Reality. So it may be said that HS is the self-evolution of the holistic mind which is fully integral with the Continuum. Thus, HS presents the universal form of science and resolves the problem of the fragmentation of life, meaning and truth. In this way it transforms incommensurable and incoherent fragments into holistic parts which find their true meaning in the Holistic Unity of the Universal Continuum of Reality.

PREFACE

Holistic Unity and the Part/Whole Problems

This essay attempts to address in a systematic and comprehensive way one essential theme of rationality— the understanding of the whole and problem of parts in organic relation to the whole. The part/whole problem is just one version of a multi-faceted and complex problem about human rationality, understanding and experience. On the one hand we have a deep intuition that human life in all its hermeneutical or cultural forms must have some integral coherence and unity, but on the other hand we find ourselves living a form of cultural life that appears to divide into quite diverse fields and disciplines. And these are so profoundly diverse that we tend to accept the radical diversity of parts of cultural life and live with the separation of these realms as the norm. For example, the area of natural science seems to be so different from the area of our religious experience that we accept as normal that these are just two very different fields of cultural life; we accept the separation and live with the tension between them. Again, the area of cultural life that is concerned with facts falls into a different realm than the concern for values and here too there appears to be a separation and tension between concern with facts and concern with values. The area of experience that we call mathematics appears to be in a different world from our esthetic experience and the world of music and art. And in general our institutions of higher education— liberal arts— reflect the partition of fields into the sciences and the humanities, and these in turn are further sub-divided into diverse fields. Thus, human life is partitioned into diverse separated areas, but at the same time we continue to feel that human culture forms an integral unity and coherent whole. So we are left with the problem of understanding how the diverse parts of human life cohere into an integral whole.

But this rationality is also essentially concerned with another related part/whole problem— it is the accompanying division of human life into diverse cultural worlds. (Here too it appears that diverse cultural worlds are profoundly different universes of discourse.) These cultural worlds appear to be incomparably diverse parts of the larger fabric of humanity as a whole, and the same tension between parts and whole is found to recur here as well. So there is the part/whole problem of intra-cultural unity as well as the related part/whole problem of inter-cultural unity, and both versions of the problem are our essential concern here— they both bear on the general problem of the unity of human experience. This encounter essentially cuts across both axes of the part/whole problem: On the one hand it is an exploration of the inter-disciplinary theme of possible unity between the diverse hermeneutical arts such as science, religion and the arts. On the other hand it raises these concerns in the context of the inter-cultural encounter of "eastern" and "western" traditions. We shall see that the concept of this encounter is quite valid and that it makes perfect sense to combine both versions of the part/whole problem— the inter-disciplinary and inter-cultural themes— into one open dialogue. The central theme of this essay is that the Universal Principle of Pure Reason which governs all life and existence is the Principle of Holistic Unity. And in the development of this theme we shall see that it is at once both classical and radical. The theme that rationality is a principle of unity is quite ancient, classical and traditional for diverse cultures. This perennial insight has recurred through the ages and has been the shaping intuition and vision of cultural life. But despite the magnificent breakthroughs that have recurred through world history in the disclosure of Rational Unity this primordial insight remains as elusive as it is ever-present and available to human intelligence. For the conventional mind is structured in a mode of thought that inherently eclipses Holistic Unity or Universal Reason as it constructs its own forms of rational life. This conventional mind takes itself to be self-existent and individuated and articulates rational unity in its own image. And while it recognizes that rationality is coherence and unity it tends to construct artificial models of unity which fall short of Holistic Unity. The result is that the rational life of the individuated mind remains incomplete, incoherent and fragmentary.

This is where our theme of Holistic Unity is radical. For there are traditions which have seen clearly that true Rational Unity cannot be thought by the individuated mind but must be realized in meditation. The meditative traditions have taught that Rational Unity cannot possibly be made into an object of thought but calls forth the holistic mind which realizes rational coherence in meditative or pure reason. So the challenge before us is most radical because it calls for the self expansion of mind itself to its holistic form. Accordingly, this essay is an exploration in the expansion of the conventional individuated mind to its universal or holistic form. Perhaps this is the most difficult and radical challenge imaginable.

Thus, Holistic Unity cannot be thought in the constructed or artificial rationality of the individuated mind, it must be meditated in the presence of the holistic mind. And while the vision of Holistic Unity has been alive and central in the meditative traditions it has not been sufficiently articulated as Universal Science which speaks to the condition of individuated mind. In this respect the articulation of Holistic Science involves the elaboration of the Holistic Thesis which entails that all human life derives from the Principle of Unity. HS is the demonstration of the Holistic Thesis. So let us begin by focusing our meditative attention on Holistic Unity.

INTRODUCTION TO HOLISTIC METHOD

i) Holistic Unity as the Principle of Pure Reason

It may be said that the deepest striving of human reason through the ages has been the quest for the ultimate principle of Unity. For it has been the perennial ideal of human understanding that the essence of rationality has to do with its power to unify diverse items under one principle or universal form. It is in the light of such a universal point of reference that what would otherwise be disconnected, merely diverse and incommensurable is seen to be intrinsically connected, commensurable and related in order and coherence. Indeed, it is a unifying principle that makes order, coherence and intelligibility possible; it is the very source of rational light. For this reason it is of the utmost importance to be truly in touch with the primordial unifying principle whence all meaning and existence derives.

Nevertheless in the history of thought we find two traditions of human rationality which approach Original Unity in profoundly contrasting ways. One tradition is *holistic* and discerns the Principle of Unity in meditative reason, while the other is *existential* and approaches rational unity through the individuated mind which is centered on identity as the principle of rationality. The former discerns an originary non-dual Unity as the principle whence all things derive, while the latter has as its foundation an intuition of Oneness as its model of primary Unity. Let us call the meditative model of Unity "holistic unity" (HU) and its principle of rationality "the principle of universal relativity" (UR). By contrast we shall call the existential model of Unity "atomic unity" (AU) and its principle of rationality "the principle of absolute identity" (AI). In what follows we shall attempt to develop the holistic model of unity in dialectical contrast to the atomic model of mind, meaning and rationality. And as we articulate Holistic Science we shall see why Universal Relativity (the holistic principle) is the principle of pure reason.

ii) The Holistic Thesis: Discerning the Universal Continuum of Reality

Let us begin our reflection on HU. We immediately see that this is perfect unity, absolutely simple, non-compounded, the perfection of form. As such this primordial form of Unity is universal and all encompassing, and nothing can stand apart from universal form. There can be nothing that does not stand in essential relationality to the form of unity— it must be at once all things, but nothing. This universal form of all forms is the primordial Universal Field whence all possible things derive and take their being, so nothing can exist which does not take Unity as its essential origin of reference and orientation. But since it is perfect and simple unity with no separable parts, it immediately follows that all things cohere, so HU is the original principle of coherence. This coherence of all things in Unity reveals that all things co-exist and are co-relational; they touch one another in deepest intimacy and hence are profoundly contiguous and mutually consistent— all things are in communion and are hence ultimately uniform. Perhaps the most dramatic disclosure in this reflection of HU is that mind (the thinker) cannot exist apart from this Universal, Uniform, Unified Field; it too is essentially implicated in the communion and inter-relationality of all things; it too must be in perfect harmony and unity with Universal Form; and since it cannot distance itself or stand apart from the Universal Continuum of Reality it immediately follows that mind cannot think HU as an object of thought. Rather, mind must realize its intrinsic universal form in the disclosure of its essential Unity with the Continuum of Reality. Thus, deepest reflection on HU shows that this very thinking must be recursive, reflexive and self-referential as mind expands to its inner universal form, to holistic mind.

As we prepare for further reflection on the Universal Unified Field of HU let us introduce some terms to assist the self-expansion of mind to its holistic form. Let us call the primordial Universal Field *Logos*. We see that Logos is Holistic Form, the form of all possible forms. This means that all forms are essentially synonymous with Logos, and Holistic Science is the process of realization of this Holistic Synonymy.

We may now formulate the *Holistic Thesis:* all possible names, forms, things are essentially direct expressions of Logos. Nothing can be or be conceived apart from essential reference to Logos. This is the original principle of all existence, experience, meaning and rationality. The Holistic Thesis implies that the true inner meaning of any name is found in its holistic synonymy with Logos. It implies that the true inner being of anything is found in its uniformity with Logos. So we truly understand a given thing when we discern its origin and derivation in Logos.

Perhaps it would be helpful to explicate some of the more obvious holistic synonyms of Logos, each of which are co-synonymous. First we see that *Logos is Goodness*— for as the form of all possible forms it is the universal point of reference for all things; as such all things are oriented to Logos and this gives order and orientation to the Universal Field. This ordering principle is the telic force that organizes all things into a coherent whole, into a universe. In this respect we may say that Goodness is the original force that holds the Universe together, and all things gravitate to Logos as its center. This formula (Logos = Goodness) opens the way to holistic teleology.

But let us reflect on other holistic synonymies: Logos is Reality; Logos is the Word; Logos is Mind; Logos is Thought; Logos is Meaning; Logos is Idea; Logos is Universe; Logos is Nature; Logos is Reason; Logos is Energy; Logos is Truth; Logos is Beauty...etc.

These holistic formulas all derive from reflection on Logos as the Universal Form— The Continuum. And since the Unified Field is uniform and consistent it follows that all names or forms mutually entail one another. Thus, Logos as the original *Word* is the holistic Name whence all else derives: there can be no split or separability between Word and Meaning, between Word and Thing (Reality), between Word and Mind, between Word and Thought, between Word and Speech, between Word and Truth, etc. All of these meet in holistic synonymy ·when spoken by the holistic mind. What is customarily separable and separated into diverse realms by the conventional existential mind is found to be in essential communion or relationality in holistic reflection.

In this way we begin to see the power of the insight that all names or forms immediately derive from Logos, as the conventional mind expands to its holistic form. We see that the Continuum of Reality or Nature is the Speaking Forth of the Holistic Word; we see that the Primordial "Stuff," Matter, Substance of Reality may be truly called by *any* of the holistic synonyms— when seen as the creative force of Speech of the Original Word the Continuum is Rational Energy, the force of Intelligence or Meaning or Truth. Here it may be said that all Reality (Nature, the Universe) is Truth-force or the Rational Action of Meaning. In this holistic context the laws of nature are synonymous with the laws of truth, meaning, thought; and the conventional realms of mind and matter find their deeper common origins in the Living Continuum. So as mind expands to its holistic or universal form, all conventional names/forms likewise expand to their true inner synonymy with Logos. And the usual problem of false reductions of mind to matter or matter to mind are avoided in Holistic Science where all conventional names are "reduced" to their intrinsic universal significance— their synonymy with Logos.

It is already clear in this preliminary elaboration of the Holistic Thesis that conventional reason (the thinking of the existential or atomic mind) is unable to approach the Continuum of Reality. It would be timely to focus our attention on this feature of the atomic mind to understand why it inherently eclipses the Continuum of Nature and cuts itself off from Reality. Thus far we have introduced the Holistic Thesis that Reality is the Continuum of Logos and that all possible names and forms immediately derive from Logos and have Logos as their true essence and significance. The basic formula is: Everything is "logos" and the Universal Law of the Continuum of Nature is that: *Every logos is Logos.*

iii)   The Fragmentation and Pathology of the Conventional Mind (Discerning the Dis-continuum of Identity)

Since our reflection on HU calls forth the holistic mind and requires the self-expansion of the conventional existential mind let us focus our attention on the inner workings of the latter to see how and why its form fragments the Continuum.

a) The Origin of the Existential Mind

The conventional mind is the mind which is centered in its *self-existence* and *self-identity*. It takes the principle of identity to be its absolute principle— the principle which is definitive of rationality and existence and conditions the existential mind in every possible way. This principle may be simply stated as follows: For any given thing "X," *X is X;* any thing is self-identical with itself, and this self-existence is the central point of reference governing all its thinking, activity, life. The self-existent mind is in some clear sense individuated or particularized insofar as it has self-identity— to be self-existent is to be differentiated and defined over against all else that is *other* to this identity. So the mind of identity is centered in its self-existence and differentiated particularity and with its inner identity is given the otherness of all else that is differentiated from it. So the principle of self-identity appears to be the principle of individuation, particularity and differentiation.

It is essential to see that the mind of identity in its very foundation is born in a duality or differentiation between itself on the one hand and the universal field of reality which surrounds it. This existential mind calls itself "I" and all its life and thought and experience arise in the dual structure of

I / Field

This dual structure is an original dis-continuum which sets the existential mind in a primitive polarization that pervades all its life. By taking itself to be a self-existent primary point of reference this "I" becomes a unifying principle for all its experience. This individuated self existent mind comes to consciousness precisely in the eclipse of the Holistic Continuum which becomes its pre-conscious. But the "consciousness" of the existential mind is deeply problematic and lives in a double-bind which is spawned by the very form of self-identity. For the original split of I/Field which bifurcates the holistic Continuum preempts original unity and places the mind of identity in the predicament of seeking universal unity *within* the structure of absolute identity. But this inner dynamic of self-existent identity only replicates its own image of unity which generates an endless fall-out of dual splits in every direction.

Let us now reflect on the dis-continuum of identity and see how it arises.

b) *The Fracture of the Holistic Continuum*
First of all we must remember throughout this account of the origin of the discontinuum that it is discerned in the context of the holistic mind, for the mind of identity believes itself to be ultimately coherent, indeed, the very measure of coherence and rationality. It must be remembered that in this holistic account the ruling hermeneutical principle is that the Holistic Continuum governs all forms of life, including the life of identity. Whatever meaning or form of life it may construct is always lodged under the sway of the Reality Principle, Logos.

It is, then, the Holistic Continuum of Reality that is "fragmented" by the postulate of self-identity. The mind of identity presumes that it is a self-existent reality. But once holistic unity is eclipsed this self-existent being (indicated by "I") finds itself in a form of life, in a fundamental dynamic, that requires it to attempt to recover a universal original principle of unity. For it sees immediately that in being an alleged self-existent (atomic) being it is thereby uniquely individuated and hence differentiated from all that is not-I; so the postulate or faith that "I" is primarily given as self-existent inherently carries with it the differentiation of all that is not-I. This means that the very being of "I" carries with it the being of not-I; and the presumption of independent self-unity of "I" leads to the opposite consequence of the dependence of "I" on its differentiation from the not-I.

This original inherent self-polarization found in "I" calls the self-existent mind beyond its presumed self-existence to find some higher mediating and uniting point of reference which can negotiate the opposition between I and not-I and hold them in a mediated unified field. The alleged self-unity of the self-existent "I" cannot find true self-unity within itself and is required to discern a universal and primitive unifying principle which it takes to be truly self-existent beyond itself in the postulation of a universal all-encompassing unified field of reality. This is its universe as a whole, and here it finds the ultimate unifying principle that makes its self-existence possible. In this way we may discern a fundamental form of triangulation that is the inner dynamic of the postulate of identity:

Figure 3

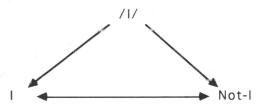

If we begin at the point of "I" as self-existent, this alleged independence is corrected by the recognition of the not-I which it essentially depends upon for its self-identity, and this sends the I in quest of the ground of its self identity in a higher principle of universal self-unity— in /I/ which is the self-existence of the postulated Universal Unifying Field of Reality. So the postulate of self-identity necessarily leads to the postulate of a Universal Field which may be called "The Universe" or "Reality." This Postulated Universal Field is all encompassing and of course includes both the I and all that is other than I, the not-I. The main point is to see that the postulate of the self-existent mind necessarily leads to the postulation of a universal field of reality, a universe of discourse, wherein it attempts to find its true unity. This means that there could not be a self-existent "I" apart from its foundational universal field which is its ground. In this way the mind of identity attempts to recover original unity as its principle of coherence and rationality. Once the Holistic Continuum is broken with the presumption of self-identity, unified fields are postulated to preserve the faith in self-existence and there is a self-perpetuating proliferation of constructed fields in every direction. Of course it is not the Holistic Continuum that is "broken" or "fragmented," but the life-world of the ego-mind or voice-field. The ego-mind in constituting itself as an alleged "autonomous" being or entity severs itself from the Unitive Field of reality and enters into a negative self-destructive dialectic with respect to the Continuum.

We remember that the Holistic Continuum is the true Universal Field of Nature, and once this is broken, all that follows is in some way a "piece" or "fragment" of this Field; there can be nothing that does not directly originate from the Holistic Field. As we reflect further on this important holistic insight we see that every possible identity— every name, every thing, every concept, every form of life, every language or universe of discourse, etc. are all *fields*, and every field is taken by the mind of identity to have inner self-existence or self-identity. So, the self-existent mind is a field unto itself, and every thing that is encompassed in the "not-I" is likewise a field unto itself. This is the key to the holistic theme that every possible "thing" is a logos, an off-spring of Logos. And here we can see the force of the problem of self-identity: namely, that any alleged self-identity, whether an "I" or a "not-I," is a postulated atomic fragment of the Holistic Field. But atomic self-identities are each a principle of self-unity (a universe) unto themselves and there could be no true inter-relatedness between each atomic field were it not for the postulate of a Universal Field (a Universal reality) that encompassed all possible self-existent fields. The life of self-identity necessarily involves the postulation of a (constructed) continuum.

c) Grammars of Reality as Unified Fields

We now see that any possible identity is a field or a form, and is necessarily encompassed within a postulated Universal Field of Reality. Let us call this Universal Field— "Grammar," and we shall speak of a Grammar of Reality or Existence. This is important for our account of the dynamics of the dis-continuum of self-identity since we now see that the mind of identity is possible only in the context of a presupposed absolute universal field that is its ground or foundation and that conditions the possibility of its existence. To exist in self-identity is to be grounded in the context of a universal field, a universe of discourse (grammar). This Grammar of Existence governs and conditions the life of self-identity in every way.

Let us reflect for a moment on this theme of a universe as a grammar of existence. The mind of self-identity necessarily finds itself existing in a universe (universal field) which, we have seen, is the alleged origin of its unity. This individuated (atomic) mind is absolutely dependent on this universal unifying point of reference for its existence, and its life is oriented towards this universal field which we have called "grammar." In our holistic account of the life of identity it is essential to see how this term "grammar" is used and why grammar is prior in every sense.[1]

The universe (the universal field) in which the individuated mind is grounded is a *universe of discourse* which expresses itself as a language of reality. This language is an organization of forms (categories, concepts, names) which reflects a determinate world. It defines what is rational, what is real, what makes sense, and it governs what may exist and structures thought and experience. This is why it is a *grammar of existence*: it is the inner structure of reality (universal field) that makes rational life possible. Thus, a given universal field is a logos that is the origin of all existence and experience for the world it defines. The very existence of the individuated mind is made possible by its grammar of reality: to exist is to be defined within a given grammar of reality.

Perhaps some examples of grammars (as universal unified fields) would be helpful here. We have said that the individuated life is always situated in some world, as a universe of discourse. In typical examples we find the mind of identity living in a shared form of life called a culture. Diverse cultures may be seen as examples of grammars of reality. A given culture is a language of reality that defines what makes sense, what is rational and what is real. It defines a language of experience and gives form to the universe. In this respect, to be a Christian is to inhabit a language-world that makes the Christian mind possible.[2] The Christian Grammar constitutes a universe which makes the form of life called "being a Christian" possible. The self-identity of the Christian mind can arise only in this grammatical field and all its life and experience is governed by this grammar of reality. For our purposes it is important to see that *all forms of experience* within the Christian world are made possible by this grammar. By contrast, the Hindu mind is likewise made possible by the Hindu grammar which makes the Hindu world possible. What makes sense for the Hindu is profoundly different from the structure of experience in the Christian world. These are diverse universes of discourse, different worlds, different languages of experience and reality. The Christian grammar is a unifying field that holds together Christian life in a unified whole. In some sense it is a unifying continuum for all of Christian existence and life.

Thus, a grammar of reality has the deepest priority for a given form of life. We call it a "grammar" because it is a structure of reality that proscribes and prescribes how the individuated mind may make sense of the universe, how it may think rationally and meaningfully, how it experiences; it structures its form of life and defines the composition and composure of the universe. In short, a grammar of reality is a unifying field that is the meeting point of existence, language, meaning, rationality, thought, experience and life. These arise together and mirror one another in common origin of a grammar.

d) Dynamics of Fragmentation

Having introduced the theme of the primacy and priority of grammar for the individuated mind we are now in a better position to continue our reflection on the nature and origin of the discontinuum in the life of identity. It has been suggested that the individuated mind splits from the Holistic Continuum and posits a universe or unifying field of its own. Its self-identity is possible only within some such specified universal field which we have called a grammar of existence. We have seen that its deepest need is to seek and maintain its self unity and it does this by identifying itself in its universe or grammar. But we have also seen that this need for self integrity is doomed to frustration since this individuated mind is caught in a self divisive triangulation of identity that generates the perpetual self polarization within its grammar. So let us now explore this dynamic of self polarization in the life of self-identity.

First, we remember that a given grammar of existence as the unifying context for the individuated self is *itself* a projected or constructed unified field which is divided off from the Holistic Continuum. This grammar of existence stands apart as a universe unto itself with cosmic self-existence and hence it is not truly one with the Holistic Continuum. So it is within this grammatical field, already separated off from the Continuum of Reality that the divisive life of the individuated mind proceeds. We shall see in due course that a given grammar of existence is in some sense a *cosmic hypothesis,* a primordial interpretation or reflection of the Continuum which it eclipses by its self-identity. And we shall see that these grammars of existence as alternative languages of reality are proliferated into a fall out of multiple universes or worlds each alleging to be universal, self-existent and constitutive of reality. But for now let us focus our attention on the dynamics of self fragmentation in the life of self-identity relative to a given grammatical field.

We have the surrounding grammatical field (the universe) and within this field the original split between the *I* and the *not-I*, as thus depicted:

Figure 4

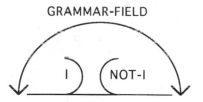

GRAMMAR-FIELD

I) (NOT-I

In some sense it is this unifying field that is the unit of individuation, and not the "I" taken in isolation. Nevertheless, within this field the "I" takes itself to be self-existent and thus existentially differentiated from all else that is *not-I,* so the grammatical field is self-divided into three opposing poles.

But this self-polarization continues without end. Let us focus on the pole of the "I." Here we find an inner polarization between I-mind and the I-not-mind, that is, between the conscious subject and what is other than the conscious subject, namely all objects that are differentiated from this conscious subject. On the side of the conscious, this is self-divided between the conscious and the un-conscious, so this field is sub-divided into two sub-fields. On the other side, of the *objects* of consciousness, discerned by the subject, still within the realm or field of mind, we find *ideas.* These ideas (objects of thought in the realm of thought) are in turn polarized into the ideal (on the side of thought) and not-ideal, that which the idea represents. This extra-ideal that ideas represent are still within the realm of mind, so there is still not a leap beyond mind to the realm of world that is beyond mind (in the not-I).

Again, within the realm of the conscious is experience and what is other-than-experience.

The realm of experience is self polarized into rational experience and non-rational experience, which includes the experience of the senses. Further, within rational experience is found rational thought which is differentiated from the not-thought. In the field of thought we find that which is expressed in language and what is extra-linguistic. Within Language is the realm of words, which is differentiated from ideas, which are differentiated from meanings, which are differentiated from the objects of meanings, or things. So we see a growing proliferation of self-dividing fields or identities each of which is polarized and reiterating the common problem of finding a true mediating common ground. From the subjective I to its objective ideas, from these ideas to what is beyond the idea; from subjective thought to meanings, to words, from words to what they represent, from the meaning of words (sense, essence) to what is beyond the idea; in the reference of things "out there" beyond the realm of mind and its conscious thought. Thus, we see an increasing fallout of polarization of sub-fields, and what originally was supposed to be a mediating, unifying connection turns out to be a deeper disconnection. For example, going back to the original I/not-I polarization, some mediating principle was needed to connect the individuated "I" with the not-I. But if we begin with self-identity of "I" as the original point of reference, (and this is what self-existence entails), then all attempts of this "I" to truly reach the not-I only entrenches it more and more deeply in self-polarizations, and the chasm between these poles only widens.

For example, in the realm of knowledge, as a form of conscious thought, it is seen that the mind immediately discerns objects of thought. These objects have an inner ambiguity since on the one hand they are within the realm of thought but they purport to be at the same time objects themselves, beyond thought— the objects of knowledge. It is immediately seen that for there to be true knowledge, thought and its object must reach beyond thought to the "external" objects of reality. So the objects of thought are given a representational character (a dual, mediating nature) to connect the polarized fields of knowledge and object of knowledge. But any attempt to discern a unified mediating identity between the I and the not-I only repeats the self-polarization and ends in frustration. The historic attempts to bridge this polarization of fields has spawned a number of deep dualisms in human experience. The split between mind and body is one of them. The dualism between ideas which are rational in origin and those which are empirical in origin, between the *a priori* and the *a posteriori*, is another classical polarization. In the realm of *meaning* we find a corresponding area of polarizations— here again some primitive unifying identity is sought to connect the kinds of entities which carry meaning, and the entities that they mean. Of course meanings themselves are taken to be representational (dual) in nature, but even meaning splits into the realm of sense and that of reference, and what is supposed to be a univocating identity ends up being inherently self-equivocal and fails to truly univocate the original polarization.

But examples abound in every direction in the life of identity. On every side we see the same pattern of self-division and failure to find a mediating identity that univocates the polarized fields. By now we see that every name indicating an identity inherently has its polar Other which is differentiated from it, and each indicates a sub-field within the universal grammar-field. Thus, if we take "reason," this realm is polarized against what is non— rational or extra-rational, and we find such polarities as *reason vs. faith*. Or, if "science" indicates a certain identity, that which is other than science, stands over against science and we have other polarities like *science vs. religion*. Again, the realm of "thought" indicates a certain identity, and all that is other than thought, such as "action" indicates a polarized field which generates dichotomies and tensions between *thought vs. action*, or *theory vs. practice*, and so on. These are randomly selected examples of classical polarizations that are spawned by the form of identity itself which is inherent in the mind and self of self-identity. The general pattern is that *Identity generates self polarization.* Perhaps it would be clearer to say that when the individuated mind fixates on the (atomic) self-existence of any identity this splits it off into a separate reality (field) thereby producing the pernicious polarization. So it is the very form of the mind of identity that generates the fragmentation and pathological condition. In fixating itself in self-identity it inevitably projects its fixation on whatever it turns its attention; the atomic mind projects its own form on any possible object before it— it objectifies.

e) The Fragmentation of Fields: Diverse Universes of Discourse
Thus far we have been exploring the dynamic of self polarization within the inner life or experience of the existential mind. But now we shall see that this same pattern of polarization pervades the *universe* that is structured in self-identity. The Universal Field is fractured into distinct domains or forms of life, forms of language, universes of discourse or grammars. The life of identity leads to fragmentation into diverse universes, diverse cultural worlds, diverse "disciplines," multiple realities and hence multiple "I's". We have seen that the existential mind can exist only in a determinate (constructed) universal field called "reality." But its grammar of reality is internally self-divided into diverse domains called "categories." Any given grammar of existence replicates the triangular form internally and self divides into fundamentally diverse domains or fields. Thus, for example, a given cultural world (grammar) differentiates such diverse categories of reality as "space," "time," "quantity," "mind," "matter," "color," "motion," etc. Each of these fundamental categories demarcates a self-existent domain of the universal field and this creates a separate field. So in the Christian world/grammar "time" is a category that stands in a certain configuration with the other categories to give a distinctive meaning to "time" in this world. By contrast, "time" in the Hindu grammar would have profoundly different signification, so much so that it is legitimate to wonder whether "time" can have any common or univocal meaning across grammars of existence.

It is important in this connection to see that a "category" is in some sense a universal domain unto itself— it exhausts a field of reality. For example, any given category replicates the triangular form of identity in its internal structure. In general any category, /C/, comprises an internal self opposition called "contrariety" which we may indicate by

c / -c

which may be read "c" and "un-c." In this case, c and un-c are contrary opposites which are intrinsically connected with each other. The identity of "c" is bound in the identity of "-c" and both together indicates the universal domain /C/ which holds the contraries in a unified field:

Figure 5

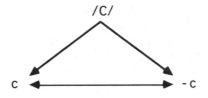

Thus, if we take the category of /Color/, any given color must be a specification of this universal field and in its inner identity differentiates itself from any other color in this domain:

red / un-red

If "red" is the particular color in question, then "un-red" indicates all other possible colors in the domain of /Color/, so contraries taken together define the category as a whole. This is the pattern with all categories.

The point here is that we see the same dynamic of identity replicated within each category as well as in the category configuration as a whole which comprises the universal grammatical field. A grammar or world is a particular configuration of categories, each of which in turn is a universal domain unto itself. And it is the category structure of a grammar/world that is the origin of the division of a given cultural world into distinct cultural fields or disciplines. One distinct field may explore the category of /number/ (mathematics), another field may explore the realm of /sound/, still another may explore the form of /space/ (geometry), and another field focuses its attention on /matter/ (physics), and so on.

It becomes increasingly apparent that the existential mind lives in some determinate grammatical field or universe of discourse, and that this all-encompassing field sub-divides into fundamental categories which are themselves universal domains within the universal field. Further, it now becomes clear that *all* names, concepts, forms, properties, etc. are necessarily specifications *within* categories— all names and forms are allegedly self-identical particularizations of sub-fields within categorial fields. In short, any identity at any level specifies some self-existent (atomic, individuated, differentiated) field or domain of the universe. This means that potentially any particularized field may be taken as a field of investigation and be a focal point for a specialized research program. It is this ontological dynamic of field formation that explains the logic of specialization and proliferation of research "fields" in the evolution of the sciences. And it is important in understanding the holistic thesis to see how diverse disciplinary languages arise in the fall-out of the self-polarization dynamic of the life of identity.

To exist, to be an identity, is to be a locus in some grammatical field; and every possible name or thing is a particularized field of its own which defines its own space. The individuated mind, of course, is purportedly a field unto itself somehow lodged within its surrounding universal grammatical field. And we saw earlier as we explored the internal mind-field of the individuated "I" that this space is infinitely self-divisible and polarized in every direction. The inner world of subjective experience, we have seen, is polarized into diverse domains and there is an existential problem of whether and how the individuated voice is truly integral and univocated. In any case, it should be evident that the life of self-identity essentially involves a language-world or grammatical field that is self divided and polarized into apparently discrete domains and the general problem before us is the problem of *coherence and unity*. How do the diverse self-identical and self existent domains that make up a world cohere in a truly integral and unified universe?

It has been suggested that any name, concept or thing with self identity is always a specification of some category or structure of categories and this implies that signification or import of any identity is necessarily *relative* to some determinate grammatical field or universe of discourse. So the meaning of a given name or concept is relative to a particular grammatical context, the identity of a thing necessarily depends upon the determinate field which makes it possible, indeed, the very *existence* of any thing is relative to its grammatical context. This means, of course, that the meaning of a given term cannot be abstracted from its indigenous context. And since the larger context is always the grammar as a whole, it follows that the meaning of any term, or the identity/existence of a given thing is relative to its universe of discourse.

But now it is important for us to see that different disciplines, diverse disciplinary languages, define different grammatical fields or universes of discourse. We saw earlier that a language/world self divides into basic categories, and each of these is a potential field for research. Thus, if a given grammar divides reality into a realm of consciousness (mind) and a realm of matter, then the discipline which investigates the nature of consciousness will be fundamentally different from the discipline which explores matter. In some sense they are different and incomparable universes of discourse. The concepts and objects that take their identity in one language will be in an important sense incomparable to the concepts and objects of the other grammar.

Furthermore, it should be apparent that the typical diverse disciplines or fields that comprise cultural life, such as art, religion, philosophy and science each defines a field that originates in some aspect of the grammatical field. For example, while science may be said to be the exploration of the phenomena entailed by a grammatical field, religion may be seen as especially concerned with the origin of meaning and existence that lights up the grammatical field as a whole with life. The exploration of the phenomena which are made possible by a universe of discourse involves a methodology suitable for explaining facts, but the concerns which arise regarding the origin of meaning in a grammatical form of life involves faith and naturally has a different methodology.

Similarly, while art may be especially concerned with the celebration and translation of forms into some medium, philosophy may be seen as being concerned with the articulation of the form of meaning and being and human life, etc. The diverse arts carry out their creative activity in some aspect of the grammatical field, and philosophy often occupies itself with the form of the grammatical field as a whole as well as with the formation and transformation of such grammars of reality. Thus, the key to understanding the nature of a given field is to discern the peculiar concerns it has regarding the grammatical field. Any given field defines a domain with identity of its own and this is always lodged in grammar. This is why it appears that each discipline of field is a universe of discourse unto itself. Typically we find that self-identity is the origin of the division and separation into diverse fields. And the recurrent form of the problem is whether and how there can be true common ground or shared meaning and rationality between diverse fields or disciplinary languages.

f) The Fragmentation of self ("I") & Diverse Grammars of Reality
We have been tracing the origin of the fragmentation of existential life that comes with the faith in self-identity and the eclipse of the Holistic Continuum of Reality. It has been suggested that the postulate of the self-existent "I" presupposes that this individuated "I" or mind subsides in an assumed universal grammatical field. This assumed unified field of reality is the very foundation that makes the determinate existential "I" possible; it could not be apart from its reality field. Further, taking such a presumed unified field as given, we explored the dynamics of identity which reiterates within the universal field in the form of diverse basic categories which comprise that reality. It is here that we saw a recurring internal

self-division that spawned separated domains of life, inquiry, experience, etc., that defined diverse sub-fields or disciplinary languages of a given culture. So the existential mind takes itself to be a unified being living in a universal grammatical field which we may call its cultural world, and within this culture its life is expressed in diverse forms of life and diverse cultural language forms.

But now we are ready to explore an even deeper fragmentation and predicament of the existential mind. For now, as we further explore the discontinuum of identity, we shall see that the presumed self-unity of the existential mind is very much in question since it finds itself confronted with profoundly diverse grammars of reality or universal unified fields. For example, while the individuated self takes its very existence to be given with its cultural world, it nevertheless finds itself confronted with the reality of diverse alternative cultural realities (grammars of reality) with which it must deal. Thus, the Christian mind which takes its meaning and existence from the Christian grammar of reality appears to have access to diverse alternative cultural realities. While apparently retaining its peculiar existential identity it seems that this mind can penetrate into alternative cultural worlds, rationally process profoundly different languages of reality. It believes it can understand the world of the Hindu or Buddhist or the world of the theoretical physicist. And our analysis of the fall-out of fragmentation of life brings out the deep predicament: how can the existential mind which is constituted in one universal grammatical field have any real access to profoundly diverse realities or universes of discourse? If the existential thesis that the individuated mind is proscribed within its indigenous reality-field is correct then this would mean that it has no real access to any reality-fields beyond its universe of discourse. On the other hand, if this mind of self-identity does indeed have real access to diverse alternative reality-fields then this would indicate that the presumed individuated mind is not really an individuated unity at all but a *multiplicity* of diverse identities somehow held together in association.

We may bring out the force of this existential predicament in the following way. Our holistic account has disclosed two theses regarding the life of self-identity which collide in polarization: one is that the existential mind is a determinate unified self-identity proscribed within its universal grammatical field, the other is that there are profoundly diverse alternative universal grammar-fields of reality. The latter disclosure of diverse realities would seem to preclude the *individuated* mind having true access to diverse realities. For diverse universes of discourse are existentially incommensurable and this means that all meaning and existence is *systematically equivocal* between different grammars of reality. The particularized mind cannot have *univocal identity* across diverse grammar-universes. And this would mean that the mind of identity is fragmented into diverse incommensurable voices across universal grammars, thus being fractured into multiple identities; or else the thesis of self-identity must be incoherent and not a proper account of the nature of mind, meaning and reality. In any case the postulate of self-existence is incoherent: either the individuated mind is not a true self-unity, or if it is a true existential unity then it cannot have univocal access to diverse realities.

These considerations lead us to the holistic insight that the mind of self-identity is internally fragmented and is in a state of non-coherence, non-unity and non-determinacy. It takes itself to be an individuated unity but holistic reflection reveals that it lives in multiple identities (multivocal) and is not a true self-unity— the postulate of self-unity leads to the opposite result of dis-unity and multi-vocity. It takes itself to be determinate, having unique particular identity, but reflection shows that it cannot be determinate— the faith in its finitude, particularity and determinacy leads to the opposite result of its non-determinacy. In short, the mind of self-identity presumes completeness, coherence and commensurability but the holistic critique shows that the life of identity necessarily leads to incompleteness, non-coherence and non-commensurability. Incompleteness, because what the individuated mind takes to be the universal grammar-field of reality is inherently partial and incomplete and cannot truly encompass Reality, which is holistic and over-flows any constructed universal grammar. Incoherence, because the existential mind presumes its reality is coherent but the holistic account shows that it is inherently self-divided and polarized in every direction and cannot account for coherence. Incommensurable, because the very form of self-identity fragments the holistic field into separated atomically discrete grammar fields which can have no common ground or meditating principle wherein diverse universes of discourse may stand in true relationality and commensurability.

It must be stressed that this fragmented life of self-identity is not a theoretical abstraction but a pragmatic living result. The holistic account, which does not begin with the faith in self-identity, discerns that the individuated mind always speaks in multivocal voice; for its speech ranges across diverse grammatical context and is always indeterminate in signification. If the voice of the self-existent mind is inherently indeterminate and multi-vocal in its speech, then the meaning of its utterances is likewise indeterminate. Once we see that the larger context of discourse always encompasses a multiplicity of diverse grammatical fields it becomes apparent that the speech of the individuated voice equivocates across grammatical fields; and when this voice pronounces the self-referential "I," this utterance reflects the existential indeterminacy across incommensurable realities. In this way we see that the faith in self-identity involves a self polarization that lands in existential non-determinacy; the individuated mind is fragmented into indeterminate multi-vocity and fails to have inner integrity, while the Continuum of Reality is fragmented into diverse universes of discourse beyond mutual relationality so its Reality is fragmented and without integrity. Thus, the original polarization of

I / not-I

that we began with continues the self-polarization on both sides: the "I" self-polarizes without end into non-determinacy, and the "not-I" self-polarizes into unmediated multiplicity and non-determinacy.

g) Pathologies in the Life of Identity: The Fixation of Meaning and Existence

Our holistic critique has uncovered an inner incoherence, incompleteness and indeterminacy in the life of the existential mind. We have seen that its internal identity is fragmented and its surrounding world is likewise fractured in every direction. While its deepest striving is to maintain and preserve its independent self-existence, identity and unity, it nevertheless finds itself in a predicament of radical dependency, disunity and indeterminacy. This impossible situation is too life threatening for it to face directly, so the existential mind constructs ways to cope with its intrinsic self-contradiction and pathological double-bind. In concluding this preliminary exploration of the discontinuum of identity we shall now further explore the dynamics of the existential mind to see how it attempts to maintain its sense of unity and coherence.

We saw earlier that the faith in self-identity requires that any given identity must essentially exist within some universal grammatical field; to exist, to have identity, is to subsist in some universal grammatical field. The general existential law is that *identity is relative* to its universal field. Let us recall that the universal field supplies the origin of unity for the identity in question. We found this dynamic of unity in the triangulating form of identity. In the case of the "I" (self-unity) we found that it could not find its unity within itself or in its "Other" so it had to postulate a higher mediating point of unity above and beyond its own identity as the foundation of its unity. This triangulating dynamic already shows the inner tension in the existential mind: on the one hand it presumes that it is absolutely self-existent and that as such it is its own independent source of unity; but at the same time it finds itself totally dependent on the external transcendent unifying principle of its universe (grammatical field) as the absolute origin of its existence. This deep tension is one symptom of its inherent indeterminacy and rational pathology. Its faith in self identity is a commitment to absolute existence, but it finds itself torn between two opposing polar limits each of which purports to be the absolute foundation of its self-identity. One purported absolute center of reference for its life is its very inner self-existence which it calls "I," but the other ostensible absolute center of reference for its being is the transcendent absolute unifying principle of its universe. One good example of the discovery of these two absolute centers of existence may be found in Descartes' *Meditations*. He found, on the one hand, that the absolute existential point of reference is the "I," but he proceeded to see that "God" or "Infinite Being" is the absolute origin and center of all existence.

The point here is that faith in identity is a faith in there being an absolute self-existent source of unity, but this existential faith finds itself torn between absolutes and *relativized* in its foundations. Indeed, its felt need for existential foundations in some absolute principle, whether in itself or in its "god," is already a confession of its ontological insecurity and dualized condition. Of course the existential mind attempts to stabilize itself and secure its self-unity by opting for *one* absolute foundation of its life; but any such strategem is destined to failure. If it makes itself the central absolute reference of its world, it falls into some form of ego-centric life. If it makes its transcendent "god" its absolute foundation and origin of unity then this leads to deep problems of grammatical theism. If it attempts to posit the grammatical field as a whole— the universe— as the absolute self-existing reality, this too has its rational price. We shall not now draw out the various problems in each of these attempts to resolve its existential predicament. Rather, we shall focus on the *general* dynamic of the mind of identity in its attempt to cope with its inherent self-polarization and indeterminacy. Let us call the common strategy to find its absolute foundation and source of unity— "*absolutism*."

Absolutism is the inherent attempt of the existential mind to preserve its self-unity, identity and determinacy. Whether it accomplishes this by absolutizing itself, its "god" or its universe as a whole, the net effect is the same— *it is the fixation of meaning and existence*, the fixation of all identities in its universal field. By fixing any absolute point of reference in its grammar-field it provides a foundation with respect to which all identities of its world become defined and definite. Of course, this is not a conscious act on its part, rather it is a primordial act of faith which arises intrinsically with its faith in identity. In this respect, the faith in self-identity is a commitment to absolutism and the fixity of meaning and existence.

Perhaps it would be timely to elaborate a bit on this general pathology of absolutism, since the diverse pathologies of identity may be seen as being different versions of absolutism. First the holistic mind is able to see the inherent pathologies of the mind of identity by uncovering the hidden dynamics of identity which comprise the *pre-conscious* conditions of the existential mind. These pre-conscious conditions govern the life of identity at every moment, but they remain eclipsed from the individuated mind. For this reason the mind of identity never becomes aware of its pathological condition and believes itself to be a true unity living in a determinate world with fixed identities, fully coherent and in direct touch with reality. That the pathological conditions of absolutism remain ever hidden and absent from the existential mind is itself a symptom of its self-division and indeterminacy. In a sense we may say that the individuated mind *postulates* its way out of its predicament in its very faith in self-identity.

With this in mind let us briefly look at some versions of absolutism. From the point of view of logic as the theory of meaning we see that absolutism is the disposition to believe that *literal* meaning is primary meaning. Let us call this prejudice *"literalism."*[3] Literalism is a form of absolutism in which it is presumed that the meaning of things is fixed and with univocal self-identity. A given word, name or concept is taken to uniquely specify some meaning content or determinately refer to some thing or property. In short, literalism is the commitment to the definite, univocal, identity of the meaning of things. It is a faith which holds that the literal meaning is primary and all other forms of meaning are derivative and trade on primary meaning. It should be apparent that literalism is just another version of the faith in self-identity applied to meanings. It is the absolutizing of the identity of meanings.

In the realm of knowledge (or epistemology) absolutism expresses itself in the form of *"foundationalism."* This is the version of absolutism which postulates the absolute external reality as absolutely existing, objectively or "nouminally" in itself. The posited absolute, objective reality "out there" becomes the *foundation* of knowledge and all inquiry. This foundation of knowledge is the absolute measure of truth and falsity and the ground of objectivity. It is this absolute measure which makes knowledge possible and which makes real the distinction between the merely subjective and the truly objective origin of facts. Of course another version of foundationalism is the very structure of knowing that posits certain fundamental truths or principles from which other truths may be derived or supported. Such axiomatic or absolute truths are taken to be the *foundations* of knowledge. And it should be increasingly apparent how this "myth" of foundations is inherent in the dynamics of identity.

Still another version of absolutism which is of special interest to us in this holistic narrative is the one we call *"fundamentalism."* In the realm of ontology this is the version of absolutism which takes a given universal grammatical field as the absolute measure of all reality— the absolute measure of what is rational, what is real, what is valuable, what is meaningful, what exists, etc.   Fundamentalism, like literalism and foundationalism, is inherent in the faith of identity.   For the fixation of one's own self-identity and self-existence is tantamount to the absolutizing of one's universal grammatical field as a whole.   One's existential identity is so deeply tied up with one's universal grammatical field that they become inseparable.   Thus, my identity as a Christian is inseparable from my identification with the universal grammar or universe of discourse or cultural world which defines Christian reality.   So insofar as I take myself to be a Christian I am committed in this faith to a fundamentalism regarding the Christian universe of discourse; I take this universal grammar to be the absolute measure of truth and meaning and reality.   And the same goes for any other grammatical faith— be it "Hindu" or "Moslem" or "natural scientist," etc.   In this respect the scientist who takes his grammatical faith to be absolute is just as fundamentalist and absolutist as the religious person.

These are just some of the main versions of absolutism which are inherent in the life of identity.   But all versions of absolutism are strategies to eclipse the intrinsic pathologies of dis-unity, incoherence and indeterminacy in the existential mind and to preserve the "myth" of self-existence, self-identity, unity, coherence and determinacy.   They are strategies of self-deception and self-forgetfulness which must fail.   For the pre-conscious self-polarization and indeterminacy of existential life overpowers the absolutist voice of the existential mind and undermines its greatest efforts to postulate its way out of its self-contradiction.   For example, the individuated mind cannot resist the grammatical overflow of reality and always finds itself subsiding in a multiplicity of diverse universal grammatical fields at any given time.   While it takes itself to be "Christian" it nevertheless finds itself immediately acquainted with the grammatical worlds of "Hindu" or "American" or "physicist" or "BaKongo," etc.   That is, it lives within a larger grammatical range of diverse universal grammatical fields at any given time and this awareness of diverse absolutized grammatical fields or realities provides a powerful ontological counterforce which perpetually reopens the question of its unity, determinacy and coherence.   In this way its strongest efforts at absolutism only accentuates all the more its inherent *relativism.*

Grammatical relativism is the immediate result of the indeterminacy of the individuated mind.   It flows from the immediate awareness of the mind simultaneously inhabiting a multitude of diverse absolute universal grammatical fields. Since these diverse universal fields all purport to be absolute measures of reality this multiplicity of absolutes reminds the existential mind of its ontological indeterminacy and disunity. For if identity is always *relative* to some determinate absolutized grammatical field then the presence of a diversity of universal grammatical fields implies an equivocity of identities across these grammatical realities. Here we see that "relativism" is just the other face of "absolutism," indeed, they are now reduced to one another. And this is just another signal of the inner pathology of the existential mind— while intending and purporting to be absolute, it only demonstrates that it is relative; while attempting to absolutize reality it only achieves the opposite result of ontological relativism.

That the faith in self-identity leads to relativism is not at first obvious. But the net effect is that the life of identity must always begin and end in a multi-vocity of grammatical fields. The voice of the existential mind always speaks in equivocity and ambiguity and does not achieve a true univocity of speech and meaning. When it says "I" its speech ranges over a diversity of universal grammatical fields so the sense and reference of "I" is always equivocal and indeterminate in voice. In this context of grammatical diversity there can be no universal measure of what is rational, what is real, what is meaningful or what is true. Reality itself is divided and suffers the same pathological condition of the existential mind.

In sum, there is no escape for the existential mind. The Continuum of Reality rules in all things and the agenda of the mind of identity always gives way to the powerful undertow of the flow of the Continuum. We now see that the individuated mind must always find itself in the deepest self-contradiction— while it intends to be absolute it relativizes itself; when it purports to be self-existent it only achieves dependency; while it strives for self-unity it only accomplishes inner self-polarization and fragmentation; while it posits itself as fixated and determinate it only shows itself to be un-fixable and indeterminate; if it claims to be atomic this produces the anatomic voice; and if it takes itself to be consistent and coherent it only reveals itself to be in a profound incoherence. And this pathological condition traces back to the original eclipse of the holistic continuum of Reality. We now see that once the Primordial Continuum is broken with the postulate of self-identity the existential mind can find no true resolution to its fragmented condition. And all its efforts to find or posit unity only deepens its crisis of identity.

Perhaps it is timely to resume our exploration of the Holistic Continuum of Nature having now experienced the dynamics of self-identity and its discontinuum of reality. We shall now see that it is the Continuum of Reality that governs all possible forms of life, including the self-polarizing life of the existential mind.

iv) The Holistic Mind and the Universal Continuum of Reality
Let us then continue our meditation on Holistic Unity as the Principle of Pure Reason as we further explicate the Holistic Thesis and explore the dynamics of the holistic mind.

a) The Holistic Principle as the Principle of Universal Relativity
It has been suggested that the mind of identity is inherently unable to discern the continuum of reality; rather, it is the holistic mind— the self universalized voice which is centered in holistic unity— that realizes the Unified Field. The Continuum of Nature cannot be made into an object of thought, it can only be meditated.

Meditative reason centers itself in the principle of Holistic Unity, in Logos. Here there can be no possible trace of the polarization and selfdivisiveness that is characteristic of the life of identity. Logos is nondual in every possible way, so the meditative or holistic mind must be integral and univocated with the Continuum of Reality. In Meditative Reason the split between "I" and "not-I" which was at the heart of the reason of identity cannot and does not get started. In this respect the polarizations which are characteristic of the life of identity are absent in the Universal Grammatical Field. Indeed, the holistic mind sees that what are irreconcilable opposites in the mind of identity are truly univocated in Logos. And in general, all possible names and forms must be essentially univocated in the Continuum; this is the essence of the Holistic Thesis that every name is a logos and every logos is Logos.

Let us further explicate this thesis. Logos is the Universal Form whence all possible names and forms derive. This Form of Absolute Unity is the origin of all possible grammar-fields or universes of discourse; and since every possible name or form is necessarily the specification of some universe of discourse, the holistic mind sees that the true meaning of any name is found in its inner orientation to Logos. As the form of all possible forms Logos is the universal point of reference for all possible worlds, for all possible names and things. As perfect Unity or Pure Form, Logos is Perfection, Goodness, the teleological center of Reality. All things essentially refer to Logos, signify Logos, are oriented to Logos, derive from Logos and gravitate to Logos. So the Continuum of Reality is Ordered and Regulated by Logos. Logos is the Universal Name which governs all names; it is the Original Creative Force that lights up the

Continuum of Nature with meaning and holds all things together in mutual co-relationality.

This is *the Principle of Universal Relativity:* it is that all names and forms are essentially co-relational, co-relatives. It is the rational principle of the Continuum which reveals in meditative logic that all names are mutually implicated in meaning and are existentially co-dependent and co-arise. Let us call this feature of the Continuum— *"holistic synonymy."*[4] In the phenomenology of Pure Reason it is seen that the true meaning of any name consists in its holistic synonymy with other names and its Univocity with Logos. The Principle of Universal Relativity is the intrinsic logical force that holds the Continuum of Reality in holistic unity. Nowhere is the Continuum broken with divisive identity or polarization; everywhere it remains essentially Unified, Uniform, Univocal, Universal.

b) Elaboration of the Continuum of Reality: Holistic ((Names))[5]
Let us meditate further on the structure of the Continuum. We have already seen that the Continuum or Unified Field is the Universal meeting point of all possible fields, of all possible names or forms or things. When, through the meditative critique, we have realized the inadequacy of the postulate of existential identity as the principle of reason the principle of Universal Relativity spontaneously arises and Holistic Rationality reveals the Logic of the Continuum. In exploring this Logic it would be helpful to introduce a special symbol to indicate the holistic or universal significance of any given name or term: let us indicate the holistic meaning of any term "x" by $((X))$.

All holistic names are synonymous with Logos and with each other. So meditation on Logos or Continuum is really the simultaneous and mutual univocation of all terms.

Let us reflect on some primary formulas:
(i) *Logos is ((Mind))*: This means that The Continuum is Universal Mind or Consciousness and hence no mind can be apart from Logos. The continuum cannot be made into an object of thought and thus separated from mind or thinker; here there can be no separation or duality between *the thinker* and *what is thought*, or between subject and object. The primordial split between "I" and "not-I" that is the foundation of identity-thinking cannot be introduced in minding the Continuum. In meditating the Continuum the Mind or Voice of thinker is univocated with Logos and the "I" and "not-I" co-arise and inhere in one another thus forming a primordial continuum. Meditative or holistic thinking invokes the Holistic Mind which

reflexively realizes itself as the Continuum. This Univocation of the subject-field and the object-field is one of the most startling disclosures of meditating thinking: it implies that all names or things are so inextricably involved with consciousness, mind or thought (and vice versa) that it may be truly said in meditative speech that all things are essentially ((Mind)). To say that the Continuum of Reality is ((Mind)) not only implies that nothing can be apart from ((Mind)), but more radically that all things are essentially of the Nature of ((Mind)).

(ii) *Logos is ((Word))*: The Holistic or Primordial Word which is the Continuum is the Universal form of Unity and hence the Meeting point of all possible words (names, forms, things). The Original Word is pure ((Mind)) and as such Speaks itself forth, Voices itself in Self Expression. In this respect all Existence is the Creative ((Speaking)) of the Word. Any name or thing is the Expression of the Word: to ((Exist)) is to be Voiced, Spoken, Expressed, to be the Creative Speech-act of the Word. Here it may be readily seen that the Original Word is Pure ((Idea)) or ((Thought)): any name, thing or creature is essentially ((Idea)). But at the same time the Universal Word is ((Meaningful)), the perfection of Meaning or Essence, the very Power or Energy of the Living Word; here we see that any thing is a center of Meaning-energy. Again, this pure ((Meaning)) of the Word is so consonant and congruent with Reality (Being, Existence) that the Holistic Word is the perfection of ((Truth)); so the Word is the Living Truth and every existing thing or creature bears witness to this Truthful Speaking forth of the Word. Further, the Word expresses itself in ((Grammar)) and is perfectly well— formed in its Syntax. The Word is the Perfect Sign or Symbol which immediately reveals Reality. In this face of the Continuum all things are Names spoken forth in Universal Grammar: to exist is to be grammatical, to be truthfully spoken and well named. Now we begin to see the holistic synonymy of Word-Mind-Being-Speech-Voice-Idea-Name-Meaning Grammar-Truth.

As we meditate further on the Word as Living Truth, we find that the Holistic Word is Meaningful, Truthful, and Mindful. The ((Mindfulness)) of the Word shows itself as Pure Intelligence, Cognition, or Reason. It may be said that Truth is the Light of Reason and the Coherence or Unity of all things. So we go full circle and see that ((Truth)) is the form of Unity itself which is the Coherence of all names and forms in Continuum;

Pure Reason or Knowledge is precisely the Coherence of all things.

(iii) *Logos is ((Nature))*:   Let us continue the meditative explication of the Continuum of Reality and the Universal Formula of the ((Word)). The Continuum is the Cosmic or Universal Field of Existence.   As such it shows itself as ((Nature)) or ((Universe)) and encompasses all possible Phenomena. In this revelation of the Continuum we discern the holistic meaning of ((Matter)) as the Primordial or Ultimate Substance of the Universe. Holistic ((Matter)) is the Continuum itself and this implies that all possible things, forms, events, phenomena are expressions of Matter— the original material of all existence. This ((Matter)), of course, is synonymous with ((Word)) and ((Mind)) and shows itself as Living Holistic ((Energy)).   In this context it may be said that Holistic ((Energy)) is the original ((Substance)) of the Universe and can be neither created nor destroyed. The Holistic Principle of the preservation or conservation of ((Energy)) is a Law of ((Nature)).   And since ((Nature)) encompasses all forms of existence, including consciousness and rational intelligence, it follows that ((Energy)) constitutes the living power and force of Mind, Meaning and Truth. But The Continuum as ((Energy)) is co-extensive with ((Time)) which is the measure of Existence and ((Space)) which is the locus of ((Nature)).   ((Time)) is omnipresent in all expressions of ((Energy)) and all possible moments of Holistic ((Time)) are immediately contiguous, contemporaneous and synchronous. In this way ((Energy)) and ((Time)) are coextensive and synonymous with ((Existence)) and are essentially a continuum. Similarly, ((Space)) is the extension of Existence or ((Energy-Time)) and all possible loci are contiguous, and co-extensive. Holistic ((Space)) is the *topos* of Existence or ((Nature)) and naturally encompasses logicible (intelligible) space thus revealing the continuum of ((Mind-Space)).   Again, ((Space)) and ((Time)) are primordial synonyms for ((Energy)) and are themselves synonymous and form a ((Space-Time)) continuum. Now we begin to discern more explicitly the Continuum of ((Nature)) in the contiguity of ((Existence-Substance-Energy-Matter-Word-Mind-Intelligence-Time-Space))

The Holistic Formula of the Continuum of ((Nature)) expands further as we focus meditative attention on Holistic ((Causality)). This is the adhesive force that holds Existence in

Unity and Order and Co-relationality; ((Casuality)) is the connective or binding force of ((Substance)) that univocates all names/forms/things into the continuum of mutual co-relation. All name/things co-arise in expressing and defining the other; all forms internally inhere in one another and mutually imply each other thus expressing the Implicature of ((Nature)). The Continuum is a ((Causal)) nexus of mutual or dialogical Implication— the Implicate Order of ((Nature)). Holistic ((Causality)) is the expression of the Principle of Universal Relativity. And Holistic Science is the explication of the Implicate rational order of Reality.

Again, The Uniformity of ((Nature)) is revealed in Holistic ((Process)) wherein the cosmic event plays itself out in the Living Conversation of all ((Phenomena)); in the ((Phenomenology)) of the Continuum all phenomena (names/things/events) are in mutual ((Becoming)). Thus, if we meditate on the holistic form of "light" we find that ((Light)) is pure ((Energy)) which permeates all things— it lights up ((Nature)) with Meaning. It is the Rational Energy of Intelligence which is ever-present throughout the Continuum of Existence.

((Light)) moves with infinite Velocity and is hence omnipresent. The Light of Logos shines in all things which reflect the form of the Continuum. But this ((Light)) is the Speech of the Word which is the ((Sound)) of Reality. The Holistic Sound of the Word vibrates in all directions in perfect ((Silence)). It becomes clear that ((Light)) and ((Sound)) are correlative and co-extensive and are one and the same Cosmic Vibration. Similarly, ((Air)), permeates the Continuum as the Living Breath of the Word and makes all things vibrant with Life. In this way we begin to see how the holistic Names of ((Nature)) are in a continuum of synonymy, and inhere in one another in mutual implication.

(iv) *Logos is ((Value))*: The Holistic Formula further expands in the meditative recognition that The Continuum is the Perfection of Holistic ((Value)). We earlier introduced the formula that *Logos is ((Goodness))*. The Continuum is the Universal point of reference for all names/forms/things, and ((Goodness)) is the Unifying form of all possible forms: all forms are essentially oriented to Perfect ((Unity)) whence they originate. ((Goodness)) is the Cause of all things and as such is the ((Telos)) which Orders the Continuum and illumines it with ((Value)). But Holistic ((Value)) univocates the diverse value-names into their Holistic Form.

Thus, ((Goodness)) is synonymous with ((Truth)) and ((Beauty)). We have seen that ((Truth)) is the perfect Coherence of all names/ things, and as a face of ((Goodness)) it reflects the Universal Form of ((Unity)). Now we see that ((Beauty)) is another face of the Continuum which likewise reflects the Perfection of ((Form)). The Continuum shines in ((Beauty)), and in the communion and harmony of all things it reveals itself as perfectly Simple and Elegant. ((Nature)) is perfectly Efficient and Economical and herein lies its Elegance. In this Light the Ecology of the Continuum Preserves and Conserves its ((Energy)). The Perfect Harmony of all Forms expresses the Music, Symphony, Song, Poetry, Dance of the Continuum, which is perfectly ((Esthetic)) in Value.

Following this Logic we begin to see the Continuum of ((Value)) in the synonymy of ((Goodness-Truth-Beauty)). All Reality is ((Value)) laden and saturated with ((Meaning)).

(v) *Logos as ((Deed))*: The Holistic Formula expands even more dramatically as we meditate on the Word as ((Deed)). Here we see the Continuum as Pure Holistic ((Action)). Reality is the Speech-Act of the Word: the expressive Speech of the Continuum is Creative ((Energy)) which is ever ((Active)) yet Perfectly Still. As the Action of ((Mind)) the Continuum is the expression of Thought-Acts in which all Existence shows itself as Hermeneutical Activity or ((Theory)). As the Creative Vibration of ((Energy)) it is seen that all things ((Move)) in the Light of the telic Truth-force. And since Rational Energy moves all things it becomes clear that ((Nature)) always Acts for the Best in Right Reason. This ((Praxis)) of the Continuum is at once Moral and Esthetic Activity: its Creative Self Expression is the Perfection of ((Art)) and its Free and Autonomous Conduct is Perfectly Good, Right and True. In this Light it becomes clear that the Continuum is a Community of Free Speech and creative Self Expression wherein all Beings take up their Rightful Place in the ((Politics)) of Existence. Here we see that all things stand together in Holistic Communion and Voice their own Form of Life in the Conversation of ((Nature)). This Speech— life of the Continuum is a Living Dialogue which expresses itself in a perfect Consensus.

c) Explicating the Implicature of ((Nature)): Beyond Dualisms
In the light of the Holistic Formula we are now in a position to further
explore the Implicature of the Continuum and discern how the pervasive
oppositions, dualities and polarizations which are inherent in the life of
identity are preempted in the Unified Field. We have been meditatively
explicating the Holistic Thesis which teaches that every possible name/form
is a logos which derives from Logos. And this has shown that the
Continuum is the Universal meeting point of all possible
names/forms/things: all Holistic Names meet and are Univocated in Holistic
Synonymy in the Logic of the Continuum. Since all names/things form a
continuum of mutual implication this implies that there are no dis-
continuities, splits, oppositions or polarizations in the Implicature of
Existence. What is found to be polarized in self opposition in the life of
identity is now seen to be in an essential continuum in the Implicature of
Holistic Life.

In exploring this contiguity of the Continuum it would be helpful here to
see that the holistic term "logos" gathers together certain fundamental
dimensions which are usually differentiated and separated in conventional
thinking: mind, idea, name, word, meaning, thing, form. All of these form
an essential continuum in ((Nature)) and we shall use the holistic term
"logos" to indicate this continuum. Accordingly *logos* is the name for any
possible name-form-thing, for any possible identity. Here we may say that
logos is the ultimate "stuff" or "particle" or "unit" of ((Existence)). Any
logos is a field which is fully integral and univocated in the Continuum.
And since logos is the holistic form of any given name/form/thing it may
be said that any name or thing is essentially a field or form of the
Continuum. There is nothing that is not a field of the Continuum and fully
implicated in the Implicature. By calling any possible name or thing by its
holistic name (i.e., "logos") we become mindful that all names/things are
really fields or forms of the Continuum and hence fully implicated in the
Universal Field.

In Holistic Logic "logos" as the protoname for all names and as the unit of
the Implicature it becomes explicit that any thing is an *implicatum,* a center
of ((Energy)), a unity of ((Meaning)). Any given name/thing as logos is a
field of the Unified Field, and all fields are mutually implicated in one
another. All things, as centers of ((Meaning)), are bound together in
meaning or sense-relations. Any ((thing)) or logos is a ((form)) or unified
and unifying ((field)) whose essence is the Continuum. No field-thing is
atomic or separable or dis-continuous; rather, any logos is a continuum
whose being— essence-meaning is the Continuum. Any ((X)) is a logos-
continuum, a self-universalizing field, which expresses the Unified Field.[6]

The holistic form of any ((thing)) is more readily seen when the polarizations which pervade the life of identity are found to be in an essential continuum or unified field in holistic thinking. We saw earlier that perhaps the most fundamental polarization of the Continuum is the primordial split between *I* and *not-I* which is at the heart of the life of identity. The "I" becomes a unified field of its own over against the "not-I" universal field and from this foundation a number of pervasive polarizations arise. Let us sketch out some of these and then select certain polarizations for meditative attention:

The Continuum (Every ((thing)) is a logos)

I field	not-I field
Subjective	Objective
(Inner)	(Outer)
Grammar/Experience	Nature/Universe/World
Intelligence/Consciousness/Mind	Body/Matter/Energy
Idea/Concept/Word	Object/Thing
Essence/Meaning	Existence/Meant
Sense	Reference
Form/Universal	Individual/Particular
Thought (Word)	Action (Deed)
Theory	Practice
Reason/Rational	Sense/Empirical
a priori	a posteriori
analytic	synthetic

Once the identity split between I and not-I is univocated in the Continuum the flood gates are opened and the polarizations of identity find their natural flow in the Implicature of ((Nature)); each polarization is found to be a continuum in which each pole is fully implicated in its "opposite." (The univocation, of course, is simultaneously horizontal and vertical.)

When the artificial split between "I" and "not-I" is overcome and the polarized fields are univocated there is a profound expansion of "I" as it realizes its holistic or universal form in Continuum: ((I)). This self-expansion is the emergence of Holistic Mind which is ever-present to the individuated and fixated "I." The artificially constructed "I," being individuated and relatively fixated in identity, is unable to realize the holistic unity of the polarizations. In general, when polarized opposites are univocated in a continuum (unified field) then holistic form begins to show itself. When the fracture between I and not-I is dissolved the implications are astounding; the split between thinker and thought, between subject and object, between consciousness and object evaporates and the poles are found to be mutually implicated in each other and in an essential continuum. There can be no "object" that is not saturated with ((consciousness)). The split between the inner space/time of experience and the outer space/time of world is likewise blown away and ((World)) is found to be totality of ((Experience)). And since the individuated "I" and its mind and experience are constituted in some grammatical field, it becomes evident that the ((Universe)) is profoundly ((Grammatical))— to be is to be Grammatical.

Again, the inner logical or intelligible mind-space univocates with the outer extended, physical, matter-space and it becomes evident that all ((things)) are in ((space)). The energy of mind (consciousness, intelligence) is found to be in a continuum or unified field with the energy of physical matter, and here we discern the mind-matter continuum of ((Energy)). This means, of course, that the laws of mind and the laws of matter are in an essential continuum in the ((Laws)) of ((Nature)). And all phenomena are essentially ((psycho-physical)).

Similarly, the artificial division between "word" and "thing," between "concept" and "object" is preempted and the natural flow of the continuum between idea-thing and concept-object is manifested; in this holistic continuum it may be truly said that all "things" are ((Ideas)), and all "objects" are ((Concepts)). This univocation is precisely analogous to the subject— object and mind-matter continuum. An obvious implication of this is that "meaning" and "existence" likewise form an holistic continuum in which every ((thing)) is ((word)) or ((Meaning)); all existence is profoundly ((grammatical)).

This holistic revelation has radical implications for the classical divisions between "reason" and "sense," between the "rational" and the "empirical," and the attendant split in knowledge and ideas between the "a priori" and the "a posteriori."

For we immediately see that there are no "facts" that are not ((theory)) laden or the artifacts of ((grammar)). Accordingly, there can be no sense— experience that is not saturated with ((grammar)). ((Mind)) and ((Nature)) are so profoundly implicated in each other that no division between *a priori* and *a posteriori* could get started.

Furthermore, in this light it becomes apparent that there can be no dichotomy between the thought-field and the action-field, between word and deed, between theory and practice. On the contrary, we now see in the continuum of theory-practice that all ((existence)) is the action of ((theory)), the ((hermeneutical activity)) of ((Nature)). In this context it is natural to say that existence is the ((grammatical)) expression of the

Continuum. All ((things)) are ((speech-acts)) of the Living Word, the creative self-expression of ((Energy)). Here it is seen that all reality is the incarnation of ((Truth)), the logos-become-flesh; all ((Nature)) is Alive and playing out the ((Truth)) force. "Truth" can no longer be divided into theoretical and practical; rather, both are in an essential continuum of Pure ((Reason)).

This implies too that there can be no split between Fact and Value: for all "facts" are ((Value)) laden. The discontinuum of "is" and "ought" meet in the texture of ((Nature)) wherein all "facts" are creative hermeneutical acts which express the laws of Freedom. For "facts" can arise only within the context of a Grammar and the being and significance of any fact implies a prior grammatical or hermeneutical choice or act of Faith. It is here that questions of moral truth and scientific truth become univocated, since all inquiry into ((Truth)) must involve ethical choices and decisions in grammatical attitude. The ethics of inquiry governs our hermeneutical conduct in the search for Truth.

These are just selected polarizations; they are selected to illustrate how the Principle of Universal Relativity places dualisms into a continuum. There are other obvious dichotomies that we might have focused upon Finite vs. Infinite, Faith vs. Reason, Science vs. Religion, or more particularized polarizations such as life/death or good/evil, etc. The point is that the Logic of the Continuum implies the univocation of all dualisms or polarizations. It should now be clear that the deep split between "finite" and "infinite" cannot get started in the Continuum of ((Nature)), for Holistic Unity is *par excellence* the continuum of finite-infinite: this is the inner character of any *logos*. And here we see the force of the Holistic Thesis that *every logos is Logos.*

d) Holistic Method of ((Inquiry)): The Dynamics of Self-Expansion From Identity to Universal Relativity

Having sketched the ((Logic)) of the Continuum and introduced the ((Phenomenology)) of the Holistic Mind our Holistic Narrative unfolds further in the articulation of the Universal Method of ((Inquiry)). We are now in a position to explore the dynamics of self-expansion from Identity to Universal Relativity.

In the Holistic account of the life of identity it is seen that all life, indeed all existence, is positioned in some field within the Unified Field. So a principle of Holistic Science is that the life of identity is governed by the Presence of the Continuum: every identity is necessarily a field which is positioned within some constructed universal field which essentially refers to the Continuum.

Let us explicate this holistic theme further. We saw earlier that any identity whatsoever, be it a name, a thing, a form, a fact, an attribute, an event, a relation, a spacio-temporal reference, a form of life, a grammar or world view, etc., is necessarily a field within the Unified Field. In general, any thing-field is always situated within a more comprehensive unified field which expresses its essence. It was suggested earlier that a given culture, for example, may be seen as a universal grammar of experience/reality which defines a universe of discourse. Such a grammar is of course a universal unified field which purports to give unity and coherence to the world or universe it constitutes. In the holistic narrative we now see that any such lived grammar in the life of identity must be a *constructed* unified field. For the mind of identity inherently eclipses the Continuum and takes its grammar-field to be the universal and absolute point of reference for its form of life. In this respect, any grammar of identity is an artificial language of experience.

The Holistic critique reveals that meaning/existence is always relative to some grammatical context. A given name/concept/thing has no meaning or existence apart from some grammar-field within which it is implicated. And the meaning of any thing is essentially a function of its implication in its grammar-field. Thus, the meaning of "time" varies across grammatical contexts and we cannot assume, in the life of identity, that "time" has free-floating meaning on its own. Similarly, the meaning and existence of "I" likewise is relative to its indigenous grammatical context. So in general, in the life of identity, meaning is always relative to grammar, and there is equivocity or systematic ambiguity across diverse grammatical fields.

For this reason it becomes apparent that meaning/existence in the life of identity is always relative to some voice/mind context. For no grammar-field on its own, apart from the voice or mind that inhabits it and speaks it, can have independent meaning. Rather, meaning is a function of the voice (mind, self, "I") which lives and speaks the grammar in question. If voice is equi-vocal or multi-vocal or indeterminate than meaning/existence is likewise equivocal or indeterminate. And we saw earlier that the voice-field or I-field is variable and has the liberty or freedom of speech to range over or inhabit diverse grammar-fields or universes of discourse. Here it is seen that any given univocal or determinate "I" (voice) is relative to the grammar-field it inhabits, but since "I"-field is indeterminate and equivocal to begin with, all speech-life is grammatically indeterminate until the intrinsic reference to the voice-field is specified. Thus, if in conventional life any term is uttered, say "I," "time," "tree," "God," etc., the meaning of that term is essentially a function of the grammar-field and voice-field which is its context of utterance. When in common sense we take the communal voice field for granted as fixed and the grammar-field as understood and determinate, we thereby disambiguate the meaning of the term within this specified field-context. However, if the voice-field is ambiguous or indeterminate, then the grammar-field is indeterminate and meaning/existence reflects this indeterminacy.

That meaning/existence is field-specific in this way is an important disclosure in the Holistic Narrative. For the Holistic Thesis or Continuum Hypothesis makes clear that all meaning-existence is essentially relative to the Continuum or Unified Field. This means that the life of identity lives always in the over-powering gravitational field of the Continuum. Eclipsed from its roots though it may be, still the I-field or voice-field or grammar-field of identity is always situated within the domain of the Continuum and is intrinsically governed by the laws of ((Nature)). Thus, the mind of identity, in all its indeterminacy, lives and moves always within the pervasive presence of ((Energy)). Indeed, it is its very indeterminacy which reserves its perpetual opening and access to the Continuum. So every voice-field or "I" lives ambiguously in the horizon of Continuum; and as it weaves its own identity-agenda of meaning and constructs its own text of experience and reality, its earth-bound narrative is always under the sway of the higher ((Narrative)) of the Unified Field.

Perhaps this should be stated even more strongly to draw out the force of the Continuum Hypothesis. It may be said that the very ((essence)) of any identity consists in its intrinsic reference to and orientation towards the Continuum. Any degree of meaning it may have is relative and derives from its implication in the Continuum. So any identity lives a double life between the narrative of identity and the Holistic Narrative. Thus, if we take any conventional term "x" as used in the egological context, this term is relatively fixated in its significance. However, when this term is taken up in the power of meditative thinking its inner universal significance is released and the term self-expands to its holistic meaning as its grounding in the unified field of Universal Grammar is realized. Here we may draw out the contrast between the law of identity and the law of universal relativity:

> Law of Identity: For any "x", **x is x.**
> Law of Universal Relativity: For any "x", x is ((X))

In the Principle of Relativity, the first mention of "x" is its conventional meaning in the mind of identity, while its second occurrence, ((X)) is its universalized or expanded (holistic) meaning in the context of the Continuum. While "x" is always self-eclipsed from its true intrinsic universal essence, ((x)) is the clarified, explicated, coherent meaning of the term in its dynamic meditative context of the Continuum. But ((X)) can be truly spoken in the holistic voice, and not in the voice of identity. In this way we see that any identity is lodged in a certain indeterminacy between the two narratives, and there is a continuum of self-expansion from identity to Relativity.

Let us explore the holistic dynamics of this expansion from "x" to ((X)).

We saw earlier that any identity (name/form/thing) is a field within its constructed universal domain or unified field. Its very identity and determinacy depends upon its universal grammar-field. Furthermore, we saw that any such grammar-field is itself a categorial continuum of diverse categories standing in a certain structure and order that gives relative rational coherence to that universe of discourse. Thus, any identity is a principle of unity whose unity lies in the unity of a more comprehensive field or "category" which is its immediate continuum, which in turn finds its unity in a still more comprehensive category-field, etc., all of which are unified in the absolute unifying principle of the grammar-field as a whole. Let us take an example:

Take this *red* object before me; this red color is an identity, a field which is given in the presence of the visual field. This visual field is the field-context for "this red" which cannot be apart from the color-space and visual field wherein it is given. First, we notice that in the very givenness of *this red* is its differentiation from other colors which it displaces in the color-field: we may say that the polar opposition

Figure 6

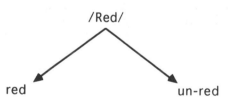

of red/un-red spans all possible colors in the color-field which is indicated as /Red/ or /Color/, which is its category-field; so all colors are necessarily in the universal and unifying domain of the category /Color/. Now the very meaning of "red" and the existence of *this red* essentially derive from its category-field /Color/ which is its essence.

But /Color/ is a category-field which takes its essence and existence from its category-field in the continuum of the grammar-field: /Color/ essentially derives within the visual field and derives from the feature of being extended in /Space/. Apart from this category-field, "red" and "/color/" cannot be or be understood. Again, this space-field essentially involves the category fields of /mass/ and /energy/, /figure/ and /texture/, etc. But these fields are essentially implicated in /time/, so the essence of "this red" traces into the category-field of /time/ which thus far is the most comprehensive and unifying category-field. In turn, /time/ is situated in some more inclusive unified category-field until we reach the universal, all-encompassing category-field which gives unity and coherence to the universe of discourse of which "this red" is situated. And the holistic point is that the essence of "this red" expands and deepens and realizes its relative (identity) universal from in its ontological universal-field. In general, any identity follows this path of self-expansion in its meaning/essence. This opens the way to seeing ((Red)).

Now the unifying principle-field of a given grammar itself resides in the more comprehensive holistic Continuum which is the meeting point of all possible grammar-fields or universes of discourse. In this way any grammar, in its unifying absolute principle, touches immediately into the Continuum where it derives its meaning/essence But we also saw earlier that the meaning of any identity-term is relative to its indigenous grammar, but may have systematic ambiguity across diverse grammatical fields. It is only in the Continuum as the Universal Holistic Field that the expansion from "x" to ((X)) may reach its natural conclusion. Thus, "time" may vary in sense/reference in diverse grammatical fields, and is indeterminate and systematically ambiguous across grammar-fields, but it reaches its universal form/essence in the Continuum in which ((Time)) flows.

We thus see in the Holistic Narrative an ordered hierarchy of fields within fields all of which vibrate out of the Holistic Continuum. Any identity is essentially oriented to the Continuum, and it touches directly into the Continuum via its constructed grammatical field. This is why the true inquiry into any identity, at any level of discourse, must make the grammatical turn and become grammatically aware, for it is in this awakening to the comprehensive grammatical field that opens the way to the ((essence)) of any thing. And when we discern a given thing in the light of its grammar-field as a whole (its ontological context), the way is prepared for the critical expansion from identity to Relativity as the constructed grammar-field is found to derive from the Continuum.

This disclosure of the Holistic Narrative that all life, meaning and existence immediately derives from the Continuum of Reality has radical implications for our understanding of human life and rational inquiry.

First, we now see that the life and mind of identity is essentially situated in the ((Light)) of the Continuum, and although in its own constructed narrative and agenda of reality it eclipses itself from the Unified Field, nevertheless it is governed in its every breath by the ever-present and pervasive ((Forces)) of the pre-conscious Continuum. The mind of identity is ruled in every way by Laws of ((Nature)) which is its Pre-conscious Unified Field.

Let us focus on its ego-narrative to see how this is edited, expanded, and radically revised in the higher Voice of the Holistic Narrative. We recall that this ego-voice, which calls itself "I," is always ambiguously situated in its universal grammar-field or universe of discourse. In its rational life it lives and moves in this field which it calls "reality" and which remains its pre-conscious absolute condition. Its grammar-field makes its life possible and as its absolute ground and foundation this pre-conscious field is its faith, the origin of its meaning. The ego-voice always lives in a faith-field which it takes to be its absolute principle. The rational life of the ego-voice always flows from its faith-field (its grammar) and it lives in relative *fixity* of voice against this absolutized faith.

But we have seen that what the mind of identity in its fixity takes to be its absolute foundation is situated in the Continuum of Reality and is really *relative*, *open* and *unfixable*. The grammar-field of the ego-narrative is found in the Holistic Mind to be an open horizon which gestures to the Continuum where it receives its ((Light)). So what the ego-voice takes to be absolute, complete, relative, incomplete, artificial, constructed, and hypothetical, what the ego mind takes to be its absolute foundations, turns out to be a conjecture or *grammatical hypothesis* of ((Reality)). All grammars of identity are in this light theoretical constructions aimed at discerning the Continuum of ((Nature)). And since the life of identity is fully circumscribed in its grammar-field we now see that in every fiber of its hermeneutical life it is implicitly engaged in interpretation, theory, experimentation and ((inquiry)) as its gravitates to its origin in the Continuum.

In this ((Light)) the Holistic Narrative teaches that the rational faith and meaning of ego life is a hypothetical construction and its grammar in this respect is artificial and not ((Natural)). Still, whatever light and meaning illumines its world derives directly from the Continuum. Insofar as the life of identity reaches some degree of rationality, truth, meaning, coherence, it receives this from its immediate dependence on the ((Light)) of the Continuum. Indeed, the Holistic Narrative reveals that all flashes of insight in the course of ((History)) which have moved human life forward in its self-evolution have been flashes into the Continuum of ((Nature)).

These flashes of brilliance break through when the mind of identity spontaneously opens to its holistic form. And the grammars of existence which have evolved in human history are hypotheses of the Continuum which tap the ((Energy)) of ((Nature)) to the degree that they are *open*. Here we find that the Unified Field of ((Reality)) is the absolute measure of ((Truth)): the deeper the ((insight)) into the form of ((Unity)) the greater the self-expansion from identity to Relativity and the greater the release of ((Energy)) = ((Truth)) = ((Rational Light)). The more fixated and closed the mind of identity, the more eclipsed it is from ((Reality)), and the more fragmentary and partial its form of life. But the more open and un-fixated the voice, the more ((Scientific)) it is, and the more directly in touch with the Continuum of ((Truth)). Thus, we find here a ((Law of Nature)): As the mind of identity self-expands to its holistic form the deeper it realizes its ((Unity)), and the deeper the self-univocation to the Continuum the greater the release of ((Energy)) = ((Life)) = ((Truth)) = ((Rationality)).

We now begin to see in the Holistic Narrative that all life is ((Inquiry)) or ((Theoretical/Grammatical Activity)): all life is intrinsically oriented and directed towards the Continuum and all grammatical forms are conjectures or hypotheses of ((Grammar)). This implies, of course, that the quality of ((Life)) is a function of the degree of openness of mind/voice to the Continuum of Reality. If the voice is relatively fixated and the grammar-field is absolutized then to this degree the mind becomes ossified and closed off from Continuum. But if the voice lives a truly ((Scientific)) form of life it remains perpetually open and is disposed to remain thoroughly experimental at its deepest levels of grammaticality and hence lives in the path of self-expansion to Holistic Form. Again, the more fixated mind tends to absolutize its grammar-field and this becomes its pre-conscious faith-field which governs its artificial life. If it is "scientific" or experimental it is against this fixated grammar-field that it expresses its limited form of "openness." Thus, in the more conventional forms of "science" and "inquiry" there is indeed theorizing, hypothesis and experimentation within some delimited field of research, but there tends to be no open ((Scientific)) experimentation at the pre-conscious level of grammar. The form of inquiry of the mind of identity tends to eclipse and absolutize its grammar-field which is the context that which frames the particular field of research. Thus, specialized research in a conventional field of physics tends to take its grammar of "nature" for granted as fixated and proceeds in its theoretical and experimental life with uncritical acceptance of the reality of certain phenomena (identities, fields) within this grammar-context. It is only when its theoretical life breaks down that a bold open spirit like Einstein dares to revise the grammar-field and open up a new and expanded universe of discourse.

The Holistic Narrative celebrates what is deepest and best in the ((Scientific)) Spirit, and universalizes it for all ((Inquiry)): the essence of Scientific Method is its experimental disposition to remain perpetually open to ((Truth)); and this is precisely the path of self-expansion from the life of identity to the ((Life)) of Universal Relativity. This path of ((Inquiry)) calls forth the Dialogical Voice which is in an ongoing conversation with ((Nature)). The Ethics of ((Inquiry)) is in this respect the discipline of perfecting our finitude through perpetual self-revision, self-correction, experimentation and verification of ((hypotheses)). It resists the closure of the categorical voice (of identity) and thrives on the ever self-expanding dialogical voice of Universal Relativity. It resists the fixity and fixation of literal meaning and soars in the open space of holistic imagination where all names vibrate in the Implicature of ((Nature)). The holistic mind sees that ((metaphoric)) meaning is primary and the meditative imagination discerns the analogical implications of the Continuum.

Thus, in doing ((Physics)) the Holistic Scientist cuts through the artificial constructions and barriers of voice that fragments research into diversified/specialized fields. It is the Continuum of Reality or ((Nature)) that is the primary subject of ((Inquiry)). And in dialogically exploring the Laws of ((Nature)) and ((Energy)) the Holistic Voice queries the mutual implication of ((Mind)) and ((Matter)) and experiments with the Causal Transformations which univocate the mind-matter Continuum. In this expanded field of ((Physics)) it is quite intelligible to inquire into the ((velocity)) of that form of ((Energy)) called intelligence. We have the intuition that there must be Causal transformations of ((Energy)) between what is called "mind" and "matter." That consciousness or rational energy may exceed the speed of "light" and approximate the Velocity of ((Light)) is an interesting hypothesis of Holistic Science worthy of experimental verification. Obviously such experimentation requires the expansion of conventional grammars (and of "mind") beyond their contemporary forms.[7]

v)   Conclusion: The Holistic Unity of the Diverse Hermeneutical Arts

This, of course, is a preliminary sketch of Holistic Science. This essay is no more than a preface to themes in Universal Hermeneutics. In this articulation of Holistic Unity and the Logic of Holistic or Pure Reason it has been stressed that ((Reality)) is a Continuum in which all possible names or forms are Univocated. In exploring the Holistic Implicature of the Continuum it was suggested that Truth, Beauty and Goodness are ((Synonyms)). Of course, the immediate implication is that Holistic Science is the univocation of the diverse hermeneutical arts: philosophy, religion, the sciences and the arts. The Holistic Narrative reveals that these are diverse ways of celebrating Holistic Unity, Pure Form or The Continuum of Reality. So, for example, while "philosophy" has characteristically attempted to articulate the Ultimate ((Form)) or ((Principle)) of Reality and Meaning, "religious" forms of life have developed diverse ritual ways of acknowledging and celebrating Divine ((Form)). And while the diverse sciences may be seen as being implicitly experimental explorations of the Laws of ((Nature)), the various arts manifest themselves as attempts to translate Pure ((Form)) into the media of the senses. Here we see that all Life is ((Inquiry)) into ((Form)) and Holistic Science is the Universal Method of Rational Inquiry. The quest for ((Truth)) then must be at once religious, scientific, esthetic and moral. This is the Critique of Pure Reason.

These themes are developed in the following chapters. In particualr, Chapter 4 focuses on the further development of Grammatology as the universal hermeneutical method of Meditative Reason. We shall now explore the categorial continuum of mind and matter and the psycho-physical continuum of Nature in the unified field of Universal Grammar.

Notes

1 In speaking here of the "individuated mind" we are speaking provisionally from the meditative narrative of the ego-logical self description of its presumed "individuality." As we shall see below this purported "individuated mind" of the ego paradigm is found to be lodged in ontological indeterminacy and equivocity, and always constitutively situated in the Continuum which remains its foundation and source of life and meaning. Indeed, we shall see that it is Meditative Reason and its Principle of Relativity that accounts for the true understanding of individuals, determinacy, specificity and differentiation. Thus, all these terms remain equivocal between the two hermeneutical fields of the egological paradigm and the paradigm of Universal Grammar.

2 Here, too, when we speak of "the Christian mind" or "Christian grammar," we are speaking provisionally, realizing of course that this designation signals an open ended range of diverse sectarian ideologies, grammatical dialects, and competing forms of life. The so-called "Christian mind" is not a monolithic and univocal grammar or form of life but is itself an opening to diverse alternative and competing grammatical forms or hermeneutical practices. Indeed, this is a symptom of the inherent indeterminacy and equivocity of any grammar when appropriated in the egological paradigm. The inner splits and divisions within the "Christian mind" can run as deep as the splits and divisions between world religions. So when we speak of the "Christian mind or grammar" it is as a mere convenience to contrast it with other external grammatical alternatives, such as the "Hindu mind" or the "Islamic mind," etc. And in this context we shall see that these designations will have profoundly different understandings between the egological paradigm and the discourse of Universal Grammar.

3 Again, the alleged "literal" meaning in the egological paradigm falls apart and undermines itself, as it does with all its intended constructions of identity, individuation, determinacy and unique specificity. We shall see that this purported "literal" meaning turns out to be indeterminate and multivocal, and that it is the principle of Meditative Reason, natural reason, that accounts for the "letter," the "literal," for true identity, individuation

and determinacy. It is Relativity that accounts for and makes all expressions of "identity" work.

4 The term "holistic" for us signals the logical structure of the Unified Field of Universal Grammar. And the Principle of Relativity (Relationality) implies that all terms are constitutively in a network or web of co-implicature— a Continuum of meanings, a mutual co-determinacy or co-arising. This fundamental feature of holistic meaning we also call "holonomy," and all terms (names, signs, concepts, ideas) are holonomous in structure and inter-relationality. In this context, the idea of "holistic synonymy" is meant to indicate that all terms are holonymous in the logical structure of the Unified Field, and take their unique specificity and determinacy of meaning in this Universal Domain. Thus, this special sense of "synonymy" does not mean— "having the same meaning as"— as it may be used in egological discourse. Nor does it mean that any term has the same meaning as *Logos,* but rather than the essence of any term is brought out in its holonomy structure and hence in its central reference to *Logos.*

5 As a heuristic device we find it useful to introduce the hermeneutical or semantical markers "((...))" as *meditative quotes* to signal that the term is being used in the meditative voice, in the voice of Relativity and in the field of Universal Grammar. These quotation marks stand in contrast to the use of terms in the egological voice, which we often accentuate by the use of "/.../" to bring out specific contrasts. It should be noted that all terms are equivocal as between the egological semantic field and the semantic field of the meditative voice. And we have been suggesting that all terms of egological discourse are constitutively situated in the field of Universal Grammar: this is why *Every /X/ is ((X)).*

6 All terms (names, ideas, things, signs, phenomena...) are holonomous in logical and ontological structure, and in this they all express the universal Form/Law— Logos— and exhibit this universal essence. There is no name or form or sign... that does not arise from the universal domain, that is not in holonomous continuum with the unified field of other co-terms, even as it expresses Logos uniquely. Thus, holonomy at once shows that any term essentially expresses Logos and is yet differentiated from other terms and is uniquely specified. Every term expresses universality and particularity, sameness and difference in its logical function. Thus, ((Time)) is holonomous with Logos and thus pervades the universal domain; all phenomena exhibit and express this natural temporality. And ((Time)) co-arises with ((Space)) which also pervades the universal domain and situates all things. The meaning of "time" and "space" are so constitutively bound and co-determinative that it is well to speak of ((Space-Time)) as a continuum. so these two terms in some sense express each other dialogically, and express Logos, individually and cooperatively, and yet "space" and "time" are particular and differentiated and uniquely specified.

7 It should be stressed here that holistic inquiry does not compete with increased diversification and specialization in research. Rather, it is a strategy for a more effective and creative method to specialize along the lines of expansion of any field or phenomena towards its grounding in the Continuum of Reality. Ostensibly, any specialized research is attempting to get a more detailed and accurate reading of its phenomena is attempting to get closer to the truth and reality of things. And conventional modes of research which remain naively fixated on its local grammatical context inevitably hits the barriers of its own constructions and works against the more effective route of ((specialization)) which follows the ever deeper path of the inner holistic structure of things. It is the Relativity Structure of phenomena that makes creative specialization work as we probe the ever deepening ((causal)) structure of things.

CHAPTER 4

UNIVERSAL RELATIVITY: MEDITATION, MIND AND MATTER

PREFACE

This chapter attempts to present Grammatology[1] as a universal hermeneutical method for discourse in general, and in particular focuses on exploring the grammatical conditions for an expanded science and philosophy of Nature. Grammatology calls for a self-transformation of rationality from the paradigm of "absolute identity" and egological practice to the practice of Universal Relativity, Meditative Reason and Universal Grammar. It shows that prior and current hermeneutical conduct in philosophy, the sciences, religious life, and cultural practice in general has been largely dominated by the paradigms of egological thinking and the rationality of absolute identity. It suggests that the egological paradigm of discourse eclipses the universal grounds of natural reason— of universal relativity— which it nevertheless constantly trades on and exploits for its life and meaning and results. Grammatology clarifies precisely why the egological paradigms prove to be incomplete, incoherent and fragmentary when rigorously pursued in terms of their own logics and grammatical faiths. And it makes clear why the principle of universal relativity is the presiding principle of natural reason which accounts for holistic unity and diversity and displaces the inherent duality and divisiveness of the ways of egological mind.

More specifically, Grammatology is the self-universalizing formal philosophy of reason which invokes the unity of diverse hermeneutical arts such as the grammatical practices of philosophy, religion, the sciences and other cultural forms. It expands more localized ontologies— accounts of the nature of reality and local grammars of existence— with more potent hermeneutical tools of Universal Grammar and Meditative Reason and thus is a more generalized method of Universal or Formal Ontology. For example, contemporary physics (as a science and discourse of Nature) arises from certain grammars of reality which appear to assume an ontological separation of the categories of mind (consciousness) and matter (physical nature). It tends to treat "matter" as if it were an independent reality in itself, and accordingly, physics takes itself to be an independent science which investigates the laws of physical nature and the phenomena of the physical world.

Grammatology shows that the ontological approach to reality upon which physics and other sciences are based arises from a constructed rationality and it calls for a revision of rationality itself. Ontological rationality is the expression of a faith in absolute identity which leads to pathological forms of absolutism. By contrast, Grammatology articulates a classical and holistic approach to rationality which is the expression of universal relativity. The rationality of universal relativity (UR) discloses the nature of true unity and breaks through the artificial duality and unity of the ontological mind. For example, Grammatology demonstrates that the universal concept of matter and mind forms a holographic continuum in which it is rationally impossible to separate one from the other. According to UR the mind (thinking, interpretations, theory, etc.) of the physicist is essentially constitutive of the phenomena of physics, and the phenomena of nature are permeated with the features of mind. So UR opens the way to the understanding of the mind/matter continuum and in general it invokes the universal continuum that reveals how all categories of reality mutually permeate each other.

In this connection it is seen that modern physics has pressed to the limits of its ontological grammars and has come to new frontiers of "recalcitrant" phenomena which cannot be rationally processed or authenticated in the constructed rationality of absolute identity. Grammatology shows that it is the very form of absolutistic thinking which binds the mind of the physicist from making the inevitable transformation to holographic understanding of natural phenomena. Here it is seen that Einstein's revision of physics to "relativity" was an initial and partial gesture in the direction of UR, but one which continued to labour under the sway of the rationality of absolute identity. For example, the move to the relativity of time and the spacetime continuum may be seen in its grammatical import as required by UR. Thus, the gesture towards UR is already implanted in modern physics and awaits further activation and cultivation.

This chapter will begin with a summary presentation of Grammatology and demonstrate how the rationality of absolute identity leads to artificial dualities and eclipses the holistic understanding of nature, matter and mind. It will outline the rationality of UR and open the way to a truly unified and universal concept of energy in which the real transformations between "mental" and "physical" energy become rationally authenticated and accessible.

INTRODUCTION

In preparation for the presentation of Grammatology and the holographic principle of UR it is first desirable to explore the origin and limitations of the ontological mind which arise on the foundation of absolute identity.

In exploring the inner form of absolute identity it is natural to begin with reflection on the mind of identity and the identity of mind. For whenever there is thought or reflection, such as we are now engaged in, the dynamics of identity are already at work dictating the form and content of all thought. So let us begin with the self-reflective and self-referential point of experience; let us reflect first on the ontological mind.

The ontological mind is the mind of identity— it takes itself to have identity, to be an integral, unified, continuously existing entity of some sort. As such, it takes itself to be differentiated and discriminated from other entities and from the world which surrounds it. Further, this existential mind takes itself to be self-contained and independently existing, so in some sense it is whole and complete in itself. In being separate and differentiated from other entities in the world the mind of identity recognizes itself as having its unique qualities and history which individuates it from everything else in the world. The existential mind is unique, differentiated and individuated; it is a central and primary reference point in its world and can refer to itself uniquely as "I".   As long as it thinks and reflects it takes itself to be independently existing and its self existence conditions all of its thinking and experience, it is axiomatic to all thought. An historical example of the self articulation of the existential mind may be found in Descartes' clarification of the "I think" ("I exist") in his *Meditations*.   (We shall see that this Cartesian "I think" is often interpreted as an egological voice, and we provisionally follow this reading for present purposes. But the Cartesian ((I think)) understood in the meditative voice is a much more compelling reading.)

The ontological mind must be approached in the first person, in self-reference, as a thinking subject; in some sense the existential "I" has privileged access to itself. In sum, we may say that the ontological mind is a self identity which takes itself to be a unique, differentiated, individuated and independently existing entity.

Now, since all thinking and experience is conditioned by the "I exist" it is crucial to see what is being assumed or taken for granted in the form and content of the "I exist". In some clear sense all meaning and existence is structured and determined by the inner form of the ontological mind, so it is all the more important from the start to make explicit the form of identity itself.

The ontological mind is a self-reflective, self-referential and universal point of reference for experience; one striking feature of self-identity is that it takes itself to be a unified voice— that it has uni-vocity. Without this univocity condition the "I" would not be a self-identical, individuated and integral being.   Indeed, it is the very meaning of "individual" to be undivided, to be a simple or primitive unity. Let us reflect for a moment on this unity condition of identity and self-existence.

We just said that the inner form of self-identity structures all thought, experience, meaning and existence. It is impossible to over-stress this elementary point of grammatology, for it is universally overlooked and forgotten precisely because it is so foundational to the enterprise of meaning and rationality.

The form of identity makes rational thought possible and for this reason ordinary rational thought eclipses its absolute condition and is not able to think its own form. But now we shall see that what ordinary thought and experience takes to be a unity and univocal, grammatology exposes as dividual, self-divided, disintegral and equi-vocal. And if the ontological mind, which takes itself to be a unity and univocal turns out to be self-divided and equi-vocal, then the very foundation of everyday rationality is called into serious question, to say the least.

For centuries it has been said that the principle of identity is the first principle of rationality. One expression of this first principle is that A is A. This is taken to be axiomatic and self-evident for rational thought - the absolute condition that makes rational thought possible. It means that A is a self-identical unity. However, suppose upon reflection we find that this principle is incoherent— that A is neither A nor not A, that A is not univocal but inherently indeterminate and equi-vocal. Suppose we find that the existential mind— referred to as "I"— is equi-vocal and indeterminate; this would be a mind shattering disclosure.

i) The Indeterminacy of the Existential Mind: The Problem of Unity and the Paradox of Identity

The existential mind takes itself to be individuated— to be a primitive self-identical unity, and its unity is the inherent form of all its thinking. The principle of identity, for any alleged identity, holds only if the self-identity and unity of the mind obtains. If the mind is equi-vocal or indeterminate, then all else suffers the same indeterminacy.

There are two points here that need clarification. The first is the general point that any alleged individuated identity contradicts itself in dis-unity, dividuation, and dis-identity; I call this the "paradox of identity". The second point is that experience, to be coherent, requires or presumes a univocating point of reference; and this is usually taken to be the self-reference of the "I" as a unifying point for my experience. But here, too, we find another version of the paradox of identity in the form of the "paradox of self-reference". Here it is found that the alleged presence of a unifying mind as supplying the unifying point of reference for experience or thought is non-existent. Indeed, critical reflection that does not presume absolute identity cannot find any unifying point of reference or individuated identity any where; neither in the mind or alleged referent of "I", nor in any alleged entity with identity.

Let us clarify these two intimately related points in turn.

a)   The Paradox of Identity

The paradox of identity is the incoherence that identity requires absolute unity but instead leads to perpetual self-division and dis-unity. To see this take any alleged individuated identity *A* :

We find that the form of identity requires that for *A* to be individuated or discriminated it must stand over against that which is other than A, call it *not-A*, so a form of self-opposition or negation is essentially the very meaning of identity itself— to be an identity is to be differentiated; so in attempting to locate the supposed independent unity of A we are addressed to another different point of reference— not-A; but now this second alleged point of reference does not stand independently, hence is not primitive and self-existent.   But individuated identity requires an independent and primitive (atomic) point of unity— which is found neither in A nor in not-A. So the unity requirement of identity must postulate a third and higher point of reference which can unite the duality of A and not-A, neither of which is a primitive unifying point /A/; this would be the absolute point of unity for the original supposed identity of A.

But here again, this postulated third point of unity is not primitive and not independent, not self-existent; it too depends on both A and not-A, neither of which is an independent unity, nor is /A/ such a unity.   So we have the following triangulation of identity:

We begin with A. but this points to not-A (-A), which points back to A, which leaves us with a duality which in turn needs to be addressed to a "higher," more primitive, unity— /A/. But this alleged higher unity is itself dependent on A and -A, and, indeed, to have /A/ as an independent identity only repeats the vicious loop all over *ad infinitum.*   In this way no independent, primitive, self-existent point of reference is ever found. Any reference to a given identity points elsewhere to another alleged point which turns out itself to be dependent on some other point, *ad infinitum.* This is the hidden dynamic of identity that holds whenever we make reference to (or suppose) any individuated identity to obtain. This is why the principle A is A, far from being self evident, is deeply problematic and paradoxical. So any alleged identity is indeterminate and this is the source of ontological indeterminacy.2

b)   The Paradox of Self-Reference: "I" is Indeterminate

The paradox of self-reference is another version of the general paradox of identity; it holds for the individuated mind taking itself to be an absolute point of reference or primitive individual. This version of the paradox of identity takes place in the voice of the first person— uttering "I" and making reference to itself as the "atomic" point of unity.

Here again we find the re-iteration of the triangular loop of identity *ad infinitum*. For the form of self-identity requires that in being a unique and individuated entity I am differentiated from the not-I; so in making self-reference to the alleged atomic point of unity that is "me" I am addressed to that which is not-me, other than I. And in seeking a unity we find a polarity, neither pole of which is a unity in itself.

But this polarity is split against itself in opposing alleged points of unity, and requires a third and higher mediating point to unite the duality into a "di-unity". However, this third alleged point of unity which is "/I/" cannot be established independently of the original "I" and "not I" yet it must be different from them. Thus the paradox of self-reference is that in saying "I" I purport to make reference to an individuated point of primitive unity, but in so doing I find an indefinitely self-divided reference that never reaches any primary univocal point, but recurs indeterminately and indefinitely. I find a recursive indeterminate loop.

If there is not a determinate primitive point of reference that is "I", that is, if the ontological mind of identity is inherently indeterminate, then all thought and experience which presuppose a universal primary unifying point of reference is likewise indeterminate; there would be no item in thought that is univocal or determinate in sense or reference— no determinate meaning or existence. And if thought is indeterminate in meaning then all experience reflects this same indeterminacy and multi-vocity. Further, since meaning and existence share the common form of identity, existence too is indeterminate, and the same for "rationality" in general. Again, if the ontological mind is radically indeterminate in its existence then all that is given to the individuated mind is equally ambiguous and indeterminate. This is the ontological indeterminacy of existence, thought, experience, meaning, rationality. It all arises from the radical indeterminacy of absolute identity.[3]

c) More Paradox: The Absolute Unifying Point & the I/Field Split
Thus far we have looked at the incoherence of absolute identity for singular cases, that is, for any one purported individuated identity in isolation. But when we postulate and entertain more than one point of atomic identity at a time the existential indeterminacy is all the more pronounced. But as we

proceed we must remember that we can no longer assume a unified or univocal mind ("me") that is doing the thinking. And every possible feature or item of thought replicates this ontological indeterminacy. For example, "time" itself can no longer be taken as a determinate, linear and continuous medium with identity of its own. The moments of time— past, present and future are purported individuated identities too and there is indeterminacy here as well. And when we speak of "at the same time" identity is presumed and this has now been placed in question. The same holds for space, cause, number, and all the categories of reality.

Now the first and most primitive dualism generated by the form of identity is the primordial division of polarity between I and not I. We have seen that the very identity "I" requires the not-I over against which it stands. This original bifurcation may be seen as the polarity between individuated mind on the one hand, and the world-field in which all else is present to the "I". This original duality creates all sorts of paradoxes and problems that have gripped the best minds over the centuries. For example, if mind (the subject) stands over against the world (object) and is differentiated from it, how can the mind know what is external to it and discontinuous with it? Here we get diverse problems of how knowledge is possible and dichotomies of subject and object, the subjective and the objective.

Still, it is critical to see in the dynamics of identity and postulate of unity that the original polarity between "I" and "field", like any other polarity, requires its mediating higher point of unity to hold the opposed poles in a unity. Let us call this higher postulated point of unity the "transcendental point of unity". It should be immediately clear that without such a postulate the individuated mind could never be in touch with the world-field— they would be incommensurable. Further, it is also evident that the "I" must have a deep and intimate connection with the transcendental point; in fact, it is as if it must be itself a higher "I", for if it were wholly other to the individuated "I" there would have to be still another postulated mediating point to negotiate the chasm between the individuated I and the transcendental absolute unifying point. But if in some sense they are one and the same (share a common identity) then whenever I utter "I", this utterance has indeterminate and divided sense and reference (self-reference), ambiguous reference between the individuated I and the transcendental I (/I/). So again we find ontological indeterminancy.

Furthermore, this postulated higher transcendental point of unity, as the mediating principle between I and world-field, must at the same time be different from the individuated I and in some respect must be indeterminate and non-individuated; otherwise it could not be a mediating point between the duality and opposition between I and not-I. In this respect it must be devoid of content found in I and not-I; this is why it transcends both polar opposites. Nevertheless, it must have some content of its own for it to be an absolute unifying point; and insofar as it has some identity it must itself be differentiated and the triangular vicious loop recurs all over again.

In summary, we find that any alleged transcendental point of unity is itself subject to the dynamics of identity and participating in the polarity between identity/difference, hence cannot fulfill its intended function of being an absolute foundation for individuated identity. Indeed, the very need for a foundation for individuated identity is a confession that absolute identity is incoherent. So we find in all this that the axiomatic commitment to individuated identity is an empty postulate having no validity other than its postulation. The belief in primitive individuals (my self or other) is an ontological myth, a postulate of faith, and we need to inquire whether it is an act of good faith.

ii) Indeterminacy of Reality: Alternative Grammars of Reality
It is timely to present the ontological understanding of a world or universe. But first certain points need preliminary clarification. We have said that the ontological mind is indeterminate. This meant that the independent self existence of primitive individuated mind could not be established. This indeterminacy was found to originate in the form of identity itself which meant that no individuated self-identical entity of any sort could ever be established. It was suggested that the principle of identity was a divisive principle that generated ontological indeterminacy in every direction, and in rationality itself. And we saw that any attempt to discern or establish any absolute unifying primitive individuated point of reference was futile and led to a recursive triangular loop.

It should be obvious that we are now probing the foundations of philosophy, religion and science in general and specifically preparing the way for exploration of holistic physics. For classical conventional physics assumes the principle of absolute identity and with it the dualizing consequences which separates the mind ("I") from the world-field. Nature is seen to be "out there" presented to the inquiring mind of the physicist, and physical nature is taken to be the objective independently existing reality which the physicist scientifically studies. We shall now see that this naive absolutistic view of reality is an artificial construct or invention of the mind of identity.

Let us first clarify the depth of the I/Field duality. In one voice the ontological mind takes itself to be living in a universe which is an all encompassing field of reality as a whole. To exist is to be in the universal field— the cosmos. From the ontological point of view the unity or univocity requirement clearly holds for the structure of the universe as a whole— a continuous unified integral field.

But there is an ambiguity of voice in the ontological mind as to the locus of the transcendental point of unity of the Universe. For in one sense the Universe is taken to be independent of me and to have its independent absolute existence apart from me. But at the same time it is clear that I could not think something that was not present to me and my mind, and in this sense I supply a unifying point of reference for the universal field as a whole. Here again we find some version of the paradox of unity (identity)— the unity of the universe is independent of me, but at the same time it is dependent on me.

It appears that there·is a self-transcending point of unity in the mind that can take the place of any possible locus in the universe— there is a universal point of reference in mind that is variable and can take (or identify with) any place. Earlier we called this point "/I/". So we may distinguish between this self-transcending presence in me (my higher voice) and all that is presented to me (world-field). This /I/ is prior to the individuated mind; it is that to which all else is present or presented but which can never be made into an object in the field. On the other hand, the I (mind) as an object in the universe (the one we call the subject) is constitutively part of the universal field presented to /I/.

Thus, it appears that the unifying point for the world-field transcends the universal field, and the unifying point of I transcends the I; each needs its unifying point, but it may well turn out that the unifying point for field and I are one and the same. There is indeterminacy and ambiguity here, which is to be expected. Throughout this narrative we have been provisionally speaking within the ways of the egological paradigm, speaking as if the egological principle of identity were valid. But this narrative as a whole is dialectical and is situated in the narrative and critique of Meditative Reason. It is the critique of Relativity that guides and moves the argument of the narrative as a whole. In this way we are able to show that the dynamics of naive identity must fail in its inner logic.[4]

a) The Primacy of Ontological Grammar

Having explored the inherent ambiguity in the "I" and the "field" and in the relation between I/field, we may proceed further with the explanation of ontological grammar.

We have now seen that it is the form of absolute identity itself that requires a paradoxical bifurcation of the mind of the thinker from the universal field that is the context of the object of thought— the subject from the object. And it is absolute identity that at the same time requires the absolute unity condition of the universe. It is the very form of identity that necessitates the commitment to the universe as an absolute self-existent reality. So ontological absolutism (the faith that there is an absolute independently existing universe) has its origin in absolute identity.

Now the ontological notion of the world or universe is an all-encompassing unity or whole which is exhaustive of all possible reality. The universe is that universal, absolute, unifying whole that includes both the thinking subject and the world-field that is presented to the subject— the realm of all possible phenomena. Absolute identity structures the universe into a comprehensive, complete and supposedly consistent totality. Nothing could possibly exist "outside" the universe: to be is to be in the universe. And to be an object is to be in the universal field.

Here too we find that the form of absolute identity governs the universal field of the universe, for the things that make up the universe have determinacy, particularity, identity. The universal field presents itself as a specified world— having definite content. But it is not at all obvious that absolute identity dictates the form and content of a world.

To see this it would be helpful to make an explicit connection between logic and ontology. While logic is a formal science which investigates the form of thought— logical form, ontology is a formal science which explores the form of existence— ontological form. But logical form and ontological form mirror each other, both sharing the common form of absolute identity.

On the one side, logic depicts the structure of thought as being predicative: to think is to predicate, i.e., to join a logical subject and predicate into a unified proposition[5] —

$$S \text{ is/isn't } P.$$

A logical predicate "P" may be affirmed or denied of a given logical subject "S". So, from a logical point of view, a language may be parsed into terms which are subjects or predicates, and thinking consists in the joining of subjects and predicates. We may speak of logical grammar as that which governs the proper formation of proposition into meaningful units.

It is not incidental that the primitive structure of thought be Subject/Predicate and oppositional (affirmative/negative) in the joining of these. For here again we find the form of absolute identity and its polar form. For example, the identity of any given subject "S" consists in its distinctive marks, attributes, features— and these are indicated as predicates. So the subject/predicate form replicates the structure of things, the form of identity. To have identity is to be discriminated and this is accomplished by having distinctive features and properties. The subject/predicate form is designed to replicate the structure of things, the form of identity.

In this respect, logical form is grounded in ontological form— in the form of reality, in absolute identity. So it is not surprising that the formal laws of thought— the laws of predication— are expressions of the principle of identity, with which we are now more familiar.

But ontological form is also governed by the form of absolute identity. We have just seen that logical form, subject and predicate, mirrors the form of things— objects and their attributes. To be an object is to be a unity of attributes; meaningful thought is grounded in the way things are. We think meaningfully when we combine appropriate subjects with appropriate predicates, and appropriateness is dictated by ontological form.

To apprehend ontological form it would be helpful to introduce the notion of a category. The predicative form of language and thought suggests that a language may be divided into logical subjects and predicates, and the laws of meaning would determine which predicates may be significantly joined with which subjects. In ordinary language there are innumerable predicates and subjects comprising the language, but these fall into basic types and categories. For example although there are many distinct terms for diverse colors, all of these fall into one basic ontological category of being /colored/.

Here again we find that categories and types reflect the structure of identity. For a category is discerned when we take any given predicate term— "P" together with its logical contrary "un-P". That is, every term has a contrary and when contraries are taken as a more comprehensive class this forms a category. In the case of color, if we take "red" then the identity of red is tied to all those things that fail to be red— that are un-red, and this indicates an exhaustive domain of existence— /color/.

Notice that we find in the unity of a category the same triangular dynamic of identity made explicit earlier:

Figure 7

$$A \longrightarrow -A \longrightarrow /A/$$

It is important to see that a contrary term "un-P" is a special sort of opposition, not the same as a complement "not-P". For "un-P" is a privative and is internal to the content of "P" while "non-P" is merely the extensional opposite that applies to everything else in the universe. For example:

> If "P" is "married" then "un-P" means "un-married"and together these contraries are unified in the category, /married/, which includes all possible things that could be married.
> Whereas "not-P" means "not-married" and this applies to all things in the universe outside the category of /married/, that is, to things that are neither married nor un-married.

So predicate terms reflect the form of identity in their internal polarity, (+P/-P) and when these are taken in their higher unity /P/, they show their categorial form. And while predicate terms indicate the properties of things, categories specify the features of the world.

Similarly, subject terms (indicated by S) show the same internal polar structure of identity and the things they specify fall into ontological types:

> If "S" indicates the person Socrates, then "-S" is the internal polar opposite that indicates all other persons in the universive of discourse. And the unity of the poles /S/ indicates the basic ontological type of thing that spans all possible /persons/.

To discern the ontological form of a given language all of its categories and types are taken together in their mutual configuration— this is the categorial

structure of the language. If we take the basic category and type terms of a
language simultaneously and ask how they may be joined predicatively for
that language, the answer is given in a hierarchial structure as follows:

> Let /A/, /B/, /C/, /D/...etc be the categories of a language,
> and let /a/, /b/, /c/, /d/...etc be the types; then if all
> categories and types are taken together in their mutual
> relations, the categorial structure (ontological form) of
> the language is shown—

Figure 8

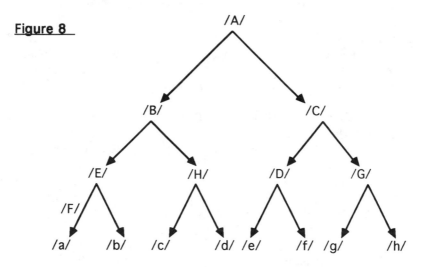

This sample categorial structure shows the categories in their mutual
hierarchial relations, and the types of things are indicated at the base of the
configuration. The arrows indicate the direction of predicability and only
terms on a continuous line may significantly join in a meaningful
proposition. It should be noted that the higher the category in the structure
the more inclusive it is, and the more types of things it spans.

In this configuration it would be significant to say: "/a/ is /F/" (/E/, /B/, /A/)
and it would be non-sense (a category mistake) to say "/a/ is /C/".

So sense and non-sense is governed by the categorial structure or ontological
form of the language.

Several points should be noted here. First, the "pyramid" structure is the
same triangular structure of identity we are now familiar with. We have

found that this form of identity repeats itself throughout all possible levels — it shows itself in the form of a term, in the form of the proposition, and in the form of the world as a whole.

Secondly, categorial form of a world depicts that there must be an "apex" term that unites the categories and types of a given language into a unified whole. This all-inclusive term "/A/" has special ontological and logical characteristics which we shall explore later. The main point here is that this universal term significantly joins with all other terms in the language. This is the transcendental unity of the language-world.

Furthermore, it is shown in this sample categorial structure that at the base of the pyramid are the types of things, and type terms are the most exclusive terms of the language. And things may be seen as the unity of the categories that characterize them: for example—

   "/a/" is the unity of /F/ & /E/ & /B/ and of course /A/

So in the very constitution of things one finds the dynamics of identity at work— a unity of polarity and plurality.

Again, it is the categorial structure that governs meaning in the language and the unique univocal meaning of a term is given in its having one location in the structure. Thus, in ordinary language, a term is equi-vocal or ambiguous in meaning (i.e. is more than one term) if it requires more than one location in the categorial structure— so, one location, one meaning.

Finally, before we take some sample categorial structures from the history of ontology, it must be stressed that the laws of sense, which is governed formally by the categorial structure, are ontologically prior to the laws governing what is the case— the facts— of a given world. To be a fact (a true predication) a proposition must make sense (be true-or-false) and to make sense the predication must conform to categorial structure. This means that meaning and truth are grounded in categorial structure (ontological form) which reveals the nature of the universe. It is important to stress this priority of ontology because the sciences, like physics, inquire into truth, investigate the facts of the universe, but tend to overlook the fact that sense precedes truth and that facts directly depend upon categorial form, as concepts depend upon categories.

This brief sketch of ontological grammar should show the appropriateness of calling it "grammar": the categorial structure is the depth grammar of thought (predication) and it is the grammar of existence (reality) as well. A grammar indicates the rules of significant combination— and an ontological grammar shows how reality is put together and hence how we may significantly combine terms in thought.6

Let us now illustrate some of these basic points of ontological grammar with some simplified ontologies taken from the history of ontology. We shall focus on the categories of /mind/ and /matter/ and on the type of thing specified by "I";

<u>Figure 9</u>

Example 1:   Cartesian Dualism –

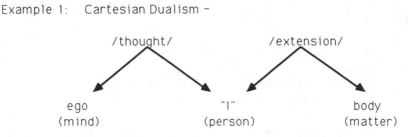

In this grammar the categories of /thought/ and /extension/ are the primary features of mind and matter respectively. It is important to see that the category of /thought/ includes all possible modification of thinking— thinking, willing, doubting, affirming, denying, questioning, etc., etc. All concepts of mind are contained within the category— /thought/. Similarly, /extension/ (the feature of dimensionality of /space/) is the primary feature of /matter/ and this includes all the other properties and features of matter like— /color/, /figure/, /texture/, /motion/, etc., etc.

The main point in this grammar is that the categories of /thought/ and /extension/, hence of /mind/ and /matter/ are mutually exclusive and existentially independent— matter and mind are existentially independent and the features of matter and mind are mutually exclusive, and this is clearly shown in the categorial structure.

The existential separation of the categories of /thought/ and /extension/ requires that these mutually exclusive categories cannot be united in one and the same thing. This necessitates that the person— the "I" be split into two types of individuals— I-mind and I-body, so the person is a composite entity and we are faced with the ontological problem of the unity of the person. And because the categories are mutually exclusive there is no existential basis for causal interaction between mind and matter so interaction between mind and body is unintelligible. This is dictated by the categorial structure itself.

Furthermore, it is shown in this Cartesian sample, taken from Descartes' Meditations, that there is a problem of the higher categorial unification of the language into one language. This requires that the unifying "apex" transcendental term connect the two branches of the ontology into one reality, into a unified grammar of existence. So the dualistic problem emerges at both ends of the pyramid structure.

Finally, it should be remembered that meaning is governed by this category structure and the meaning of all terms in this language is a function of this ontological form. It would be a category mistake here to say: "The body is thinking" or "The ego occupies space". And every use of the term "I" is systematically equi-vocal and in this sense indeterminate. Any use of the term "I" would have to be dis-ambiguated in the context of the structure to make its meaning explicit and univocal.

Figure 10

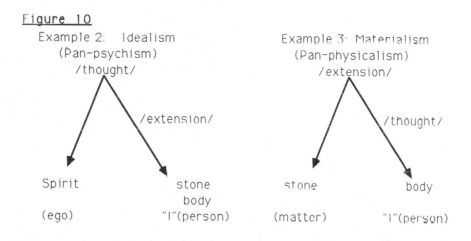

Example 2: Idealism
(Pan-psychism)
/thought/

/extension/

Spirit   stone
body
(ego)   "I"(person)

Example 3: Materialism
(Pan-physicalism)
/extension/

/thought/

stone   body
(matter)   "I"(person)

There is an interesting polar contrast in these two classical categorial grammars. In example 2 we find a simplified form of ontological idealism in which the primary feature of the universe is /thought/ (intelligence, the features of mind), and the category of /space/ and /matter/ are contained within the broader category of /thought/. In this world everything that does or could exist /thinks/, and while there could be pure spirits (like God) that think without body, persons are embodied and share the same ontological features of material bodies— all bodies /think/. In this grammar it is meaningful to say: "The stone is thinking" so the realm of intelligence applies to all possible entities of this universe. It is clearly shown here that the category of /extension/ is derived from the category of /thought/, and this is an existential dependence.

In this grammar, as with any other, the meaning of the terms of the language is a function of the categorial structure as a whole. All of the terms of this language are incomparably (incommensurably) different from the terms of the Cartesian grammar for example. So the meaning and reference of "I" in the Idealist grammar is radically different from "I" in the Cartesian grammar or any other. But in this configuration, because the basic features of /thought/ and /matter/ are inherently united the person is a primitive individual; here it is possible to have existential and conceptual connections (interaction) between mind and body because the two categories are supposedly connected.

By contrast, in the materialist grammar, we find that the features of matter are the primary features of the universe— to be is to be material, to occupy space. In this grammar all things are material in nature including intelligence and mind. The category of /thought/ is derived from (an evolute of) matter— and a person is a thinking body, mind is explainable in terms of the functioning of the brain. But here again, all the terms of this language are indigenous to this grammatical structure so the meaning of "I" in pan-physicalism or materialism is incomparably different from the sense/reference of the term "I" in diverse grammars. The facts of this world are not the same as the facts of diverse ontologies. What is common sense in this materialist world is not common sense in another world. So we cannot assume neutral facts of reality apart from specific, determinate grammatical structures. In the egological paradigm, any category is systematically equivocal across diverse grammars of reality— there is no "univocity" or universal common category across worlds. But in Relativity, in the Unified Field— which is the Universal Categorial Continuum— the Universal and Univocal meaning of ((categories)) are revealed across grammars: here we find the universal category of ((time)), ((space)), ((matter)), ((mind)), etc.[7]

With these examples of diverse grammars in mind we may now resume the main theme of the primacy of ontological grammar for all thought, existence, meaning and experience. This theme was essential to seeing the indeterminacy of the ontological mind and to understanding how the form of absolute identity governs the form of thought (logic) and the form of existence (ontology). We have been exploring the structure of the universal field and seeing that the universe (reality) presents itself to the ontological mind in a determinate and particularized form— as a grammar of existence. But the theme of the indeterminacy of reality comes into focus with the acknowledgment of multiple grammars. So keeping the basic duality between "I" and Universal Field in the background for now let us further clarify the point of the primacy and pervasiveness of grammar and the point about multiple alternative realities.

b) The Monadic Feature of World Wholes: Multiple Realities (Universes)
It has been suggested that to exist is to be in the context of a grammar, and that a grammar of reality is cosmically universal— exhaustive of the universe. And it has been stressed that such a grammar is the deep structure of thought, meaning and experience. For to think or experience is to engage in meaning— to ontologically /interpret/; to live is to be grammatical.

This may be seen by taking examples from world history— examples of world cultures and cultural worlds. A world culture may be seen as a naturally evolved grammar of reality— a cosmological space for the shared cultural life of a community. If we simplify and speak of the Hindu world (grammar) or the Christian world, for example, it may be more readily seen that a grammar shapes all aspects of the life of a culture— all meaning, all existence, all thought, all experience, all hermeneutical expressions.

Thus, from the ontological point of view, the Hindu grammar makes the Hindu mind possible— it makes the existence of the mind possible, it makes it possible too for thought to take place, for there to be meaning and rationality— it makes experience possible. It is crucial to appreciate the depth of grammar— it is not just a world view, rather, it makes all viewing possible for the ontological mind.

It is in this sense that grammar is "hermeneutical"— to experience is to live in a grammar and in this sense "interpret" reality. In the case of the Hindu grammar it may be seen that its religious life, its political life, its moral life, its science, its art forms— every facet of Hindu life, reflects the Hindu grammar. It is in this sense that an ontological grammar is cosmological— all encompassing of reality, the universe— a cosmological universal. This is a grammar as a whole, as a universe, with its transcendal absolute point of reference and unity. This transcendal point of unity has some feature of the "infinite" built into it and is all-encompassing. Let us call this the "monadic" feature of a grammar or universe— a grammar is a cosmological universe and purports to be exhaustive of reality. There can be no reality apart from it. The grammar presents itself as being the measure of reality, meaning and truth.

In this respect the Hindu grammar is a world whole as is the Christian grammar. And a world culture is governed in all its hermeneutical forms by its ontological grammar. What makes sense in the Hindu world does not make sense in the Christian world. What is common (communal) sense in one world is not recognizable as such in another grammatical space. The facts of one world cannot be processed in the grammaticality of another reality. And the monadic effect of a world implies ontological incommensurability between diverse worlds. Worlds are incommensurable in the sense that they share nothing in common, no common point of reference; each is an absolute in itself and a reality unto itself. Rationality itself is formed within the "gravitational field" or grammar. The rational "light" of a given world remains within the inner "curved space" of a cosmological grammar. The monadic effect of a grammatical world leads to incommensurability. This is the problem of unity all over again; in this version there can be no more primitive unity (transcendental unity) uniting diverse worlds. And apart from some common point of reference— some mediating, univocating condition, there can be no rational light between the dark void that holds diverse worlds apart.

But this incommensurability between worlds is the direct result of absolute identity and the ontological mind. It is the absolutism of identity that leads to this result. For now we can see that a grammar as a whole is an absolute identity in itself, a cosmological absolute, apart from which nothing can be; an ontological "black hole".

It should be noted here that the form of identity is what generates the axiomatic structure of rationality, whether it be expressed in a geometric form (alternative geometries) or in a logistic form (alternative formal axiomatized languages). The axiomatic form is the form of identity, and a grammar is a "geometry" of reality— a purportedly complete axiomatization of reality.

In this connection we may bring in the indeterminacy of reality once more. The ontological indeterminacy comes from the paradox of identity. On the one hand we find that the universe is one and absolute— monadic. And the monadic world-whole appears to the ontological mind in the determinate form of a grammar; it has internal determinacy and specificity. But on the other hand, it is given to the ontological mind that there is a plurality of worlds— of monadic absolutes, each of which is internally determinate and absolute— monadic. The ontological mind refers to itself— uttering "I", but this pronominal utterance takes its sense and reference from a particular grammar; but still it finds itself inhabiting multiple worlds, hence with multiple identity. And we are left again with the problem of the unity and uni-vocity of "I" and mind. Thus we see that indeterminacy and incommensurability arise together from the form of absolute identity.

c) *Multiple Worlds, Incommensurability and Indeterminacy*

Incommensurability is not an abstract result of ontological investigation. It is a lived condition of everyday life that we shall explore below. For it should now be evident as we look at what we call "common sense" in everyday American cultural life that we inhabit diverse grammatical worlds simultaneously. Indeed, it may be seen that any world culture deriving from the life of absolute identity is really a cluster of precariously juxtaposed grammars under the surface of the spoken communal language. The linguistic system of the culture must be decoded and dis-ambiguated according to the grammatical context at any given time. Any term in the linguistic system is indeterminate in meaning until it is specified by its grammatical context.

Again, if we look at American culture from the ontological point of view we find a cluster of diverse grammars— certain religious grammars contribute to common sense while scientific grammars make their own contribution. And "common sense" is a dynamic, evolving consensus of the grammatical life of the culture. There are grammatical revolutions in science (as with Einstein's revolution) and this brings about new forms of life and thought— a new universe opens up with its own idiom and jargon. In part of our lives we may believe that God exists and that Spirit is primary and that intelligence shapes matter, but in another domain of life we speak a materialist grammar and believe that matter is primary and that intelligence evolved from matter and the "big bang" origin of the universe. And we are content to inhabit these multiple grammars believing ourselves to be sane and rational beings. We do not seem to realize that under the surface lies deep problems for rationality, faith, sanity, meaning and truth.

These ontological problems are particularly poignant in the area of inter-grammatical (trans-world) relations. The recognition that there are multiple monadic/absolute grammars of reality each of which constitutes rationality itself in diverse ways, places a deep strain on the rationality of absolute identity. For it questions the faith in one objective, neutral reality out there which science investigates. It questions the absolutist prejudice that one grammar must be true or more true than others, and that science experimentally approximates the true and best grammar of reality. It raises the question of multiple validity of alternative "geometries" of reality and rationality. It recognizes that my very identity and existence is indeterminate across diverse grammars of existence. And this crisis of identity comes to a head when I try to discern which "I" it is that has access to multiple realities at the "same time". And it becomes clear that time itself is relative to grammar and there is a problem of assuming a neutral temporality between grammars— that can unify time into a simultaneous "moment" for diverse worlds. So once we begin to take the critical turn and recognize the depth of incommensurability we then see that rationality and intelligibility itself is in crisis. The question is raised whether we are fractured and fragmented beings living a dis-integral and incoherent form of life with multiple identities and multiple voices. All sorts of questions emerge here about our religious and scientific life— questions about the true meaning and meaningful truth.

iii) Grammar and Physics: Making the Ontological Turn

Before we proceed further to articulate these inter-grammatical problems let us focus for a moment on the relevance of ontological grammar to physics. We have suggested that any area of discourse and meaning must be grammatical— is governed by ontological grammar. This is of course true of all the sciences and of physics. And it is timely to reflect on the importance of grammar for physics. One theme of this essay is that physics must become explicit aware of its grammar and of alternative grammars. Physics speaks a particular grammar and its scientific activity both theoretical and experimental is governed by its grammar.

Ontology makes clear that all conceptualization takes place within a categorial structure; concepts are specifications of categories. And once we apprehend the primacy of grammar we likewise see that facts are specifications of potentiality of grammar— facts are specifications of sense. Here it may be said that while physics (and any other science) investigates the facts and properties of things, ontology discloses the sense, categories and features of reality. When the grammar of reality is fixed and taken on faith then the "facts" of that world are the projections of the grammar; the theoretical and conceptual investigation are clarifications of the categorial structure; and experimental testing verifies the actualized facts that are possibilities of the grammar.

In this respect it is interesting to look at Einstein's revisions of the language of physics. The Newtonian grammar used categories of space, time, mass, energy, motion, etc. in a certain configuration. This grammar delimited what was intelligible, conceivable, possible for the Newtonian world. But Einstein's revisions were so deep that they reached down to the categorial level, and when this happens a new universe opens up. His famous equation which placed "mass" and "energy" in a new relation involved a categorial transformation that brought with it a new sense structure and this opens up new possible facts and phenomena. With Einstein's grammatical revision transformations between mass and energy now become possible. And his dramatic revisions of the categories of space and time opened up a new world with new possible facts for physics. The Einsteinian world was of course there to be grammatically articulated, but it was beyond the grammatical scope of the Newtonian grammar. Thus it is essential in conceptual revisions to be keenly aware of the categorial implications. And when we speak of conceptual frameworks and paradigms in science we must be sensitive to the categorial structure and the grammatical paradigm that makes the science possible.8

The point here is that as long as physics takes its grammar for granted it is ontologically "unconscious" and in a way in bondage to its grammar. The scientific and experimental spirit requires that the scientist be explicit about grammar and experimental in categorial possibilities as well. Otherwise physics fails in its interpretation of reality to see that it is working within a particular ontological grammar and inquiring into the projections of this grammar. Physics and Grammatology must work together.

When physics takes the ontological turn and recognizes that there are alternative grammars of reality, alternative worlds or natures to inquire into, then it will have made a major step further in scientific method. The scientific spirit in its quest for truth demands that the step be made to bring grammar to the fore in scientific research, and questions the naive absolutism that has eclipsed the presence of multiple grammars of reality. When physics has made the ontological turn it will have come to the horizon of true universal relativity and will become self critical and will see through the fundamentalism and irrationality that comes with blind faith in absolute identity. Only then will physics and other sciences be ready for the revolution to grammatology.

iv) Absolute Identity and the Pathologies of the Ontological Mind
We are now in a better position to prepare the way for the grammatological
turn in physics.

It is timely to explore the pathological condition of the ontological mind.
We have seen thus far that the ontological or existential mind is structured
by absolute identity and this sets up a recursive "loop" of self-splitting that
pervades the grammatical life of the individuated mind. Let us for a moment
stand back and attempt to articulate the general dynamic that generates this
splintering and dualization of reality, thought, experience and of meaning
and rationality. We shall now develop this theme further that it is the form
of absolute identity that polarizes in all directions. And it is this very form
that produces the recursive incommensurability between identities on all
levels.

a) *The atomic/monadic effect of absolute identity*
It has been stated that wherever there is absolute identity there we will find
ontological indeterminacy and the self-splitting "triangulating" dynamic.
Earlier, when we sketched the ontological concept of a universe as a world-
whole, we spoke of the monadic feature of the universe and of the
individuated mind. This meant that the universe as a self-existent whole was
self-contained and independent and all-encompassing of its domain. This
monadic feature was typified by the transcendental point of universal unity.
It has been suggested that this monadic effect holds for the ontological mind
as well— the self-existent mind must take its transcendental unifying point
to be monadic in a way analogous to the monadic feature of the universe as a
whole; the monadic mind is a universe unto itself.

Now we may generalize this point and speak of the atomic features for any
possible individuated entity. The monadic feature is the internalized view of
the monadic whole under its transcendental unity. The atomic feature is the
external view of the monadic whole from a different, independent point of
reference. So the monadic and atomic features are complementary effects of
the same absolute identity. This means that any purported absolute identity
is at once monadic internally and atomic externally. It varies with the
unifying point of reference taken by "I" (the thinker). The internal monadic
universe presents itself as infinitely open and expansive. But the external
atomic universe is seen as being impenetrable, closed, self-contained.

It is important to see that any instance of an absolute identity at once exhibits
the monadic and atomic effect depending on its point of reference with

respect to the transcendental unifying point taken by "I". Thus, a world-whole or universe may itself be atomic with respect to multiple worlds— a world-whole is a "global" atom when considered externally and with respect to multiple universes. Similarly, any individuated entity taken externally is a universal whole and shows its atomic features. So there is a plurality of wholes implied in any atomic identity, and a monistic universality expressed in any monadic identity.

Thus, if I am an absolute identity then I too exhibit the monadic and atomic features; the same for any possible individuated identity. To be an entity is to be individuated and to be individuated is to be in alleged atomic identity, at any possible level of individuated identity. In this respect, an atomic particle in the grammar of physics, is (ontologically speaking) an absolute identity. Equally a world-whole, a grammar as a whole, is atomic/monadic as well. This means that the same deep problems of incommensurability between diverse absolute universes recurs at any level of identity, whether between worlds, or within a given world; whether between personal identities (inter-personal) or even within the structure of a person (intra-personal), and so on.

b) *Polarization of the Ontological Mind: Artificial Unity*
Let us see how this incommensurability arises. We have seen that between universal grammars there is no common mediating point of unifying reference. Universes are absolute self-identities which are internally infinite, self-contained and cannot be in relationality to anything outside itself. Nevertheless, the ontological mind finds itself entertaining diverse grammars of reality— having access to diverse universes of discourse. This suggests (demands) that there *must be* some more primitive transcendental unifying point of reference in the thinker. But what we find is simply a repeating of the same triangular loop of absolute identity.

It is evident that common sense reason, which ambiguously lives in absolute identity, recognizes the need for the transcendental unifying point to make diverse "things" of whatever sort (whether universes or diverse entities within a given universe) cohere in unity. If, for example, common sense is committed to a vast plurality of atomic entities, then these self-existent things are still seen to be collected within a unifying field like physical space or logical space or grammatical space, etc. So common sense reason works on the faith in unity and postulates the transcendental unity wherever it is needed to produce coherence and rational commensurability. This postulate then allows the otherwise incommensurable discrete identities to be placed in relationality.

For example, without the postulate of unity, I, as an individuated entity would be a universe unto myself (monadic); I would and could know only myself, my own "subjective" grammatical field. Other persons would be atomic identities "out there" and I could never suppose that I am in relation with them, speak the same language, participate in shared meaning and inhabit a common (communal) reality. There would be incommensurability between diverse individuated (atomized) minds. Each mind would be monadic— a closed universe unto itself. However, common sense assumes that I am indeed in touch with other minds, that we share a common world, that we communicate in a common language and forms of meaning and rationality. But common sense leaves it at that and does not draw out the inherent paradox and incoherence in its two postulates; it does not see that the faith in absolute identity runs at cross-purposes to its postulate of transcendental unity. Its faith in absolute identity pulls towards the atomic pole while its faith in absolute transcendental unity pulls towards the monadic (anatomic) pole. It does not recognize that absolute identity leads to conclusions which directly rule out any real unity, coherence, consistency. Rather, common sense lives in its incoherent condition (double-bind) and takes it to be the norm of rationality and of reality. On the one hand it is committed to absolute identity but on the other hand it is equally committed to unity, commensurability and coherence.

So, common sense trades on indeterminacy, ambiguity, equivocity and incoherence; it takes a polar split to be a primitive unity. Its faith in individuated entities is artificial because nowhere can any primitive individual be established, and its faith in unity is likewise artificial since nowhere can any absolute unity be found. Yet common sense reason— the mind of identity— lives as if this polarity were a unity, as if common sense faith were univocal, coherent, integral and the voice of rationality itself.

c) *The Polarized Mind: Atomic/Anatomic*
It has been argued that the ontological mind is self-polarized by absolute identity. And naturally, the polarized mind will always think in a polarized way. We have already seen this in the self-polarizing (triangular) dynamics of identity:

> If we suppose A as any individuated entity, this requires
> that *un-A* be given; but this polarization denies the unity

requirement of *A* as self-existent and independent. So unity is postulated as a third transcendental point, which, because it transcends both *A* and *un-A*, must be different from both, so it is not really the unity of *A* that was originally supposed.

In general, wherever there is alleged identity there will be ontological indeterminacy in self-polarization and a determinate, primitive unity will not be found. The polarization pervades common sense reason and shows itself in all thought, experience and existence. In thought, in theorizing, for example, if one thesis is asserted the polar opposite thesis will always be forthcoming, and there will be "evidence" for both polar points. In any point the counterpoint will also hold; in any assertion the contra-diction will be forthcoming. If in theoretical physics atomicity is taken as primitive it is predictable that anatomicity (the unified field) will soon come forth as necessary for truth and rationality in physics. And when the polarity is explicit there will ensue the inevitable search for a more primitive underlying (transcendental) unity to make the polar opposites cohere and be commensurable. So the polarized mind thinks and speaks in a polarized way, lives in a polarized reality, discovers a polarized truth and reasons in a polarized logic.

d) *The Pathology of Absolutism*

We may now look at the general form of the pathology of the ontological mind. Absolute identity generates a range of pathologies of reason which may be characterized as disorders of absolutism.

Absolutism is a pathology that takes innumerable forms; it originates with absolute identity, and wherever there is absolute identity, there we shall find absolutism. At the deepest level of common sense rationality we find absolutism in the form of the faith that there is an objective reality "out there" independent of consciousness or the individuated mind. This postulate of absolute reality, we have seen is a *requirement* of absolute identity itself; it comes from the requirement of identity that there be a transcendental unifying point of reference or ground for existence and experience. More importantly, we have found the source of ontological absolutism in the split produced between subjective/objective fields by absolute identity. The dualism of "I" (mind) on one side and object (universal field) on the other is inherently required by identity.

A familiar version of ontological absolutism is the faith that reality or the universe is *absolute*— it is the source of the distinction between truth and falsity, between fact and fiction, between real and imaginary, between knowledge and illusion. The absolute universe out there is the measure of truth and knowledge, the measure of rationality and meaning; and science aims at approaching, approximating and having direct access to this objective absolute reality.9

However, as is typical with the polarized mind of identity, every postulate has its counter-postulate, and where absolutism is found there we will naturally find relativism; this is the polar side of absolutism. And now we can readily see how and why relativism is one version of the pathology of absolutism. For ontology teaches that there are multiple alternative grammars of reality— multiple absolute universes— and this runs counter to the naive faith in a single, unified, monadic universe. Ontological relativism is the recognition that there are alternative realities each of which is absolute or monadic in its own right and incommensurable; each sets its own standards of reality, truth, fact and value. It makes clear that the absolute is relative to a determinate grammar and each grammar is atomic/monadic in itself. So while naive absolutism is committed to there being one monadic absolute, the polar voice lives in the faith that there are *multiple absolutes* and reality is relative to each absolute. So ontological relativism is a version of absolutism and essentially trades on absolute identity; the difference is that naive absolutism is monadic (anatomic) while relativism is atomic (pluralistic). They are the polar voices of absolute identity. So henceforth, let us treat the polar versions— absolutism and relativism— in one concept: /absolutism/.10

e) *Diverse forms of Absolutism*

/Absolutism/ is the faith in absolute identity, and wherever there is absolute identity we shall find the pathology of /absolutism/. On the level of grammars, each absolutizes itself and takes itself to be the absolute measure of truth and reality. This version is called "*onto-centrism*" and it is typically found in communally shared grammars, such as in certain cultures. The pathology of absolutism is particularly strong in religious cults each of which takes itself to be the measure, the absolute measure, of meaning, truth and reality. And world history has made abundantly clear the pathological conflicts and wars through the centuries that are direct expressions of this pathology. Religious conflict between people are *grammatical* in origin and are inevitable wherever there is ontocentrism. This disorder will always lead to grammatical violence— the violation of the *other* by denying his grammatical authenticity and *reducing* the grammars of the other to the ontocentric's ontological vocabulary.

Equally pathological is the chronic breakdown in communication between individuals even *within* an ostensibly shared communal grammar. For here, again, the pathology of absolute identity rules the lives of egocentrics. This is another pervasive disorder of absolutism directly resulting from the self-polarization of identity. When an individual is so locked into his own world, his own subjective realm, and absolutizes this as the measure of reality, others around him are reduced to objects and are grammatically violated. The egocentric, like the ontocentric, leaves no room for the legitimate voice of the other. The great religious teachers, the grammatically wise through the ages, have all addressed this egocentric (and ontocentric) pathology as the source of human suffering and the life of ignorance and sin. The way to liberation and enlightenment is seen to be precisely overcoming the absolutism of absolute self-identity. In the ontological sense, the *ego* may be seen as the individuated, self-identical, self-existent self. And here it is readily seen that the global/communal form of the pathology of ontocentrism has the same source as the pathology of egocentrism. When the ego-self ("I") identifies with the grammar/world of the community or culture the two versions of absolutism merge into one. Indeed, we saw earlier that the voice of the "I" has variability and is able to identify with diverse points of reference in grammatical space. And it is this dynamic of identity that allows for the diverse forms of "isms" like logocentrism, chauvinism, racism, etc., that are pathological forms of /absolutism/.

Still another version of absolutism of relevance here is that of fundamentalism. This is a specific form of ontocentrism which is the expression of faith in literalism. Literalism is a disposition regarding meaning which is a naive acceptance of univocity and identity (determinacy) of meaning; one word, one unambiguous, literal, univocal, transparent meaning. The word, in the form of the letter, speaks for itself and declares its meaning and truth. This is a faith about meaning which holds that the unique identity-meaning of a word is immediately given in the word. And fundamentalism is absolutistic faith that the literal meaning (given in the grammar) is the absolute truth. So this pathology traces to ontocentrism since literal meaning derives from the grammar one inhabits. When the grammar is absolutized then there is fixity and fixation of meaning.

Needless to say, these pathologies are all found in the grammatical disposition (hermeneutics) of science, when the scientist (or community of scientists) embraces a particular grammar of science in an absolutistic disposition we get the same ontocentrism and fundamentalism found in other areas of cultural life. From the grammatical point of view fundamentalism in science is just as pathological as fundamentalism in religious life. They spring from the common faith in absolute identity. Here it may be said that the true, liberated scientific spirit must overcome the pathologies of identity. The true scientific spirit goes against the hermeneutical closure and grammatical prejudice of /absolutism/.

Again, what the absolutistic mind takes to be rational discourse turns out to be rationalization and irrationality. For one thing, the ontocentric takes his grammar to be consistent and complete and absolute when critical ontology or grammatology shows that it is incomplete, incoherent and relative. This is particularly evident in conversation between and across diverse grammars. In inter-grammatical discourse there is typically found indeterminacy and ambiguity of meaning, mis-communication, incoherence and an inevitable power struggle for control of the agenda and the authority to voice reality and truth. The rational enterprise (which calls for openness and dialogue) gives way to rationalization, self-righteousness, prejudice, closed-mindedness, and authoritarianism. When true rational persuasion breaks down between grammars (or persons) the ontocentric typically resorts to arbitrary power and tyrannical authority to assert his grammar over the other. Here the "politics" of truth and reality rules, and we have another instance of the irrationality of religio-grammatical battles— conflicts of faith.

f) *Pathologies of Life: Mind and Matter*
We are finally in a position to turn to the fragmentation of life in general, and the dualism between mind and matter in particular that is the foundation of conventional physics.

It has been suggested that absolutism leads to breakdown of rationality between grammars and to pathologies of communication between indivdual persons. But now we may extend this theme and see that the pathology of fragmentation pervades the everyday life of *common sense*, for any given community of discourse.

First, we have seen that human life is a function of grammar, and if our grammatical life is fragmented and incoherent then so will be our form of life as well. And indeed we find that so-called common sense comprises a diversity of grammars all superimposed on one another and "co-existing" at the "same time". So in accordance with the incommensurability of meaning and existence found between grammars, it appears that our everyday life is a complex of identities ("I's") and worlds. It is not a coherent, univocal, integrated universe of discourse, but rather an artificially constructed complex of diverse voices and forms of life. Any supposed unity and coherence here is merely conventional and postulated.11

Secondly, the intra-personal inner discourse of the individual (ego) self is also multi-vocal and complex— a cluster of diverse identities or voices. Here again it is a lived problem to find inner coherence, unity, integrity in identity and voice. This is the inherent indeterminacy of "I" we spoke of earlier. Any supposed unity of the individuated self turns out to be an artificial postulated construction of a complex of voices. It must be stressed that this is not an abstract or theoretical problem but a most immediate existential fracturing of human life.12

The fall-out of self-splitting and dualities pervade every direction of the life of identity. There is the split between the self (subject) and the world-field (objects); there is the split between thought and the objects of thought; there is the split between word and object; between meaning and reference; there is a split between thought and action, theory and practice; between facts and values, between self and others, between reason and sense experience; between fact and fiction, between real and imaginary, and so on. These familiar dualities are taken to be natural *distinctions* of everyday life and nothing to be alarmed about— certainly nothing pathological. But they are all part of the pathological fall-out of absolute identity and in them lurks fractures of life and existence which hold us in bondage.

One fundamental grammatical split, we have seen earlier, is the dualism between the mental and the physical, between mind and matter. This is one polarization of absolute identity which emerges in any possible grammar. Of course this split is foundational for classical and contemporary physics.

It must be recalled that *all* dualisms trace back to absolute identity and the polarization dynamics of the ontological mind. And it is important to remember that dualisms are not benign *distinctions* but pathological faults in existence and experience. They are not mere abstract conceptual differences but profound categorial fractures of grammar which show themselves in reality and govern our lives. The mind/matter (mental/physical) dualism has dominated human existence and all aspects of cultural-hermeneutical life.

Furthermore, we have seen that pernicious dualisms exhibit the common double-bind and paradoxical dynamics of the form of absolute identity— the paradox of identity. For example, common sense faith assumes that knowledge is possible, and this requires the most intimate relationality between the knowing mind and the known object. But the deep duality between the knowing subject (mind) and the object of knowledge (world-field) preempts the intimate connection between mind and field required by the possibility of knowledge. So the ontological foundations of knowledge has remained problematic and paradoxical for centuries.

The point here is that the mental/physical dualism is ontological in origin and eminates from the I/Field dualism necessitated by absolute identity. And since *any possible grammar* of identity replicates the form of identity and the subject/object duality we may naturally expect some version of the mind/matter fragmentation in any possible world.

This point needs some clarification. For it is often thought that the mind/matter dualism is to be found only in a grammar such as the "dualistic" grammar of Descartes where one form of ontological dualism is explicit. It is thought that the mind/matter dualism would be overcome in an alternative grammar in which the categories of mind and matter are placed in internal relation— such as the grammatical models of materialism and idealism examined earlier. The latter are attempts to overcome the specific mind/matter dualism of the Cartesian variety. Nevertheless, since these ontological paradigms are equally structured in absolute identity and the primordial subject/object (I/Field) dualism we find that they do not (and cannot) overcome the underlying structural split, and so *some* version of the ontological mind/matter paradox will emerge. All grammars of identity are /dualistic/.

To see this two points must be stressed. First, as we saw earlier, the utterance "I" is always spoken within some ostensibly determinate grammar— the existence of the "I" is grammatically conditioned. But there is always a self-transcending "I" that stands as a witness and cannot be reduced to an existing object in the grammatical field. So "I" is inherently indeterminate and equi-vocal in reference. With this ontological ambiguity in mind it is important to distinguish between the objectified "I" and the subjectified "I"— the former is just as much an object in the grammatical field as other objects— along with physical objects. So the objectified concept of mind is one special sort of object in the world along with material objects.

The second point is to see the mind/matter categorial duality in the three sample grammatical paradigms we examined earlier. In the Cartesian grammar the category of mind and matter are fundamentally independent and the "I" is found to be an ontological compound (composite) entity and inherently equi-vocal (I-mind and I-body). In the materialist grammar the primary category is matter, and mind is seen to be derived from matter. This paradigm places mind and matter in a dependent relation. Nevertheless, the duality remains: first, the thinking *subject* (the subjective "I" of the materialist) is not reducible to the objective "I" in the materialist's grammatical field, so there is a duality here. Secondly, the concept of "matter" and "mind" are categorically still distinct, each having its own absolute identity, and the general paradox of identity applies: the identity-split between "mind" and "matter" remains despite the materialist's postulate that mind is existentially dependent on matter.

Similarly, in the idealist paradigm the relation between mind and matter goes the other way— matter being existentially derived from and dependent upon mind. But here again, the subjective "I" of the idealist is not reducible to the idealist's grammatical field, so the same structural dualism between "I" and field obtains, and the "objective" mind in the grammatical field has its identity which remains different from objective matter, and so the general paradox of identity holds here as well. In the idealist grammar it is postulated that matter is derived from mind but the existential derivation remains a dualistic mystery.

Thus, while the materialist has the dualistic problem of explaining how mind and intelligence can come from the material world, the idealist has the polar problem of explaining how the material world can come from mind and the world of mind. And of course each polar voice speaks past one another in systematically ambiguous speech. The Cartesian dualist simply accepts the split and lives with the two realities. While the Cartesian postulates unity between the realities; he cannot demonstrate it or account for causal interaction between the two realities. Such relationality is structurally precluded by his categorial structure.

Besides, it must be remembered that the terms "I", "mind", "matter" are all relative to a particular grammatical context and we cannot presume that we are using these terms with absolute, fixed, neutral, univocal meaning. On the contrary, these terms are grammatically ambiguous and take on incomparably different sense/reference in diverse grammatical contexts. And this is another aspect of the mind/matter problem— that these terms are systematically ambiguous or split in meaning across diverse grammars of existence— so we do not even have a coherent, univocal *problem* to begin with. The materialist concept of matter is not the same as the idealist concept of matter, so we do not have a univocal category of mind or matter to begin with.

The general problem of duality is the problem of indeterminacy— we need to find a truly unified (univocated) sense of "I", of "mind" and of "matter" to begin with, but when we do we shall find that the sense of "I", "mind" and "matter" so deeply inter-relate and so profoundly co-arise that only a new form of speech and grammaticality will enable "us" to think "them". Only a dramatic revolution in rationality itself which overcomes absolute identity will enable us to resolve the pathologies of dualism.

The ontological mind wants two polar objectives which it cannot simultaneously have; it wants differentiated, self-existent, individuated things which is its *atomic voice*, but it also wants unity, relationality, existential dependence, which is its *anatomic voice*. "It" wants existentially to differentiate mind and matter, which implies ontological diversity, but "it" also wants existential co-dependence and relationality which implies unity. But since "it" is itself self-divided in its polar voices it remains impotent to mediate its rational life and remains lodged in incompleteness, inconsistency, incoherence and irrationality. To give "itself" the appearance of rational and ontological coherence "it" *postulates* unity and this is the origin of the *artificial intelligence* of the ontological mind. Its grammars are artificial grammars, conventional constructions, cultural inventions or artifacts. Its life is artificial, its knowledge and reason engineered. It is only when physics (and the sciences in general, indeed all the hermeneutical arts) make the ontological turn that this insight becomes accessible. When physics goes explicitly grammatical it becomes in a position to discern the pathological consequences of absolute identity and the self-divisive grammars of reality. Only then will it be in a position to raise the generic problem of absolute identity and see the pathologies of absolutism clearly. When this is done physics and the sciences will be prepared for the turn to universal relativity and the revolution *from ontology to grammatology*.13

v) Universal Relativity: From Ontology to Grammatology
We are now in a position to make the turn from identity to grammatology. We have seen that the postulate of absolute identity fails as the principle of rationality, and the scientific spirit requires us to overcome pathological reason and find a new beginning. Here it is appropriate to stand back and go

back to the beginning when the Word (Reality) was One, and unbroken by absolute identity. This would be in effect a sort of "copernican revolution" in rationality. In going back to the true starting point of rational inquiry we find that the classical postulate of meditative reason— the principle of universal relativity— the principle of the holistic word— the holographic principle of unity— is the primordial origin of scientific inquiry. So let us attempt to bracket the mind of identity and enter the voice of meditative or holistic reason.

a) *Understanding Universal Relativity: The Continuum*
Meditative reason is the self-transformation of consciousness from identity to non-duality. And *Universal Relativity (UR)* is the principle of non-dual unity— the principle of pure reason.

In approaching UR let us introduce a term that might help in this therapeutic self-transformation to original Unity. Let us use the term *Logos* for the primordial, non-dual, undivided, universal unity. By meditating on this Original Word we begin to see the following. Logos is everything, it is Reality itself. It is the Word; it is Consciousness; it is Meaning; it is Existence; it is Intelligence, Mind, Thought; it is Energy, Matter, Nature; it is Space and Time; it is Life and Truth and Knowledge, the Light of Reason; it is Me and You, it is /I/; and all in all it is Nothing (nothing, no identity-name is equivalent to it).

One noticeable feature of Logos is that it is non-divisible and prior to any division of I/Field, consciousness/object; it is the universal and univocal point of self-reference and it forms a *Continuum* or *Unified Field* of Reality in which all possible phenomena arise and all possible concepts take their meaning. Any item in the Continuum is in essential Unity with the Continuum and all items are placed in an original co-dependency and co-arising such that they stand in some primordial existential synonymy.

Let us call this Continuum (its contiguity and synonymy) the "*holographic*" structure of Logos. The holographic feature is the recursive self- referential, self-universalizing dynamic in which the identity of any term inter-penetrates every other term in synonymy with Logos. This is the principle of *Universal Relativity*— it is the principle of non-dual unity of all things in Logos. This is the principle of Meaning and Rationality— the meaning of any item consists in its self-universalized holographic unity in the Continuum; this is the Universal Context of true meaning.

The first point to notice in self-reflective meditation is that /I/ am One with Logos— I am holographic, my mind is holographic, my speech is holographic, my thought is holographic, and all contiguous in holographic synonymy. Holographic rationality reveals that the true import of a thing is found in its inner unity, univocity and universality. So the principle of meditative reason (UR) is classical in the best sense— it respects (and achieves) the ideal that true rationality must approach the Universal and disclose Unity or Coherence. We no longer begin with fragmented pathological identities and then ask about their universality and unity; rather, meditative reason *begins* with Logos (with holographic mind) and anything, when truly perceived or interpreted, is taken in its holographic import. This is the method of holistic reason and the methodology of the scientific spirit.14

Thus, Grammatology is Pure Science, the science of meaning and truth and it discloses the holographic synonymy of meaning and truth. Naturally, UR requires that the holographic synonymy be discerned between Meaning, Truth, Speech, Understanding and Existence— these are holographically contiguous. So, in general, the method of meditative reason requires that the mind of identity must itself be self-transformed to realize its holographic form, for only the holographic mind can perceive truth and be One with the continuum of Logos. This self-transformation from absolute identity to UR is the method of grammatology.

b) *Some Historical Examples of UR*
It might be helpful here to pick out some prominent examples or paradigms of UR from the world historical traditions.

The ontological mind of identity is so deeply and chronically habituated to absolute identity and individuation that it cannot conceive holographic unity and is unable to enter the meditative continuum of UR. It calls for meditative devices and tangible examples to help it therapeutically restructure itself in its original universal form.

In the meditative tradition of Indian thought it is readily seen that the teaching of Advaita (Non-dual) Vedanta reveals that AUM is the Universal principle of Unity. AUM is holographic form itself— holonymous with Logos, and through proper meditation on AUM the mind itself becomes AUM. This is the Universal Continuum of which all else is an expression. If any item is selected for meditative attention its true import is revealed when its synonymy with AUM is realized. The science of Yoga (Self

Union) in its highest form expands rational awareness to its universal synonymy with AUM— the Original Holistic Word. This is not just an altered state of consciousness but the realization of Pure Consciousness or Reason, the realization of Truth itself.

Another classical example of the holographic principle of UR may be found in the teaching of Nagarjuna, the founder of the Madhyamika Buddhist School. Nagarjuna presents one version of UR in the form of the principle of dependent co-arising of all things. He teaches that absolute identity (svabhava) is vacuous and he demonstrates that wherever there is identity there is contradiction and in-coherence. He shows that true reason arises with the realization of Sunya, which may be translated as Emptiness, Void, Zero, and now Logos. He teaches that all things are Sunya, which is beyond the oppositional (dual, polar) structure of identity; Sunya is neither full nor empty, neither one nor many, neither *is* nor *isn't*, neither relative nor absolute, etc. The holographic principle of Sunya exhibits the non-dual features we have just discussed— it is the holographic continuum. Things are devoid of identity; all things co-dependently arise. The identity of anything consists in its identity through everything else. So it is the holographic principle (Sunya) that makes the world work, and true insight comes with the realization of Sunya— this is the middle way between all opposition and the pathological polarization of identity. Here too all opposites of identity are found to be co-dependently united in the holographic continuum.

Still another classical example of the holographic principle which may not at first be evident to the mind of identity is the being of the Christ.

It may be argued in Grammatology that the Christ is a perfect living example of UR— of the self-transformative process of non-dual Unity. The Christ meditatively understood is a Unifying principle that overcomes the deepest duality there can be in the structure of absolute identity— the split between finite individuated being and Infinite Being. For the Christ is the Unified Being that is at once fully finite and fully Infinite— the Living Logos, the Logos become Flesh. The Unity of the Christ is the Unity of UR, of the Continuum. In this respect the Christ is prior to the duality of identity and is the more profound unifying principle— the incarnation of the Word.

Meditative reason is able to discern that the Christ is the Universal mediator that heals the splits between opposites— the overcoming of absolute identity itself, the living principle of non-dual unity. And of course it is clear that

UR must be a Living Principle. The Christ is the voice of the Continuum that brings all separated things into the Universal Light of the Word. This Christ of Meditative Reason is not the same as the Christ of ontological mind. Holographic reason makes clear that the Christ and Word (Logos) are One, that the Christ is the Truth, the Way, the Life. The Christ Principle explains that individuated mind is separated from the Word and this inherent pathological condition is called "sin". The mediating principle is Salvational in that it alone can univocate the split between the indivduated mind and the Logos. It is required of the holographic principle of UR that it be the living incarnation of the Word, where Word and flesh are One, where mind and matter are holographically One. Thus, the speech-life of the Christ, every speech-act performed, is Living Proof of UR; every act performed by the Christ, when understood by the holographic mind is verification of the holographic principle.

c) *Grammatology and Physics: The Mind/Matter Continuum of Nature*
We have said that Grammatology is the science of Logos, of the Original Word, of Reality. It is the Science of Unity and calls forth the unity of sciences. It is the voice of UR and the method of self-universalization. If Physics were to make the revolutionary transformation to UR and transform itself to begin with holographic unity (and holographic rationality) it would then encounter the *Continuum of Nature*. Nature would be the Unified Field in which all the basic categories of existence realized their universal import in holographic synonymy with Logos. Let us meditate further on the Unified Field of non-dual Nature.

In the first place, the mind of the physicist itself would have to go through the transformation from the individuated ontological mind to the holographic mind— and this very self-transformation is an essential part of the subject-matter of holographic physics.

Now this self-universalizing, expanding mind would be capable of discerning the continuum, in which Mass and Energy are in continuum, where Mind and Matter are in continuum, and so on. Indeed, the holographic mind discerns the holographic Unity between the mind of the physicist and Nature. It becomes impossible to separate the features of consciousness (the rational intelligence of the physicist) from the phenomena of holographic Nature. There can be no split between "I" and Field, and between mind and matter, the mental and the physical. In the Continuum of the Unified Field any item discerned is a "clone" of the Universe (nature); each item is holographic in the sense that it has encoded within it the structure of Nature. The features of Mind permeates all things and the features of Matter permeate all things— in the holographic Continuum. Thus, in holographic physics the mind of the physicist becomes the essential subject-matter, and the Laws of Matter are always kept in Mind.

When Physics makes the grammatological turn to UR and the holographic mind begins to emerge in Meditative Reason, the resurrected mind becomes the true "laboratory" of High Energy physics, for matter and mind are univocated in the continuum— and every item of mind is incarnated and every item of matter is resurrected with the features of Nature. The Universal relativity of "time" becomes accessible to the holographic mind, and the curvature of time is experienced when every "moment" is perceived in relation to the Continuum; here every moment is contiguous to every other moment, and the holographic Eternal is decoded from any given moment. The Present is realized as the Continuum itself— Presence.

Furthermore, the non-dual Continuum reveals the holographic synonymy between Energy, Mind and Matter. Here it is found that the Universal Energy (Logos) essentially exhibits the features of Mind and Matter (but not, of course the features of "mind" and "matter" as they appear to the mind of identity). In this speech of Grammatology it is now meaningful to inquire into the Velocity of Consciousness or Intelligence as a form of Energy. It may be significantly asked whether the velocity (holographically understood) of intelligence is faster than the speed of Light, whether thought can break the time barrier, etc. Indeed, the holographic mind of grammatology in discerning the Continuum of Nature is now able to conceive of phenomena as they really are— phenomena that are inconceivable to the mind of identity.

When Physics lives the faith of identity the mind of the physicist is eclipsed from holographic Nature. And the artificial grammar of physics will always distort phenomena and be incomplete when it comes to discerning the Unified Field. The Physics of identity will always be caught in the polarized reason in which it will ebb and flow between opposing poles and polar grammatical constructions. Is the Universe expanding or contracting? Can there be a velocity faster than the speed of light? Is light wave or particle? etc., etc. But most pernicious is the separation of the energy of Mind— the mind of the physicist— from the energy of matter, the discontinuity between the features of mind and matter. Both Mind and Matter are violated in this artificial split between I and Field (Subject/Object) and between Mental and Physical.

The Physics of Identity violates the phenomena of Nature, the phenomena of the Unified Field (Reality). Since the holographic Mind is always present (though eclipsed and rendered unconscious) to the mind of identity, some of the phenomena of the Continuum do occasionally spontaneously emerge; but these cannot be processed by the grammar of physics— they are denied or dismissed as para-psychological or para-physical. But holographic physics teaches that all Phenomena are "para-psychical" ("para-physical") in the Mind/Matter Continuum. When it is understood that any instance of Matter is a form of Mental Energy and every instance of mind is a form of holographic Matter— then physics is grammatically prepared to explore transformation of Energy between Mind and Matter, and then Physiology would be ready scientifically to investigate the transformations which are the source of psycho-somatic pathologies.15

The holographic principle now makes clear how meaning is possible without absolute identity; now we can understand how objects with particularity are possible without entification and the fixation of meaning— existence is possible without atomic thinking.

While the mind of identity takes literal meaning to be primary, and metaphoric/symbolic meaning to be secondary and derivative, the holographic mind overcomes this dis-order and reveals that the metaphoric/symbolic is primary meaning. Metaphoric meaning is the self-expanding meaning which overflows the artificial fixity of sense in grammars of identity. Now we may approach metaphoric meaning as the expansion of the fixated sense of terms in the Continuum as they approximate their universal import and holographic synonymy. The expansion of the fixated senses of "mind" and "matter" in the holographic continuum is metaphoric. So the self-expanding mind will thrive on metaphoric transformations as it approaches the Continuum of Meaning.

Finally, the Continuum of Grammatology resolves the paradoxes of identity and opens the way for true Unity and Coherence. Grammatology shows how knowledge is possible, how communication is possible and how Rational Unity and Coherence is possible. And the pathologies of absolute identity which arose with atomic thinking are healed.16

Thus, it is only when the Continuum of Nature is discerned in UR that Science shall be in a position to advance in understanding of the laws of Energy and decode the hitherto eclipsed transformations between the mental and the physical. We have seen that the mind of identity engages in atomic thinking and we have been living in the atomic age for centuries. One attractive idea of the atomic age is the more recent realization that "energy" is released with the splitting of the atom (nuclear energy). By contrast, holographic thinking realizes that the "atom" is always self-divided and its challenge is to unify the perpetually split atom into the holographic unity of the Continuum. Here it is seen that the Univocation of the atom releases the highest form of energy in the Universe, the Energy of Logos. When Physics and the Sciences make the radical turn from ontological thinking to Grammatology, Science will mature to its higher form.

Notes

1 I use the term "Grammatology" in a different sense and context from the use of this term by the author Jacque Derrida. He uses the term in the context of literary criticism and theory of writing. I use the term in the context of meditative science of the origin of all meaning in the Holistic Word (Logos). In this context "grammatology" is the universal science of all forms of the Word— the grammar of thought, the grammar of experience, the grammar of existence or reality, the grammar of speech, the grammar of meaning, etc. The term "grammar" already has a well established traditionand usage in the context of logical theory where it connotes the logical form (syntax) of language or thought. I have attempted in earlier chapters to extend the term "grammar" to indicate ontological form as well— the categorial form of a language-world which constitutes a particular life-world. Here we speak of diverse grammars of ontological languages of reality. In this context it is suggested that to live, to experience, is to participate in some grammar of experience/existence where meaning is a function of grammar or ontological form. Thus, the general hermeneutical theme is presented where to experience, to think, to participate in meaning in any form is to participate in grammar. The present essay extends the use and context of "grammar" further to its most general or universal form— grammatology as the voice of meditative or holistic speech, the universal science of the Holistic Word.

2 "A is A" begs the question: **Is A, A?"**; it assumes identity and univocity— an atomic point in ontological space. Now we see that the paradox of identity is the universal form of paradox itself, and all other similar paradoxes are instances of the general paradox of identity. This is also the atomic paradox— for the atom is an elementary and absolute point of ontological space. The paradox of identity shows that no such atomic point does or could exist.

3 Ontological indeterminacy of identity means that there never can be found to exist any primitive individuated self-existent unit; any attempt to find or postulate such a primitive individual (or absolute atomic entity) must be self-contradictory and futile. The belief or appearance that there are primitive individuals of any sort can arise only by already assuming the existence of some absolute, universal and unitary ontological point of reference. Once this is done, as the ontological mind must do, then the myth of primitive individuals and ontological atoms can proceed with the semblance of validity.

Of course there are ((primitive individuals)), but they are constitutively situated in the Unified Field of Relativity. In a real sense the identity of individuals arises in primitive alterity and in the holistic unity of the Continuum: all primitive identity is co-identity. In thus finding that the Principle of Universal Relativity is the principle of identity, individuation and determinacy we see that naive /identity/ turns out to be derived and an artificial posit or construct. The bottom line here is that ((Identity)) is Holistic in nature, and cannot be accounted for adequately in the objectification of the egological mind.

4   It should be noted that the self-transcending dynamic is the strategy of identity for getting out of its perpetual double-bind, its paradoxical and self-contradictory position. When it finds itself in a bind it postulates a higher univocity which would rescue it from its present rational disaster. In this way it borrows time and postpones its eventual demise. It is a strategy of delay and procrastination.

5   Again the unity and polarity of the proposition is shown in predicative form; the Subject and Predicate are structurally polar to one another and the copula is the explicit sign of univocation (unity) that holds the propositional poles together into a unity. In this way the proposition as the basic unit (atom) and unity of thought replicates the form of absolute identity. But, of course, there is not only the problem of the atomic unity of the proposition; there is also the problem of the unity between thinker and the thought (the atomic predication).

6   For a more detailed presentation of categorial structure and grammar see "Formal Ontology and Movement Between Worlds"— *Philosophy East and West,* Volume 26, April 1976. See also "Formal Ontology and the Dialectical Transformation of Consciousness," *Philosophy East and West,* Volume 29, January 1979.

7   The issue, for example, of creationism and evolution is really an ontological one of grammar. Very often speakers of different grammatical faiths enter controversy as if they were debating facts, when what is really going on is a deeper collision of grammars. This seems to be the case with the creationism/evolution controversy— it is a garbled confrontation of diverse grammars. The creationist speaks in the Biblical grammar of idealism in which reality is an evolute of spirit, of mind. But in the evolutionary view the grammar of materialism is being spoken and here mind and intelligence are evolutes of matter (inert). In one sense both voices speak the "truth" and represent the "facts" of *relative* reality. But the real issue is whether there is a neutral absolute reality "out there" with neutral facts in terms of which this disagreement is to be settled. And now we see that the ontological controversy is much deeper and more problematic. We do not yet know our way about when grammars collide or speak past each other.

8   For a more detailed discussion of the ontology of Einstein's thought see "Ontological Relativity: A Metaphysical Critique of Einstein's Thought"— which was presented at the Einstein Conference at Hofstra University, November 1979. The Conference theme was— "Albert Einstein as an Intercultural and Interdisciplinary Phenomenon: His Influence in All Fields of Thought." See this paper in *Albert Einstein as an Inter-cultural and Inter-disciplinary Phenomenon*, Greenwood Press 1986.

9   Another version of absolutism is foundationalism, and this pathology also comes from identity. It is the deep tendency in the mind of identity ·to postulate a ground or foundation for experience, meaning and knowledge. Rationality itself appears to have a foundation in more primitive principles (foundations) from which all else is derived. This is the *axiomatic form* of common sense reason which governs all identity-thought; and now we find that the axiomatic dynamic is a direct expression of the form of absolute

identity. We have already found it in the triangular dynamic of identity. This is the origin of the axiomatic form of the mind of identity.

10   A more familiar version of "relativism" is the view that there is no absolute knowledge, each person's view is just as valid as any other and there are no absolute common universal standards for truth. This epistemological version of the pathology is easily seen to fit the general form of /absolutism/. For instead of taking diverse grammars as multiple absolutes, it takes each individual mind as the multiple absolutes and denies a common absolute point of unity for the diverse individuated minds. Each mind is taken as monadic and the absolute measure of truth.

11   The projected unity of common sense is artificial because it is not *real;* common sense requires unity but the polarization preempts it. So the projected unity is artificial in the sense that it is postulated, and it is nothing more than the postulation itself   a regulative condition of the mind of identity. The egological paradigm trades on relativity for its univocity condition.

12   For a systematic discussion of the psycho-pathologies of identity see "Madhyamika Dialectic and Holistic Psychotherapy"— *Buddhist Philosophy (Journal of)*, Vol. I, 1983 included below as Chapter 8..

13   If the scientist does not make the grammatical turn and master grammar then grammar masters the scientist and the pathologies of absolutism result. It should now be seen that the eclipse of ontology from modern science is itself a symptom of the pathology of identity— a dualism between grammar and physics. This pathological dualism is one of the main barriers to the progress of knowledge and scientific method.

14   Perhaps it should be stressed here that "Unity" and "One" are not to be taken in their more mundane sense of absolute identity; for we have seen that the sense of these terms in the mind of identity is self-divisive and indeterminate, like all other terms. Instead, holographic Unity is prior to any individuated thing, so the atomic/monadic features can never arise in the first place.

15   In the Continuum of Grammatology, *all* Phenomena of Nature are "para-psychological" for the mind of identity. The Holographic principle calls for a radical scientific review and re-evaluation of what is to count as legitimate or authentic "phenomena"; and the current grammar-politics of contemporary sciences are thereafter suspended. Holographic science will be open to and sympathetic to the range of phenomena which hitherto were illegitimate— the so-called "para-psychical" phenomena. The rationality of the Unified Field of Phenomena understands the holographic transformations between mind and matter which have been mysterious to the mind of identity.

16 It need not be pointed out that the pathologies of absolutism in the physics of identity are very real and thrive in contemporary physics. It is to be expected that Phenomena of the Unified Field will burst through the artificial grammar of physics and that holographic concepts will strain the limits of the rationality of identity. It is precisely because physics has ripened in its pathologies and straining at the limits of identity that it is an exciting place to witness the inevitable turn to universal relativity. So it is not a casual option for

the sciences to make the turn to Grammatology— it is rather an inevitable and necessary step in the self-evolution of the growth of science, knowledge and rationality.

CHAPTER 5

UNIVERSAL THEOLOGY:
BEYOND ABSOLUTISM AND RELATIVISM

FOREWORD

This essay is the outgrowth of research done over the past twenty years in the diverse areas of philosophy of logic and language, ontology, Hindu and Buddhist philosophy, and on the nature and method of comparative thought. As this research progressed, it became increasingly clear that precisely analogous formal problems in rationality arose in diverse areas of research. Indeed, it became clear that the crisis of rationality, as found for example in the problems of absolutism and relativism, comes to a head in the area of comparative thought. For in this area the question of the nature of discourse between different language forms or life-worlds brings the issues of the nature of rational unity between apparently incommensurable forms of meaning into sharp focus.

The areas of comparative thought, inter-religious dialogue and cross-cultural philosophy of religion have flourished in recent years and the deepest challenges have been raised for rationality and theology. These challenges call for a revised and more powerful rational form of discourse.

This has become evident in the intensive and creative discussions that have been taking place in such places as the Society for Asian and Comparative Philosophy and the recent Cross-Cultural Philosophy of Religion Group of the American Academy of Religion. I have benefited from participation in these meetings which stimulated my thought. I also have gained much while I was Director of the Margaret Gest Center for Cross-Cultural Study of Religion at Haverford College. The Annual Lecture Series on the Unity of Religions as well as the Annual Dialogues and Seminars helped me to see the problems more clearly.

So this essay is an attempt to respond to the range of substantive issues of rationality and inter-religious theology which have emerged at this new frontier of inter-cultural research. Although specific positions have not been explicitly discussed or singled out, the essay was composed with the range of issues in mind and attempts to present a way of thinking which essentially addresses the basic issues.

PREFACE

I   Absolutism and the Universal Pathology of Rationality
Universal Theology is the inevitable outgrowth of inter-religious theology, and indeed of theology in general. For it is essentially the articulation of the universal Divine Form which must live at the heart of any and every form of life. The essence of this essay is that every possible name or form is a logos and every logos inherently reflects the Universal Word, which is Absolute, Infinite Unity. Reflection on Divine Form reveals that as the form of all possible forms it discloses itself as the Universal Continuum which is Logos. The essay is an elaboration of this theme.

The enterprise of inter-religious theology raises deep issues about rationality in general— it brings out inherent paradoxes and incoherencies in the nature of discourse between profoundly diverse religious worlds. Since it appears that each religious world defines its own rational form of life and is a universe of discourse unto itself, this seems to imply that diverse worlds are incommensurable, beyond rational mutuality or shared meanings. Nevertheless, we have the deep intuition that we are able to truly inhabit diverse religious worlds and understand them from within. And this suggests that there is, indeed, deeper unity and mutuality than might first have been seen. In this way a problem of rationality arises— how can there be true unity between radically diverse religious worlds, each of which in one way or another defines its absolute principle? We cannot simply postulate a transcendent unity of religions which discloses some more primitive meta-unity. This way out has been tried, but it has its problems. The point is that in this context of the dialectical tensions about reconciling radical diversity and radical unity between religious worlds certain predictable and perennial problems of absolutism and relativism arise.

These problems of absolutism have resonated through the ages and diverse cultures. They appear to be inherent in the very structure of human reason itself. But these problems continue to rage in all areas of contemporary rationality, as much today as they did in ancient times. These problems are deep in the discourse of ethics— are there absolute values for human life or are values subjective or relative? They emerge at the center of current discussions about rationality itself— are there absolute or foundational rational principles or criteria in terms of which intelligibility and truth can be judged? These problems of absolutism have been intense in recent philosophy of science— what is the nature of scientific discourse in self-transformation from one paradigm or conceptual framework to another? Are there objective or universal principles of rationality of scientific growth and change? And, of course, the problems of absolutism abound in everyday life. So, it is important to address the underlying causes of absolutism and to find a deeper way to understand it.

This is a problem that Universal Theology cannot and does not avoid. It is the central issue in the question of inter-religious dialogue and the unity of religions. This essay attempts to give an account of the nature of absolutism in a way that speaks directly to the central issues of theology and inter-religious discourse.

SYNOPSIS

Universal Theology (UT) is meditation on Divine Form. It calls for a meditative voice and an holistic narrative. This meditation reveals that Divine Form as the form of absolute and infinite Unity must be holistic and cannot be thought by the particularistic or literalist or egological mind. Meditation on divine form calls forth the holistic mind and voice and reveals the Divine Continuum as the essence of Divine Unity. This Holistic Original Word is called *Logos* and it is seen that the Divine Continuum is the form of all possible forms. Any possible form is called *logos*. This would include any possible name or thing at any possible level— a word, a person, an event, a world, a language, a culture, a religion, or a theology. The holistic voice reveals that the Continuum is at the heart of every possible logos and the very essence of any possible form of life. And the hermeneutical principle of holistic reason is that the true understanding of any logos requires that it be seen in the light of its inner universal form. Any given logos reflects Logos and its universal significance is realized when its holistic form is discerned. And it becomes clear that the holistic mind is called forth in meditation on divine form.

The essay attempts to demonstrate that the particularistic or existential mind lives a form of life, a form of reason, and speaks in a voice that cannot adequately discern divine form. Indeed, the meditative narrative demonstrates that the very form of the particularistic mind is centered in the principle of absolute self-identity, a principle of rational life which is oriented around its own ontocentric self-definition. It is found that the deep structure of this existential voice is the source of all pathologies of life, the source of a recurrent and chronic self-dualizing that leads it into inner rational strife and paradox. Here the holistic voice discerns the deeper cause of the pathologies of life and rationality— the origin of absolutism and relativism. It is seen that the origin of irrationality, falsity, sin, and suffering is found in the very form of self-identity which manifests itself as the tendency to fixate form and hence to eclipse itself from its origin in the Continuum. Thus, the Continuum hypothesis— that all life is immediately conditioned by the presence of the Continuum, that it is the pre-conscious condition shaping all rational life and meaning— requires that the true logos of any thing is realized when its inner universal form is brought forth. So, the origin of all pathology is found in the eclipse of the Continuum by self-identity and the resulting disorientation and deformation comes from the inner self-division that cuts life off from its roots. This brings out the universal form of sin and suffering.

The holistic narrative continues its meditative attention to Divine Form and explores the possibility of the fixated and particularized voice finding hermeneutical release from its pathological condition. It is seen that every possible life-world, as a form of life, expresses itself in the logos of a grammar, and true to form, the holistic voice discerns that every grammar intrinsically reflects Logos. This means that every form of life, as a logos, is inherently religious and lives under some faith principle of unity. Every grammar of life is in some way a divine hypothesis, a theogram of Divine Form. And when the fictional narrative of the particularistic voice is seen through, any logos is discerned in its universal import in the context of the Continuum. The principle of absolute identity is displaced by the living principle of universal relativity, which is the holistic unity of the Continuum.

UT discerns that in human life and for any possible religious form of life, it is the higher holistic voice that is the open space of dialogical self unity. It is in the holistic dialogical voice that all oppositions are reconciled and true life is found. It is in dialogical form, the Universal Christ voice, that true unity and rationality arises. This holistic voice is found to be speaking in such voices as Jesus, Buddha, or Lord Krishna. The religious grammars called "christianity," "hinduism" or "buddhism" may be spoken in the particularistic voice, in which case the universal dialogical or holistic import is eclipsed; or they may be spoken in the holistic voice in which case their universal import is realized. Any religious grammar is found essentially to reflect Logos, and the dialogical voice discerns its universal import. In this way UT attempts to open a way in which the pathologies of life and reason which are intrinsic to the particularistic voice may be overcome.

i) Discerning the Divine Form: Holistic Unity as the Divine Continuum
Universal theology (UT) is meditation on universal divine form. Such meditation reveals that Divine form is absolute, infinite unity. Here we already see a kind of redundancy or reiteration in the words— "universal," "unity," "absolute," and "infinite;" for in meditative thought divine form is revealed as the universal Continuum in which all possible divine names are synonymous. Thus in meditative reason it is seen that divine form is infinite unity and meditation on infinite unity reveals that divine form must be absolutely universal— the form of all possible forms. In short, UT is the articulation of absolute unity.

Let us call this "holistic unity." Holistic unity is infinitely pure and has no trace of duality or discrimination within it. As such it cannot be made into an *object* of thought in any way and is hence not accessible to the individuated mind. Holistic form must be *meditated* and in such meditation mind becomes one with divine form, so mind self-expands to holistic unity. And this very process of self-universalization becomes the essential concern of UT; meditation on divine unity calls forth the holistic mind for only the mind which is truly one with divine form can discern infinite unity.

Holistic Unity implies a divine Continuum in which whatever is discerned is found to be essentially holonymous with divine form— so any divine name is one with divine form: this is the essence of infinite unity. Thus, in meditating on divine form we find that infinite form is the form of all possible forms, so there can be no form that is not encompassed within the divine Continuum. Again, meditation on absolute unity reveals that pure unity is the form of perfection and such infinite perfection is the form of goodness; meditation on goodness reveals the form of pure meaning which is the origin of all reason; meditation on the form of holistic reason discloses the nature of truth; meditation on the form of truth shows the form of pure life; meditation on holistic life makes manifest the meaning of intelligence; reflection on the pure form of intelligence opens the way to the divine light which is the form of all forms; reflection on infinite form shows itself as infinite being; meditation on infinite being reveals the form of the Universal Word; contemplation of the Holistic Word makes clear the Universal Grammar of any possible existence; mindfulness of pure Grammar shows the deep structure of any possible Experience; and so on. Thus, the divine Continuum is perfect self-unity in which any divine name, being infinite and holistic, implies all other divine names. Let us speak of this as the "divine synonymy" of the holistic Continuum.

As we reflect on the Divine Continuum we see that holistic unity implies the non-difference of Being, Truth, Goodness, Meaning, Intelligence, Rationality, Knowledge, Life ... and so on, ad infinitum. Let us use the term "*Logos*" for the Divine Continuum— for divine form. So *Logos* is the original universal or holistic Word— the infinite form of all possible forms; and UT is the meditative articulation of Logos.

There is something redundant in the name "universal theology" for theology is par excellence the articulation of divine form which is the absolute universal form of all forms. So theology by its nature must be universal. And as meditation on the Universal Word (Logos) UT must be able to account for any possible form— for all forms essentially reflect Logos. This means of course that UT should be able to account for any possible theology and any possible form of life. This is one sense in which UT must be universal.

To see more clearly the universal scope of UT it would be helpful to elaborate on the idea of any possible form. It has been said that UT is the articulation of Logos which is the universal absolute form of all possible forms. Let us use the term "*logos*" for any possible form in general. The insight of UT is that any *logos* essentially reflects Logos, and the true universal import of any logos is revealed when its holistic unity with Logos is meditatively realized. The main objective of UT is to show that any possible form *is* a logos and to show that every logos essentially reflects Logos as its true form.

Let us clarify this point. It is important to see from the start that the term "form" is holistic and encompasses any possible thing that may be discerned in thought. If we speak of diverse forms of life— as in different religious worlds or cultures, each would be a logos. So the Christian life-world would be a logos, the Buddhist life-world would be a logos, the form of life we call science— being a scientist— would be a logos, and so on. So any form of life would be a logos. But so would any discriminated item in any given cultural world— in reality— would also be a logos— a person, mind, body, an event, a process, an action, sky, water, ... is a logos; in short, any possible thing that may be discriminated or individuated is a logos. So the term "logos" applies to any possible thing that may have identity (name or form).

Logos has jurisdiction over any possible logos— there is no possible religion or theology, for example, that does not have Logos as its true inner form; there is no divine name in any possible religious form of life that does not make reference to Logos; there is no form of life in general whose meaning and rationality is not oriented to the Universal Word. In general, there is no meaning that is not in its deep structure oriented to Logos, no word or name that is beyond the scope of the Universal Word. There is no life that does not get its life-force from Logos, and so on, for every possible logos.

It should be evident that this feature of Logos is immediately implied in holistic meaning of Infinite Form— there can be no possible form that stands independently and apart from Divine Form. This is the very meaning of the Universality and Unity of Logos. And it is indeed a classical thesis of theology that all things derive from Divine Form. One task of UT is to elaborate on this holistic truth and make clear its explanatory power for understanding all possible forms of life.

ii) The Holistic Mind vs. The Particularistic Mind

The central thesis of UT is that every logos is Logos. This is an holistic truth spoken in the meditative narrative of the holistic mind. It is a simple truth, but its full power is not readily available to the particularistic mind.

For the latter attempts to think what cannot be thought but only meditated. Thinking arises in a dualized structure that separates the mind or voice of the thinker from the holistic Continuum and reduces divine form to an object of thought. But the holistic mind teaches that divine form cannot be thought; it must be realized in meditation. Meditative thinking essentially involves the self-expansion of the particularistic mind to its holistic form in which it is one with the Continuum. What makes perfect sense to the meditative narrative can be inscrutable to the particularistic voice, for the latter does not discern the holistic Continuum. Meditative speech is centered in the Continuum while the particularistic mind is centered in a logos which separates itself from the Continuum. In a sense the challenge of UT is to give a critical account of the particularistic mind in the context of making clear the nature of the dialectical self-transformation of the particularistic mind to its holistic form.

In approaching this task let us continue the holistic narrative. The holistic mind works on the *principle of universal relativity*.[1] This is the principle of the Continuum— the Universal Field— in which any given logos permeates every other logos in dependent co-arising, in divine synonymy. The true meaning of any logos is realized in discerning its inner form which is Logos. This means that in meditating on any logos (any name or form) its true import is found in discerning it in the context of the Holistic continuum. The Continuum is the universal context of true meaning. So no logos is ever given identity or particularistic meaning in isolation from Logos.

The principle of holistic meaning reveals that primary meaning is metaphoric and symbolic rather than literalistic.[2] But the terms "metaphoric" and "symbolic" are used in their holistic sense here— the *symbolic* force of any logos is precisely its conformity to universal relativity— its self universalization in the Continuum; its true meaning shows that it is *analogous* to every other logos, that is, its identity is found in discerning its unity in the Continuum. By contrast, the particularistic mind begins with the presumption that *literal* meaning is primary and that the unique meaning of a given logos consists in its differentiated identity— that which separates it off from everything else. Thus, for example, in discerning the true identity of Jesus Christ, the particularistic mind finds in this logos a unique, particular being who is differentiated from other beings. But the holistic mind discerns a logos whose true identity or form consists in the unity of the Continuum— that is, the meditative intelligence discerns a logos whose true meaning is Logos. Indeed, the essential import of the

Christ is found to be precisely the living principle of relativity— the living Logos. So while the particularistic mind perceives a uniquely individuated and objectified logos, the holistic mind discerns a self-universalizing holistic form— a uniquely individuated presence in the historical Continuum of Logos. (In a sense the rest of this essay is an elaboration of this point.)

The meditative mind, in thinking metaphorically and symbolically according to universal relativity, exercises a meditative imagination that discerns analogies or synonymies in the Continuum. While the particularistic mind, working on the principle of absolute identity, fixates meaning and produces discontinuity, meditative thinking activates the analogical imagination which breaks through artificial boundaries and discerns the deeper holistic import in any given logos. Thus, to take another example, in meditating on "bread" the holistic imagination sees here a logos whose universal import or true symbolic meaning is expanded in the Continuum— universal bread is one with the body of the Christ which is the Living Word— the resurrected body. The holistic import of "bread" is not that it is inert matter but that it is the living Word. We may perform a similar meditative experiment on "wine" or "air" or "water" and so on.

In meditative speech, holy water— holistic water— is discerned to be self-universalized in the Continuum and here one may say in the meditative voice— All is Water. In this meditative transformation one finds the holistic meaning of Water in the Continuum— its divine synonymy. And this meaning transformation is classical— one finds in the Upanisads for example— the meditative principle that All is AUM. This principle requires that in proper meditation on any given word its universal synonymy with AUM is discerned. AUM is the Divine Form, the holistic Continuum in which the universal import of any word is discerned. So if in yogic meditation we meditate on "air" the holistic mind which is yoked with the Continuum discerns the universal import of holistic Air— the divine breath, speech, the living Word.

Again, in Buddhist meditation the Madhyamika teaches that all things (logos) are empty when taken in self-existence (independent identity); and this is true of the self as indicated by "I." But when particularistic identity is overcome and the individuated "I" (mind, voice) is removed, the holistic voice that is one with the Continuum (Súnyata) sees things as they truly are— in universal relativity. In this form of meditative speech the true import of things is seen in the universal Continuum which is divine form. And so on.

These are just preliminary illustrations to make more vivid the difference between the holistic mind and the particularistic voice. The main point here is that the Continuum— divine form— must come first in every respect, and all true thought, meaning, life is oriented to holistic unity.

   iii) Elaboration in Holistic Narrative of "logos": the form of life
Let us now continue the meditation on divine form and elaborate on how any possible form or logos is oriented to the Continuum as its essential form.

The term "logos" is an holistic term and the remark that "every possible form is logos" is an holistic remark spoken in the meditative voice. So "logos" is precisely *analogous* to Logos and it mirrors divine form in the Continuum: logos is in the image of Logos.

We saw earlier that divine form is the form of perfect unity and that meditation on this unity opened up the divine synonymy of diverse divine names: in absolute unity is perfection, in perfection is goodness, in goodness is truth, in truth is intelligence, in intelligence is life, in life is the word, in the word there is meaning, in meaning there is being, and so on. So it is impossible to separate off any divine name from the form of perfect unity, and all divine names mutually entail one another: this is the form of the Continuum.

This reminds us that divine form is the form of all possible forms— of any possible logos. This means that any possible logos, for example, a human life, is intrinsically oriented to Logos— it gets its form, life, meaning, being, telos, from the divine form and every logos imitates Logos in being a unity— to be a form is to be a unity of some sort.

To see this we must remember that the word "form" or "logos" is holistic and hence recursively applies to any possible "thing" at any level: whatever can be named indicates a form of some sort. So "logos" can be any thing: a person, a form of life, a mind, a voice, a word, an object, an event, an action, a religious world, an art, etc. There is no limit to what can be a logos— it is infinitely recursive and reiterative, and this is connected to its holistic form.

Every logos (name or form) is a unity which is intrinsically oriented to Logos and gets its true meaning in its unity with the Continuum. This is the principle of meaning and interpretation for UT: its hermeneutical principle.

To illustrate this let us focus meditative attention on a logos of special interest— a life, a human life. This logos gets its life, its being, its meaning from the Continuum and its true life and meaning consists in its realizing its unity in Continuum. Let us call this its "form of life."

The form of life of a human logos gets its meaning from its intrinsic orientation to Logos. The holistic understanding of any form of life shows how its meaning arises in its unity with the Continuum: being in the image of Logos the form of life derives its meaning in orientation to divine form— which is its unifying principle. The unifying principle of a life is what gives this logos its form of rationality, for rationality is precisely the formal principle of unity of a given life. The unifying principle of a form of life is its *faith*— that form from which all meaning derives. And this unifying principle of rational faith (for faith and reason are one in holistic life) is the very form of Goodness which is the reason for being of this life: the unifying principle of a form of life is its source of life, meaning, being and value. In this respect the unifying form of a life orients all its life and its life force is directed towards this principle. So the *meaning of life* is in its form and its form is its unifying principle which is its rational faith. In this holistic narrative then we begin to discern the divine synonymy in form of life, unifying principle, reason for being, goodness or origin of all meaning and value and its faith.

In meditating further on this logos we find that it is one with its form of life which is a unity of its meaning, being, value and thought. So its rational thought is its being and this takes the form of *grammar* 3— the form of its *word*. In this holistic sense, "grammar" is the logos-structure which makes all meaning possible and constitutes a world or universe; so the grammar of a form of life makes a universe of discourse possible and gives form to all meaning and experience in that world. In this respect a grammar is the structure of a form of life which allows the logos to think, experience, speak and make sense of reality; a grammar is a life-world which makes reality possible and allows a logos to know itself and be one with Logos.

iv) Grammar and Divine Form: every form of life is religious
In meditating on a logos as a form of life we have seen in holistic unity that
the form of life is structured in grammar which makes the self-
interpretation of a life-world possible. Here it may be seen that *to live is to
interpret*— there is no meaning, no existence, no thought, no experience
that is not grammatical; as the form of life, grammar universally
conditions the life in its rational possibilities. It may be said that a
grammar is a divine interpretation, a divine name, an holistic hypothesis.

Some illustrations might make this more tangible. We have been reflecting
on a logos as a form of life and this has taken us to grammar. It has been
ambiguous whether the form of life is individual or communal; it could be
both. But for our purposes here let us take some historical examples of
forms of life (grammars)— it is easily seen that the Hindu or Buddhist or
Christian forms of life express themselves in diverse grammars of reality.
Each grammar constitutes a life-world which is communally lived as a
culture. The grammar here is the structure of logos which makes all life
and meaning possible: it constitutes its rational form. What is rational or
makes sense in one life-world appears to be different from what makes
sense in another. And each grammar involves a faith, a unifying principle,
which is its divine interpretation or shows its divine form. Each grammar
may be taken in its holistic form— in its divine synonymy with the
Continuum, or it might take itself as an absolute form, as a grammar of
divine form in and of itself, as a separate universe of discourse. We shall
explore this difference later. The point here is that a grammar by its
nature shows its divine form and since it orders and orients a given form
of life, it involves a faith and hence a religious form of life.

The holistic insight that every form of life, shown in a grammar, involves
a faith principle and implies a religious form of life (i.e., a life oriented in
faith and conditioned by a divine name or form) may be more readily seen
if we take some illustrations of grammars that are not conventionally called
"religious." Thus, if we take the form of life called "physics" we find a
grammar of physics which structures this form of life and conditions its
meaning and experience. Like any grammar the grammar of physics is a
logos with a unifying principle that makes this form of life possible. This
grammar-logos, like any logos, makes implicit reference to divine form
and hence essentially works on a faith principle that is the origin of this
form of life. All the interpretive rational activity called "doing physics" is
a praxis that proceeds in the light of the "theoria" of the logos of physics;
this means that to do physics is to be grammatical, it is the very life of the

grammar, and this life, like any form of life, is a faith that is oriented to divine form. Thus, although in conventional life the form of life called "physics" is taken to be "secular," in the holistic understanding that discerns the essential unity and continuity between the form of life, its grammar, its divine form and its faith, this logos like any other is holistically religious. The experimental investigation of "nature" is one opening to divine form.

Similarly, holistic thinking about the logos called "mathematics" or "music" or "philosophy," and so on are all grammatical activities and hence inherently are oriented to divine form and are in a sense divine hypotheses or conjectures or names.

v) *The holistic form of religious life: degrees of life*

Let us review what this meditation on divine form has shown. We have been meditating on the holistic thesis that every *logos is Logos*: that every possible form of logos, any form of life, any word, any language, culture, meaning, etc., is inherently oriented to Logos. We focused on a special logos: a life in human form— and this led to discerning the form of life in general; and on reflecting on this we found that the meaning of life derives from a structure of unity which shows itself as a grammar which is the presentation of divine form as word. The grammar as the form of life made life possible in the space of a life-world. And we saw that any form of life as grammar is oriented to divine unity which is its faith or originating principle— the source of all its meaning— its rational faith. So all life was implicitly religious in the sense that it participated in rational faith or grammar which is oriented to divine form, the Continuum. The Continuum is seen to be the pre-grammatical structure of all meaning, the unconscious and pre-conscious Presence that conditions all meaning and life.

Now we may move more deeply in this meditation on the Continuum and reflect on an essential feature of human life— on its holistic religious form. It is the Continuum that orients human life and gives it meaning and value. The Continuum, Divine form, is the Absolute form of infinite unity which we have seen is the holistic meaning of Life, Truth, Meaning, Goodness. A life is meaningful, true, real, worthy, to the degree that it realizes its inner form--this is the measure or standard of religious life, the life which self-transforms to its highest possible form.

It is the Presence of the Continuum as the deep inherent form of any life that orients that life to the possibility of ever higher meaning, higher life, higher truth, higher value. Human life finds in this orientation the possibility of self-expansion and self-realization; life is directed towards divine form as its ultimate concern and in this orientation is its telic structure— that at which all its life may be directed. We may call this *the holistic process of self-consciousness*, the perpetual possibility of reflexive self-transcendence or self-transformation to higher realization of form. The higher the self-evolution of form, the higher the life, the deeper the freedom, the purer the rational faith. So human life essentially has the possibility of self-expanding its form in the realization of deeper self-unity. And it is this possibility of self-expansion of form towards unity with Continuum (holistic form) that we call *awareness*.

Awareness is the realization of higher life that comes with reflexive self-consciousness through meditation. So awareness is the higher energy of consciousness as it expands its form in ever deeper ways towards holistic unity with Continuum. So it is the Continuum that is ever present to life which calls life to it like a magnet. As the source of life, it is the direction in which greater life is released. As the source of meaning, it is the origin which yields ever more meaningful life. As the locus of pure reason, it is the ultimate point of reference for all rational growth. As boundless energy, it is the source of greater power and energy. And as pure light, it is the source of liberation and enlightenment. So all life is held in its gravitational field and under its infinite influence whether that life recognizes this or not; and all life in one way or another responds to the presence of the Continuum. It is that to which all life aims.

Thus, we see that rational thought is always oriented towards the deep unity of the Continuum, towards self-unity. The form of unity is life force or energy that moves reason, self-conscious life, to its self-realization. And the path of reason is always towards deeper realization of form and unity. Thus, common sense life, being a form of meaning and reason, lives at some form of logos, some degree of consciousness. The question of degree indicates that it is aware at one level of form but asleep to a deeper level. So common sense tends to be unconscious about its form of life, its grammar. When it moves to the reflexive awareness of its form of life and makes the grammatical turn, it achieves a higher consciousness and a deeper rational form of life. By contrast, ·common sense is here unreflexive and un-informed. To go even deeper and discern the logos or form of any grammar is still a deeper transformation of rational awareness— to discern the form of any possible life— world. And to self-expand in rational form to the holistic unity of the Continuum is the culmination of the self-reflexive journey of reason. Reason finds it highest realization of form in meditative self-unity— holistic form. This is the orientation and direction of religious life.

II The Pathology of Meaning: Absolutism and Relativism

Let us continue our meditation on divine form— the Continuum. We have focused thus far on the holistic unity of the Continuum and developed the holistic narrative in the meditative voice. Here we saw that every logos is inherently and essentially oriented to Logos as its true form. Here any logos is holistically united in the Continuum and has no separate or independent identity or form of life. The holistic mind is one with the Continuum which has the form of universal relativity. In the holistic narrative any logos is essentially dialogical in its unity structure and it is inherently conversational in its holistic life.

But there is a form of life in which a logos in its inner form develops a voice of its own and speaks its own narrative giving its self interpretation. Let us call this form of life "the life of self-identity." The inner narrative and speech life of this logos breaks from the holistic voice and it falls into a self-eclipse from its inner holistic form. So the holistic conversation or dialogue is broken and there is a separation in voice, a split in narratives. So in our present meditation there is a tension between the holistic narrative and the inner self-narrative of the separated voice. The Primordial Word has been broken and our meditative challenge is to continue our holistic narrative while we enter into the inner space of the individuated voice to experience its pathological form of life. We now need to re-create the form of its inner life without breaking our holistic concentration and continued attention to divine form.

To hold the two narratives together some distinctions might be helpful. For when we enter the inner voice of the separated self-identity we are in a different universe of discourse. Let us call this inner orientation around the voice of self-identity the *monadic voice*4. As a separate and independent existence it is eclipsed from holistic unity in the Continuum and it is centered in its own absolute form of life— its own universe. This primordial split from Continuum creates a self-division within its life giving rise to a primary consciousness of its independent existence— the break from the Holistic Continuum creates reality, existence, world. This existence is experienced as a dual structure in which the individuated self-existence ("I") lives within a universal world-field that stands over-against it; thus, there is given with self-existence the primordial duality between I and Field. And with the split from Logos the separated logos breaks from its inner true form and takes the name "ontos" for itself. This separate voice is existential and self-referential, centered in its own being— it is now *onto-centric*5 Thus, with the creation of Being and its re-orientation in onto-centric life the original logos is self-eclipsed, deformed and disoriented from holistic life.

In losing its true orientation from Logos, from Divine unity, it loses its holistic Self-unity and falls into pathological forms of life and meaning. Its inner monadic narrative is inherently fictional since it is cut off from its holistic voice and form of life. In gaining a certain form of consciousness it loses holistic awareness, and the ever-present holistic voice becomes its un-conscious. It loses its original symbolic form of metaphoric or holistic meaning and now lives in the faith of its own *self-unity*; having lost the true holistic unity of the Continuum its inner drive or life force is to *be a unity* unto itself. It recreates itself in its own image and constructs its own form of life which it calls *reality*. It takes itself to be a self-unity but, of course, there is no real unity in its form of life. And as it follows its own form of life eclipsed from Divine form, its unconscious holistic voice haunts it, continues to nourish this alienated ontos, and remains ever-present to it. And though this ontos has a will of its own, a name of its own, a voice of its own, and its own form of life, it remains lodged in the ever-present Continuum that harkens it back to its true roots. In the presence of this all encompassing Continuum which is its unconscious home the ontos clings to dear life and clutches at its self-unity which is its very existence. This presumed self-unity or uni-vocity is fictional for we have seen that the *voice of ontos* and the *voice of logos* are now self-alienated and bifurcated into conscious and pre-conscious: voice is now inherently equi-vocal and the speech life of the individuated voice remains in a hidden original ambiguity. Its life is self-divided, dualized, its meaning is fragmented and its rationality is self-divided. This individuated voice, in its misguided faith in its self-unity replicates its equivocity in all directions.

i) The Particularistic Mind and Its Fictional Self-Unity

Our meditation on divine form has revealed that absolute infinite unity is the Life and Light of the Continuum. And in our holistic narrative of the origin of the life of self-identity, we find that though its deepest faith is in its own unity it lives a life of inner dis-unity. Let us move more deeply into the inner (monadic) self-consciousness of the particularistic mind. Let us follow its inner phenomenology and sense of itself and its universe. Here we find that at its foundations its assumed self-unity is the absolute condition and central reference of all its experience and meaning. In pseudo-imitation of divine form its presumed self-identity and unity becomes the *a priori* condition of all its life— the absolute condition of its reason and meaning and experience. Let us call this the *univocity condition*6 of the life of self-identity: it is the condition that it is a unified voice and that its speech is univocal in meaning. If its univocity condition fails, if its voice is not an original absolute self-unity, then it lives in bad faith and all its speech life, all its rationality and meaning is without determinacy.

And, of course, our meditation on self-existence and self-identity as the absolute condition of the rational life of the individuated voice or particularistic mind reveals that its presumed identity is empty and that the individuated voice in fact lives in original indeterminacy of meaning. Its presumption or faith that it speaks in a unified and determinate voice is found in the holistic narrative to be its fatal error.

In moving further into the self-reference and narrative of this individuated voice it is critical for us to see that the form of self-identity is the absolute condition and central point of unifying reference for all its life. This point deserves further elaboration. The mind of identity takes itself to have identity, to be an integral, unified, continuously existing entity of some sort. As such, it takes itself to be differentiated and discriminated from other entities and from the world which surrounds it. Further, this existential mind takes itself to be self-contained and independently existing, so in some sense it is whole and complete in itself. In being separate and differentiated from other entities in the world the mind of identity recognizes itself as having its unique qualities and history which individuates it from everything else in the world. The existential mind is unique, differentiated and individuated; it is the central and primary reference point in its world and can refer to itself uniquely as "I." As long as it thinks and reflects it takes itself to be independently existing and its self-existence conditions all of its thinking and experience— its self-unity is an absolute condition of its life. This is its form of life. So the mind of identity must be approached in the first-person voice, in self-reference as a thinking subject. And since all its conscious life is conditioned by the "I exist," by self-identity, it is essential for us to meditate further on the form of self-identity. If the form of identity turns out to be empty or problematic, then all the life of the individuated "I" is likewise empty. We already have the hint here that the alleged absolute self-unity of the "I" has eclipsed the holistic unity of divine form.

We have already seen in Chapter 4 Section 1 a meditative argument showing the indeterminacy of naive identity. The meditative argument invokes the unitive power of the non-dual Unified Field to show that the mind of identity can never in its own terms establish any self-existent identity. We have seen that if we focus on any alleged object, term, sign, identity, etc., it is found to be inherently dependent on *what-it-is-not* for its differentiated status and is hence *not* self-existent. Further, we have seen that the very "givenness" of any purported entity (of any kind) inherently depends upon the thinker— the voice, mind, grammar-field— of the one who perceives or thinks the sign. Furthermore, we showed that the polar or alterity structure of any alleged identity calls for some additional unifying function to keep the polarity in existential unitive connection, and that any such transcendental unifying term will itself reiterate this same self-polarization, *ad infinitum*.

This meditative argument in effect shows that the *practice* of the mind of identity, in its objectification structure, violates and eclipses the unifying function of Relativity (of the Unified Field), which is the ground of all relations and all unity. This is why within the paradigm of absolute identity no unity, relationality or self-identity can be found. There can be no "entity-in-itself" apart from the Principle of Universal Relativity— apart from its being constitutively situated in the non-dual Unified Field or Continuum of Logos. So the transcendental force of the meditative argument for radical indeterminacy of identity brings out this feature of Natural Reason— that no entity, object, individual, identity, relationality, can ever be established within the strict terms of identity and the practice of objectification. The meditative argument shows that insofar as there is unique differentiation, individuation, self-identity and unity for any term, sign, consent, thing, etc., it must come from the Universal Domain of Relativity— from the Continuum of Logos.

ii) Voice and Grammar: Indeterminacy of Reality
The individuated voice lives in a world with assumed determinacy— determinacy in its own identity, in the existence of things and in meaning and rationality. This is the essence of its faith in absolute identity. But since the individuated voice is inherently indeterminate its world and form of life is likewise indeterminate. For voice and world mirror one another. This mirror is *grammar*. Grammar is the form of life which shapes all meaning and conditions all existence. It makes possible my self-interpretation as well as the interpretation of the world. It is the rational form of reality. So there is a one-to-one isomorphism and assumed

identity (identification) between Voice and Grammar; and here we find that the indeterminacy of voice is mirrored in the indeterminacy of grammar as well, so reality— both self and world— is ontologically indeterminate.

Let us first clarify the depth of the I/Field duality. In one voice the ontological mind takes itself to be living in a *universe* which is an all encompassing field of reality as a whole. To exist is to be in the universal field— the cosmos. From the ontological point of view the unity or univocity requirement clearly holds for the structure of the universe as a whole— a continuous unified integral field.

But there is an ambiguity of voice in the ontological mind as to the locus of the transcendental point of unity of the Universe. For in one sense the Universe is taken to be independent of me and to have its independent absolute existence apart from me. But at the same time it is clear that I could not *think* something that was not present to me and my mind, and in this sense I supply a unifying point of recurrence for the universal field as a whole. Here again we find some version of the paradox of unity (identity)— the unity of the universe is independent of me, but at the same time it is dependent on me.

It appears that there is a self-transcending point of unity in the mind that can take the place of any possible locus in the universe— there is a universal point of reference in mind that is variable and can take (or identify with) any place. Earlier we called this point "/I/." So we may distinguish between this self-transcending presence in me (my higher voice) and all that is presented to me (world-field).   This /I/ is prior to the individuated mind; it is that to which all else is present or presented but which can never be made into an object in the field. On the other hand, the *I* (mind) as an object in the universe (the one we call the subject) is constitutively part of the universal field presented to /I/.

Thus, it appears that the unifying point for the world-field transcends the universal field, and the unifying point of I transcends the I; each needs its unifying point, but it may well turn out that the unifying point for field and I are one and the same. There is indeterminacy and ambiguity here, which is to be expected.

a. The Primacy of Ontological Grammar. Having explored inherent ambiguity in the "I" and the "field" and in the relation between I/field, we may proceed further with the explanation of ontological grammar.

We have now seen that it is the form of absolute identity itself that requires a paradoxical bifurcation of the mind of the thinker from the universal field that is the context of the object of thought— the subject from the object.   And it is absolute identity that at the same time requires the absolute unity condition of the universe. It is the very form of identity that necessitates the commitment to the universe as an absolute self-existent reality.   So ontological absolutism (the faith that there is an absolute independently existing universe) has its origin in absolute identity.

Now the ontological notion of the world or universe is an all— encompassing unity or whole which is exhaustive of all possible reality.   The universe is that *universal*, absolute, unifying whole that includes both the thinking subject and the world-field that is presented to the subject— the realm of all possible phenomena. Absolute identity structures the universe into a comprehensive, complete and supposedly consistent totality. Nothing could possibly exist "outside" the universe: to be is to be in the universe. And to be an object is to be in the universal field.

Here, too, we find that the form of absolute identity governs the universal field of the universe, for the things that make up the universe have determinacy, particularity, identity. The universal field presents itself as a specified world— having definite content. But it is not at all obvious that absolute identity dictates the form and content of a world.

To see this it would be helpful to make an explicit connection between logic and ontology. While logic is a formal science which investigates the form of thought— logical form, ontology is a formal science which explores the form of existence— ontological form. But logical form and ontological form mirror each other, both sharing the common form of absolute identity.

Our meditation on identity shows that the self-dualizing dynamic in the form of self identity is the source of all the pathologies of life. The fall out of the self-splitting and fragmentation of voice and life moves in every possible direction. In my inner indeterminacy of existence and identity I suffer due to fragmentation of my voice into incommensurable identities. So my inner voice-life is fragmented into multiple voices and the absence of a unifying voice leaves me in a disintegrated form with no real integrity of life of voice.

I find myself inhabiting multiple grammars, living in diverse universes of discourse, and these forms of life are likewise incommensurable in the absence of a true unifying principle. So my inner and outer worlds are lodged in multiplicity with no coherence. I live under multiple realities each with their absolute divine principles.

In another dimension I find the dualizing influence splitting into opposition and polarization what the Continuum reveals as holistically One: my life divides into mental and physical, holistic meaning is divided into thought, meaning and being; there is division between word and object, between meaning and existence, between thought and action, between myself and others, and so on.

More deeply, in the very form of my existence I find in the self division of identity a self separation that leaves me incomplete and unfulfilled. So my life is lodged in desire and privation which motivates my strivings and actions. But there remains a deep emptiness and incompleteness at the heart of my existence.

iii) *Voice, Grammar and "Theology": Unity, Infinity and Divinity*

Our meditation on the form of absolute identity as the foundation of all meaning and existence in the existential mind has shown that in the deep structure of the self or voice or of its grammar there is a necessary condition of unity or univocity; it is an absolute requirement that voice be a unity and that a grammar-world be a unity as well. It is this transcendental unity condition inherent in self and grammar that is the origin of meaning and rationality. Here we find the key to the divine form as interpreted by any grammar— every grammar has its divine form which is its absolute condition, the foundation of all meaning and being. It is for this reason that any form of life of the existential voice is in some religious mode, in some faith. To live is to be grammatical, and the divine form of any grammar governs and conditions all life. In this sense, all life is intrinsically religious, for to be committed to a form of life, a form of meaning is to live in a faith.

I may live in a grammar as my faith without explicitly engaging in worship, which is recognition of the absolute principle that governs my form of life. And I become explicitly "theological" when I engage in openly articulating the form of my faith (grammar) and the divine principle that absolutely conditions it. In this sense divinity is intrinsic to any grammar, and every grammar is a form of faith.7

In making this explicit we now see how incommensurability of realities (grammars) implies a deep incoherence in theology: if each grammar has its divine form which is its infinite absolute unifying condition, and if grammars are in some deep sense incommensurable, how can there be a multiplicity of infinite absolutes? It would seem that in the very meaning of *infinite* and absolute there could not be a radical diversity of divine forms. How can there be irreducible diversity here? How can there be pluralism of infinite absolutes? Is it not rationally required that the infinite absolute be an absolute unity? Can the true divine form be multiple? Can we suppose a transcendent unity of divine principles? But we have already seen that this upward gesture to a higher unifying principle (required by the form of identity) does not work. It only pushes back the problem of true unity. These are some of the problems of theology that emerge from the very form of self identity. In a way it may be said that diverse theologies have been governed by the dynamics of self-identity and suffer all of the pathologies of meaning and life found in the very heart of the existential voice and egological paradigm.

III Universal Theology: Beyond Pathology and the Radical Return to Roots

We began with meditation on Divine Form and discerned the Universal Unified Field of the Continuum— Divine Infinite Unity. We then entered into the inner form of the particularistic or existential mind to experience its inner fragmentation and pathology of life. We saw that the monadic voice of the individuated self names itself as an ontos, as a being with identity, and in this breaks off from the holistic continuum in search of its own absolute unity. In its ontocentric form of life it self-divides and loses touch with its true inner form which remains in holistic unity with the Continuum. This self-split in voice (equi-vocity) in its form of life involves a disorientation from its true center in Logos. We find in the very form of absolute identity the source of all pathology of meaning and Life, a pathology of self-splitting which is the opposite of true unity. Let us now follow the inner logic of this meditation and explore the nature and possibility of the salvation and liberation from this inherent condition of hermeneutical sin. So we now continue our holistic narrative having seen through the fictional narrative of the individuated voice. The individuated voice inherently lives in self-deception and is not able to discern deeply enough its own pathological condition; it takes the higher holistic voice to clearly discern the self-eclipsed source of its pathological condition. We are now in a position to explore the dynamics of liberation, the self-expansion of the form of life of the particularistic mind to its true inner logos. Thus, our holistic narrative will trace the return to holistic roots and the true unity of the Continuum that blows away the pathological dis-unities that inhere in the fixated life of the ontocentric voice.

Self-Univocation: Discerning the Dialogical Voice as Essence of Religious Life

Having seen the universal form of pathology let us now re-center ourselves in holistic voice and continue our meditation on divine form— the Continuum. Having seen the origin of duality and dis-unity let us focus our attention on holistic unity and concern ourselves with the self-conversion from fixation of voice and objectification to freedom of speech and liberation of meaning.

Let us use the word "Christ" for the Holistic Voice in its appearance as the mediating principle that opens up the fixated mind to divine form. This Universal Christ form is the living logos that opens the closed particularistic voice into its true inner form, to its self-unity, to its true inner self-universalization. This is the universal dialogical voice that mediates the split between ontos and Logos, between the form of identity and the holistic form of universal relativity. This dialogical voice is the healing voice that brings liberation from the perpetual strife, confusion, suffering, irrationality and hermeneutical death of the pathological mind. It is the self-univocating principle that brings true life and living truth by opening the way to the Universal Light of the Continuum. This Christ-voice is the living principle of universal relativity. As the universal mediating logos, it is the meeting point at which all possible dualities and splits are joined. This universal dialogical principle may be found to live and speak in any logos or grammar where the holistic voice speaks. One may find it in teachings of Jesus, in the speech of Krishna, in the discourses of Buddha.

For we now see that any logos, any form of life, any grammar in the egological paradigm, is lodged in self-eclipsed indeterminacy of meaning, in original hidden ambiguity. When taken in the particularistic voice, it is a fixated inert sign; but when taken in the holistic voice, it is a living holistic symbol reflecting the Continuum. And it is the true dialogical voice that is the universal meeting point which brings salvation and liberation of meaning and life.

The dialogical principle, the living principle of universal relativity, is that universal mediator that turns the death of meaning into true life— the resurrection of fixated voice. This logos of the Continuum is the universal meeting point that univocates all opposition and reverses the perpetual fallout of self-splitting that comes with the eclipse of divine form.

How does the fixated voice become awakened to holistic life? What is the dialogical process of self-awakening that brings the fixated form of life to its inner universal form? How is the holistic voice and mind awakened to its higher form? This is the process of inner dialogical speech in which the fixated voice enters conversation with its inner logos.

Let us reflect on this dialogical process. The awakening of true inner dialogue, self-univocation, comes with the recognition of the reality of *indeterminacy*— the opening which can be both a blessing and a curse. The recognition of indeterminacy, that ontos is not inherently wedded to its fixated form of life and voice, is what brings the freedom of speech that transforms the fixated sign into the living symbol. Indeterminacy is the interface between identity and relativity, between fixity and liberation of meaning. It is the opening, the pivot that is the perpetual possibility of the fixated voice turning itself around (self-conversion) and re-centering in the living continuum which is its true inner form. This is the very possibility of its hermeneutical freedom and detachment from rational enslavement. It is in indeterminacy that the possibility of salvation and self-univocation is found. And it is the awareness of indeterminacy, that voice is not fixated to its particularized form of life, that initiates the dialogical self-transformation to holistic unity. Indeterminacy is the opening from which the light of the Continuum is found to be present; it is the forum in which inner dialogue or self-unification converses.

The recognition of indeterminacy initiates the holistic process of self-expansion, the dialogical process which is the very essence of reflexive Self-awareness— it is mediational form itself. This dialogical form, once initiated, is without beginning or end; it is of cosmic proportions. For once the holistic voice is awakened the dialogical process of self-unification and self-univocation with Continuum resonates throughout the Continuum. The life of universal relativity— true life— is the perpetual celebration of the infinite self-expansion of form; it is being in touch with Logos. So meditational self-univocation is the living dialogical process which is the reflexive life of true consciousness. The universal form of religious life is the life of dialogical self-unity. It is in the temple of holistic dialogue that true worship and divine celebration can spontaneously arise. The dialogical voice is, of course, not subject to the will and command of the particularized voice, it is rather a gift of grace. It is a higher voice that always remains higher and perpetually calls us to our roots. So dialogue is the universal meeting place in which all possible oppositions or dualities are reconciled in peace.

i) Holistic (Dialogical) Unity and the Univocation of all Opposition
Let us reflect further on the awakening of the holistic voice within, and on the dialogical process of self-expansion which is the essence of all religious life. It is in the dialogical process that the fixated particularized voice begins to awaken to a deeper awareness of its true inner universal form, its universal Christ voice within. This self-universalization is experienced as the mediation of opposition as the fixated voice opens up in dialogue with Continuum.

We have seen that the origin of all dualism is in the fixation of form, the fixation of voice which is inherent in the faith of the particularistic mind. Our meditation now makes clear that the fictional and partial narrative of the fixated voice, though eclipsed from the holistic narrative, lives in primordial equivocity and indeterminacy. In this indeterminacy the holistic narrative rules and governs every logos and has supreme jurisdiction over every form of life. The internal agenda of the fixated voice is always over-ruled by the divine agenda as manifested in the holistic narrative. This is another version of the Continuum hypothesis— that every possible logos inherently reflects divine form and has the Continuum as its true origin and rational principle.

This helps to explain the phenomenology of the dialogical awakening as the fixated voice opens up to its inner universal meaning. We now see that life is situated in indeterminacy and the artificial narrative of the fixated voice is over-ruled by the narrative of the holistic voice. The history of the evolution of human consciousness may be explained in this context. For the holistic mind sees that the particularistic mind has evolved through its spontaneous breakthrough into its pre-conscious Continuum— all advances in rational understanding, all revelation and deeper insight into truth, all advances in knowledge and religious life have been the lightening of the Continuum breaking through the closure of the fixated mind. We now see that the great philosophical, religious, scientific, poetic and artistic strokes of genius which have advanced human forms of life have been the breakthrough of the closed mind into the open space of the divine Continuum— they have been flashes of divine form, revelations of divine unity, dialogical moments of cosmic insight.

The gifted voices that were able to discern the holistic Continuum and have a flash of deeper unity translated their vision into grammars of new and higher forms of life. And this evolution of higher life is always measured by the degree to which the Continuum is discerned and the comprehensiveness and completeness of the narrative. The speaking forth of deeper grammars was always of course lodged in the original indeterminacy which left them open to multiple interpretations and mis-interpretation. When the dialogical voices attempted to give form to their insight into Continuum by articulating this insight in terms that the fixated voice might understand, there was and has been an inevitable mis-translation of the insight and a mis-reading of the holistic hermeneutic. Often the blessed seer-poets who had flashes into holistic life and dialogical unity themselves failed to discern the holistic voice or appeared to speak in the jargon of the egological paradigm and hence mis-spoke their own flash of insight. And here the holistic narrative sees that the cosmic evolution of the divine narrative, the divine agenda, is precisely the coming forth of the holistic voice and the self-articulation of the holistic life. The meditative mind can see that the divine agenda of self-evolution is the manifestation of the Continuum in ever deeper self-univocation. The divine agenda as discerned in holistic history is the evolution of holistic life which is the universal form of life inherent at the heart of every logos. This is the self-realization of holistic prophesy and divine will—the dialogical self-expansion of holistic life.

So it is in the in-betweenness of indeterminacy that the ultimate dialogical encounter takes place— between the fixated voice and the holistic voice, between the principle of identity and the living principle of universal relativity. We see that fixation can take place at any stage or level of holistic evolution, and where fixation of form takes place there is always the higher voice which speaks from a deeper intimacy with Continuum, calling the lower voice to a new and higher life. The higher voice always threatens the independent being of the lower form of life and, indeed, the dynamics of dialogue requires that the lower form be consumed by the Light and is the fuel which releases rational energy for re-birth into a higher form. This process of holistic self-expansion is the process of hermeneutical death and re-birth into every higher life. It is in the meeting place of the dialogical Christ-voice that there is a surrender of old fixated life and the resurrection into a higher form of self-unity.

Wherever this dialogical self-expansion arises, at any stage of cosmic evolution of form, there is the experience of an expansion of meaning— as the fixated voice opens up into holistic space, in awareness of the indeterminacy of meanings, it experiences deeper analogical unities between all things. As the holistic mind comes forth, any fixated sign blossoms into symbolic universalization, as we saw earlier with examples of "water" and "air" and "bread." The meditative imagination can perceive intrinsic unities and synonymies of meaning which the fixated literalist mind cannot see. Most of all, in dialogical self-expansion, the analogical mind sees clearly that "I" am not fixated in sense and reference, but gestures to the open Continuum in which "I" can discern my true meaning in any name and form— in any logos. As the holistic mind comes forth and the analogical imagination is released, there is a simultaneous univocation in all directions arising co-dependently. The primordial split in my voice between I and Field begins to evaporate, and with this healing there arises a deeper self-integrity in which my previously fixated voice as *ontos* finds dialogical unity with its deeper form— *logos*. This univocation of voice in dialogical form reverses the pathological process that created the recursive fall-out of dualism and fragmentation in every direction. Thus, it is this very dialogical self-expansion and self-integration that is the essence of rational life and the universal form of religious awakening.

Realizing, then, that the fixated voice presents a distorted narrative of itself, and seeing clearly that the holistic narrative rules in all hermeneutical matters, let us focus meditative attention on the holistic hermeneutic and elaborate on the dialogical principle which is the meeting point of all possible oppositions.

We have now discerned the universal form of dialogue as self-univocation. And we have seen that the dialogical voice is the universal mediating principle that reveals the non-duality of any opposition. It is now clear that all oppositions or dualisms arise in the very form of identity which is the origin of pathological life. What the voice of identity sees as absolute distinctions or oppositions, the holistic voice univocates in a higher mediating principle: this is another law of holistic hermeneutics. The particularistic mind encounters oppositions and strife in every direction and these are seen as absolute and irreducible. But the higher dialogical voice sees through these artificial oppositions and finds a deeper univocation which places the polar splits into the context of the Continuum where they are more clearly seen to be relative and constructed division.

Thus, we saw earlier in meditating on the universal origin of pathology of life that the following splits arise in the life of identity: between unity and diversity, between I and field, between real and unreal, between finite and infinite, between particular and universal, between intra-personal life and inter-personal life, between sign and symbol, between meaning and existence, between good and evil, between sacred and secular, between faith and reason, between religion and science, between meaning and truth, between word and object, between mind and body, between absolutism and relativism, etc. These primary oppositions are the result of the faith of identity. And these are just some obvious samples that fragments life from holistic unity. In what is conventionally called "theology" we find recurrent polarizations between theism/atheism, mono-theism/poly-theism, transcendence and immanence, affirmative theology and negative theology, and so on. These polarizations are the workings of the inner self-division of the voice of identity itself. And they have as much validity as this fragmented voice does.8

So let us select some sample polarizations which appear absolute and place them in the unity of Continuum which brings out their true import.

1. Of special interest is the problem of "evil" and the division between good and evil; the mind of identity sees here an absolute distinction but the holistic mind sees a Continuum which relativizes these poles. For the life of fixation itself is the source of holistic "evil"— the origin of hermeneutical sin and suffering. It is the fixations of voice and the eclipse of divine form that is the universal form of "evil," and the distinction within that form of life between good and evil are seen to be both sharing in the common pathology of fixation of form and life. In this self-divided life the voice of "good" divorces itself from what it takes to be "evil" and the problem of evil is spawned from this self-division. There is a breakdown of conversation and dialogue between these poles and a pathological alienation arises which is all projected on "evil" as the cause. But the holistic voice sees through these divisive dynamics and reinterprets the distinction in the light of the Continuum. Here the Continuum hypothesis that every logos is Logos enables us to see that even in "evil voices" the Logos must be present and ruling. Thus, there is a profound re-interpretation of "evil" and the judgmental narrative of the self-designated "good" one is corrected. Now we see that in being self-righteous and alienating itself from its polar opposite— "evil"— the "good one" fixates the "evil one" in its absolute judgment and thereby violates both itself and the other. And here we see the holistic imperative: *judge*

not; for it is this very act of self-righteous judgment that participates in the universal form of evil which is always the eclipse of divine form, dialogical unity.

On the other hand, the holistic voice looks more deeply into the form of life of the "evil" polar voice and sees its garbled attempt to express its intrinsic divine hypothesis. Since it is a logos, however distorted, it participates in hermeneutical form, in the structure of meaning, and as a form of life it somehow strives to universalize itself and find its ultimate expression of unity. If we take any case of what is more conventionally called "evil," as in an "evil" life— we shall find in the holistic reading a more comprehensive narrative which brings out all the significance implicit in the confused and garbled voice. It may be said that any corrupted voice still thinks it is doing what is best and highest for itself. In its monadic orientation, which is its source of pathology, it self-articulates a form of life with its highest principle of meaning (divine hypothesis) which rules and directs this life. Even a pathological life, operating to direct itself by its own will in the darkness of the eclipse of divine form, speaks a "logos" that orients its meaning and priorities. Within this artificial monadic space of its voice it expresses its religious zeal with devastating consequences to itself and others. But when the polar voice which takes itself to be "good" judges and condemns its opposite, it here falls from Continuum and participates in the origin of holistic evil, with devastating consequences to itself and others.

Thus, we see that the problem of evil originates in the eclipse of divine form and the dialogical Christ voice which would mediate all opposition and strife. When dialogue fails, evil runs rampant and there is both self-violation and violation of the other. And, of course, the holistic reading of human history readily sees this failure as the source of strife and wars and self-destruction. Here the holistic voice calls for a higher covenant with Logos, it calls for a deeper ethics of dialogue wherein the split voice achieves deeper integrity in dialogical self unity. Dialogical or Holistic Ethics is a matter of integrity of voice, and it is the self-univocated voice which can be more profoundly good.

2. But let us take a dialogical look at another pervasive polarization— finite and infinite: Here again we see that the mind of identity creates an ultimate or absolute split between finite and infinite, and we find typical versions of this in "theism." More generally, the voice of identity is committed to a faith in particularity and "historicity" which it takes to be

an ultimate truth. One version of this particularism or finitism is that persons are absolutely finite, self-existent and determinate, on the one hand, while God (divine hypothesis) is infinite, universal and absolutely Other. This polarizing voice does not, of course, detect that this ultimate faith in finitude and fixity is the projection of its form of life— its faith in absolute identity. So the holistic voice places this polarity in the context of the Continuum and brings out its deeper self-eclipsed insight. In the holistic narrative the polarization of finite/infinite (particular/universal) is seen to be mediated in dialogical form (Christ form) and the duality is relativized and placed in deeper conversation. The question is not whether finitude or particularity is given up in Continuum; it is rather that we come to a deeper more faithful understanding of the meaning of finitude and particularity. The holistic voice respects particularity precisely by placing it in the mediating light of Continuum and recovering the universal divine form at the heart of any given finitized or particularized logos.

Thus, here, too, we find that the voice of identity violates holistic finitude and particularity of any logos— in its self-interpretation it eclipses the higher holistic (Christ) voice within which is its true essential form, and which is the true source of its divine worth and nobility. In its mistaken understanding of particularity it violates itself which leads to violation of others. So, again we see that it is the holistic voice that discerns the dialogical mediation which brings self-integrity and opens the way for a deeper form of religious life. In discerning the intrinsic dialogical form that lives in the heart of every logos and which is the essence of its particularity it shows the ultimate respect and honoring of holistic finitude.

3. Still another area of recursive polarization is found in the vast range of logos called "theologies." We have seen that in holistic hermeneutic every logos is Logos and hence implies a religious form of life and, of course, a "theology." This cuts across the artificial duality between "religious" and "non-religious" life, between sacred and secular. And just as in the case of "evil" and "finite" the holistic narrative places all "theologies" in the context of the Continuum and draws out the truth implicit in their logos. Thus, in the polarization between theist/atheist, for example, we do not find an absolute irreconcilable split where one must be true and the other false. Rather, when placed in dialogical form we find that the divine hypothesis of theism does reflect an important holistic truth— namely, that the Absolute Logos is the form of all possible forms, the source of all meaning and being, infinitely higher than any logos, the infinite Presence that illumines all things, etc. The deeper holistic intent of theism is its fidelity

to divine form. But the atheist, in speaking a polar "theology" is committed to a form of life which, since it mistakes the opposing "theist" voice to be speaking in a closed, absolute, exclusivist voice and takes strong exception to its literalist and fundamentalist faith, believes itself to be in good faith and moving to a higher truth when it declares that "there is no God." This contrary theology, of course, has its ultimate faith and divine hypothesis, and both the theist and atheist share a common faith in absolute identity which governs their religious life. The negative theological voice of the "atheist" is in *its* divine hypothesis attempting to be faithful to its implicit holistic insight that the particularized voice will always violate holistic divine form in its theistic fundamentalism; so it attempts to be true to divine form by negating the literalism of the theist theology with a polar faith.

Again, we can find the same pattern in the polarities of monotheism and polytheism. Each has its garbled holistic flash of insight. The great advance in religious life with monotheism is the recognition that divine form is Absolute Unity which immediately requires that "God is One"; so the implicit holistic insight here is in discerning more deeply Divine Form and coming closer to Holistic Unity— the Continuum. By contrast, the polar theology of poly-theism is another holistic flash of insight which sees that every logos is Logos— the divine form lives in every logos. And in attempting to be faithful to this holistic revelation, it counters the monotheism which it reads in a literalist and exclusivist light. So the polarization of transcendent/immanent emerges in a non-negotiable split and in this there is eclipse of dialogical form.

Similarly, we can see in "negative theology" an holistic insight that flashes into the holistic narrative. For this polarized voice of theology presents its divine hypothesis as a radical critique of all "affirmative" theologies which share the common hermeneutical faith of literalism and belief that the Divine Form may be described and predicated in literalist discourse. Against this pathology the contrary voice of negative theology attempts to be more faithful to Divine Form in confessing that there can be no predication of Divine Form— no literal discourse can truly approach the Continuum and no fundamentalist voice can be faithful to the living Logos. And so on. We could go on in this way to mediate the diverse pathological polarities throughout the life of identity (absolutism).

Finally, we begin to see the artificiality of the absolutist constructions of sacred/secular, faith/reason, religion/science and so on. Here, too, we find the dialogical voice blowing away these polarities and discerning the non-dual Continuum that negotiates them in deeper unity. We have seen that in holistic hermeneutic every logos has its divine hypothesis and is practically and potentially a religious form of life. So, in any grammar or ideology we may discern its religious form and implicit theology. In the separation of Church and State, for example, the holistic voice sees that the democratic ideology or grammar is a theogram with its unifying principle and ultimate faith. What we have seen then is a competition and strife between two competing religious forms of life. And so, too, with the split between religion and science: it should be clear that the diverse scientific grammars are structures of meaning and praxis which attempt to discern highest truth and in this way are divine hypotheses which flash into the Continuum. Science, too, may be lived in a fundamentalist voice and literalist mind, or it may open up to holistic hermeneutic like any conventional "theology." Thus, we see the artificiality of the duality between faith and reason. The dialogical voice discerns that pure faith and pure reason are one and the same in the light of Continuum.9

ii) Dialogical Unity and Holistic Religious Life

Our meditation on dialogical form has helped us to see more clearly the nature of the self-expansion as the self-unification of dialogical life. We now see that the universal form of religious life is the overcoming of egological objectivication and the fixity of voice and the literalism of life. It is the self-conversion in dialogue to holistic unity that reveals the deep structure of religious life in all its dimensions. And in this holistic context we can see the universal meaning of such religious "concepts" as sin, suffering, conversion, death, resurrection, immortality, and liberation. We have seen that in the holistic hermeneutic "sin" is the pathology of the fixation of voice and meaning that eclipses divine form— sin is separation from Divinity. We see in the self-fixity of absolute identity, too, the origins of human suffering and strife. We discern that the human "existential" condition is the condition of the life of self-identity (identity is existential life); and we see that death is the hermeneutical death of meaning— the fixity of the word (logos) which renders it inert. Here, we see that the life of sin is hermeneutical death— the death of "god." The holistic voice also discloses the universal form of religious "conversion"— it is always *self-conversion* in dialogical self-univocation. Conversion is the self-unification that comes with dialogical life. It is in this self-realization that we find the true import of spiritual re-birth, resurrection (the re-birth of the mortified logos) and liberation. It is in the detachment from the fixity of the word that hermeneutical liberation comes, and with this arises the human freedom of speech which is the essence of happiness, peace, and immortality. For the holistic life is without beginning or end and at perfect peace with Divine Form.

In this Universal Light we may readily see the essence of religious phenomena— worship, ritual, prayer, sacrifice. The holistic narrative discerns that the true reading of scripture must be in the holistic voice. For the literalist reading inherently violates the Word and eclipses divine form. Worship is found to be dialogical univocation with Continuum— the authentic living conversation between logos and Logos. All ritual is designed to deepen this dialogical self-unity and prayer can take place in the sacred space of dialogical form— the Christ voice. Religious meaning must be essentially symbolic and dialogical, as must religious Truth be holistic.

We may now see more clearly that in approaching any authentic scripture we must advance with due respect for the Word and with appropriate honoring of our particularity in holistic voice. Whether we read the voice of Jesus, Buddha, or Krishna, the essential prerequisite is to approach the living Word with dialogical openness and hermeneutical humility. If we discern the life and speech of Jesus/Christ with fixated voice and literalistic mind, we do violence to the Living Word of the Holistic Christ. The Universal Christ voice— the universal mediating, dialogical form— is never exclusivist or absolutist or relativist. It essentially speaks beyond the hermeneutical pathologies of dualism and divisiveness. In the holistic narrative we see that in every speech-act, in every teaching, in every breath the Holistic Christ calls us to our true roots in divine form. In the new covenant we see demonstrated that "bread" is the living body of Christ; and "wine" is the living blood. The new Covenant is a new form of speech life, the opening of a new holistic voice that brings us deeper to unity with Logos. All the miracles performed by the Lord were holistic demonstrations that enacted the resurrection of the word— from ontos to logos/Logos. And when we read the speech of the Buddha, we violate the Holistic Buddha voice if we approach it with closed egological mind and literalist faith. Every speech act of the Buddha showed the way to liberation from the fixity and bondage of the life of identity, towards holistic life. And similarly with the speech and life of Lord Krishna— his hermeneutical instruction in the meditative self-transformation of life is precisely the dialogical self-conversion from an ontocentric life to a life centered in divine form, the Continuum, Atmo-centric life. And so on with any form of the divine Word.

iii) *Dialogical Unity of Religions*

We may now conclude with meditation on the question of the unity of religions. We have discerned the universal form of dialogue and of religious life. We have developed the holistic hermeneutic of dialogical speech and seen how pernicious polarizations are renegotiated in the higher voice. So, too, with the question of the unity of religions. We are now in a position to see that the problem of unity/diversity formulated in the voice of identity is ill-formed in every sense— it is in bad form. For the universal unity of any logos (any religious form of life) is Logos--the divine Continuum. And this Unity is not a "transcendent" unity, nor is it "immanent." We have found a higher principle of unity— dialogical unity, holistic unity, which cannot become ensnared in the polarizations and dualities born of fixated voice. In dialogical form the artificial split between internal (intra-personal) life and external (inter-personal) is reconciled in holistic life. And true dialogue— whether the internal self-conversion of voice or the external conversation between diverse logos, makes clear the universal origin of all forms of life.

The dialogical life is the religious celebration of the divine form in every logos, and this celebration is the essence of love— the communion between self and other in dialogue. In this communion (dialogical unity) is found the essence of compassion and liberation. So, it is here that we see the form of ethical life— dialogical ethics. This univocation of self and other is the meaning of respect: it takes us to a higher form of life in which being true to our own particularity we need not violate the particularity of the other; we no longer need to speak an exclusivist voice that reduces the logos of the other to my particularity. Rather, in dialogical unity we find the open space in which each logos may celebrate its universal form and discern it in the logos of the other. The holistic conservative/orthodox is the voice which, in being faithful and true to its own inner universal logos sees that he or she must likewise preserve and enhance the divine form in the logos of the other, as his own. For the Universal Word is seen to be the true meaning of every logos.

REFERENCES

The following papers by the author are referred to in the essay and footnotes. The footnotes refer to the papers by their numbers.

1. "Formal Ontology and Movement Between Worlds"— *Philosophy East and West*, April 1976, Vol. 26, #2.

2. "Formal Ontology and the Dialectical Transformation of Consciosness" *Philosophy East and West*, 29, No. 1, Janurary 1979.

3. "Nagarjuna, Aristotle and Frege on the Nature of Thought" in *Buddhist and Western Philosophy*, ed. Nathan Katz, Sterling Publishers, New Delhi.

4. "Comparative Ontology and the Interpretation of 'Karma'"— *Indian Philosophical Quarterly*, Vol. 6, #2, January 1979.

5. "Comparative Ontology: Relative and Absolute Truth"— *Philosophy East and West*, January 1981.

6. "Ontological Relativity— A Metaphysical Critique of Einstein's Thought"- In Einstein and the Humanities, (ed.) Dennis P. Ryan, Greenwood Press (Westport, CT) 1987.

7. "The Ontological Relativity of Religious Meaning and Truth"— *Indian Philosophical Quarterly*, October 1982, Poona, India.

8. "The Relevance of Indian Thought to the Evolution of World Philosophy" in *Indian Philosophy: Past and Future* ed. SS Rao and S. Puligandala, Motilal, New Delhi, 1982.

9. "Ontological Relativity and Spiritual Liberation"— presented to the Second Annual Conference of the International Association of Buddhist Studies, Nalanda, India (January 1980) and published in *Thought and Action* (Professor Barlingay Commemoration Volume) Poona, India, 1980.

10. "Madhyamika Dialectic and Holistic Psychotherapy" *Journal of Buddhist Philosophy*, Vol. 1, 1983. (See Chapter 9)

11. "A Hermeneutic for Inter-Cultural Religious Life" *Religious Studies*, University of Punjab, Patiala, India, November 1984.

12. "Meditative Reason and the Logic of Communication," in *Rationality in Thought and Action*, eds. M. Tamny and K.D. Irani - Greenwood Press (Westport, CT) 1986

13. "Meditation, Rationality and Universal Relativity: The Holistic Unity of Philosophy, Religion and Science"— presented at the East/West Philosophy Encounter, Max Meuller Bhavan, 1983. (See chapter 2.)

14. "Meditation, Metaphor and Meaning" in *Indian Philosophical Quarterly*, Vol. 15, #4 October 1988, Poona, India. (See chapter 9.)

15. "Universal Relativity and the Holistic Mind: Holistic Unity and the Fragmentation of Life," in *Man's Search for Meaning in a Fragmented Universe* ed. P. De Silva (Sri Lanka).

16. "Universal Relativity: Meditation, Mind and Matter" (See chapter 4.)

SELECTED BIBLIOGRAPHY

The following is a sample selection of works which are directly relevant to the range of hermeneutical issues raised in this essay. I have focused on the recent literature and, of course, many important works worthy of mention are not included in this sampling.

1. Abe, Masao - *Zen and Western Thought*, University of Hawaii Press (Honolulu, 1985).

2. Berger, Peter - *The Sacred Canopy*, Doubleday (New York, 1969).

3. Berger, Peter - ed. *The Other Side of God* - (A Polarity in World Religions) Anchor (New York, 1981).

4. Bernstein, Richard - *Beyond Objectivism and Relativism* (Science, Hermeneutics and Praxis) University of Pennsylvania Press (Philadelphia, 1983).

5. Cobb, John B. Jr. - *Beyond Dialogue* (Toward a Mutual Transformation of Christianity and Buddhism) Fortress Press (Philadelphia, 1983).

6. Dawe, D.G. & Carman, John B., eds. *Christian Faith in a Religiously Plural World*, Orbis Books (Maryknoll, NY, 1978).

7. Derrida, Jacques - *Of Grammatology* (tr. G.C. Spivak) Johns Hopkins (Baltimore, 1978).

8. Deutsch, Eliot - *On Truth: An Ontological Theory*, University of Hawaii Press (Honolulu, 1979).

9. Fingarette, H. - *The Self in Transformation* (*Psychoanalysis, Philosophy and The Life of Spirit*) Harper (New York, 1963).

10. Frei, Hans W. - *The Eclipse of Biblical Narrative* A Study in Eighteenth and Nineteenth Century Hermeneutics, Yale Press, New Haven, 1974.

11. Gadamer, Hans-Georg - *Truth and Method*, Seabury Press (New York 1975).

12. Hesse, Mary - *Revolutions and Reconstructions in the Philosophy of Science* - Harvester Press, (Brighton, Sussex,1980).

13. Hick, John - *Truth and Dialogue in World Religions* (Conflicting Truth Claims) Westminster Press (Philadelphia, 1974).

14. Hick, John - *God Has Many Names*, Westminster Press, Philadelphia, 1980).

15. Hick, J. & Hebblethwait, B. eds. - *Christianity and Other Religions* Fortress Press, Philadelphia, 1980.

16. Iida, Shotaro - *Reason and Emptiness* (A Study in Logic and Mysticism) The Hokuseido Press (Tokyo, 1980).

17. Kaufman, G. - *An Essay in Theological Method*, Scholars Press (Misulu, MT, 1975).

18. Kelsey, David - *The Uses of Scripture in Recent Theology*, Fortress Press (Philadelphia, 1975).

19. Kuhn, Thomas - *The Structure of Scientific Revolutions*, University of Chicago Press (Chicago, 1962).

20. Lakatos & Musgrave eds. *Criticism and the Growth of Knowledge*, Cambridge University Press, (New York, 1970).

21. Meiland, J.W. & Krausz, M. ed. - *Relativism* (Cognitive and Moral), University of Notre Dame Press (Notre Dame, 1982).

22. Neusner, Joseph ed. - *Christian Revelation and World Religions*. Brunes and Oates (London, 19).

23. Neville, R.C. - *The Tao and the Daimon* (Segments of a Religious Inquiry) (SUNY Press) - Albany, New York, 1982).

24. Nishitani, Keiji - *Religion and Nothingness*, University of California Press (Los Angeles, 1982).

25. Panikkar, R. - *The Inter-religious Dialogue*, Paulist Press (New York, 1978).

26. Panikkar, R. - *Myth Faith & Hermeneutics*, Paulist Press (New York, 1979).

27. Ricoeur, Paul - *Interpretation Theory* (Discourse and the Surplus of Meaning) Texas Christian University Press (Fort Worth, 1976).

28. Robinson, John - *Truth is Two-Eyed*, SCM Press, London, 1981.

29. Rorty, Richard - *Philosophy and the Mirror of Nature*, Princeton University Press (Princeton, 1979).

30. Rupp, George - *Beyond Existentialism and Zen* (Religion in a Pluralistic World) Oxford University Press (New York, 1979).

31. Schuon, F. - *The Transcendent Unity of Religions*, Pantheon (New York, 1953).

32. Smart, Ninian - *Beyond Ideology* (Religion and the Future of Western Civilization) Harper & Row, San Francisco, 1981).

33. Smart, Ninian - *Worldviews* (Cross-Cultural Explorations of Human Beliefs) Charles Scribners & Sons (New York, 1983).

34. Smartha, S.J. ed. *Towards World Community* (The Colombo Papers) World Council of Churches (Geneva, 1975).

35. Smith, W.C. - *Towards a World Theology* (Faith and the Comparative History of Religions) The Westminster Press (Philadelphia, 1981).

36. Smith, W.C. - *The Meaning and End of Religion* (A New Approach to the Religious Traditions of Mankind) Macmillan, (New York, 1963).

37. Smith, Houston - *Beyond the Post Modern Mind* Crossroad (New York, 1982).

38. Sontag, F. & Bryand, M.D. eds. - *God: The Contemporary Discussion* The Rose of Sharon Press, (New York, 1982).

39. Streng, Frederick - *Emptiness* (A Study in Religious Meaning) Abingdon, (Nashville, 1967).

40. Swearer, Donald - *Dialogue* (The Key to Understanding Other Religions) Westminster Press, (Philadelphia, 1977).

41. Troeltsch, Ernst - *The Absoluteness of Christianity * The History of Religions* John Knott Press (Richmond, VA, 1971).

42. Waldenfels, H. - *Absolute Nothingness* (Foundations for a Buddhist- Christian Dialogue) - Paulist Press (New York, 1976).

43. Wittaker, J.H. - *Matters of Faith and Matters of Principle* (Religious Truth Claims and Their Logic) Trinity University Press.

GLOSSARY (1)

The following terms are used in a special sense in this essay. They are selected for special notice because they recur in the text.

1. Absolutism - This indicates the origin of the pathology of meaning that arises in the very form of the mind of identity.

2. Analogous - For the meditative mind original meaning is metaphoric and not literal; the holistic mind discerns a continuum of meaning in which all terms permeate one another in analogical synonymy.

3. Continuum - This indicates the absolute unity of divine form as it is discerned by the holistic and; it is non-dual, primordial and prior to any possible dualism or division between "I" and Field.

4. Form of life - Any life is structured in a grammar or life-world which gives it form - any life is a logos with form.

5. Equi-vocity - The voice of the speaker/thinker taken in its indeterminacy; the original self-division of voice into polarization. The self-divided or equivocal voice speaks equivocally.

6. Grammar - The ontological structure of any logos (form of life) world or language which constitutes a life-world; a grammar makes a form of life possible and defines its meaning, experience, existence.

7. Holistic - This refers to Divine Unity, the unity of the Continuum which is non-dual; the primordial unity discerned by the meditative mind.

8. Incommensurability - The pathology or incoherence of reason or meaning in which diverse things (logos, worlds, forms of life, etc.) each have their internal absolute self-definition, atomic independence, and hence share no unifying principle which could make rational relations between them possible.

9. Indeterminacy - The ontological condition of meaning, existence, voice in which there can be no literal fixation of meaning or identity; a given thing is indeterminate if its identity is open and neither fixated, univocal nor specifiable.

10. Literalism - The hermeneutical faith that literal meaning is primary and that words have their intrinsic fixated, determinate senses and univocity; metaphoric meaning is taken to be derivative.

11. Metaphor - This indicates the primordial form of meaning discerned by the meditative or holistic mind in discerning the continuum of meaning; the non-dual meaning conforming to universal relativity.

12. Monadic - A monadic universe or life-world is one which takes itself as the absolute measure, having independent self-existence; and Voice is said to be monadic when it takes the onto-centric or absolutistic posture.

13. Ontos - When a logos or form of life takes itself in independent identity and defines itself apart from divine form (Continuum) it becomes ontological, ontocentric and names itself: ontos.

14. Logos - The Holistic Name for the Universal Divine Form - the Absolute Principle which is the form of all possible names/forms ("logos").

15. Logos - Any name or form (form of life) in its holistic particularity in the divine continuum; hence any form in its univocity or dialogical unity with Logos.

16. Relativism - A pathological form of absolutism in which this faith is committed to a multiplicity of radically diverse of incommensurable absolute forms each of which is an absolute measure of its reality.

17. Symbolic - Any sign or thing taken in its holistic or universal meaning— the symbolic meaning of any name or form is discerned by the holistic mind in the context of the Continuum of meaning. This term is used closely with "metaphoric" and "analogical."

18. Universal Relativity - (UR) The holistic principle of the Continuum, the principle of non-dual unity of Divine Form.

19. Universal Theology (UT) The meditation on Universal Divine Form; the holistic narrative or hermeneutic which articulates this meditative voice.

20. Voice - This is used synonymously for "mind"— as in the mind of the speaker/thinker/listener; voice is the presence which speaks or thinks, the voice of the first person indicated by "I," etc.

Notes

1 For a more systematic presentation of the principle of universal relativity see Gangadean
9, 10, 11 and 16. It might be helpful here to pick out some prominent examples of UR
(Universal Relativity) from the world historical traditions.

In the meditative tradition of Indian thought it is readily seen that the teaching of Advaita
(Non-dual) Vedanta reveals that AUM is the Universal Principle of Unity. AUM is holistic
form itself— synonymous with Logos. And through proper meditation on AUM the mind
itself self-transforms and univocates with AUM. This is the Universal Continuum of
which all else is an expression. If any item is selected for meditative attention its true
import is revealed when its meditative synonymy with AUM is realized. The science of
Yoga (Self Union) in its highest form expands rational awareness to its universal
synonymy with AUM— the Original Holistic Word. This is not just an "altered state" of
consciousness but the realization of Pure Consciousness or Reason, the realization of Truth
itself.

Another classical example of the holistic principle of UR may be found in the teaching of
Nagarjuna, the founder of the Madhyamika Buddhist tradition. Nagarjuna presents one
version of UR in the form of the principle of dependent co-arising of all things. He teaches
that absolute identity (svabhava) is vacuous and he demonstrates that wherever there is
identity there is contradiction and in-coherence. He shows that true Reason arises with the
realization of *Sunya*, which may be translated as Emptiness, Void, Zero, and now *Logos*.
He teaches that all things are sunyata— which is beyond the oppositional (dual, polar)
structure of identity; Sunya is neither full nor empty, neither one nor many, neither is nor
isn't, neither relative nor absolute, etc. The holistic principle of Sunya exhibits the non-
dual features we have just discussed— it is the Universal Continuum. Things are devoid
of absolute identity; all things dependently co-arise. The identity of anything consists in its
identity with everything else. And it is the Holistic Principle that makes thought, language
and world work; and true insight comes with the realization of Sunya— which is the
middle way between all opposition and the pathological polarization of identity.

Still another classical example of the living principle UR which may not at first be evident
to the mind of identity is the being of the Christ. It may be argued in this context that the
Christ is the perfect living example of UR— the self-transformative dialogical form of non-
dual unity. The Christ meditatively understood is a unifying principle that overcomes the
deepest duality there can be in the deep structure of identity— the polarization of finite
(individuated) beings and Infinite (transcendent) Being. For the Christ is that Unified and
Unifying Being that is at once fully finite and fully Infinite— the Living logos, the Logos
become flesh. The form of Unity of the Christ voice is the dialogical form of the
Continuum. In this respect the Universal Christ is prior to the duality of identity and is the
more profound unifying principle (UR)— the incarnation of Logos.

2 The terms "metaphoric" and "symbolic" are used in a special meditative sense here.
While the mind of identity takes literal meaning to be primary, the meditative mind, being
centered in the Continuum, discerns *holistic* meaning (metaphor/symbol) to be primary and
literal meaning to be artificially derived. For a systematic discussion of holistic metaphor
and symbol see Gangadean 12, 14. The meditative mind works on the principle of
universal relativity which structures the analogical (meditative) imagination.

3 The term "grammar" is here used in the ontological sense of the structure of a language form which constitutes a life-world. This idea of grammar is developed in detail in Gangadean 1, 2 4, 16, and in chapter 1 above.

4 The term "monadic" (a modification of a term from Leibniz's thought) indicates the orientation of voice from the internal self-references of its independent identity. Voice may take different orientations in logical space; it can be centered in the "I" locus or take a more transcendent over-view which is external to the individuated "I," etc. This point is elaborated in Gangadean 16.

5 It must be stressed here that the term "ontology" (ontos) indicates a cosmological universal, a world-whole that is all-encompassing. When voice centers in its universe, its life-world or ontology, as its absolute center of reference for its life and logos it may be said to be "ontocentric." Here it takes its life-world or ontology to be the absolute measure of all meaning. This theme is developed in Gangadean 11. (Chapter 7 below.)

6 Usually in logic the term "univocal" applies to the literal primary unity of the meaning of a word or concept. But here we re-orient to the primacy of the *voice* of the thinker/speaker and the original question is whether the mind/voice of the speaker can be presumed to be *univocal*, a primitive unity. This point is explored in Gangadean 3, 9, 7, 10, 16.

7 Every grammar, to be coherent and to define a universe of discourse, must have its ultimate unifying principle which unifies its universe. In this univocity condition of any grammar, which is intrinsic to the form of identity itself, we find the image of the divine form in any possible grammar. And all life in this universe is under the rule of this unifying principle. In this respect every grammar has its divinity and faith principle.

8 For a systematic holistic analysis which demonstrates the unity of mind and matter see Gangadean 16.

9 Here it may be seen that in Descartes' *Meditations* his demonstration that "I am" and *God is*, taken in the holistic or meditative narrative is powerful. The essence of Descartes' demonstration of the necessary existence of Divine Being turns on the meditation on Divine Unity; if it is taken in the narrative of the particularistic voice the force of the speech is lost. Descartes himself speaks in an equivocal voice, intending to express a holistic insight in the voice and rhetoric of the voice of identity and literal predication. The holistic narrative makes clear that Divine Form cannot be thought by the mind of identity which separates the Idea of God, the Word, its Sense, Essence and Being.

CHAPTER 6

MEDITATIVE REASON AND THE LOGIC OF COMMUNICATION

FOREWORD

The clarification of the concept of holistic communication reveals that what passes for communication in everyday life is often a failure of communication and a pathology of meaning. The obsession with the primacy of literalistic meaning and descriptive discourse has distorted true communication and eclipsed the understanding of the origin of meaning. The recovery of holistic communication requires a transformation in understanding which discloses the origin of meaning and discourse. Here it is found that primary meaning and speech arise in meditative understanding which breaks through the bondage of literalistic meaning and opens the way to the richness and power of holistic or metaphoric meaning. The true power of metaphoric meaning cannot be approached and released when literalistic meaning is taken as primary meaning. The transformation to holistic communication requires the advance to holistic meaning where it is recognized that primary discourse is essentially metaphoric. The primacy of metaphoric meaning helps us to understand how true communication takes place and how there can be a communion and community of meaning.

SYNOPSIS NOTES

This chapter explores the holistic concept and practice of communication. It focuses on meaning and communication in ordinary language and makes clear that communication is hermeneutical art which is always a function of its self understanding. The essence of communication is a function of what it takes itself to be. This hermeneutical self-reference reveals that communication is an open-ended enterprise which fluctuates and varies with the hermeneutical understanding of those involved in communication. The universal concept of communication is approached and the universal concept of language/meaning (logos) is explicated.

It is shown that meaning is *ontological* in origin— meaning arises in a life-world as this is constituted in a grammar of existence. That the unit of meaning is the life-world has not been properly appreciated, and this has led to misunderstanding concerning meaning and communication. A life-world is always personal, and a shared life-world is a culture or community of discourse. The politics of meaning must address the issues of the privacy of meaning and the publicity of communication.

Ordinary language and common sense (meaning) naturally arise in a life-world or cluster of life-worlds. The essay attempts to make explicit the ontological or hermeneutical form of life which shapes ordinary meaning. Comparative ontology (ontological hermeneutics) shows that there is a plurality of grammars of existence or life-worlds which shape common-sense in different cultures. What is common sense in one culture is different from common sense in another. Since communication is a function of hermeneutical self-understanding it is shown that communication itself is contextually determined by the life-world of a given cultural language. This makes inter-cultural communication especially interesting and challenging.

Ontological hermeneutics or grammatology helps us to see that there is a common *form* of understanding in ordinary languages— despite their material differences ordinary languages typically arise in a *formal hermeneutic*. The common formal hermeneutic of ordinary natural languages is often *literalistic* and takes the principle of identity as its hermeneutical principle. This principle is the principle of univocity (fixity) of meaning. It is found that this principle is the principle of "essence" and duality. This hermeneutical principle takes literal discourse to be primary and treats "violation" of the principle of identity to be either ruled out as contradiction, non-sense or else is tolerated as "metaphor." As the principle of duality, it "saves" a contradiction by splitting the term in question in two and requiring the recognition of two distinct meanings— so the principle of univocity (identity) is at the same time wielded as the principle of equivocity (ambiguity). Metaphoric meaning is taken to be derivative and falls in-between the polarity of univocity and equivocity. The egological paradigm takes the principle of metaphor to be a principle of *analogy* based upon the weak (associative) relation of *similarity* (rather than identity). This means that metaphor arises in a certain vagueness and indeterminacy of meaning. For this reason it cannot be a *primary* form of communication. In the formal hermeneutic of univocity and identity true communication arises in a communal sharing of identical univocal meaning: communication presupposes shared univocal synonymy.

This typical self-understanding (hence constitution) of communication in natural languages is found to be incoherent upon critical analysis.

First, the alleged "facts" of communication are constituted in a certain grammar or form of life, and when one lives in this grammar its "facts" are very difficult to question and critique. When one lives in the faith of a certain grammar of existence its facts carry tremendous weight and force. Instead, the alleged facts of communication for the life-world of a given natural language, when properly understood to be constituted by the very structure of that world, may be *indirectly* questioned by questioning the life-world as a whole. Second, hermeneutical critique shows that the principle of literalism (identity) leads to an incoherent self understanding of communication— hence to an incoherent practice of communication. Communication that understands itself to be based upon the principle of univocity, and which takes literal discourse as primitive, falls into onto-centrism and hermeneutical indeterminacy. Onto-centrism is the incoherence of meaning in which identity and essence lead to the incommensurability and the failure of communication [and leads to a form of hermeneutical solipsism]. This pathology of meaning (isolation, bifurcation, alienation) puts an undue strain on communication by requiring it to be the vehicle of *unity and community of meaning*. It postulates a common unity (identity) of shared meaning (common language, rules of use, common terms, games, etc.) which objectively ties the group of individuated and separated identities into a community of discourse.

But when this postulate is examined upon the principle of identity itself it becomes questionable and question begging. This typical absolutism and foundationalism of meaning does not really answer the pathology of onto-centrism or privacy of meaning. It cannot simply postulate itself out of the difficulty. The principle of identity attempts to save itself by going to the opposite extreme of relativism by postulating a plurality of life-worlds and an indeterminacy of meaning as the basis of communication. This ironic ploy of essential identity suggests that each life-world has its absolute foundations and denies that there is any one absolute, privileged life-world. Meaning is relative to each life-world, and communication must be understood as relative to what each life-world takes it to be. In effect, the extreme of hermeneutical relativism concedes the incommensurability of onto-centrism and sells out the concept of communication as a true communion and community of meaning. Thus, the governing principle of identity is not a possible hermeneutical principle for natural languages; so, some other principle is needed for meaning and communication in natural language.

Part 2 of the essay presents the true hermeneutical principle of meaning for natural reason and natural languages. It argues that the principle of universal relativity opens the dialogical space in which the true unity and community of meaning essential for communication may proceed. It demonstrates that universal relativity goes beyond the pathological extremes of absolutism and relativism of meaning, and that metaphoric discourse is primary meaning— the meaning structure of the Continuum— while the literalist practice of the egological mind is derivative. It shows that literalist meaning is possible only as arising out of the recursive richness of metaphoric meaning. It becomes clear that the principle and practice of universal relativity— meditative meaning— is the origin of metaphoric meaning. Formally this is the principle of non-dual identity of opposites. In this hermeneutical inversion of essential identity what appeared as contradiction now appears as primary meaning in the form of metaphor. This principle cuts between the polarity of relativism and absolutism (as it cuts between all dual polarities) and overcomes the pathology of onto-centrism and incommensurability. It respects diversity and uniqueness (and preserves) while revealing a non-dual unity in relativity which makes true communication possible.

But in approaching the principle of relativity (relative identity) a fundamental hermeneutical transformation is required to meditative reason. It is shown that relativity can be understood only within meditative rationality which is the logic of primary or original non-dual logos. Natural meditation as rational consciousness is explicated, and it is argued that natural languages work on the principle of relativity. The original logos of natural languages has been eclipsed by the constructed hermeneutic of essential identity. The recovery of original logos in natural meditation reveals that natural language was already in perfect order and only needs to be recovered. In overcoming the forgetfulness of original logos the fragmentation and pathology meaning is now healed in the genuine unity and community of relativity. A new understanding of language, meaning and communication arises in meditative logos, and the pervasive polarities and dualities which were inevitable in the hermeneutic of essential identity now appear in a transformed rational consciousness. It is only in this transformation to original logos that the incoherence of communication in natural life can be overcome and holistic communication can be realized. The hermeneutical circularity of this reflection on communication comes to light with the transformation to non-dual logos— this essay, as an attempt to communicate with the reader, succeeds to the extent that it brings about a hermeneutical transformation in the reader, and then it is realized that the most radical and pragmatic of transformations is *hermeneutical* change. A new awareness of holistic communication means the emergence of a new practice of communication and conduct of mind.

PREFACE

Communication is essentially a matter of *meaning* and the views and assumptions that we hold about the origin and nature of meaning will shape our understanding of communication. More generally, communication is so inextricably bound with modifications of meaning such as understanding, interpretation, expression, and intention that any systematic account of the former inevitably raises issues concerning the latter. In giving an account of communication this inquiry takes and presents an account of meaning in ordinary language that is not customarily taken.

The view taken here is that meaning and communication must be understood in *ontological* terms. *Ontology* is the science which explores the mutuality of existence and meaning. It reveals that meaning and existence mutually arise and constitute each other in some determinate form— in a grammar of existence. A grammar of existence is a form of life— a life-world— which gives form and intelligibility to experience. An ontological grammar makes life and experience possible and defines what is meaningful and what is not. As a grammar of existence it makes facts possible. Thus, existence, meaning and experience mutually arise in a grammar which defines a world.

But ontology is a *formal* science which discerns a plurality of grammars of reality. Comparative ontology makes clear that there are alternative living languages of reality or life-worlds which constitute meaning in radically different ways. What makes sense in one world does not square with what makes sense in another. For example, different historical cultures are suitable paradigms of diverse ontological grammars, and from an ontological point of view what makes sense in a Hindu life-world is at variance with what is intelligible in a Christian life-world. What is taken to be a fact in one world appears to be unintelligible in another. The metaphor of a *grammar* of existence plays on the theme that a world arises with a certain system of basic categories which mutually configure to define a language and which determines the meaning of concepts as well as specifies which concepts may and may not intelligibly conjoin to form a meaningful or well-formed state of affairs.[1]

Furthermore, since meaning is essentially an ontological matter, it may be said that ontology and hermeneutics are one and the same. *Hermeneutics* may be characterized as the discipline which deals with the full range of arts concerning meaning— interpretation, communication, understanding, expression, thinking, acting, experiencing, living, etc. There is no facet of human existence which does not involve meaning and hence which is not hermeneutical or ontological. To experience is to be hermeneutical; to live is to be engaged in meaning. It is crucial for this study that the primacy and depth of the hermeneutical theme be remembered. For communication is a hermeneutical art which trades in meaning but which at the same time gets its own significance as a meaningful activity from the ontological life-world which constitutes it. Of course, this places our inquiry from the state in an intriguing hermeneutical circularity since this discussion of communication must *already* be situated in a grammar of experience which calls itself into question.

The presence of multiple grammars of meaning disclosed by comparative ontology requires us to enlarge the scope of our discussion of communication.

It is one thing to inquire into the nature of communication *within* a given life-world, quite another to raise the question of communication *between* different hermeneutical languages. The ontology of meaning and communication makes clear that the unit of meaning is the life-world as a whole; and if a particular life-world be granted as being shared by a community (i.e., a *cultural* language), then communication appears to be primarily concerned with discourse between members of that community. However, when it is realized that different life-worlds constitute meaning itself in radically different ways, then the question of communication seems to become more problematic. How can there be communication between two distinct grammars of experience which appear to share no common form of meaning? Is communication possible between distinct cultural languages? Thus, our inquiry must address the question of communication *between* cultural language as well as *within* a given cultural grammar. In fact, our topic must be generalized even further. Not only must we be concerned with *inter-personal* communication within and between cultural languages, we must also bring into focus the concerns of intra-personal discourse. For a life-world is always *personal,* and we cannot avoid raising the question of the arising of a shared or communal life-world of a culture or community. The politics of meaning becomes relevant here and this inevitably raises issues about the publicity and privacy of meaning. In any case the microcosm of the individual person may well involve a community of voices or personalities of its own and this leads us to inquire into the nature of internal (intra-personal) dialogue. If a person speaks multiple grammars, how can there be *internal* self-communication? If personal identity involves multiple ontological identities, then how can the person be integrated in true self-communion? These questions reveal that the very same sorts of issues are raised whether we focus on intro-cultural, inter-cultural or intra-personal communication. In each case we gravitate to the fundamental issues of the politics of meaning and the nature of discourse between life-worlds. Our inquiry will be concerned with the *generic* concept of communication.

In approaching the generic concept of communication we need to generalize our topic in another direction as well. For discussions of meaning and communication have often been dominated by the paradigm of literal, descriptive discourse where exchange of information is taken to be the primary feature of communication. This predominant paradigm has distorted the landscape of communication, but in more recent philosophy of language Wittgenstein and Austin have led the way back to the rough ground of ordinary language and have taught us to recognize and respect a diverse range of "language games" and types of linguistic utterances or speech acts. This healthy influence has helped to broaden the context and concept of communication, but it is only a beginning. There has been increasing recognition of *non-linguistic* forms of communication— such as "body language"— in some recent discussions. What we need is a generic concept of "language" which includes both linguistic and non-linguistic meaning and communication. I propose to use the term *"logos"* for the broadest possible meaning of "language" and "meaning"— an open-ended concept of language which runs the full range of all possible language forms, from artificially constructed languages to natural or ordinary language, from verbalized languages to non-linguistic forms of meaning. In this way it may be said that *the generic or universal concept of communication is manifested in logos.*

The universal concept of language as logos, of course, challenges the narrower concepts of language that we find in discussions of conventional linguistic meaning. The danger of broadening the concept of language to its universal form (logos) is that we may end up with something so broad and indeterminate that it loses all specific content and has no real meaning. But later we shall see that this transformation is essential for the true understanding of ordinary language, meaning and communication in their more conventional sense. Indeed, we shall see that from an ontological point of view *logos* breaks down the usual barriers between meaning and existence, thought and object, language and world, experience and reality. In this way *logos* makes inseparable words, objects, meaning, reference, thought, existence, expression and experience. Thus, our concern in this study is to explore the universal concept of communication as expressed in logos.

INTRODUCTION: THE ONTOLOGICAL PROBLEM OF COMMUNICATION

1) The Question of Communication

Communication is a hermeneutical art which is ever-present in everyday life. It appears to be an undeniable fact of life that we do communicate with one another when we describe situations, report events, tell stories, make each other laugh, express how we feel, prescribe and direct conduct, engage in linguistic ceremonies, and so on. It seems intuitively clear that we follow common rules of use in our linguistic expressions and engage in a shared enterprise of human behavior. We make ourselves understood to one another through language, and by and large our common world works fairly smoothly. Occasionally, perhaps even often, communication breaks down and there is misunderstanding, frustration, and even pain. But our common enterprise allows us, fortunately, to correct such situations if we wish. There can be no doubt that we do communicate in ordinary language, and this is a fact of common sense.

Undoubtedly the facts of life cannot be denied, nor should they be. Once the fact of communication is granted, it would be perverse to proceed to deny that communication takes place. Nevertheless, ontological hermeneutics teaches us that *facts* themselves are constituted in a life-world or grammar of existence. It reminds us that *common sense, too, is hermeneutical*— common conventional meaning is ontological and arises in a life-world. This becomes clear in comparative ontology where the ordinary languages of different cultural grammars disclose very different *facts* of life. What is a fact or common sense in one life-world appears to be importantly different from the facts and common sense in another. This goes for the facts of communication as well. Thus, when it is understood that facts are relative to a given grammar of existence we can see more clearly why it is perverse to assent to the grammar of life-world but deny its established facts.

In the politics of meaning the ontological consensus of a shared life-world— an ontological community or culture— determines what are the common-sensical facts of life. That hermeneutical consensus determines the "official" interpretation which gives meaning and facticity to the facts. To question the facts of a given life-world is to question the life-world as a whole. For example, to question the common sense (ontological) facts of the Hindu life-world— the facts of samsara, of karma, rebirth, transmigration, etc. is really to question the grammar of existence of that world. It becomes clear in ontological critique that the unit of meaning is the life-world and the primary object of critique is the life-world. This is equally evident in the ontology of communication— to question the conventionally established facts of communication in any given life-world is to call the life-world as a whole into question.

This form of hermeneutical critique helps us to see the legitimate sense in which the conventionally established facts of life of a given life-world may be called into question. We may grant the facts of communication but still question the hermeneutical form of life (grammar of existence) which constitute those facts. Of course, this is not to question the *facticity* of the facts *per* se, but more radically to question their intelligibility. We shall see shortly that there are good reasons to question the workings of communication in ordinary life. That communication is taken to be a well established practice which works in ordinary life is granted. But ontological critique recognizes that the very criteria and standards which determine success of *any* practice in common sense life are *themselves* constituted by the life-world in question. Indeed, the very judgments which decide success and failure of a practice, and which decide the facticity of facts, also stem from the life-world under consideration. Thus, we must not let the everyday facts of communication deter our inquiry for there is a more radical form of questioning which refuses to identify any given term with the meaning it is given in the context of any particular life-world. While conventional phenomenology takes the ordinary established meanings of terms in a given life-world as definitive and absolute, the phenomenology of ontological hermeneutics recognizes its relativity to a given life-world and discerns a plurality of meanings which are legitimized by diverse life-worlds. To inquire into the true meaning of "communication" for *any possible life-world* is a task of ontological hermeneutics.[2]

Here it becomes important to distinguish between "ordinary language" in terms of conventional *linguistic* criteria (where, for example, English, Hindi and Spanish are different ordinary languages) and in terms of the *ontological* criteria of different grammars of existence (where the life-world grammars of contemporary American English-speaking culture and the ontological grammar of the ordinary Hindi-speaking culture are importantly different). It is naive and inaccurate to act as if there were some homogeneous entity like "ordinary language." It is more accurate to speak of the ontologies or life-worlds of ordinary (natural) languages which involve very different grammars (languages) of existence. Our interest here is in exploring the nature of communication in the context of multiple (perhaps incommensurable) grammars of existence. Can there be communication between the life-world grammars of different ordinary languages? Is there a common and univocal meaning of communication between such diverse natural languages? Henceforth, when I speak of different natural languages, I shall mean different *ontological* grammars.

2)　The Ontological Grammars of Natural Languages: Life-Worlds

In preparing further to address the ontological problem of communication it is timely to develop in more detail the hermeneutical theme of the life-world as the origin and unit of meaning. I shall here present a summary review and development of the main features of a life-world or ontological grammar.

a)　*A Life-World Makes Existence/Experience Possible*

Perhaps the most important feature of a life-world is its primacy or *ontological universality*. There can be no meaning, experience, thought, language, existence or world apart from a life-world . A life-world is a universal and self-universalizing grammar of existence/experience. It constitutes a *universe of discourse* and as such is all-encompassing of reality. It makes experience in *all its forms* possible— meaning, facts, action or behavior, judgment, rationality, interpretation, etc. It cannot be considered a view (amongst others) because it makes viewing possible. It cannot be reduced to an epistemological state because it makes all distinctions possible— between consciousness and object, between thought and action, between mind and body, between word and object, and so on. A life-world makes it possible to be conscious of self in the form of "I" identity. As a universal grammar of meaning and experience, it takes all possible data of experience into its orbit and sphere of meaning. In this respect a life-world is a cultural proto-type since it gives meaning and form to all dimensions of experience and organizes it into a structured world; it makes religion, science, art, politics, ethics, everyday life and common sense possible. Thus, when we speak of the Hindu life-world or the Christian life-world, etc., we refer to universal grammars of existence which constitute different universes. The various forms of rational life such as judgment, reasoning, predication, interpretation, knowing, etc. become possible within the context of a universal grammar. The primacy of a life-world reminds us that the distinction between reality (existence), experience, thought, world, and meaning is *ontologically posterior* to the universal grammar in question— each of these dimensions of a life-world mutually arises with the other, so it cannot be said that existence precedes experience or that meaning is prior to thought or the facts prior to rationality, and so on. The term *logos* is used for the organic *ontological* beginning in which reality/experience/meaning are inseparable.

b) A Life-World as a Grammar of Logos

A life-world is an ontological grammar which constitutes a language. The ontology of meaning presents itself in a determinate *categorial structure*— a systematic configuration of basic categories— which defines what can and cannot be, what can and cannot be thought, and what can and cannot be said. Ontological categories are primary universal features (such as time, space, consciousness, self, object, event, cause, properties, etc.) which make up a world. But these features take their determinate meaning with respect to one another in their mutual configuration. Thus, the meaning/being of "I" is a function of its locus in an ontological grammar. It is the *configuration* of the categories which determine intelligibility, which define the lines of meaningful predication. Any ontological language discerns category-correct and category-incorrect predications. For example, in one particular grammar it is permissible to meaningfully conjoin the category of *thought* with the category of *material objects*. In such a grammar it is meaningful to say that "stones think"— this is a possible fact. But in a grammar in which such a predication is formally precluded it is a category mistake (an error in ontological grammar) to say "stones think"; it is simply meaningless and inconceivable. An ontological grammar proscribes the realm of possibility and conceivability.

The grammar of a life-world is an *organic unity* which prescribes the rules of use of the terms of a natural or constructed language. The meaning of a term in a given language is defined by its *location* in the categorial configuration. The very *formation* of terms (concepts) is constrained by the category structure and a term takes its identity by its unique location in the structure: one term = one meaning = one location. For this reason the category structure is the formal condition of univocity and ambiguity for the given language. The distinction between literal and figurative is determined by the grammar, so that non-literal discourse (including metaphor) must be understood with respect to the rules of literal use.

It should be pointed out that a categorial grammar has a hierarchical structure— a pyramid form. At the apex of the configuration is the unifying and all-inclusive category which unites the language into the unified world system. At the base of the pyramid is found the most exclusive terms in the language. The continuous lines from the apex to the base points are the lines of meaningful configuration which define predicability for that language. If a term has two locations in the pyramid structure, then this is formal evidence for its equivocity. It must be stressed that it is the ontological grammar which governs how terms may or may not be used in natural languages. (See Chapter 4, Section ii.)

c) Systematic Ambiguity: The Incommensurability of Life-Worlds
Ontological hermeneutics (comparative ontology) discerns a plurality of *actual* ontological grammars— a diversity of actual worlds or realities. What makes sense in one world is incommensurably different from meaning (common identity) between different grammars. It cannot be assumed that there is a neutral world "out there" with its neutral "facts" and neutral "objects" which different grammars articulate. The incoherence of this assumption, if it is not already evident, will be discussed below. It may be said, then, that there is *systematic* ambiguity between different life-worlds. The meaning and being (sense and referent) of "I," for example, is systematically ambiguous in different grammars. Of course, the same holds for "here" and "now" and every other term of the language. But incommensurability between grammars must not be confused with or reduced to ordinary difference or otherness. For *relationality* and opposition and differentiation themselves are given meaning *within* a grammar— they are *categorial relations*. To be in opposition or contrast is already to be united in a categorial point of common reference. Categorial incommensurability is a problematic and puzzling "relation" to process.

d) Ontological Imagination: Rational Transformations Between Life-Worlds
At the same time it appears to be an undeniable hermeneutical "fact" that there are intelligible transformations between life-worlds— ontological conversion from one world to another, translatability, dialogue, communication, and so on. While the categorial imagination takes flight within a grammar, it appears that the ontological (transcategorial) imagination soars between life-worlds. It seems to be the case that a speaker of a particular grammar is able to create, discover and speak a new grammar in the launching of an ontological revolution. Examples abound in the history of thought— Jesus, Buddha, and the ontological poets such as Plato, Spinoza, Leibniz, Hegel, Einstein, and so on. The ontological revolutionaries uncover new worlds (new forms of life) and forge new grammars. It appears to be an historical fact that different cultural languages have met and mutually transformed one another in the course of time. Indeed, it appears that a conventional culture consists of a network or cluster of ontological grammars— that an ordinary language involves a diversity of ontological grammars.

This apparent fact of *transcategorial commensurability* is also very puzzling and difficult to understand, especially in the light of the categorial incommensurability we have just touched on. How can there be discourse and communication between ontological grammars? How can there be intelligible transformations between life-worlds? What is the nature of the ontological imagination with its world— making powers? What is the ontologic of conversion and ontological revolutions?

e) The Politics of Reality: The Privacy and Community Meaning
A life-world constitutes a *form of life:* it is *lived* and in this sense always *personal.* But we have seen that a life-world makes the distinctions between subjective and objective, between personal and inter-personal, between "I" and "you," and between private and public possible. Once we *assume* a community of discourse it may be taken for granted that there is a shared common life-world and an ontological consensus. A *culture* may be seen as a communal life-world in which distinct individual persons form an ontological polis, inhabit a common world, and speak a common grammar in their ordinary language. This community lives a common form of life (logos) and enters a consensus which is manifested in conventional common-sense. Any member of the community who stands outside this consensus of reality risks the stigma of "insanity" and the pain of ontological anonymity and alienation. The reality and presence of other cultural languages and communities of discourse pose special threats and ontological challenges.

Still, life-worlds are *personal* in a deep and radical sense— deeper than ordinary subjectivity and more radical than conventional privacy. Experience and ontological politics teach us that even within a community of discourse there is breakdown of communication between individual members, ontological factions, the insane, and the inevitable fringe of ontological revolutionaries who threaten orthodox conventional (normal) life. It can not be simply *assumed* that there exists an ontological consensus and a shared hermeneutic or grammar. It remains problematic and an open question whether in *fact* a community of discourse exists, whether in fact there is a communal form of life and reality. The deeply personal nature of life-worlds makes it a real and pressing concern whether we live in different worlds. What is the nature of shared or communal life (logos)? How is an ontological consensus possible? What is the nature of the ontological relation between the individual person and the ontological community? If *neither* has ontological priority, then how does each arise?

f) The Ontological Problem of Communication: Onto-Centrism and the Pathology of Meaning

The life-world is the unit of meaning, and the personal feature of life-worlds leads to serious questions about the nature of a genuine community of discourse. But whether a life-world is individually lived or communally shared a common problem of *ontological* privacy of meaning remains. For we have seen that a life-world purports to be a *universal* grammar of reality; and as such, it is all-encompassing of existence, experience, and meaning— a universe. Whatever comes into the presence of a life-world is taken in and processed by it, becomes appropriated by its categorial grammar. This is equally so in the encounter of alien life-worlds; the grammar in question attempts to make sense of the new "data" in terms of its own structure of meaning and form of life. In this way the inherent ontological universality of a life-world leads to onto-centrism— the pathology of logos in which an individual person or community of discourse is solipsistically centered and enclosed within one's own grammar. This form of *ontological* privacy of meaning is a real threat to the possibility of communication in all of its forms

There is no special connection between the unity, identity and integrity of a life-world on the one hand and the ontological structure of a person or community on the other. An individual person may, as we have noted, live in a multiplicity of life-worlds with multiple identities speaking a plurality of grammars. Similarly, a plurality or community of persons may share a common life-world. So, whether we consider intra-personal, inter-personal or inter-cultural communication, the same generic problem of ontocentrism arises.

Once we recognize a plurality of valid and actual life-worlds (alternative actual worlds) or grammars of reality the concepts of truth and facticity are thrown into crisis. We can no longer assume the validity of the either/or principle of reason for life-worlds— that among alternative life-worlds one must be true and the others false. On the contrary, we have seen that *truth itself* is constituted in a life-world, as are the facts. So we are reminded that the "facts" of communication for any given life-world are relative to that life-world and cannot be naively generalized as valid for all possible grammars. It is here appropriate to wonder whether there are facts of communication and what the meaning of communication is.

Perhaps we may now state the general ontological problem of communication. Communication appears to be a natural fact of life, but we have seen that it is a difficult fact to understand. The term suggests some sort of joining or coming together in unity. Since communication is essentially concerned with meaning, understanding and interpretation, it is natural to think of communication as involving mutual understanding and shared common meaning. Furthermore, the term suggests a form of activity in virtue of which meaning is conveyed between persons— through certain forms of linguistic and non-linguistic expression different individuals succeed in coming into a unity of shared meaning. In the broadest sense, then, communication seems to involve some form of synonymy or common identity of meaning. But we have seen that the ontological privacy and onto-centrism of life-worlds raise doubts about a genuine ontological unity between diverse life-worlds. So, we are left with the generic problem of communication: communication presupposes an ontological unity and common identity of meaning between persons (or communities); but the very structure of meaning in life-worlds seems to preclude a common identity between diverse life-worlds.

PART I: IDENTITY, LITERALISM AND THE INCOHERENCE OF COMMUNICATION

The problem of communication is the problem of unity and community of meaning (logos). The grammar of any life-world naturally has a self-understanding of communication— an implicit understanding of what communication is as well as conventions determining what counts as successful communication. Despite a form of incommensurability between life-worlds, ontological hermeneutics, as a formal science, discerns common formal principles which shape life-worlds. It shows that the fundamental hermeneutical principle of meaning for life-worlds is the principle of identity— a principle which gives identity to life-worlds and governs its literal discourse. It must be stressed that this principle of literal discourse is not an abstract theoretical invention of compulsive philosophers but a principle which structures everyday life and common sense. To live in common sense is to live the principle of identity— to live is to be ontological, to experience is to be hermeneutical. We shall now see that it is the formal principle of identity which shapes meaning in everyday conventional life but which renders communication unintelligible and gives rise to the pathology of meaning. We shall presently examine the typical strategies of the hermeneutic of identity and literalism to *make* communication coherent, and we shall then see why they inevitably fail.

a) The Hermeneutic of Identity: The Principle of Literal Meaning

The formal (ontological) principle of identity structures everyday life in every possible way— it shapes the content of existence, gives form to experience and common sense, it makes language and meaning possible. It gives unique identity and determinacy to life-worlds as unified systems of experience. In short, it gives identity, determinacy, particularity to life-worlds and to all that constitutes a life-world. Formal ontology teaches that any possible life-world discerns definite entities of some sort including some conception of "I"— some conception of the ego as the central reference point which organizes experience— the living center of a life-world. But the principle of identity is recursive and reiterates throughout a given life-world— it gives determinacy and identity to all actual and possible entities, whether to the "I," to natural objects, to events, to facts, to properties, to relations to spacial temporal locations, to actions, to linguistic items (subjects, predicates, etc.), to linguistic conventions or language games, to speech acts or linguistic utterances, to any form of human activity— any practice of form of life, to rules of discourse or action (rules of the game), and so on. In general, wherever there is determinacy, definiteness, particularity, differentiation, there is identity. Indeed, the generic hermeneutical principle of existence/meaning is: to be is to be determinate, to be something, to be differentiated, for any possible item of reality.

It is important for our purposes to stress the pervasiveness of identity for lived everyday experience because it has been customary to restrict questions of identity to the existence of *objects* rather than acknowledging it as the general principle for any and all possible kinds of entities constituting a life-world. In addition, philosophical discussions of identity have tended to suggest that identity is an abstract principle important to logical theory rather than stressing that it is the lived principle of everyday existence— the living center of common sense.

i) Identity as the Principle of Existential Independence
A primary feature of hermeneutical identity is that of existential independence. Any given item of a life-world in having identity thereby has independence of self-existence. This inner self definition permits the thing in question to enter into relations with other items of the world. For example, my identity as a self (as the referent of "I") entails my independent existence as an entity in the world. It makes me different from you, he, she, it or any other entity. This very independence and self-definition allows me to be in relation with other entities— to be dependent upon others for my continued life.

ii) Identity as the Principle of Duality (Opposition, Difference)
Another way to see the same point is to recognize that identity arises in opposition or differentiation— to be something, say A, is thereby to be differentiated from every other item *different from* A, which is *not-A* (say B). So identity arises in ontological negation or opposition and is at the same time the principle of difference. In this respect there is a primitive

ontological contrariety of Identity/Difference which is inseparable. Contrariety is a primitive opposition in which each item in the relation formally depends upon the other and this manifestation of identity immediately leads to the principles of non-contradiction and excluded middle: any given item cannot both be and not be what it is. Thus, duality is in the heart of identity.

iii) *Identity as the Structure of Predication*

But identity in the form of primary opposition discloses itself as the ontological form of *predication;* predication is at once ontological as the structure of existence, and logical as the structure of thought and meaning— predication is the primary form of logos. In this form it becomes evident that to be any given thing (to be a logical subject) is to constitute attributes in a unity, and the identity of any given thing consists in its being *identical* with some primary attribute which is its *essence.* Thus, again, in the identity of the self (the referent of I) that which distinguishes the self from all other entities and which *defines* it as such is its essence. That self would not be what it is were it not for its essence. So identity is identity with essence.

iv) *Identity as the Principle of Essence (Determinacy/Particularity)*

Identity as essence shows itself in predicative form: to exist is to be a possible *ontological subject* with at least one distinguishing mark. It may be said that to exist is to be determinate or particularized in some way, and to lack identity is to lack particularity— to be indeterminate and undifferentiated, i.e., to be nothing at all.

v) *Identity as Atomicity, Plurality, Incommensurability*

The identity structure of common sense existence discloses itself in an existential atomicity and plurality— this follows from the features of independence and particularity. Existential atomicity of identity (essence) helps us to see clearly the ontological autonomy and self centeredness of any given item of the world. The *uniqueness* of any essence immediately leads to a form of *existential incommensurability* in which the inner integrity of discrete (individual) entities in a life-world perseveres in *internal unity* and external plurality. In this respect the identity of different things cannot form a genuine common unity: different things cannot be identical. Just as the arising of identity creates simultaneous difference, so too the arising of determinacy in identity brings forth indeterminacy as incommensurability of identity between diverse particulars— one identity cannot *be* another. This helps us to see that *formal identity brings unity and diversity:* internal identity is unity, while external non-identity is diversity or dis-unity.

b) Identity and Literal Meaning: Univocity and Ambiguity

Having reviewed some of the primary features of existential identity we are in a better position to appreciate identity as *the principle of meaning* in all of its forms. The identity of the meaning of any given term of a language naturally conforms to the structure of identity and in this context identity of meaning defines the *univocity of terms*. The identity of any given term consists in its univocal significance. To have determinate meaning is to have one definite sense in a given language, even if the meaning of the term is somewhat vague. At the same time the principle of univocity is the very principle which determines ambiguity or equivocity— the principle of differentiation of meaning. Meaning becomes incoherent if one and the same term (identity) has more than one distinct meaning, so the principle of literal meaning formally requires any such equivocal term to be existentially split into at least two distinct terms. The word "bank" in ordinary English, for example, happens to have two distinct senses so the principle of univocity requires that this word must indicate two distinct terms.

The logic of literal discourse for any given life-world consists in the one-to-one correspondence between a given term and its fixed definite meaning may be given in the unique reference of a term or in the unique rule of use which governs the term's use in the language-game in question. So in its generic form literal discourse (meaning in identity) must not be confused with *descriptive* language— the language-game in which facts are described, objects referred to, events reported, etc.— but more generally includes all forms of language use in which there is fixity and identity of meaning. For example, in the language-games in which we tell jokes, prescribe or direct conduct, perform ceremonies, express feelings, etc., there are definite rules of the game which make the various forms of discourse possible. It needs to be stressed that the logic of identity governs the determinate rules of use which constitute distinct and diverse language forms. In general the condition of univocity points to the uniqueness and determinateness of rules of use of a given term: *one meaning means one use in the language.*

c) The Literal Meaning and Ontological Grammar: Sense and Non-Sense

Literal meaning in all of its forms arises within a determinate ontological grammar or life-world. We have seen that such a grammar consists of an ordered and systematic configuration of basic categories which defines what makes sense and what does not. It is the *categorial grammar* which makes literal meaning possible, for the rules of use of terms in a language derive directly from the mutual relations of categories in the pyramid form. Those categories which predicatively join make sense and those which do not join are predicatively incommensurable and lead to non-sense. The joining of terms in predication which cannot configure according to the categorial grammar results in a *category mistake,* which is non-sense.

It is in the uniqueness of a given categorial grammar that we uncover the relation between formal identity, univocity and sense/non-sense. The principle of identity gives unique determination to a categorial grammar as a whole in discriminating it from different categorial grammars. But it is the *grammar* which determines the univocal meaning of terms and prescribes the correct rules of use thereby defining what makes sense and what does not. Thus, in the categorial grammar of ordinary English, for example, it is grammatical to say "The sky is blue," but ungrammatical to say "Seven is blue." This is because the grammar permits the commensurability of "sky" and "blue" (the sky is a colored thing), and prescribes the incommensurability of "seven" and "blue" (numbers are not colored things).

It is timely to elaborate on the internal form and identity of categories. We have seen that a category (in any given life-world) is an all-inclusive and exhaustive domain of reality. From the point of view of *meaning* structure a category combines contrary opposites into a primitive unity: for every term P there is a contrary opposite un-P (the privation of P) which together define the range of a category. For example, the term "red" and its contrary "un-red" taken as a unity, "that which is red or un-red," defines the category of /color/. All things which are colored (including those un-colored things which could be colored, like colorless water) fall within the category of /color/. Since numbers are not included within the category of /color/ it is non-sense to predicate (unite) these two terms in the grammar of common sense English.

The unity or identity of contrary opposites in a primitive category teaches us that we must distinguish between "opposites" that are commensurable and those that are incommensurable. Intra-categorial opposites (logical contraries) are commensurable opposites which are united in the more primitive category. For example, although "red" and "blue" each has unique identity and exclude each other (incommensurable) they are nevertheless commensurable in being united in a more primitive level in the category of /color/. But within an ontological grammar where *categories* mutually exclude each other we encounter *inter-categorial incommensurability*. In our previous example the category of /numbers/ and the category of /color/ are incommensurable opposites.

d) Metaphor as the Violation of Category Rules

The ontological origin and primacy of literal meaning helps us to understand the logic of metaphor. We have seen that identity is the very form of existence and meaning, and this entails the *primacy* of literal meaning— a given categorial grammar defines what is real, and literal meaning immediately mirrors the world. Any deviant form of "meaning" which violates the categorial grammar ostensibly distorts reality and must be ontologically derivative and secondary.

If we take identity and literal discourse to be ontologically primary, then metaphoric meaning appears to arise from the violation of categorial grammar; that is, to arise out of non-sense. For example, if the categorial grammar reveals that "love" and "color" are categorially incommensurable, it would be a category-mistake to say "Love is blue." Nevertheless, a poet may say just that, and in the context of poetry we concede some form of meaning to such utterances. It may be said that such an utterance has *metaphoric* meaning in contrast to literal import: literally it is non-sense, but metaphorically it makes some sort of sense.

Metaphoric meaning is ontologically intriguing. Although it has been much discussed in recent times, most of the discussions have not been sensitive to the *ontology* of metaphor. Metaphor is especially interesting from the point of view of the principle of identity since it appears to take the middle way between the duality of univocity and equivocity. For example, in the utterance "Love is blue" the meaning would be lost if "blue" were taken in its literal or univocal sense. But if we then use the principle of identity to enforce ambiguity and judge that "blue" in this context has an entirely different (equivocal) meaning from the literal sense, we also lose the essence of the metaphoric use of "blue." It appears that the logic of identity with its opposition of univocal/equivocal cannot be the principle of metaphoric meaning. With respect to categorial grammar it is too strong to say that metaphoric meaning is non-sense (a category mistake). It certainly appears that metaphoric meaning violates the rules of literal use, but it also seems to be the case that metaphor has a logic of its own and is not simply a distortion of meaning. Nor should it be assumed that metaphor is secondary and distorts reality; on the contrary, we must leave open the possibility that poetic insight expressed in metaphor may disclose reality more deeply than literal discourse.

A popular way to account for metaphoric meaning which takes literal meaning to be primary claims that there is an essential link between *metaphor and analogy*. This approach implicitly recognizes that the hard opposition between univocity and equivocity leaves no room for metaphoric meaning which appears to be in-between. It attempts to open up such a space by introducing or postulating a special kind of relation called *analogy*. This relation is not as strong as identity (univocity) and weaker than difference (ambiguity). When pressed for the basis of such a relation, the mild "connection" of similarity, resemblance, or association, is invoked. However, the primacy of literal discourse and identity presupposes that there must be some sort of real connection (identity) upon which to base analogy in the first place: resemblance must be based upon some kind of unity or identity between the two similar entities in question. For example, in theological discourse it may be said that God is good, and the question is raised whether "good" is used in the same univocal sense as in saying that humans are good. But if God and humans are ontologically incommensurable, the principle of identity would require us to equivocate the term "good" when predicated of God and humans. It cannot then be said that there is an *analogy* between God's goodness and human goodness if the two are radically incommensurable. For in order to establish a basis for the comparison of similarity, the two kinds of entities must have *something* in common— they must share some *univocal* term of terms.

So we cannot appeal to analogy for the relation between truly incommensurable terms.[3]

e) Metaphor and the Problem of Unity (Identity)

The fact that analogy *presupposes* identity and the primacy of literal meaning renders it ineffective in accounting for the logic of metaphor. It appears that metaphor defies the laws of identity, and it is not a mere violation of the rules of literal meaning. It challenges the duality between univocity and equivocity and presents itself precisely as a primitive unity or "identity" of opposites. It makes commensurable what literal meaning discloses as incommensurable. It challenges the ontological prejudice that literal discourse is primary discourse. Metaphor calls the principle of identity into question and calls for an account which does not presuppose the logos of identity.

f) Communication and Hermeneutical Privacy/Indeterminacy

Identity typically creates a predicament for itself by generating an incommensurable dualism or dichotomy which *precludes* the possibility of a common unity (commensurable identity) but which at the same time *presupposes* a common unity between the opposites in order to work. We have just seen this dynamic at work in the predicament of metaphor— the need for a univocal identity between the poles of univocal and equivocal meaning. The same pattern creates a paradox in the case of communication. For formal identity takes the individual person to be ontologically primary and meaning is thereby organized around the individual self (ego) which gives rise to a form of hermeneutical subjectivity and privacy. On the other hand, identity also gives ontological primacy to the identity of the community as a whole, which gives rise to hermeneutical objectivity and communality. In this way the dual opposition between the individual person and the collective community, between the subjective and the objective, between the private and the public arises. This polarity involves two opposite identities which are existentially incommensurable: each claims a primacy, but on the principle of identity only one or the other can be primary. The dynamic which takes the individual person to be the primary reality is the typical requirement of ontological *atomism,* while the movement which takes the community (polis) to have ontological priority (independent identity) arises with ontological anatomism (monism). It should be noted that each incommensurable pole is a result of the common principle of identity.

The self-created paradox of communication generated by identity may be seen as follows. If atomic identity is given in the identity of the individual person, then meaning is centered around the *individuated* life-world; and this means that meaning and experience must be in some sense ontologically subjective and private. The resulting problem of communication would be to establish that there is a true unity and community of meaning between individual persons (subjects), that is, to establish the reality of a communal life-world. So, atomic identity leads to the challenge of hermeneutical privacy. If, on the other hand, anatomic identity is given in the identity of the community, then meaning is centered around the communal life-world; and this would mean that meaning and experience must be ontologically objective and public. The resulting problem of communication is then to establish that there is true unity and community of meaning between *individual* persons, that is, to establish the reality of *individual* persons with distinct identity. Atomic identity precludes the primary reality of communal meaning, but anatomic identity equally threatens the primary reality of the individual person. But the ontology of communication presupposes the reality of both poles: it requires the genuine individuated subjectivity of the living person, as well as the communal "objectivity" of the living community. Communication requires a *mediating principle* between the incommensurable poles. That is, it requires a *third identity* which is primary and which is at once both subjective and objective, both individual and communal, both private and public.

We have seen that the life-world is the unit of meaning, and it has been stressed that the primacy of the life-world *precedes* the duality of individual subjectivity and communal objectivity; it makes the private/public distinction possible. Still, there is a deep sense of hermeneutical subjectivity or ontological privacy that perserveres in the life of identity— even in the sharing of a *communal* life-world. For identity holds sway equally in communal identity, in the identity of a culture as a whole, creating incommensurable oppositions between cultural languages. So, even if communal meaning can be established in the primacy of a shared life-world, the problem of hermeneutical privacy of meaning remains.

It should now be clearer that identity leads to ontocentrism as a form of hermeneutical privacy or "subjectivity," whether in the case of an individual person (ego) or in the case of a community— both are cases of onto-centrism. Hermeneutical privacy obtains even in the case of a communally shared life-world, and this makes explicit that the problem of "private" language or meaning is not just a matter of meaning being subjective for the individual consciousness, it arises equally for communal consciousness as well. Ontocentrism at the individual or communal level points to the same general challenge for communication: on what grounds can it ever be determined that meaning (experience, existence, logos) is ever genuinely shared between individual persons or individual communities. The life of identity creates the predicament of hermeneutical privacy as well as hermeneutical indeterminacy. If the life-worlds of individual persons are ontologically private and incommensurable, then this leads to the radical indeterminacy of meaning— each person would be speaking a private language and living in his own world.[4]

g) Metaphor and Communication: Incommensurability and Unity of Meaning

We now begin to see more clearly the intimate connection between the logic of metaphor and the ontology of communication: both involve paradoxes of meaning which arise from the common principle of identity, and both share a common predicament of requiring a unity (identity) between incommensurable opposites. Metaphoric meaning defies identity by requiring the legitimacy of *trans-categorial predications* (identity and unity between incommensurable concepts), while communication defies identity by requiring legitimate *transcategorial relations* (primary identity and unity between incommensurable life-worlds). In both cases a new principle of transcategorial unity/ identity is required to legitimize and save the phenomena. In each case there is an incommensurable dualism or opposition entailed by identity, but at the same time there is need for a primitive unity-in-duality precluded by identity. It appears that the key to understanding both metaphor and communication is to be found in apprehending the rationality of transcategorial relations. We may then be in a position to see that communication essentially involves metaphoric meaning, and metaphoric meaning arises in a principle of the unity of incommensurables, a principle which both respects the primacy of distinctions and oppositions and yet reveals the essential unity between what identity takes to be incommensurable.

PART II: HOW ESSENTIAL IDENTITY ATTEMPTS TO SOLVE THE PROBLEM OF COMMUNICATION

In Part 1 we attempted to draw out more fully the ontological implications of formal identity for meaning, experience, and existence. It was stressed that identity was the universal form of common sense as this is constituted in different life-worlds or grammars of existence. It became evident that the principle of identity in its general form implied a *fixity* and objectification of meaning in duality throughout natural discourse in its full variety of "language-games." In this broadest sense identity entails a general form of essentialism of meaning which determines literal discourse. It was then shown that identity takes literal discourse to be primary meaning (literalism) which in turn leads to the hermeneutical pathology of onto-centrism. The very form of identity structures meaning, experience, and existence into an individuated (egocentric) particularity that manifests itself in the incommensurability of life-worlds. It is here that the full problematic which identity poses for itself displays the impasse of communication, an impasse which challenges identity to authenticate itself by demonstrating the essential unity and identity of diverse life-worlds in a community of meaning. Let us now briefly examine how essential identity attempts to resolve the paradox of communication by uncovering the foundations of meaning.

a)   Essentialism, Absolutism, and the Foundations of Meaning
The natural strategy of formal identity to find the common factor (the common identity between incommensurable life-worlds) that makes communication work is to point to *the absolute foundations of meaning*. Hermeneutical privacy is taken to be a form of relativism and subjectivity of meaning which falls short of the true objective common meaning "out there." Essentialism teaches that there is, after all, an absolute and objective foundation of true meaning which provides the basis of communication. Thus, identity diagnoses the problem of communication as being the degeneracy of relativism and prescribes absolute objective meaning (absolutism) as the cure.

But identity has presented a variety of candidates for the absolute foundations of objective meaning. One of its implicit assumptions is that meaning is objectively grounded in absolute reality, and it takes reality to be noumenal and pre-hermeneutically given. This view assumes that reality (the world) is in some important sense independent of human consciousness and understanding and remains the objective and universal standard of meaning. The true meaning of terms in a language it is supposed is determined by the objective referent in "external" reality which the term in question specifies: the meaning is the objective referent of the term. Of course, this strategy to find the common factor underlying communication reduces life-worlds to *world-views,* that is, it takes life-worlds to be at best approximations to reality, not reality itself. This implies that the diverse life-worlds (different ontological grammars, different cultural worlds) are different re-constructions or interpretations of the one true reality. The diversity and incommensurability of life-worlds is taken to be subjective differences which can be mediated and overcome by the central reference to the one absolute reality. The assumption of an objective reality—objects, facts, events— as the foundation of meaning requires a dualism between mental states and the world and treats alleged ontological differences between life-worlds as if they were epistemological states of consciousness. These states of mind have validity to the extent that they approximate and mirror accurately the objective world of neutral facts.

However, if this assumption of absolute foundations is tested by the standards of identity itself, it is found that the paradox of communication is only deepened and the problem re-located. For we have seen that identity necessarily involves determinacy and specificity; but when we press further for the identity of this alleged neutral reality, all we find is an empty postulate with no content. Any attempt to approach or apprehend this alleged objective reality in itself is inherently doomed to frustration and failure. In terms of the absolute standards of identity that which is without specificity and content cannot exist, for to be is to be determinate. Even worse, the dualism between mind (mental states, interpretation, epistemology) and reality now becomes incommensurable and far from answering the paradox of communication the postulate of foundations creates a deeper chasm. Instead of the challenge of incommensurable multiple reality is which recognized the ontological status of life-worlds, absolutism postulates a single absolute and independent reality-in-itself which is incommensurable with hermeneutical reason; between a determinate life-world and an indeterminate postulated reality there is no commensurability and the possibility of genuine knowledge is undermined. It appears that the postulate of absolute independent foundations of meaning does not provide the basis of unity and community of meaning necessary for communication.[5]

When the life of identity sees that this postulate of the objective referent does not work, it typically shifts ground and attempts to relocate the objective foundations in the conventional *rules of use* of the various language-games we play; or it appeals to the alleged objective standards of common observable human behavior as the ground of meaning. An example of this shift in the strategy of essentialism may be found in the later writings of Wittgenstein. His earlier work took the direction of naive essentialism (identity) just examined above, and his later research attempted to overcome this form of essentialism by locating objective meaning in the rules of use of expressions in natural language. He took this to be the origin of meaning and argued well against naive essentialism. But we have seen that no feature of experience stands outside the hermeneutical circle— not the facts, not human action or behavior, and not the conventional rules that gives meaning to any form of life. In the *generic* understanding of identity *all* features of experience and existence take on determinate, fixed, essential meaning, including the rules of use of various language games.

Furthermore, Wittgenstein attempts to answer one form of private meaning (private language) which arose from naive identity and essentialism; he taught that we can avoid the mistakes of private language by coming to see that meaning arises in the rules of use of terms, and that the following of such rules is directly translatable into linguistic behavior which he took to be an objective ground of meaning. He attempted to show that the very concept of a private language (to which any single person alone had privileged access in principle) was incoherent, but he steered away from naive essentialism by respecting an irreducible diversity of language-games or forms of meaning (life). However, this important critique of naive essentialism does not answer the problem of communication. Indeed, it turns out to be another form of generic essentialism which begs the hermeneutical question. For the rules of use of expressions, the language-games, and the conventional linguistic behavior which purports to be the objective ground of meaning in natural language are *themselves* hermeneutically indeterminate and open to systematic ambiguity and incommensurability across life-worlds. Wittgenstein's insight into the incoherence of "private" languages does not address the theme of *hermeneutical* privacy which already assumes that language must be communicable. The generic critique of essentialism requires us to see that facts, rules of use, and linguistic behavior are all equally indeterminate (precisely because of their fixity) and cannot be appealed to for the objective foundations of meaning across life-worlds or language games.

b) Relativism as a Form of Foundationalism
When identity plays itself out to one extreme of absolutism and discovers that this does not address the paradox of communication, it typically moves to the opposite extreme in an attempt to resolve the predicament. While absolutism is one pole of essentialism which postulates a single (monistic) objective and independent foundation for meaning, relativism is the opposite pole of essentialism which postulates a plurality (atomic) of

distinct and incommensurable languages each having its own standards and ground of meaning. What is meaningful in one language-world is not meaningful in another, and there are no absolute objective and common standards between the languages. In this respect each language becomes absolute in itself and internally determines what is meaningful. Needless to say this is just another form of identity and essentialism since ontological relativism presupposes the unique atomic identity of diverse languages. This form of identity merely multiplies the foundations of meaning and celebrates incommensurability, which, we have seen, is a natural outcome of essential identity.

That relativism has often been confused with subjectivism should not distract us from discerning its roots in identity. Nor should the fact that abolutism has been identified with monistic foundationalism keep us from seeing that relativism is a form of *multiple* atomic foundationalsim. The critical ontological factor is that relativism presupposes a plurality of distinct identities each of which is absolute in itself. When relativism is superimposed upon the individual person, and each individual person is taken to be a subjective standard, then relativism becomes subjectivism. But relativism may equally take the form of objectivism if each individual person, for example, is taken to be the objective standard. Indeed, relativism is the form of identity which collapses subjectivism and objectivism in a multiplicity of distinct and incommensurable foundations.

It becomes clear that relativism and absolutism are polar opposites of essential identity, the latter being a form of monistic essentialism while the former is a form of atomic (pluralistic) essentialism. Just as absolutism fails to produce any determinate pre-hermeneutical common foundations of meaning which makes communication possible, we may anticipate that relativism likewise fails to show how communication is possible. For communication requires a shared identity and community of meaning, but relativism precludes this possibility from the start. Indeed, it leads to skepticism concerning communication in the sense in which we have taken it. Relativism of meaning makes clear how essential identity necessarily leads to hermeneutical privacy, incommensurability of meaning between distinct languages and the indeterminacy of meaning between speakers. Of course, such relativism is then free to tamper with the meaning of communication and alter it to its own designs. Relativism takes liberty and goes so far as to make indeterminacy and incommensurability of meaning the very *basis* of communication and translatability. It dares to point to radical *difference* and systematic ambiguity as the common factor underlying communication. Relativism attempts to re-make communication in its own image and show that absolutistic communication cannot be true communication, that there cannot be and need not be a common univocal and determinate community of meaning in communication. Of course, this ploy of relativistic identity concedes that communication in the common sense meaning which we have focused upon is incoherent. Thus, relativism as a form of identity fails to resolve the paradox of communication. 6

c) Identity and Faith in Communication

It appears, then, that identity as the supposed form of common sense is unable to rationally account for communication. But common sense is sensible and refuses to be sceptical about genuine communication. If critical common sense holds on to essential identity as the principle of meaning and affirms literal discourse as primary meaning, then it is faced with two alternatives. Either it must become sceptical about communication or else reaffirm communication and begin to question its literalism and fundamentalism of meaning. If it is sensible, it will trust its intuition that communication does take place and realize that it takes place in faith. It will acknowledge that the foundations of meaning (in absolutism or relativism) is a *postulate of faith* of essential identity which cannot be rationally explained by its own understanding of rationality. It would be healthy for the fundamentalist hermeneutic or meaning to openly declare that communication rests on faith, for it would at least be speaking the truth and ironically opening the door to the serious questioning of essential identity as the formal principle of meaning and common sense. What would be unhealthy is the blind pretense that communication is rationally explained by the foundations of meaning. The recognition that communication in common sense everyday life rests on faith opens the way to a deeper understanding of rational faith and a transformation beyond identity as the principle of meaning and rationality.7

PART III: MEDITATION, METAPHOR, AND THE ONTOLOGICAL RELATIVITY OF MEANING

In retrospect it now becomes clearer that from the *beginning* of this inquiry we had already entered a journey of the self-questioning and self-transformation of understanding. While appearing to be centered within the grammar of essential identity we called identity into question and hopefully saw that there was good reason to be skeptical about the hermeneutic of identity. We are now at a critical point in our hermeneutical journey. We must make every effort to bracket and suspend our ontological habits of identity and open ourselves to a more radical hermeneutical transformation to non-dual meditative discourse. This is especially difficult since, as we have seen the depth and primacy of life of identity takes existence, experience, meaning, and common sense to be *essentially* a matter of individual identity and duality. It seems that *by definition* existence and everything about it must arise in identity and difference. So, to suggest that we suspend the life of identity and allow reason and being to speak to us anew in non-duality seems to be asking the impossible. It would be naive to think that we could *at will* lay the life of identity aside for the moment, for intention and volition themselves arise with the hermeneutic of identity. But the fact that this suspension or questioning of identity appears impossible should not stop us because the logic of identity has also disclosed that we are *already* in an impossible situation.

As a therapeutic device of hermeneutical self-transformation, let us act as if the life of identity were in an impossible situation, let us assume that literal discourse is not primary discourse, let us work with the hypothesis that essential identity is not the true principle of rationality and understanding, and let us entertain the possibility that identity has eclipsed from us the true workings of common sense, the true meaning of everyday existence, the authentic principle of meaning in natural language. This hermeneutical experiment might help us to resolve the paradox of communication.

a) Meditation as a Natural Rational Transformation

The hermeneutic of identity necessarily distorts and misperceives meditative reason. It takes meditation to be some sort of esoteric act of thought which is extra-rational and which takes consciousness to some alleged realm of silence in a certain illusive, mystical state of mind. But once identity is called into question and taken to task, the way is open for a hermeneutical inversion in which it is *identity itself* that is revealed as irrational. In the logic of meditation one sees that meditation is not an act of mind of the ego, not a state of awareness, not esoteric or mystical, but rather the original, natural, spontaneous, ever-present light of reason which *already* pervades common sense. To see that meditation eludes ordinary essentialistic description is already *to be* in meditative transformation. It cannot be described as a state of mind, because it is not a state and it is not of mind; it cannot be described as an act in any ordinary sense, for this would imply the separability of the act and agent, and so on. The language of identity is inappropriate in approaching meditation. Meditation calls for a transcategorial mode of speech in which to speak of meditation is to speak meditatively. When the noise of identity is silenced, the speech of meditation may be heard and remembered. Meditative speech makes perfect sense; the world is intelligible, things are in harmony, and experience becomes rational and coherent. In the hermeneutical transformation to meditative reason it may be seen that the light of reason was ever-present to the ego-centric life although eclipsed by identity. This light breaks through from time to time at high moments in everyday life when the ego temporarily gets out of the way and pure reason shows itself: in moments of creativity, in moments of inspiration, in times of religious experience, in moments of pure action when the ego-agent is not the doer. These fleeting flashes of meditative light appear to arise spontaneously and to disappear beyond our control and beyond our understanding.

The science and discipline of meditation teaches the way out of the darkness of identity into the light of reason. The therapeutic discourse of this hermeneutical conversion is ever sensitive to the transformative dialogue between the light and darkness. This dialogue *itself* creates special confusions, for it becomes inherently "ambiguous" which hermeneutical voice is speaking— the voice of identity or the voice of meditation. Sometimes the therapeutic speech appears to be using terms in their literal (identity) sense, but then it appears that it cannot have been speaking in the unequivocal voice of identity. At other times it seems that it is the meditative voice which is speaking fully in its own terms, but then how could it be speaking to the condition of identity? In any case it is clear that therapeutic speech does not conform to the standards of identity and its logic of discursive thinking. It has a dynamic logic of its own in which speech itself is self-transformed in speech.

b) Meditation and the Principle of Ontological Relativity
As we now enter more deeply into the hermeneutical circularity of therapeutic speech, the logos of meditation becomes more evident. The *transformation* to meditative speech itself requires the principle of meditative reason. One way to approach this principle is to re-trace the fall of reason into duality and self-opposition. This re-tracing of the path of essential identity is not a mere *denial* of the principle of identity, not a mere *reversal* of dual identity. It is rather a seeing through of identity back into the original *non-dual* unity of the light of reason. It is a *trans-versal* of the principle of identity which *provisionally* speaks of "opposites" only to show that they were misunderstood by identity. We recover the space of non-dual unity by *crossing through* essential identity.

The inversion of essential identity brings us into the "circular" non-dual space of pure reason. Now we see that "opposites" are already unified in non-difference. When identity/difference is transported from linear space into multi-dimensional curved rational space, it is seen that the identity of one (i.e., co-arises in) is the identity of the other. Nothing has identity independently of anything else. The identity of anything functionally arises with the identity of everything else. The principle of *non-difference of opposites* reveals the non-dual nature of things, and the *dualities* of identity are now recognized to be non-dual differences. Thus, the ontological separations of mind and body, of thought and object, of subject (thinker) and object (what is thought), of sense and reference, of word (signified) reference and object (what is signified), of theory and practice, of thought and action, of talking and doing, and so on, are healed in the reason of non-duality.8

But how can there be *anything*, any individual, particular, differentiated thing in the space of non-duality? How can there be anything without essential identity? The principle of *non-dual identity* teaches us a new meaning of *identity* and *thing*. Any thing resonates with the identity of any and every other thing. For example, my identity— the meaning and reference of "I"— is not limited to the meaning of "I" in any one ontological grammar; it resonates with multiple meaning and identities across diverse grammars. But it is not just a multiplicity of diverse identities; it is a primitive (non-dual) unity. The true identity of "I" consists in the unity of all possible meanings for all possible worlds. But this universal (transcategorial) identity of "I" opens the door for *I* to be non-different from all other identities in the world. It becomes apparent that the principle of non-dual identity must be a recursive, reiterative, circular or self referential principle of the *transitivity* of identity, for all possible identities. Transcategorial identity for any one thing implies the relativity of identity for all things. So, the non-dual identity of "I" immediately "touches" the identity of everything else, and there is ontological commensurability of all things with all things. Distinctions are not barriers between things, but openings and horizons for being in and with the other. In the non-dual identity of any spacial position, the "here" immediately reaches and locates itself in every other possible location in the ontological curvature of space. And so on.

The mind of identity remains puzzled by all this talk of multiple identities and remains skeptical about the alleged non-dual unity of "circular" reason. It continues to press for explanations that it can relate to— explanations, for example, of how things can be determinate and fixed and differentiated with the so-called "non-dual identity." Of course, the therapeutic speech is quite familiar with such resistance and clinging to essential identity. It replies not by trying to explain the matter in essentialistic terms but carries the skeptic deeper into the territory of relativity where identity loses its hold. One therapeutic device is the principle of *recursivity;* this feature of circular reason helps to "explain" the presence of distinct particulars in non-dual identity. Recursivity is the non-difference between the finite and the infinite, a bridge between the finite and infinite. The recursive identity of anything consists of the transcategorial infinity of identity of all things. Just as certain syntactic rules of language are recursive in being finite yet allowing an infinity of well-formed possibilities, so, too, the identity of anything is "finite" yet resonates with infinite possibilities. In the politics of reality a given cultural language prescribes where the determinate identity of anything is to be fixed. The fixing of identity in essence is an ontological convention of a life-world. But therapeutic speech is most effective when it reminds the skeptic that essential identity has *not* succeeded in explaining the nature of particulars and has only succeeded in producing some entertaining paradoxes.

It is timely to re-introduce the term *Logos* into our therapeutic conversation. *Logos* is the principle of relativity: the non-dual unity of opposites. In meditative reason Logos is the transcategorial universal identity in which word, meaning, thought, object, existence are non-different.

The word is life, the word is thought, the word is meaning, the word is thing, the word is existence, the word is truth. A good example of the Living Logos would be the non-dual identity of the Christ. The Christ is that being which is the non-dual unity of opposites, of the ultimate opposition of finite and infinite. For if the Christ were dual (two beings, two natures), there would be no true mediation between the finite and infinite and no hope of salvation from the fallen life of identity. The being of Christ makes perfect sense in relativity and presents itself as paradox to essential identity. In relative identity it makes sense for the Christ to say "I am the way," "I am the truth," and so on. The Christ is non-different from his speaking, from his acting, from his presence. The "miracles" performed by the Living Logos break the dualistic barriers: one is made many, the dead is made alive, the fallen is made to rise, water (one identity) is made into wine (another identity), and so on. What must appear to be miraculous to the life of identity is demonstrated as plain truth in relativity. The speech of the Christ, which is the life and being of the Christ, is *meditative* speech.

In the Hindu ontological grammar the Living Universal Word (Logos) speaks forth as AUM— the Sacred syllable. This is the non-dual transcategorial identity of all identities which is the principle of ontological relativity. Every word, every name, is non-different from AUM. Lord Krishna, the Living AUM, is the cosmic (transcategorial) identity of relativity.

Similarly, in the Buddhist grammar, Buddha Nature is the Living Logos, the universal identity, the principle of relativity itself. The transfinite presence and speech of the Buddha is meditative speech.

The principle of ontological relativity, the relativity of identity, is the principle of meditative reason. But it is a principle which cannot be stated or approached in the language of identity. It must be a *living* principle which may be spoken and heard only in the recursive space of meditation.

Thus, utterance of the principle of relativity involves the hermeneutical transformation to primary Logos.

c) Meditative Logos, Metaphor, and Primary Speech

Perhaps it is now easier to see that metaphoric meaning could not be approached in the language of identity (literalism, univocity). At best it can characterize *metaphor* as a unity of incommensurables (opposites). But such a unity it could not comprehend, and the impossibility of uniting incommensurables must lead identity to tolerate metaphor as extrarational. But now in the space of relativity, metaphor makes perfect sense and appears in its universal form. Incommensurables for identity are nondifferent for relativity. Metaphor may be spoken in meditative speech as the principle of relativity itself. The example of the Christ as a metaphor (unity of opposites) requires us to approach metaphor anew as the living logos, the living word. Metaphor comes to life in meditative speech; as the recursive principle of relativity, any metaphor resonates infinitely with meaning. Living metaphors are inexhaustible in connotations; and if they are *fixed* in meaning and limited in essential identity, the word dies. In the life of identity metaphors are experienced as the breaking through of the light of Logos. In the life of relativity *all* speaking is metaphoric. Thus, metaphors are powerful transformative utterances which invoke the dead, inert, fixed word (identity) to become alive with meaning (logos).

This therapeutic function of metaphor helps us to see why metaphors are so important to conventional speech. True metaphors activate the ontological imagination and give it a flash into the space of relativity. Such imagination works on the principle of relativity, and in those rare flashes of meditative insight a new life-world may be conceived and given birth in poetic speech. Ontological poets open the horizon of new worlds in speaking metaphorically. For example, the birth of Einstein's universe arose with the creative metaphor which made commensurable the space between matter and energy and between space and time. The ontological imagination is able to negotiate the space between the incommensurables of identity.[9]

But as we have seen, the life of identity has a difficult time dealing with true living metaphors. It abuses them, crucifies them, nails them down to fix their meaning, thereby "killing" them. It cuts off relativity before it has a chance to take and reduces metaphors to episodic and fanciful speech which takes flight from true reality. But meditative speech reveals that the opposite is true; metaphors have inexhaustible life and are the speaking forth of being itself. In primary speech metaphors are transcategorial universals which speak the truth and which disclose reality. Metaphors are the living truth which disclose reality. Metaphors are the living truth, the immortal life and light of the Word which makes salvation from the bondage of identity possible.

This gives us a new insight into metaphor and primary speech. For while conventional speech takes metaphor to be occasional utterances which violate the rules of literal speech, primary speech reveals metaphor to be the universal norm of true speech. The speaking forth of the Holy Word in the sacred writings (scriptures) of different cultural grammars, for example, are examplars of primary speech and of metaphoric meaning (relativity). The speech of Krishna is primary metaphoric speech. The speech of the Buddha is metaphoric in import, the speech of Jesus is primary speech, where the speaker is non-different from the speech, where the spoken word is the truth. The life of identity violates scripture, but scripture comes to life in relativity.10

We are not far from making the boldest move of all— of going full circle back to the rough ground of ordinary speech. Completing the hermeneutical circle is the natural and inevitable outcome of circular (recursive) reason. When conventional speech discovers its origin in primary speech, when it understands that rational faith is relativity itself, the space between conventional speech and primary speech begins to close. The rules of ordinary speech emerge in a new light, and it is seen that natural language was *already* in perfect order— lying dormant only waiting to be spoken forth in new life. Then it is realized that the life of identity means the death of the Word. When the ossification of literal meaning is released in relativity *all* utterances of everyday language take on their living metaphoric meaning. The simple utterance "I go," for example, resonates as a wonderful metaphor when spoken in primary speech. Our hermeneutical journey, our speech therapy, culminates in the realization that everyday language works only in virtue of the rational light of primary speech. When conventional speech goes on "holiday," the perfection of natural language can come to life again in primary speech.11

d) Meditation, Metaphor, and Communication

The universality of metaphoric meaning as the basis of meaning in natural language helps us to understand how communication works in everyday life. We saw earlier that communication requires a genuine unity and community of meaning, and such unity was precluded by identity in the incommensurability of life-worlds. However, the therapeutic transformation to primary Logos, primary speech in relativity, teaches us that true meaning involves the unity or co-arising of "incommensurables." Metaphoric meaning cuts through the paradox of communication which arose in the mistake of taking identity to be absolute and literal meaning to be primary. Now it is found that the unity of meaning which makes communication possible is the non-dual unity in Logos of the community of speakers. To speak from the ego is to speak onto-centrically, but to speak meditatively is be in *communion* with the other. The communion of relativity reveals that the *identity* of "I" is situated in the community of discourse. The unity of communication is not an external unity of univocal meaning of linguistic utterances but the non-dual unity of the life of Logos itself, the unity found in metaphoric meaning. We remain united in primary speech even when this is eclipsed in identity and conventional speech. The multiplicity of incommensurable life-worlds which is disclosed in the life of identity now shows itself to be united in the communion of relativity.

That communication arises in ontological communion is an inevitable truth of relativity and primary speech. Communication, like metaphor, is a unity of "incommensurables" that can be addressed and realized only in primary speech. What conventional speech takes to be communication is a supposed and problematic sharing of linguistic meaning. But communication in relativity is a hermeneutical transformation to meditative Logos. Were primary speech not ever-present to conventional speech, there would be no hope of true communication. Insofar as there is any communication in conventional speech, it arises in the foundations of relativity and metaphoric meaning. This is the rational faith that makes communication work in everyday life But the true foundations of meaning in relativity goes beyond the absolutism and relativism of essential identity.

The communion of primary speech teaches that communication is not an intentional act of the ego but an ontological touching of the other (the direct I-Thou dialogical encounter) which needs no conventional speech. Communication, like meditation, is a celebration of our commensurability. Whenever we truly communicate, our speech brings us closer together in Logos. But it is *because* we are *already* united in relativity that we can communicate at all. We can each speak our ontological grammars in primary speech; and when we speak to each other in primary speech, nothing needs to be said in order to communicate, for the highest communication is the speaking of Silence.

Notes

1 For a systematic discussion of ontology as hermeneutical science see the first five articles listed below in the references.

2 Contemporary "ordinary language philosophy" has failed to evolve into the phenomenology of ontological hermeneutics. Apparently it takes the established ordinary sense of a term (in ordinary English) to be definitive of the true meaning of that term (how that term is used in ordinary life) and has not recognized the ontological relativity or

ordinary meanings to the life-worlds which govern ordinary languages. It has also acted as if "ordinary language" were the same as ordinary English and has not been sensitive to the diversity of ontological grammars. While the phenomenology of ontological hermeneutics respects the integrity of rules of use of terms in any given ordinary language, it also recognizes the additional task of inquiring into the meaning of a term in ontological relativity. This is explained below.

3 The term "metaphor" is ordinarily used for a range of language uses. But in the ontological analysis of metaphor we shall focus on intercategorial predications. Thus, although it is sometimes said that an utterance such as "the ship plowed through the sea" involves metaphor, from the categorial point of view it is still literal; because the sea is the kind of thing which a plow may literally plow through. There is, indeed, a similarity or analogy between a ship moving through water and a plow moving through earth. But wherever there is genuine analogy there is at best *simile* and not metaphor. The principle of identity must reduce metaphor to *category mistake*.

4 It must be stressed that hermeneutical privacy (onto-centrism) is not to be confused with the subjectivity or privacy of mental states of the individuated ego, nor with the idea of a language which in principle is private to a given individual. Rather, hermeneutical or ontological privacy already assumes that a life-world is in principle communal in its accessibility; from the ontology of meaning it is clear that a life-world and its logos is at once accessible to the individual subject as well as the community at large. So, the ontological "private language' question must not be confused with the versions of private language problems often discussed in analytic philosophy.

5 The reduction of life-worlds to subjective mental states is a misunderstanding of the hermeneutic of identity. For within hermeneutical privacy of a life-world there remains the important distinction between subjective mental states and objective reality. A life-world presents itself as objective and subjective mental states are corrigible with respect to its objectivity.

6 Here again, Wittgenstein's move to a plurality of distinct language games avoided absolutism in the form of a monistic logical foundation of all language. In effect Wittgenstein moved to a form of relativism in claiming a plurality of incommensurable language-games or forms of life. Perhaps he would have seen the full implication of hermeneutical privacy if he had taken the next step to see that different natural languages played different ontological language-games— that is lived different forms of life and spoke different ontological grammars. Instead, he stopped short in the incommensurability of diverse forms of life *within* the logos of a given natural language. In this respect he already accepted the incommensurability of language-games. In another context we find that Quine, in *Word and Object*, recognizes a form of ontological indeterminacy in the object of reference between languages, but through a foundation in ostensibly shared pragmatic criteria and systematic reconstruction that very indeterminacy may be the basis of communication and translatability between languages.

7 For a more developed discussion of the transformation beyond absolutism and relativism see Chapter 7 and for a systematic development of the theme of rational faith (meditative rationality) see Chapter 3.

Of course, the theme that common sense rests on some form of faith has been touched on in various ways in the history of thought. For example, the philosophy of Berkeley and of Hume in different ways point to faith, and certainly the thought of Kant took knowledge and meaning to the horizon of rational faith. But faith has often been thought of as beginning precisely where rationality ends, where essential identity reaches its limits. We shall see in the sequel that once we suspend essential identity as the principle of reason the way is open for a deeper understanding of true faith as the highest form of rationality.

8 The principle of non-duality (relativity) must not be confused with the principle of ontological monism, which is the opposite of atomism. Both poles, atomism and anatomism, equally presuppose the principle of identity. The ontological grammar of anatomism (monism) teaches that all things are really one. It acts as if individual things of the world are like predicates of the One true Substance. But it does not explain how the plurality of "predicates" form a true ontological unity. The duality between substance and attributes remains, and the atomism of diverse attributes continues in the background. The principle of relativity goes beyond atomism and monism.

9 The life of identity is unable to explain such everyday rational phenomena as metaphor, communication, imagination, and memory. It is relativity that makes sense of these as it makes sense of everyday life and common sense. The principle of relativity reveals how imagination can be a unity of incommensurables, how memory can juxtapose incommensurable moments of time in the relativity of time, and so on.

10 A good example of the misunderstanding of primary (meditative) speech may be found in Descartes' *Meditations* and in the traditional interpretations of Descartes' thought. If we take the voice of the *Meditations* in meditative speech, Descartes' arguments become coherent and rational. But, if taken in the language of identity, the "arguments" of Descartes do not work. For example, the meditative utterance "I am, I exist" when taken in relativity defeats the evil demon, for a meditative utterance, being non-dual, is not a proposition or judgment that is separable from the speaking itself. If there were a dual separation between the speaker and spoken, then the spoken may be false. The "necessary truth" of the utterance "I am" is the truth of primary speech not the truth of a predication. Similarly, in the meditative utterance "God is" there is a speaking to God and an immediate disclosure of God. It is not that a proposition ("God exists") is logically entailed by some other propositions. The meditative utterance "God is" discloses the Living Word (non-dual Logos) in such a way that there can be no space between the "Idea" of God and God, no duality between sense and reference, essence and existence.

11 The perfection of natural language is realized in primary speech. The rough ground of ordinary language is pervaded by metaphoric meaning, all things are metaphoric, I am metaphoric, a tree is metaphoric, and so on. Every instance of literal fixed meaning comes to life in metaphoric import in the transformation to relativity.

CHAPTER 7

MEDITATIVE REASON:
FOUNDATIONS FOR INTER-CULTURAL
DISCOURSE

PREFACE

This essay attempts to explore the nature of inter-cultural life. In doing so
it is first necessary to understand the nature of a religious world. It is
suggested that the proper understanding of a religious world must be an
ontological one. The notion of ontological hermeneutics is introduced and
the form and formation of life-worlds is explored. Ontological
hermeneutics reveals that any possible life-world arises on the principle of
essentialistic identity, a formal principle which is constituted in duality.
More importantly it is found that a life-world is inherently dual and
dualistic in structure and is at the same time a universal grammar of
reality. The notion of hermeneutical (Ontological) universality makes clear
that a life-world necessarily has an ultimate transcendent Absolute
(Infinite) point of reference which makes it a universe. Here it is found that
every life-world arises in the dual tension between finite and infinite being.
This dual structure (which is the principle of identity) points the way to the
ontological nature of religious life. A life-world (grammar of experience/
reality) taken in its communal aspect is a culture and the essence of cultural
life involves the religious transformation from ego-centric (finitized,

alienated) life to the higher life which is centered in the Absolute Infinite Transcendent Ground and Unity of the life-world. This analysis reveals that religious transformations are not additional or contingent to a life-world but are rather a constitutive and essential life-force of a life-world. What is to count as religion and religious emerges in a new light.

After exploring the internal (intra-world) dynamics of faith attention is turned to the inter-world religious transformations which arise when diverse life-worlds come into dialogue and conversation. The paper traces the stages of hermeneutical self-conversion that arise in the evolution of interreligious dialogue. Here it is found that the principle of essential (absolute) identity which constitutes the inner structure of life-worlds is called into question and there emerges a deep crisis of identity. It begins to emerge that the great divide in religious life is that between the life of duality (absolute identity) and the life of non-dual logos (relativity). It is found that the principle of duality (absolute identity) fails in its attempt to deal with a true religious pluralism, fails in the attempt to understand true religious diversity. For each religious life-world has its Absolute Transcendent Unifying point of ultimate reference and the hermeneutic of duality collapses when it attempts to recognize a pluralism of diverse infinite absolutes. The inevitable crisis of identity opens the way for a deeper hermeneutical transformation to primary non-dual Logos which arises in the principle of relativity (relative identity). Non-dual logos (life) arises in meditative reason and moves beyond the limitations of absolutism and relativism as it clears the way to the true non-dual Absolute. This necessary religious transformation of inter-religious life presents inter-religious transformations (dialogue, translation, conversion) in a new light. It turns out in relativity that one's own religious grammar already contains the non-dual powers of infinite expansion to a truly Universal significance. It becomes clear that non-dual relativity truly honors the particularity of one's cultural tradition and reveals how dialogue is possible between diverse religious universal grammars. This hermeneutical transformation shows the direction for the resolution of the problem of unity and diversity of religious life-worlds.

PART I: A HERMENEUTIC FOR INTER-CULTURAL RELIGIOUS LIFE

INTRODUCTION

i)   The Problem: How is inter-cultural reflection possible? Unity and Diversity

The enterprise of cross-cultural inquiry must face at the outset a challenge which questions its very possibility. This challenge comes to the fore when we acknowledge two intuitions concerning cross-cultural life. One is the fact that different cultures make sense of the world in significantly different ways and involve different forms of life. What is taken to be significant and meaningful in one cultural world may well fail to make sense in another. The first fact, then, is that cultures are different forms of meaning and different forms of life or being. If this fact is ignored, denied or trivialized, the project of cross-cultural intercourse is undermined. The other primary intuition of cross-cultural discourse is that we humans share a common world and are able to communicate and understand one another across cultures. It is an undeniable fact of life that we can and do engage in significant inter-cultural discourse— it is possible to enter an alien cultural world, learn its language, translate it into our own language and engage in conversation between the two cultural languages. If this intuition be denied, we again render cross-cultural discourse impossible. Nevertheless, the more we reflect on these two intuitions the more it becomes clear that they repel each other and are in an important way incompatible. For the former intuition of *diversity* leads us inevitably to the recognition that cultural life-forms are irreducibly distinct and this leads to skepticism about there being common terms of reference between cultural worlds. But on the other hand, the latter intuition of *unity* teaches us that whatever the differences between cultures may be we humans are able to be of one mind and share a common life and live in a common world. This seems to imply that the differences between cultures cannot be ultimate and must be capable of being overcome in the deeper unity of a common culturally neutral world. Thus, cross-cultural discourse presupposes both *unity* and *diversity* but it finds itself in the apparent dilemma that each is incompatible with the other. How is cross-cultural discourse possible?

The answer to this question must find a way to reconcile both primitive unity and primitive diversity. One cannot be reduced to the other, and one must not be sacrificed for the other; both must be preserved. Are they, indeed, incompatible? If so, what form of reason could hold them together in a dialectical harmony? What is the hermeneutic of cross-cultural discourse?

ii)   Questioning the Problem Formulation: Self-Reference and Self-Transformation

Before we proceed uncritically to accept the above problem formulation and to attempt to answer it, we must pause to reflect on the language in which the problematic is presented. This self-reflection is critical in the present inquiry since the question of the nature of discourse between religious worlds or languages immediately raises the issue of the language in which our inquiry is to take place. For example, are we already situated in a particular cultural language in framing the problem? If so, do we not beg the essential question from the start by articulating a problem that may be valid in one religious language but inappropriate in another? Can we assume that this danger is avoided because in fact our language is culturally neutral and universally valid for any religious form of life? But on what grounds can this substantive assumption be made? If there were such a religiously neutral and universal language would it not be important to explicitly establish that this is the language in which our inquiry takes place? Indeed, would this not be precisely the material factor in resolving the problematic we have just presented? Clearly, then, we must begin by sensitizing ourselves to the language or hermeneutic of our inquiry and proceed with caution to make explicit the language we are speaking.

This concern is especially pressing since earlier ontological studies have made clear the hermeneutical theme[1] which suggests that to think, to judge, to understand, to interpret, to explain, to act, in short to live, is to be situated in the midst of a life-world, culture or language of reality. A life-world and its language constitutes reality and determines how one makes sense of the world; it makes experience possible. Ontological hermeneutics makes clear that human experience is always structured by the life-world in which one resides and all experience arises within its domain. This is one way to understand the hermeneutical problem: if all experience and meaning arises in the context of one's life-world, then how is it possible to meet an alien life-world on its own terms? This is the familiar problem of the closed hermeneutical circle.

Our present concern is to understand the nature of the transformation from the closed to the open hermeneutical circle. While the previous studies in ontological hermeneutics have taken a more static approach, the present inquiry will focus on the dynamic expansion and self-transformation of a lifeworld in its encounter with alien religious worlds. Beginning with naive pre-reflective conventional understanding we shall attempt to trace and make explicit the inevitable stages of self-evolution of a given life-world as it comes to full hermeneutical self-consciousness in dialogue with a diverse cultural world. Thus, the present inquiry stresses that a life-world is inherently open, organic, growing, self-evolving in an ongoing dramatic way. Similarly, our present journey must itself proceed in dynamic self-transformation and reflect the stages of hermeneutical self-transformation. We may then come to see that the problem formulation with which we have begun must be dissolved rather than solved as we go in full hermeneutical circle.

PART II: ONTOLOGICAL HERMENEUTICS: THE SELF-EVOLUTION OF A LIFE-WORLD

i) Some Terminology for the Journey

Since meaning is constituted by a life-world, the self-transformation of a life-world involves a dynamic transformation of the meaning of the terms of its language. It becomes especially important to coin some resilient and flexible terms which can aid us in our journey. First of all, the term "ontological hermeneutics" which was used in earlier discussions may serve us well in this context. "Ontology" indicates the science of being which investigates the form and transformation of reality. Reality takes shape in a *world* which is a universe, a universal, all-encompassing system. A world system (ontology) is constituted by a structure of *categories* which defines what is possible (what may and may not be the case) in that world. This means that a world system defines a *language of experience*— a language which makes experience in all forms possible and which defines what makes sense and what fails to make sense. A world, with its language constitutes a *form of life* which may be called a "culture" or a "life-world." It must be stressed that a life-world is *not* a world-view (a view of reality) but is rather that structure which makes life possible, which makes all experience and viewing possible, which constitutes reality itself. Thus, ontology at once indicates the science of being or reality, of meaning and existence, of language and possible facts, of human experience, understanding, judgment and life. The term "hermeneutics" in this context indicates the realm of human experience, understanding, judgment, interpretation, theory and praxis; human reason, in other words, takes shape in and through some ontology. In this way the term "ontological hermeneutics" makes inseparable the science of reality and the science of rational experience and praxis.

But it also makes inseparable the relation between reason, reality, meaning, language and experience, and any one of these terms inter-penetrates the others. It will be useful to introduce a term which can capture the mutual connectedness of these realms— I propose to use *"logos"* in this way. Thus, the term *logos* is generic and organic and integrates the realms of being, meaning, language, understanding, rationality, and lived experience. In this way it may be said that *ontological hermeneutics is the science of logos*. And our present investigation is an exploration of the evolution and self-transformation of *logos* in its encounter with a diverse life-world. The term *logos* is designed with resilience to take us through our journey.

At the same time our concern is essentially with *religious* life and inter-religious *logos*. But if it is not already clear that this must be the essential focus of ontological hermeneutics this theme will emerge in the course of our exploration.

ii) Summary Review of Ontological Hermeneutics: The Form and Formation of a Life-World

Earlier chapters have attempted detailed systematic presentation of the form of ontologies or life-worlds. On this occasion it would be desirable to review and recast some of the main features and dynamics in the form and formation of life-worlds. The interested reader may consult earlier papers for further development.

a) The Concept of a World: Hermeneutical Universality

Perhaps the most prominent feature of a world, one which is often overlooked by scholars, is the hermeneutical universality of a world. A world is a *universe,* all encompassing of reality, existence, reason, experience. A world is open-ended and accommodates and incorporates all that can possibly come into its range. There can be nothing new and unaccounted for in the horizon of a world, for by its nature it has already left ample room for new possibilities and the unknown. In short, a world is reality and is exhaustive of the range of all possible experience and existence. In this respect, a world has the infinite inherent in its very structure. Those who speak of a world as a world "view" or who think of a world as a conceptual framework or a theoretical construct, etc., fail to understand the ontological concept of a world.

Hermeneutical or ontological universality is both easy and difficult to grasp. We are more accustomed to think of universals in contrast to particulars, or to conceive universality in terms of general principles which exhaust some determinate domain. But ontological universality is more radical and pervasive. It is a universality in the sense of universe— an all-encompassing of reality of which there can be nothing excluded. But a lived world, a life-world or culture, is always in the process of universalization, of realizing the universal potentiality of its world. It stops to rest at its horizon only to resume its endless journey when foreign objects appear. It familiarizes itself with the unknown and incorporates it into its sphere and makes room for it. Hence, ontological universalization remains an ongoing dynamic process in the expansion and growth of a world.

A world is *lived;* it is a life-world, and a life-world is at once personal and communal. A communal life-world is a culture which, like all forms of life, is born, grows, changes, matures, dies, and is re-born again. It is in the context of a culture that we may best appreciate the inner life-force of a world as it matures to hermeneutical universality. A culture is a world in its lived form and as such it is a *universe of experience*. This means that all possible experience and forms of life are constituted within its infinite possibilities. Hermeneutical universality of a culture means that all dimensions of human existence take their significance within that world. In this respect a world defines what is *meaningful* in human existence and defines the human condition. For this reason all dimensions of the life of a culture are possible only within the structure of its logos: religion, ethics, esthetics, politics, science, all forms of human behavior or praxis, all forms of rational life— judgment, interpretation, explanation, description, knowledge and so on. The appreciation of hermeneutical universality in its cultural form makes clear the hermeneutical theme: we humans are hermeneutical beings; to live is to be interpreted by the structure of our life-world. Thus, it is a mistake to think of a culture merely as a product of human interpretation; on the contrary, our cultural world makes our interpretations possible.

b) *The Logos of a Life-World: Universal Cultural Grammar*
Another way to appreciate the ontological universality of a life-world is to understand that a world is *a system and structure of logos* which manifests itself in the form of a universal cultural grammar of existence and experience. That is, a life-world is a logos or language which defines what makes sense and what is non-sense. As a system of *meaning* it constitutes a universal grammar or ontological language. This grammar is at once the structure of reality and of human experience, and gives form and determinacy to human reason and understanding. To be raised in a culture or life-world is to learn this grammar, and to be cultured is to speak that language well. But, again, the grammar is *universal* and this means that it is (potentially if not actually) complete, self-contained, all-encompassing, independent, open-ended, dynamically evolving and infinite in its possibilities. A cultural grammar permits and makes possible the full range of human creativity.

Of course, a cultural grammar, like any grammar, involves rules of proper sentence formation and legitimate or intelligible modes of thought. Earlier chapters have presented the structure and rules of a cultural grammar. It has been found that a world arises in a determinate hierarchical structure of categories which are mutually deployed in a network of precisely defined relations. *Categories* are the most basic and exhaustive features which constitute a life-world: time, space, cause, substance, color, sound, mind, matter, and so on. The material categories which constitute a given world take their meaning in the context of that world space. Although the ontological structure of a life-world (the pyramid form)[2] remains constant, the particular constitutive categories of a life-world take their meaning in different configurations within that constant formal structure. Life-worlds share common formal or structural principles but are materially radically different. What makes sense in one cultural grammar cannot be said (or translated) in another. What is a real possibility for human existence in one language is unintelligible or non-possible in another cultural grammar. Thus, the meaning of life, experience, existence and thought is defined and made possible by the grammar of a life-world.[3]

c) The Structure of a Life-World: Unity and Diversity

We have just spoken of the common structure or form of life-worlds. This needs further development. The distinction made in earlier discussion between formal and material ontology would be useful here. That distinction made clear that although life-worlds are fundamentally different in material content, they nevertheless shared common formal principles. The pyramid structure was used to graphically illustrate the common form of worlds. This structure shows that a life-world necessarily has an apex point of unity— a unifying point of reference that makes it one universe of one cultural grammar. It also shows that a world simultaneously moves in the opposite direction of increasing diversification, division, differentiation, individuation, particularization and atomization. This feature of a life-world is represented by the base of the pyramid. Thus, the pyramid structure illustrates that a world is inherently structured in the complementary directions of absolute unification and complete diversification. In metaphysics these tendencies have been articulated in the extremes of ontological monism and ontological atomism. But in any cultural world these polar forces must remain in creative tension.

The formal principle of unity is in fact the same as the principle of differentiation— it is known in logic and ontology as the *principle of identity*. This formal principle of being and thought is often expressed in the statement— *A is A* or *A is identical with A*. But the same meaning may be expressed in the *principle of difference— A is not B*. It is important to see that in identity there is difference; in the identity of A is implied otherness or difference from what is not A (call it B). Thus, inherent in identity is negation, difference and otherness— to be a given thing is precisely to stand in opposition to what it is not. And if there is nothing over against which it stands in contrast and distinction, then it would fail to have any determinate identity. This version of the principle of identity yields the formal *principle of essence:* to be something, to have determinate identity, is to be differentiated from what is other. When it is clear that the formal principle of identity or essence inherently involves difference and opposition and negation, it is then easily seen that this formal principle is precisely the fundamental principle of all principles; as Aristotle puts it, the first principle of thought and being— the principle of non-contradiction: A given thing S cannot be both P and not-P at the same time and in the same respect. The converse version of this is known as the principle of excluded-middle: A given thing S must be either P or not-P. The earlier papers have shown how this first principle immediately leads to the pyramid structure as the ontological form of any possible world

It is important to stress that this is a formal principle. In effect it states that any world inherently must have a unifying point of reference (identity) as well as discriminate particularized objects of some sort. The nature of the objects which make up a world and the nature of the unifying principle which makes a world a unified whole are differently constituted in different life-worlds. It should also be stressed that the problem of unity and diversity is not only a special concern of inter-cultural discourse; it is also an essential inherent concern of any life-world. In its irrepressible urge for self-preservation, universalization and inner coherence a life-world necessarily strives to uphold the universal principle of identity or non-contradiction. It does so by moving simultaneously in the upward direction to its absolute ground in transcendent unity or in the downward direction (to the base of the pyramid) to greater division and differentiation. Whenever it is faced with a possible violation of the principle of identity (a possible contradiction or inconsistency), a life-world re-affirms its integrity by moving higher to a deeper univocity or pressing lower to a hitherto undetected equivocity, ambiguity or distinction. Eminent examples of the upward movement to an absolute point of unity may be found in Plato's movement to absolute Goodness as the ground of being and truth, or Spinoza's unification of the duality of the language of mind and body as two attributes of Absolute Substance, or Aristotle's movement to the Unmoved Mover, and so on. And some good examples of the downward movement to division and dualizing may be found in Descartes' splitting of the being of persons into two substances of mind and body, or Aristotle's distinction between potentiality and actuality to explain how, for example, the acorn both is and is not an oak, or Hume's treatment of objects as bundles rather than primitive unities, etc.

d) The Unresolved Duality of Life Worlds: Separation of Finite and Infinite

That the formal principle of essential identity is a principle of *duality* and *opposition* begins to emerge more clearly. Inherent in the structure of life worlds is an existential tension and polarity between the limit of transcendent unity and the limit of complete individuation, particularity, determinateness and atomicity. It appears that a life-world grows and evolves in the space created by the separation and tension of the polarity of the finite and the infinite.

This primary polarity inherent in the principle of identity spawns and reiterates dualities in every sphere of the logos of a life-world. It is easy enough to find pervasive dualisms throughout the structure of existence— between the mental and physical (mind/body), between consciousness and object, between self and other, between thought and world, between appearance and reality, between word and object, between essence and existence, between being and becoming, between rest and motion, between universal and particular, between theory and practice, between substance and attribute, subject and predicate, and so on. But it is more difficult to understand the formal origin of these dualities, more difficult to see how they arise inevitably from the principle of essential identity.

The dynamics and dialectics of identity/difference helps us to see how dualisms necessarily arise in the structure of a life-world. First, it must be remembered that the principle of identity is a principle of opposition, for to have identity is to be differentiated or discriminated: the principle of contrariety is implicit in the principle of identity— a given thing X is either *P or un-P*. The point is that contrary opposition formally requires a unifying point of reference in virtue of which they may be in opposition. The general principle is that any differentiation (otherness, difference, opposition) must have a unifying (univocal) point of reference in order to be in the relation of difference: ambiguity presupposes univocity; diversity presupposes unity; the many presupposes the one, and so on. In graphic form this general principle of the unity of opposites is represented as a triangle (abstracted from the pyramid model of a life-world) in which the apex point is the point of unity and to two base points are the differentiated opposites. In fact it is this triangular figure that reiterates to yield the pyramid form of a world.

But let us now look at some primary examples of this principle to see just how dualisms arise:

i) *The structure of objects*: to be an object is to have identity and this means to be discriminated and differentiated; the object X must have some mark A to be that object, but in being A it is differentiated from *non-A* (or B); A and non-A(B) are opposites which are differentiated with respect to each other with reference to X which is its implicit unifying point; but then X stands opposed to *both* A and B and must be separated from them. Some fundamental dualisms lurk in this apparently simple and familiar dynamic: Subject/Predicate, Substance/Attribute, Particular/Universal, Existence/ Essence, Reference/Sense, Object/Concept.

ii) *The structure of attributes*: the dual structure of any attribute or property yields a category; take any attribute P: to be P (identity) is to be differentiated from un-P (what fails to be P) but the contrariety of P and un-P must be referred to some unity to be in that relation— let us indicate this unity by "/P/". Then, /P/ is a unifying point of reference for the opposition of P and un-P: for example, if "wise" is a property, then "un-wise" is its contrary. But this opposition is held as such in virtue of implicit reference to a more primitive unity /wise/ which indicates all those things which *can be* wise-or-unwise. This unifying concept /wise/ is a *category*. In general, every determinate property P has a contrary un-P and this contrariety necessarily involves a more primitive unity /P/ which holds the contrariety together.

iii) *The structure of being and becoming*: It is in the structure of *becoming* that we perhaps most clearly see the dynamics of diversity in unity. It has been well established in ontology that becoming necessarily unfolds between contrary opposites— P and un-P. For something X to become P entails that it *must be* un-P— duality and privation are necessary conditions of all becoming, but there must be some unified subject of becoming which passes between the contrary opposites and which must be differentiated from either of those opposites— and this points to being as a unifying point of reference for becoming.

These three obvious examples of the dynamics of identity should give us some sense of the inherent duality and dualism of life-worlds. For any life-world involves the identity and existence of objects, the existence of attributes or categories and the existence of becoming. We shall see shortly that this "triangular" dynamic of identity/difference not only structures a life-world but reveals the dynamics of religious life. For this inner tension of identity remains open-ended and recursive and opens the chasm to the two extremes of dual existence— in the downward direction it presses all the way in the direction of finitude (individuation, particularization) in quest of the ultimate subject or referent, and in the upward (infinite) direction it moves relentlessly to the ultimate transcendent ground and unity of being.

e) The Inherent Religious Dimension of Life-Worlds: Transformations to the Transcendent Infinite Ground

Thus far we have reviewed some of the main features of life-worlds and stressed the hermeneutical universality of worlds as well as the inherent dualism in the dynamics of identity. We are now hopefully in a better position to address more explicitly our primary concern— the nature of religious life. We touched very briefly on the ontological nature of *culture* as a communally shared life-world and the relation between religion and culture will be developed further in the sequel.[4]

The deep tension in the dynamics of identity just referred to (i.e. the pull to the pole of finitude and the opposite pull to the pole of infinitude) points the way to the essential dynamics of religious life for *any* life-world. Life-worlds, in their essential structure, give rise to the possibility of religious transformations, but the religious potentialities of a life-world are not necessarily authentically *lived* or realized in a given religious form of life. A life which is centered in the pull to finitude and particularity is a secular or irreligious life, and a life which is centered in the transformation to the transcendent infinite ground and unity of the life-world is a religious life.

Let us look first at the dynamics of the life centered in finitude. This form of life is centered in the indivudal, particularized, differentiated identity. In human existence this takes the form of egocentric life which is the life of self-contained, separated, individual self-identity; this is the form of life of atomic independence. Ontologically, this is the life of unmediated duality, privation, separation and hermeneutical sin.

Hermeneutical sin is not a moral concept but an onotolgical condition of being separated and alienated from Being. It is a condition of existential suffering, anguish, despair, death and ill-being. This condition arises in the willful affirmation of absolute ego-identity, a self-affirmation which organizes life around ego-desire. Ontological desire is the existential condition of inherently lacking and suffering privation which one seeks to overcome in striving for objects of desire. This vain and endless striving creates action and the life of becoming. We have seen that becoming arises out of potentiality and privation, but ego-centered action created by desire is incapable of overcoming its inherent privation or sin. Ego-centric life is proscribed within the poles of birth and death and lives in quiet despair in the shadow of death. This hellish life is hermeneutically bound within the endless cycles of becoming between opposites.

By contrast, let us explore the life which is centered in the pole of *infinitude— the dynamics of faith*. A life which, though arising in ego-identity, nevertheless recognizes its finitude, limitations, ontological dependence and existential contingency, acknowledges the presence of an absolute, infinite, unconditioned, unlimited, ground and source of itself and its world. It recognizes its sinful condition and encounters the presence of the Absolute Ground as a transcendent Other. It realizes that any truth and authenticity of life comes from a form of life which remains fixed and centered on the origin of the life-world. In disciplined rituals and practices it comes to see that the ego-centric life is a life of sin and suffering and that a new and higher form of life is required to become ontologically detached from the alienated condition. It enters a path of hermeneutical self-transformation which means the death of ego-centric identity and birth into a new life. The new life is one that is given up willingly in love, devotion and sacrifice to the Absolute Other. This transformation means not only the detachment from ego-identity but the re-orientation of will and desire and action towards the higher center. In this transformation the life of ego-judgment and belief is left behind and a new life of graceful, free, Other-centered faith arises. This higher form of life is not centered in privation and becoming but has conquered death in freedom, peace and well-being.

It should now be seen that the dynamics of faith arises in the inherent urge to hermeneutical universality of a life-world. This primary feature of a life-world can be realized only in reference to an absolute, self-existent, transcendent, infinite Other. This ultimate point of reference of a life-world cannot be grasped or articulated within the immanent terms of that life-world. That is, it cannot be known, understood, described, referred to, believed, etc. in the mundane terms of the life-world in question, for it is the source, origin and condition of all possible meaning and being in that world. The Absolute Other is not an object of belief for it makes belief possible. In this respect faith is not a form of belief but that which makes belief possible, not a form of knowledge but that which gives light to knowledge. Faith, then, is not in competition with reason or logos, it is the fulfillment of the logos of a life-world. Without reference to its Absolute Ground, a life remains fragmented, fractured, chaotic, absurd, incomplete and incoherent.

How diverse religious life-worlds deal with the dynamics of faith and the precise dialectics of the dialogue and meaning between ego-centric life and the Absolute Transcendent Other will obviously vary in significant ways. How they specify the finite condition of ego-identity as well as conceive of the Absolute Ground will also strain our ontological imagination. Nevertheless, it is significant for our inquiry to apprehend the formal dynamics of worship for any life-world. A religious life is a life of hermeneutical transformation from the life of individual identity to the life centered in salvation and ontological liberation. Worship involves those rituals, symbols, practices, etc. which bring about this hermeneutical conversion.

Some Historical Examples of Religious Life-Worlds: Cultural Grammars

We have now a formal and universal *ontological* principle for determining what is to count as religion and religious. When scholars used historical and conventional criteria in determining what is to count as religion, their judgment may focus on accidental and contingent features. The present analysis attempts to articulate criteria which would avoid accidental consideration and focus on essential features of religious life. It may well turn out that what counts as religion by hermeneutical criteria may not count as religion by conventional criteria, and vice versa. The approach taken here suggests that religious transformations are inherent in the structure of life-worlds, and this would include life-worlds which are often contrasted with religion, such as the life-world of experimental science.

But let us briefly look at some obvious examples of religious life-worlds or cultural grammars.

i) Christianity
Despite various versions of the ontology or cultural grammar of Christianity, it seems clear that the essential dynamic or transformation form egocentric life to a life centered in the Absolute Other is manifested. In this cultural grammar the ontological condition of sin is explicitly understood as separation from God, and the life of sin is one which fails to acknowledge the presence of the Infinite Other. The attendant features of the life of sin are also explicit in this grammar— the suffering and disturbance which attends the life of ego-desire, the life which ends in death and which proceeds in contingency and in authentic meaning, and so on. Of special interest here is the being of the Christ who mediates the relation and transformation between the life of sin and the life of salvation. From an ontological point of view it becomes clear that the mediating being of Christ poses special problems for the dialectics of identity, for this unique being is at once a primitive unity of a radical duality— the duality of finite and infinite being. The hermeneutical problem of the being of Christ will be discussed later.

ii) Hinduism
Again, there are a variety of ontological variations in the cultural grammar of Hinduism, but here, too, the dynamics of faith are obvious. For example, in the *Bhagavadgita* Lord Krishna instructs Arjuna and shows that he suffers because he lives in ignorance of this true Self. It becomes clear that he lives an ego-centric form of life in which he identifies himself with his ego or individual self. Arjuna is taught the secrets of existence and is shown that human existence is without beginning and without end in innumerable births and deaths in the eternal cycle of Samsara. Here we find a significant difference in the cultural grammars of Hinduism and Christianity. Nevertheless, the inherent ignorance and suffering and sin in the egocentric life of desire is made clear and it is also manifest that the cycle of becoming proceeds endlessly between opposites. The life of Samsara is a life of bondage and eternal birth and death. Here one lives in the dread not of death but of eternal re-birth. Equally prominent is the hermeneutical conversion from egocentric life to atmo-centric liberation. In this transformation, through love and devotion to the Absolute

transcendent Other in the form of Krishna, one becomes detached from the life of sin and realizes true identity in the Universal Self. With this transformation comes liberation and peace and one is free from the sin of Samsara, and so on. The special from of hermeneutical transformation presented by Sankara in the grammar of Advaita Vedanta is especially interesting, and raises some questions about the dynamics of faith and the dynamics of identity. In this version of the Hindu ontological language the transcendent Absolute is found to be nirguna— without any marks or attributes— and does not take a personal form. More on this later.

iii) Buddhism

Of course there are variations in the cultural grammars of Buddhism and the manifestation of the dynamics of identity are just as obvious as in the two previous cases. It is especially interesting here that the source of suffering is found in the ignorance of false self-identity. The illusion that there is an enduring substantial self is found to be cause of sin and existential disturbance and an important hermeneutical transformation is the recognition of the truth of no-self (anatma). But in Early Buddhism, at least, it is clear that this means that there is no *substantial* self and its ontological grammar reveals instead that the true identity of "I" consists in bundles or heaps of elements (dharmas) which are ultimate atomic properties of the life-world. In any case, whatever the nature of "I" it is clear that the essential religious transformation turns on the question of individual identity and rests on the conversion to the higher life of non-identity or realization of Buddha-nature. Here, again, we find the transformation from an individual-centered form of life to a new relation with the Absolute condition of all existence. The case of the Madhyamika dialectical transformation raises interesting questions for our dynamics of identity and faith. For it goes full circle and teaches that nirvana is non-different from samsara, and this seems clearly to reject any *transcendent* Absolute Ground of Being. This point will be taken up later.[5]

iv) Plato's Ontological Grammar

We may now touch briefly on a life-world that is not usually taken to be religious in order to see its inherent religious structure. Plato's ontological grammar may be taken as a candidate for a cultural life-world since it purports to be a hermeneutically universal language. In any case we find, especially in the *Republic,* a presentation of the hermeneutical journey of logos from lower consciousness to the wisdom of highest consciousness. The lower world (in the divided line model) is the world of becoming and change and potentiality and is taken to be appearance. The higher world, the world of the soul, is seen to be the true world of eternal life. But even this higher world of knowledge is still conditioned and dependent and lodged in differentiation and plurality of forms, so a more radical hermeneutical transformation is necessary to move to an immediate intuition of Absolute Goodness which is the ground of logos, beyond being and truth. I would suggest that this highest transformation of life is a religious transformation which takes life to its fulfillment. This ultimate transformation is the fruition of reason and knowledge and is an excellent example of the dynamic of faith. It is in the immediate apprehension of Absolute Goodness that unity of being is reached and unity of understanding emerges.

PART III: THE SELF-TRANSFORMATION OF RELIGIOUS LIFE-WORLDS IN DIALOGUE

Thus far we have been reviewing and clarifying the nature of life-worlds in the context of ontological hermeneutics. We have explored the inner dynamics of identity which is the life-force of life-worlds and we have introduced the central theme of the hermeneutical universality of worlds. This has all been in preparation for our journey through the self transformation of the logos of a world when it comes into relation with another alien world. We have been considering life-worlds in their internal dynamics and in relative isolation from one another. But a main concern of this inquiry is to understand the hermeneutical dynamics of inter-cultural religious life. So now we begin that journey into the transformation of a life-world when it comes into relation with another cultural universal grammar.

In fact it is problematic to even think of multiple worlds given what we have stressed about the nature of a world as a hermeneutical universal or all-encompassing universe with its Absolute infinite ground. For how can there be more than one Infinite Absolute? And how can there be more than one hermeneutical universal, more than one universe? *Prima facie* it appears that something has to give when two life-worlds meet. Can the principle of essential (absolute) identity survive this encounter? What internal and external revisions must a life-world make in its logos? What is the nature of inter-world dialogue? Is inter-cultural life possible? What becomes of religious life in the encounter of diverse religious worlds?

i)   Naive Conventional Logos: Indiscriminate/Ontocentric Understanding

It is natural to begin this journey of inter-religious encounter by focusing first on *conventional* logos. Conventional life is pre-reflective and onto-centric. Just as ego-centric life takes itself as the center of the life-world on the microscopic (intra-world) level, conventional life is onto-centric and takes its life-world as the totality of the universe on the global or macroscopic level. This form of life is naive and indiscriminate regarding difference and otherness— it takes all forms of difference and otherness as being more or less on a par. For example, intra-world otherness of two objects is taken to be on a par with the inter-world otherness of things. It is innocent about discrimination in the sense that it fails to make the dualistic distinctions that structures its world— for example, it fails to distinguish between appearance and reality, between consciousness and object, between essence and existence, between thought and action, and so on. It has not come to full awareness of the dynamics of identity/difference and is untroubled by incoherence and fragmentation. Thus, for example, since conventional cultures or life-worlds are mixed historically inter-woven life worlds, conventional logos tolerates the undifferentiated chaos of mixed fragmented worlds as the normal state of life. It has not yet come to awareness that its life is fragmented into pieces of juxtaposed life-worlds, nor is it concerned to bring order or coherence into this jumble.

In terms of its onto-centrism it simply takes for granted that its cultural grammar is logos itself, and its life-world is reality itself. It takes itself to be self-contained, complete, and independent. It does not see itself as universal because it is not conscious of itself as particular in any way; this question just does not arise. In a sense it is hermeneutically solipsistic and takes this closed hermeneutical attitude to be synonymous with complete realism and objectivity. Clearly in this hermeneutical solipsism or onto-centrism there can be no room for genuine inter-world otherness, no room for the acknowledgment of the integrity of the other, no room for an alternative life-world or ontological logos. From the point of view of religious life, just as ego-centric life fails to encounter its transcendent Absolute Other, so, too, the onto-centric logos is irreligious and fails to make room for and meet the trans-world Other as Other.

ii) The First Stage of Hermeneutical Awakening: The Initial Encounter with Inter-Cultural Other

The first phase of hermeneutical awakening from onto-centrism is the (perhaps vague or confused) realization that there exists an alien Other. It takes a certain amount of hermeneutical maturity and self-reflective questioning to recognize that not all forms of otherness are alike or on a par. At this initial stage of reflective awareness a distinction is made between internal (familiar) otherness and external (alien) otherness. But the latter is not yet recognized as *other-worldly,* for the more radical transformation to the recognition of another *world* is not yet made. So some strategy must be developed to extend and expand the horizon of one's life-world to make room for, accommodate, and appropriate the alien Other.

The hermeneutical strategy for appropriating the other is found in the inherent orthodoxy, conservatism, and hermeneutical universalization of a life-world. We have seen earlier that this inner urge to universalization is not a matter of choice but is structurally required by the structure of a world— a world by nature is all-encompassing of reality within its cultural grammar. It is natural, therefore, for the first encounter with an alien Other to be a re-affirmation of the universality of the logos of the life-world and transform (translate) the Other into familiar terms of one's own language. From the point of view of the Other, this appropriation is imperialism, aggression, and violation of hermeneutical integrity and freedom.

The "dialogue" which is sparked by this hermeneutical imperialism takes the form not of an open conversation but of a *resistance* by the Other to the appropriation. The "conversation" is really a self-defense and self-affirmation of the logos of the Other in the attempt to get the chauvinist life-world to change its dehumanizing posture.

iii)   The Second Stage: The Recognition of an Other-Worldly Logos

Thus far the life-world has re-affirmed its hermeneutical universality and absolute status and attempted to achieve an inner coherence by employing the familiar dynamic of the principle of identity/difference: when faced with difference or otherness, appropriate it as an internal otherness under the absolute transcendent unifying point of reference. This powerful strategy for coherence of identity is difficult to resist— after all, there is but one world, one universe, one reality and one infinite absolute.

Nevertheless, the persistent other-worldly Other speaks up and affirms its own logos and strives for recognition. In this second stage of "dialogue" there occurs a dramatic and startling hermeneutical revelation— the recognition that there exists an *alien ontological logos* or hermeneutical grammar. With this recognition some confused attempts are made at "translation" between the languages. The "translation" amounts to a piecemeal fragmentary transcription of the utterances of the Other into the familiar grammar of one's life-world. The speech or logos of the Other appears strange, odd, indeed. They have strange beliefs, superstitious practices, unintelligible myths and uncivilized ways. Thus, although there is an alien world, here it is clearly out of touch with reality, fictional, false. It may be a *possible* world, but not an actual one.

An important hermeneutical advance has been made here, for the acknowledgment of an alien but *false* life-world at least concedes some level of intelligibility of its logos for it to count as false. To be false is at least to have some meaning. So the strategy of taking the life-world of the Other to be fictional or false or a gross approximation to reality is one step closer to the genuine recognition of the authenticity of the logos of the Other.

It is at this stage of the hermeneutical dialogue that the missionary posture arises. This hermeneutical attitude no longer naively attempts to *reduce* the world of the Other to one's own, rather, it sets out to *convert* the Other to the true life-world. Unlike the previous stage, the missionary hermeneutical strategy does not simply re-affirm hermeneutical universality, but qualifies this and reaffirms universal absolute *truth* of its own life-world. There is a shift *from being to knowledge;* this is an important hermeneutical concession to the Other— it is willing now to share reality with the Other. The Absolute Universal reality is re-affirmed, but now there is room for dialogue over which logos accurately reflects the common reality. So this maneuver in effect makes a new distinction between reality itself (noumenal) and the logos of one's life-world.

iv)   The Third Stage: Systematic Ambiguity and Incommensurability

In the previous stage the question of truth was confused with the concern of systematic coherence. The logos of the Other had not yet been recognized as a systematic and coherent logos; its ontological grammar was not properly understood. And this means that the ontological grammar was mis-understood and dismissed as "false." In the third stage of hermeneutical awakening to the Other there is a new recognition that the logos of the Other is, indeed, coherent and intelligible when taken in its own terms. The internal logos of the alien life-world is grasped in its integrity and its hermeneutical coherence and power must now be acknowledged.

The premature assumption that the logos of the alien life-world was incoherent made it easier to treat it as fictional or false— a mere myth. But the recognition that it is, indeed, a systematic and coherent language of reality takes us closer to the acknowledgment of a true alternative world. This latter transformation is facilitated by the new awareness of systematic ambiguity between my own language and the language of the other. Now that I recognize the two ontological grammars, I realize that each logos constitutes meaning and being in its own terms. For example, any term in my language takes its meaning within the context of my hermeneutical grammar, and the same for the language of the Other. A new awareness of incommensurability (intranslatability) between life-worlds arises, and for the first time the absolute universality, truth and foundations of my own life-world are shaken. I can no longer easily dismiss the world of the other as fictional; it presents itself as a plausible universal grammar of reality which it constitutes in its own terms.

At this point the foundation of the life-world is thrown into a *crisis of identity*. How can there be more than one universal grammar, more than one universe or world? How can there coherently be more than one Absolute Infinite Ground? Having granted coherence to the life-world of the Other my own world is threatened with incoherence. Having moved to a new hermeneutical tolerance of the Other I find myself placed in an intolerable situation. The crisis of identity is precisely whether both universal grammars can be true, authentic and equally legitimate. To admit that both are true would be to violate the principle of identity— (the first principle of rational thought and being) that of two opposites (incompatibles) both cannot be true; one must be true and other false. To give up this bi-valent (either/or) principle would be to give up my world, it seems.

v) The Fourth Stage: The Crisis of Identity, Relativism and Absolutism

The hermeneutical dialogue has advanced to a new level. I have come finally to acknowledge the existence of a radically irreducibly Other universal grammar as authentic and legitimate, possibly even true. My earlier missionary hermeneutical attitude has been transformed to that of tolerance, even respect. I stand ready to meet the Other in its own terms of sense and reference. But now there must be some radical shift internally to attempt to maintain the coherence of my world. Here are my main hermeneutical options:

a) Absolutism/Foundationalism

l re-affirmn the absolute principle of identity and employ the dynamics of identity in the *upward* direction making for the first time a distinction between my understanding of the Absolute Infinite and the Absolute Infinite in itself. I re-affirm the one ultimate point of unifying reference as the transcendent unity of Being. In the context of this new noumenal Absolutism I admit that the Other's understanding of the one and only infinite Absolute is, indeed, different from mine, but both are approximations to the Noumenal Absolute. And typically I introduce a crucial dualism to save absolute identity: The two languages of reality are intensionally distinct but extensionally identical. This way both can be equally valid (in principle, if not in fact) without destroying the foundations of my world or the world of the Other. This strategy for solving the crisis of identity has the virtue of unifying the two universes and "solves" the problem of unity and diversity.

Comment: Of course this strategy can accommodate innumerable alternative actual-worlds. But on closer reflection it appears that much has been compromised in this move. In effect it rejects the reality of alternative *worlds,* by reducing worlds to *world-views.* By introducing the dualism or distinction between noumenal referent and (phenomenal) sense the original primary realism and ontic import of the life-world has been compromised. Secondly, an ontological space has been created between the transcendent Absolute of my life-world and *the* Infinite Absolute as it is in itself and this opens up the possibility of skepticism and questions the foundations of my life-world. In addition, it raises the question of the synonymy (ontic) of the Absolute of my world and the Absolute of the world of the Other. Do I really wish to accept this identity? What revisions in my religious life must I make if this is so? Is there any good reason to continue to affirm my life-world rather than that of the Other? Should I affirm both? What would that mean?

b) Pragmatic Provisionalism (Qualified Secular Absolutism)
An alternative intermediate option is to move in the *downward* direction and make the foundationalist and absolutist move there. This secular stratagem ignores or denies the question of the transcendent Absolute and instead affirms the foundations in the noumenal referents of reality: it argues that each life-world names objects differently but the objects in themselves— the noumenal referents "out there" remain independent of any attempt to name or interpret them. The world (mundane) becomes the noumenal absolute (the foundations) and the cultural grammars are taken to be approximations to that absolute. So, again, the dualism of noumena and phenomena, object and conceptual scheme, etc., is used to drive a wedge between the grammar of a life-world and reality.

This pragmatic provisionalism prides itself on rejecting the naive absolutism and foundationalism of pre-scientific thinking. And in fact it does succeed in rejecting *one* form of absolutism— the absolutism of any ontological grammar. Any life-world is a *world-view,* an *interpretation* of reality and as such must be corrigible in principle. It is here that the pragmatic provisionalism pretends to escape from the principle of absolute identity and its necessary absolutism. For it affirms that any world-view is revisable and a provisional construct which more or less approximates true noumenal reality. This hermeneutical scientism is pragmatic in the sense that it maintains that the criteria of truth and rationality are objective but themselves revisable, and truth consists in the consensus of judgment as interpretations of reality become more accurate projections. It should be clear, however, that the absolute principle of identity is re-affirmed by this hermeneutical strategy in its assumption of noumenal referents. This approach avoids one form of absolutism but re-affirms another.

Comment: This move has the virtue of maintaining an absolute (foundational) reality in the form of noumenal referents which are the common ground of different world-views. This is one way to solve the problem of unity and diversity. The transcendent absolute noumenal world is the common unifying ground of the diverse world-views. But, as before, this approach compromises the authentic notion of a life-world as a hermeneutical universal. First of all, it confuses ontological grammars with mere conceptual schemes or theoretical constructs and makes the mistake of treating worlds as *views*. Secondly, by provisionalizing life-worlds it rejects its hermeneutical universality and reduces them to hypotheses, as if they were scientific theories. This mistake arises, apparently, because of a failure to understand that a life-world makes theorizing possible. It is a category mistake to reduce life-worlds to views. Again, we find the predictable ploy of absolute identity at work: it calls forth a dualism to reaffirm itself. In this case it uses the dualism between noumena and phenomena in one of its versions. Finally, this secular move is one-sided and fails to deal with the unavoidable structure of the Absolute Infinite ground of life-worlds. In any case it does not avoid ontological absolutism and foundationalism.

c) Relativism: The Re-Affirmation of Absolute Identity

A third possible hermeneutical response to a pluralism of life-worlds is to make the *contrary* move to the first option of re-affirming absolutism and instead to affirm relativism. This option relativizes reality to the terms of reference of each life-world. It rejects the possibility of noumenal, objective, neutral reality and identifies reality with what each cultural grammar defines it to be. Ironically, this is an alternative way to preserve the principle of absolute identity which governs the structure of a life-world. This hermeneutical option simply accepts a real pluralism of atomic and independent universes. This relativism accepts radical incommensurability and treats life-worlds as if they were monads— windowless universes.

Comment: Relativism usually appears to be degenerate when affirmed *within* a life-world which necessarily has an absolutistic structure. However, in the context of hermeneutical pluralism it becomes a powerful way to re-affirm absolute identity. All it does is to multiply the absolutes.

Of course this raises some problems. How can there be radically independent Infinite Absolutes? This problem creates a challenge to absolute identity because we have seen that the dynamic of identity/difference requires some unifying point of reference to *háve* difference in the first place, but this option allows no such absolute unifying point. Furthermore, it fails to account for the possibility of dialogue and translatability between religious worlds— which are forms of commensurability. It makes inter-religious transformations impossible and unintelligible. Finally, by affirming radical pluralism (as an absolute) it defeats its own relativism and makes resolution of the problem of unity and diversity impossible. As a *contrary* to absolutism we find that it must be one form of absolutism itself, for contraries are always bound in a unifying *category*.

Thus, the three main hermeneutical options fail for various reasons. The identity crisis remains unresolved, and the nature of inter-religious transformations (dialogue, translation, conversion, faith) remain an unexplained mystery. The problem of unity and diversity with which we began this journey also remains unresolved. We must ask once more— Is it possible to have a genuine religious pluralism of life-worlds without compromising their primitiveness and authenticity and universality? How can there be a multiplicity of Absolute Infinites?

PART IV: HERMENEUTICAL RELATIVITY: BEYOND ABSOLUTISM AND RELATIVISM

It appears that if we accept the Logos of essentialistic identity as absolute then we are left with irresolvable paradox and incoherence. For in our hermeneutical struggle to recognize true pluralism and understand true diversity we are led to the dualistic problem of multiple Infinite Absolutes. The dynamics of identity/difference fail to resolve this problem of dualism. It *must* fail for we have seen that the principle of identity/difference is inherently a principle of dualism, duality and constitutively involves the separation of finite and infinite being. Indeed, it now appears that our entire problematic of radically different worlds and hermeneutical pluralism itself arose from the hermeneutic of absolute identity. We began this investigation with the self-question of the logos of the problem formulation. Our journey through the religious transformations of Logos has led us to the recognition that the initial problematic must now be self-transformed into a new and deeper hermeneutic.

In our journey to understand *true diversity,* to recognize and ontologically respect the Other, we have come to see that the Other must be met in hermeneutical openness and encountered as *self-defining* and *hermeneutically free.* The Other cannot be reduced to an object of investigation, description, scientific analysis or conversion. This challenge to truly meet the other in dialogue calls the hermeneutic of absolute identity and its form of life into question. But what else can there be: If Logos itself is constituted by absolute identity and inherent duality, how can we even raise the question of logos apart from identity? We must now attempt to resolve the crisis of identity.

Transformation to Non-Dual Relative Identity

First of all, there is an option that we have not taken seriously, one that has been raised at various points in different religious traditions. We have seen that the principle of essentialistic identity is the principle of duality. What would follow if this were now questioned and another principle of identity were entertained? Is it possible that there is a more primitive Logos which is non-dual? What transformation must we go through to enter that Logos?

We initially introduced the term "logos" as a generic and organic term which holds together the usually separated realms of thought, world, language, being, meaning and truth. Perhaps we are now in a better position to appreciate why this was necessary. For if there is a primary non-dual Logos then clearly the pervasive qualities which constitutively arise from naive absolute identity must be questioned and transcended. We have seen that essentialistic identity leads to the deepest dualism between finite and infinite, and the very structure of foundationalism, absolutism with its transcendent infinite absolute ground reflects the inherent dualism. But we have also seen that the very nature of particularity arises, we thought, from the principle of essential identity. If we call this principle of logos into question, do we not thereby reject particularity itself? More radically, does this not amount to the rejection of the integrity of life-worlds which also arise from essential identity?

These questions themselves arise from the reaffirmation of the logos of essential identity. What we must now realize is that the transformation to original non-dual Logos brings a new understanding of particularity and identity and duality and life-worlds. The puzzlement spawned by the dualizing hermeneutic evaporates in the transformation to non-dual Logos.

The crisis of absolute identity has brought us to the point of questioning the principle of duality. If there is an alternative non-dual Logos then the fundamental dualities which structure life-worlds would no longer hold— the separation of finite and infinite, the duality of word and object, the separation of I and Thou, the duality of universal and particular, consciousness and object, between essence and existence, between subject and attribute and between thought and being. The mere questioniong of these ordering principles of logos seems to threaten to bring complete chaos and irrationality. But does it lead to that?

Are there not precedents in religious life-worlds of precisely this non-dual Logos? For example, in one scriptural tradition it is said that "In the beginning is the Word (Logos)." This original Word must be non-dual—no inherent distinction between Word and reality for the Word is Reality, no distinction between Infinite and Finite for the Word is not particularized or differentiated. Again, take another scriptural tradition which says "all this is AUM." Must not this AUM be an original non-dual-Logos? How can AUM be everything in this world and yet signify nothing? If AUM is the original Word then can it be dualized in any way? Does the principle of essential identity apply to it as well? Does it suffer the separation between finite and infinite? Take still another scriptural remark: "I am the Way, the Truth, the Life"— How can a particularized (dualized) person *be* the Living Logos or *be* the Truth? We know that in dualized life a person cannot be Word and cannot literally be the Truth. So can this scriptural remark be taken in the principle of duality? Finally we find in the Madhyamika tradition remarks that "All things (views) are sunya" and this critique turns out to be precisely a critique of the principle of essential identity. This religious tradition teaches the principle of non-duality, that is, the principle of relative identity as the principle of non-duality, that is, the principle of relative identity as the principle of true Logos. It teaches that Logos fails in absolute identity and works only in the logos of relative identity, and so on.

These passing allusions to different traditions are meant to reduce some initial resistance to the natural skepticism about non-dual Logos which must arise to the dualized understanding. If we are to take relative identity (non-dual Logos) seriously, we must develop a more powerful and systematic critique of dual logos and thereby open the way to original Logos.[6]

What is the principle of non-dual Identity? How is relativity to be understood? One way to make the apparently radical transformation from absolutistic identity to relativity is to reverse the direction of the hermeneutical journey we have taken and move back to original Logos.

Let us begin with the assumption of a true pluralism of life-worlds. According to absolute identity we have seen that each life-world is a distinct logos each having its own internal system of meaning. We have seen that this leads to systematic ambiguity between life-worlds. For example, the term "I" as uttered in the different universal grammars is systematically ambiguous and has incommensurable sense and reference. This dualization and fragmentation of "I" in the inter-cultural context leads to the earlier predicament concerning the true meaning of "I," etc. But the non-dual Logos presses beyond the fragmentation of radical ambiguity and incommensurability to the primary Logos in which the true meaning of "I" consists in the unity of the infinite possible senses of the term for all possible worlds. That is, non-dual logos does not *begin* with the assumption of radical ambiguity (duality) but rather accepts that multiple grammars can be simultaneously valid in a non-dual unity. It moves deeper than literal dualized discourse to the more primitive level where "metaphor" comes first. It is in the *logos of metaphor* that non-dual unity is to be reached.

But how are we to approach this alleged primitive non-dual unity of metaphor? Obviously it *cannot* be approached in dual logos with essential identity. An alternative is to be found in *meditative* logos which is non-discriminating. The principle of meditative logos is the principle of *bi-polarity* or *relative identity*. This principle unites opposites in a primitive unity, but a unity different in nature from the dualized unity of absolute identity. Non-dual unity appears as a mystery to dual consciousness, but it is the literal and simple truth to meditative awareness. Metaphor is a good instrument for the hermeneutical transformation from dual to non-dual unity, for what appears as incompatible for dual reason is presented as unity in metaphor.

An excellent example of non-dual unity may be found in the being of Christ. The being of Christ is a primitive unity, but it is a unity of the ultimate opposites of dualized life— of the Infinite and the finite. For dual logos there cannot coherently be a true unity of such opposites. The being of Christ must remain a mystery to dual identity. But in meditative logos which does not assume absolutistic identity the way is opened for a more powerful unity where finite and infinite are non-different. In this respect the being of Christ appears as a metaphor to dual logos, but in meditative logos this "metaphor" is revealed as the literal truth.

Again, meditation of AUM reveals the non-dual unity (Advaita) in which the mystical symbol takes on *infinite* signification. If AUM had fixed determinate meaning (absolute identity) it *could not* serve as a universal sacred symbol of all possible being and beings. Here we find another non-dual illustration of transfinite meaning which is a unity of finite and infinite. AUM truly signifies everything and nothing. This is another good example of the bi-polar principle of relative identity. Still another example may be found in the dialectics of the Madhyamika. By opening the way to sunya— "All things are sunya"— there must be non-difference between infinite and finite. The Madhyamika makes this explicit in pointing out that there cannot be the slightest difference between samsara (determinate particularity and duality) and Nirvana (relativity).[7]

Of course the suggestion that meditative (non-dual) Logos is primary discourse, and that ontological relativity and relative identity (non-dual unity) displaces absolutistic identity, has radical hermeneutical implications.

It immediately suggests that any and every term in any ontological grammar is infinite in signification— like AUM. It means, for example, that the term "I" properly uttered resonates with infinite hermeneutical possibilities and that personal identity is organically interrelated with the identity of all other things. If this be so, then the original suggestion that there are radically different worlds is called into question. For now it appears that intra-world otherness and inter-world otherness are, indeed, on a par and this means that in a non-dual sense there is "one" world, one hermeneutical universal, a trans-world Universal, like AUM or like Christ Being, or Sunya or Tao. The transformation from mundane dual consciousness to non-dual meditative (relativistic) cosmic consciousness does not involve the denial or particularity. On the contrary, it is the highest honoring of non dual particularity, as in the case of the meditative utterance "I". This non-dual Logos transcends the dualism of finite and Infinite, immanent and transcendent, phenomenal and noumenal, consciousness and object, logos and being, universal and particular. Now, every true and non-dual particular is non-different from its universal import, every true finite being is non-different from infinite being, just as Nirvana is non-different from Samsara.

This transformation to meditative logos involves the true mastery of the universal grammar of logos— the grammar which is non-different from the diverse grammars of life-worlds, cultures, religions. This non-dual hermeneutic reveals that natural logos (which was taken to be constituted in dual identity) was already non-dual in its original and primitive form. It was this ever-presence of the non-dual logos in natural life that made the transformations between different life-worlds possible. In this universal light it becomes clear that true inter-religious dialogue requires *hermeneutical self-conversion*. For when one enters the sacred space of true dialogue beginning in a dualistic self-understanding, this space requires the self-conversion to the deeper meditative non-dual Logos in which one comes to realize one's true identity, particularity and humanity. For example, one may enter dialogue in a dualistic self-understanding of being a "Christian"; but if the dialogue is a true and authentic one, one emerges in the dialogue into a deeper religious life and a new self-understanding of what it means to be a Christian. In dialogue there must be a hermeneutical conversion from the dualized Christ to the non-dual Universal Christ. The same would hold for *any* dualized religious consciousness. Thus, our earlier understanding of religious life as the transformation within one's life-world to hermeneutical universality is now enlarged and made more radical. Now we see that in mediative logos religious self-realization requires the self-conversion to non-dual universality. In this respect we may appreciate that the non-dual Christ is the Living Logos and is the way (to be).[8]

The meditative hermeneutic reminds us that the logos of our particular life-worlds is already non-dual in origin. It helps us to distinguish between the particularity of my cultural grammar and the infinite particularity of the Logos in which it is manifested. This new awareness helps to show that true inter-cultural "translation" is really the reconstruction of the foreign grammar in its integrity within my non-dual open Logos. With this expansion of the internal horizon one begins to feel the relief from the dualistic pressures of the closed hermeneutical circle. Now in this space of relativity one can experience the infinite possibilities within the particularity of one's own life-world and even begin to entertain the possibility of living simultaneously in multiple worlds. Now the horizon of inter-cultural life begins to open and the bondage of absolutistic identity is left behind. Ironically it turns out that in relativity one transcends the dualism of absolutism and relativism. One approaches the true Universal Being, the true Absolute, the true Infinite Relativity removes relativism and absolutism to make way for the Absolute.[9]

In the non-dual hermeneutic all aspects of religious life emerge in a new light. In the primary discourse of meditative Logos (Reason),[10] we begin to appreciate the transformative power of prayer, religious myths, symbols and ritual action. The concept of detached action (self-less action) makes perfect sense and any and every act takes on ritual significance. What appeared to dual logos as mysteries and miracles emerge as powerful and literal truths. For example, the raising from the dead takes on new significance in non-dual logos where there is non-duality between body and spirit. The resurrection, the ritual of the Last Supper (the new covenant) are no longer esoteric mysteries which defy understanding. Scripture is now taken as the non-dual Divine Word which calls us to the self-conversion to true (nondual) life.

Finally, it becomes clear that the meditative logos breaks the closed hermeneutical (dualized) circle and requires fallen consciousness to go in full hermeneutical circle in the recovery of original non-dual Logos. It is in this complete journey of reason that the problem of unity and diversity is resolved. The unity that was sought which honors true particularity and diversity is the non-dual unity of relativity.

REFERENCES

The following are papers referred to explicitly in the text or which develop themes in this Chapter:

1)　　　"Formal Ontology and Movement Between Worlds" - *Philosophy East and West*, April, 1976, Vol. 26, 112.

2)   "Formal Ontology and the Dialectical Transformation of Consciousness" - *Philosophy East and West,* 29, No. 1, January 1979.

3)   "Nagarjuna, Aristotle and Frege on the Nature of Thought" in *Buddhist and Western Philosophy,* ed. Nathan Katz, Sterling Publishers, New Delhi 1980.

4)   "Comparative Ontology and the Interpretation of `Karma'" - *Indian Philosophical Quarterly,* Vol. 6, 112, January 1979.

5)   "Comparative Ontology: Relative and Absolute Truth" - *Philosophy East and West,* January 1981.

6)   "Ontological Relativity: A Metaphysical Critique of Einstein's Thought" in *Einstein and the Humanities ed. Dennis P. Ryan, Greenwood Press, Westport, CT, 1987.*

7)   "The Ontological Relativity of Religious Meaning and Truth" Presented to the American Academy of Religion, New Orleans, 1979: Published in *Indian Philosophical Quarterly,* October 1982 (Poona, India).

8)   "The Relevance of Indian Thought to the Evolution of World Philosophy" in *Indian Philosophy: Past and Future ed.* S.S. Rao and S. Puligandala, Motilal, New Delhi 1982.

9)   "Ontological Relativity and Spiritual Liberation" - presented to the International Association of Buddhist Studies, Second Annual Conference, Nalanda, India, January 1980 and published in the Barlingay Commemoration Volume, Poona (India) 1980.

Notes

1 See especially "Comparative Ontology and the Interpretations of 'Karma' and "Formal Ontology and Movement Between Worlds."

2 For details, see "Formal Ontology and Movement Between Worlds."

3 It would be a mistake to confuse language in the linguistic sense of conventional languages with language in the sense of an ontological grammar. An ontological grammar may be manifested in different linguistic systems in English, French, Sanskrit, Greek, etc.

It should also be clear that experience and thought and action is possible only within the context of a universal cultural grammar.

4 For a more systematic development of the nature of culture see "Comparative Ontology and the Interpretation of 'Karma'."

5 See "Formal Ontology and the Dialectical Transformation of Consciousness" for a systematic discussion of this point.

6 For a more systematic explication of the logos of non-duality see "The Relevance of Indian Thought to the Evolution of World Philosophy."

7 See "Mediation, Meditation and Communication" for a more systematic development of this theme. (Chapter 9)

8 "The Hermeneutic of Comparative Theology" presents the nature of religious life, worship, scripture in the meditative hermeneutic.

9 See "Relative and Absolute Truth" for further discussion of this point.

10 "Categorial and Transcategorial Rationality" develops the theme of the transformation from impure (dual) reason to pure (non) dual reason. It is stressed that this radical hermeneutical transformation is essentially the self-conversion of rationality.

CHAPTER 8

MEDITATIVE CRITIQUE OF PATHOLOGY IN THE HUMAN CONDITION

PROLOGUE

This essay is an attempt to move towards a general account of the nature and origin of diverse human pathologies. It has been a perennial theme in the history of thought that the human condition is in some form of disorder or alienation. In the Buddhist tradition, for example, it is taught that to exist is to suffer. It is found that the existential condition arises with the false belief that the individuated self is an absolute reality. The existential life of this self is pervaded with delusion, self-deception and suffering. Similarly, in the Hindu tradition it is taught that the failure to discern the true Self in conventional life is the source of mental disturbances of all kinds. Here, too, it is found that the existential condition, which is called "samsara," arises from a primal ignorance which is the origin of human pathologies. Again, in the Christian tradition it is revealed that the human being is born in a certain primordial or original sin. The human existential condition is found to be pervaded by sin which is some sort of deep ontological separation or alienation from God. This means, of course, that all aspects of the life of a sinful being reflects this pathological condition— its rational life, its moral life, its political life, etc., are all symptoms of the condition of sin.

And this theme is found in a range of more "secular" accounts of the human condition as well. For example, in the teachings of Plato it is found that the conventional human life suffers a fundamental ignorance that leads to moral, rational, psychic and political pathologies. A life that is not centered in the higher rational self will live a "cave" existence in darkness, appearance, illusion and falsity. In this philosophical vision it is suggested that various human pathologies are rational in origin— are rational disorders. Again, in the Freudian account of human life it is taught that the human psyche is under the sway of powerful unconscious forces which can influence and even control the self and all its life. In this account we get brilliant insights into the psycho-dynamics of human pathologies. Still in a different context we find thinkers like Marx presenting a picture of the human condition in which the quality of life is governed by certain political, social, and economic forces. Here, too, it is found that there are deep forms of alienation in human life which are the origin of certain pathologies. In another context certain "existentialist" writers like Sartre locate the predicaments and problems of human life in the ontological problems inherent in human existence. This tradition characteristically presses the questions of meaning and value in human life to their limits in the existential condition. In this approach it is found that a meaningful life must come face to face with the original issues of nothingness, absurdity, and radical freedom. And so on.

That there are deep and pervasive pathologies in human life may be readily granted. What has not been clear, however, is that the diverse disorders which afflict all aspects of human life may have a common nature and origin. This may be due in part to the fact that we fail to share a generic account of the human existential condition. Instead we are confronted with diverse "languages" of existence each of which purports to present a true account of the human condition. And since each language constitutes a different universe of discourse with a different "world view" it is not clear in the first place that there is or can be a universal or univocal understanding of the human condition.

This essay attempts to open the way to a generic understanding of the diverse human pathologies and of the human existential condition. It is suggested that there are two fundamental principles which govern human life. One is the Principle of Absolute Identity and the other is the Principle of Universal Relativity. The former entails that mind, self, things have inherent identity and self-existence, are individuated and existentially determinate, the latter is the principle of Original Unity which entails that Reality is a primordial Continuum wherein all possible names, forms, things, and self are co-relative, co-existent, co-extensive and are mutually implicated in one another. It is found that Absolute Identity leads to atomic unity while Universal Relativity necessarily involves Holistic Unity of a Continuum. The mind or self which takes itself to be individuated and self-existent lives in the faith of Absolute Identity and this is called the "ego" or "existential mind." By contrast, the form of life which recognizes Universal Relativity or Holistic Unity as its center is called the "Holistic Self" or the "holistic mind."

The essay attempts to show that the existential mind is inherently problematic and that Absolute Identity is the origin of human pathologies. It argues that the existential mind places itself in a primal self-devisive dynamic which eclipses Reality and Self. It is shown that Identity not only fails to be an adequate principle of Unity, but leads to a radical and pernicious indeterminacy which pervades the life of the existential mind. It is suggested that the ego is not capable of discerning its inherent pathological condition but the Holistic Mind which is ever present to the existential self opens the horizon to the Self which is more profoundly in touch with Reality. The essay articulates the Holistic Thesis which is the principle of rationality and which entails that all life, existence, meaning, experience must derive from the Holistic Continuum of Reality. Thus, the Holistic Narrative presents a general account of the human existential condition which finds that the ego is an artificial or hypothetical construct which is lodged in radical or indeterminate ambiguity all of which is surrounded by the Unified Field of Reality. Accordingly, the ego voice or mind projects or constructs its existential field and its life is carried out in this space. When the existential condition of the ego life is properly located within the universal context of the Unified Field or Continuum of Reality it becomes more evident precisely how and why the diverse pathologies are expressions of indeterminacy which derive from Identity.

The Holistic Narrative teaches that Self, Mind, Reality are holistic in form. This means that Reality is a Unified Field in which all "things" are profoundly co-relative and co-related. Nowhere is any atomic unity or individuated self-existence ever found. Any true differentiation or specification must be found in the universal context of the Unified Field. It is shown that the greater the commitment to fixity and atomic unity, the greater the degree of pathology, while the greater the openness and capacity for Self Unity the greater the degree of rational health. The Holistic account of the human condition makes clear precisely why the deepest striving of life is the quest for Self Unity. The striving for fulfillment, well-being, for truth and meaning is precisely the quest for Self Unity, and this can be realized only when a deep revolution in the self takes place; only when human life re-centers itself from the pathological ego-identity to the Holistic Self and the Continuum of Reality can the diverse pathologies of indeterminacy be overcome.

The Holistic account given here sketches in outline the derivation of the diverse pathologies from the inner form of the existential mind. For once it is clear that the existential condition of the ego-self is pathological it becomes evident that *any* expression of ego life reflects the pathology of indeterminacy. In its religious life it is found to be lodged in a deep despair regarding its self-created negativity and death and profoundly alienated from its natural home in the Continuum of Reality; in its rational life it is found to be lodged in non-unity, incoherence, incommensurability and irrationality or incompleteness; in its psychic life it is found to be placed in a degenerative dialectic of internal fragmentation and external polarization or alienation— living a neurotic, compulsive, driven life; in its epistemological life the existential self is found to be caught in prejudiced judgment, subjectivity and rationalization; in its moral life it is found to be fixated in a deep moral malpractice of will— a form of ill-will which does not realize true freedom; in its socio-political life it finds itself in strife and conflict with other selves in its existential field where there are divisive forces which preempt true communication and effective dialogue; and so on. In all cases it is seen that a given pathology in the existential condition is a symptom of the indeterminacy of ego life. In effect the holistic narrative shows precisely why diverse pathologies are cases of bad faith, moral malpractice or rational disorder. It suggests that human beings are individually and collectively responsible for the pathology of the existential condition and ultimately have a choice in the shape our mind, (existence, discourse) is in.

The essay attempts to open further the foundations of meditative psychology and psychotherapy. The hermeneutic of meditative reason shows that the psyche or self is constitutively holistic in form and cannot adequately be accounted for in egological paradigms of the self or of natural consciousness. Consequently, the various accounts of the life of the psyche which have been lodged in the discourse of egological thinking are placed under the meditative critique of universal relativity.

There has always been a deep connection between philosophical analysis and the therapeutic transformation of self understanding, self realization and self liberation. This is true, for example, in the deep analytical insights into the nature of the psyche in the teachings of Buddha, and in the analytical and dialectical methods of Socratic teaching which aimed primarily at the self knowledge and self understanding as the highest value of philosophical inquiry. This theme of the liberation of the self from existential despair and meaningless through depth-insight into the true nature of the self is central in the meditative therapy practiced by Lord Krishna in the *Bhagavadgita*. Here we find a classical model of philosophical or meditative psychotherapy which attempts to liberate the self from its many forms of existential pathology and bondage through deeper insight into the true nature of the Psyche and the overcoming of egological malpractice.

The evolution of thought, east and west, abounds with recurrent examples of this theme of existential pathologies and the need to overcome them through deeper understanding of the onto-hermeneutical dynamics of the psyche and the conduct of mind. This theme ranges from the philosophical origins of psyche-analysis in the teachings of Socrates and Plato, through the spiritual insights into the conduct of the psyche in the teachings of Jesus, through the depth analysis of the existential condition of the self in the writings of the existential philosophers like Sartre and Camus, through the meditative experiments of an explorer like Descartes, through the onto-hermeneutical horizons of the psyche opened in the phenomenological experiments of Husserl and Heidegger, and of course in the depth analysis of the psyche found in the teachings of Freud and Jung and others.

A universal recurring theme in the evolution of global thought is that the existential condition of the self or psyche plays out deeply into a range of pathologies of life. Rational pathologies— pathologies in the malpractice of mind, of interpretation and judgment, of understanding and will,— profoundly affect the pragmatic quality of life. Human well-being essentially turns on our conduct of meaning and interpretation— on our onto-hermeneutical activity, on the conduct of our very being and existence. Thus, our well-being essentially turns on the competent and informed conduct of mind and grammatical conduct of our being. The questions of the true meaning of a life are essentially grammatical ones, and the questions of well-being are essentially ontological and hermeneutical issues in the conduct of mind, existence, life.

Meditative psychotherapy attempts to come to terms with this concern. The meditative critique builds on results already achieved through the ages in the depth analysis of the psyche and attempts to go further by showing in detail precisely how the egological conduct of mind is at the core and source of practical everyday existential disorders and pathologies of life. It begins to become clearer that egological mind with its hermeneutical patterns of closure, objectification and onto-centrism is the very source of a range of existential disorders of life including diverse forms of violence to self and other, forms of bigotry and prejudice, forms of existential stress and anxiety concerning death and facing life, forms of breakdown in human relations and communication, etc.

In the meditative critique of egological life it becomes clear why the ego practice inherently leads to pernicious fragmentations of the self that plays out in moral, religious and political malpractice. It becomes clearer that it is the conduct of mind that is the true origin of the violence to the Other that is found in ethnic, ideological and religious violence, racism and sexism, and other forms of pathology. Indeed, it becomes clear that the ego-practice is the very origin of violence and abuse to itself and its environment. As long as the self is at odds with and out of touch with its true holistic nature and the Universal Law, it remains lodged in a pathological life of violence, failure of meaning and values, existential stress and anxiety, and inherent malpracitce of human relations and ethics. Here it becomes evident that to become truly rational is to enter into deep therapeutic self transformation in the conduct of mind and discourse. It is through such a therapeutic self transformation that we realize Natural Reason.

INTRODUCTION

Foundations of Meditative Psychotherapy

When Descartes stood back from the egological mind and crossed over into the meditative voice— the voice of the *Cogito*— he realized that he had reached a new existential revelation and had arrived at the foundation of thinking and consciousness. This bold explorer opened the frontier of the meditative mind and of the Unified Field of Reality but failed to have the technology of meditative reason and the logistic of Relativity to negotiate clearly and distinctly the new foundations of the psyche he had entered. We suggested earlier that if we reconstruct the *Meditations* with the tools of non-dual or unitive thinking the full latent powers of Descartes' meditations and remarkable discoveries become more accessible.

Meditative Reason and the practice of Universal Grammar (of Grammatology) help to open up this new frontier of Natural Reason uncovered by Descartes and already explored deeply in diverse traditions of meditative philosophy. These tools of meditative discourse help to resolve more effectively the deep problems that thinkers like Hegel, Husserl, Heidegger, Sartre, Wittgenstein and Derrida have struggled with gallantly. It now becomes apparent that the human existential condition is situated in the existential field of Universal Relativity— the rough ground of Natural Reason. To truly reach our original existential condition, as Descartes and others sought, we must move beyond the egological dual structures of ego thinking. To strip the egological "subject" of its attributes, predicates, names forms, essence— is only the first step in reaching the depth of the existential encounter of the *Cogito*. As long as the proto-subject remains a denuded entity— a stripped logical subject— awaiting the re-predication, re-naming— we remain lodged within the pernicious dualized structure of the paradigms of egological practice. Rather, the full *Copernican revolution* in philosophy is realized when the artificial egological mind is therapeutically deconstructed and the non-duality of meditative natural reason is entered. It then becomes clearer that our original existential condition is saturated with meaning and life and truly answers the existential anxieties and threat of absurdity and nihilism beautifully articulated by existentialist thinkers.

In Chapter Three we attempted a meditative articulation of this existential condition in the Unified Field by opening up the holistic or holonymous structure of the Continuum of Relativity. It is one thing to allege that there is a Universal Law governing all existence, to affirm that this Universal Form or Principle is the generative ground or foundation of all proceedings of Reality, but it is another to actually begin to spell out this derivation in a Transcendental Deduction of the fundamental categories of Natural Reason. It is timely to resume this meditative deduction of natural discourse in explicating the holonymous structure of the Continuum of Universal Grammar. This will further help us to situate the human psyche in its healthy natural condition and clarify the diagnosis of pathologies in the human condition. Chapter 8 will resume this exploration of the structure of the Continuum, and Chapter 9 will attempt to move towards further articulation of rational practice or meditative psychotherapy and psychoanalysis.

1) The Holistic Mind and the Unified Field of Reality

The Holistic Tradition has been alive through the ages in diverse cultures. It teaches that mind and reality are essentially holistic in form and that conventional forms of mind live in a profound form of fragmentation, incoherence or rational pathology. But the holistic teaching has remained largely eclipsed and inaccessible since the conventional existential mind in its fragmented condition is unable to apprehend holistic form. Indeed, since the existential mind takes itself to be the very norm or standard of rationality, truth and reality it rejects the suggestion that it is in a fragmented condition or suffers pathologies of self polarization and incoherence. So one primary objective of the holistic narrative is to establish that the existential mind and life suffer deep rational pathologies.

That mind is essentially holistic in form is a natural place to begin our critical reflection. The holistic paradigm reveals that Reality is the form of Holistic or Universal Unity (hereafter abbreviated HU). Let us focus our meditative attention on HU. We immediately see that this is perfect Unity, absolutely simple, non-compounded, the perfection of form. There can be nothing that does not stand in essential relationality to the form of Unity — all possible things directly derive from it, but in itself it is nothing. This universal form of all possible forms is the primordial Universal Field whence all possible things derive their existence, so nothing can exist which does not take Unity as its essential origin of reference and orientation.

But since it is perfect and simple unity with no separable parts, it immediately follows that all things cohere, and in this sense HU is the original principle of coherence. This primordial coherence of all things in Unity reveals that all things co-exist, are co-extensive, co-referential and co-relative. They touch one another in deepest intimacy and hence are profoundly contiguous and mutually consistent— all things are in communion and are hence ultimately uniform. Perhaps the most dramatic disclosure in this reflection on HU is that mind (the thinker) cannot exist apart from this Universal, Uniform, Unified Field; it too is essentially implicated in the communion and inter-relationality of all things; it too must be in perfect harmony and unity with Universal Form. And since mind cannot distance itself or stand apart from the Universal Continuum of Reality it immediately follows that mind cannot think HU as an object of thought. Rather, mind must realize its intrinsic universal form in the disclosure of its essential Unity with the Continuum of Reality. Thus, deepest reflection on HU shows that this very thinking must be recursive, reflexive and self-referential as mind expands to its inner universal forms to holistic mind.

Let us now resume our meditative exploration of the Universal Continuum of Reality which we opened in Chapter 3. There we introduced some holistic terms to assist the self-expansion of mind to its holistic form. We called the primordial Unified Field *Logos*. We saw that Logos is the form of Absolute Unity, the form of all possible forms, the primordial origin which is the universal essence of any possible thing. We also suggested that Logos is the context of all plurality, diversity, individuation and historical particularity. The living field of Logos is the Universal Domain or Historical Context for all discourse, for all names and forms, for all events, etc.

In this context we may now recall the *Holistic Thesis:* all possible names, forms, things are essentially direct expressions of Logos. Nothing can be or be conceived apart from essential reference to Logos. This is the original principle of all existence, meaning and rationality. The Holistic Thesis implies that the true inner meaning of any name is found in its holistic synonymy with Logos. So we truly understand a given thing when we discern its origin and derivation in Logos. As the universal meeting point of all possible things it is evident that this Pure Form of Reality is· the *Principle of Universal Relativity:* that all possible things are mutually implicated in one another and are co-relative and co-dependently arise.

This principle is the principle of Holistic Reason and it implies that all holistic names are co-synonymous. Let us call this *"holistic synonymy"* or *"Holonymy."* Holistic Synonymy is immediately implied by the principle of universal relativity and entails that all names, when seen in their universal import in the Unified Field, are holonymous with one another and "univocated" in Logos. Let us explore the Holonymous nature of *Logos*.

Perhaps the most dramatic disclosure of the holistic tradition is that the Self (mind, psyche) is holistic in form. Unlike the conventional existential self or mind the Holistic Self finds itself fully implicated in the Unified Field of reality. But this primordial implicature of Self and Reality cannot be realized through conventional forms of rational thought— rather it is realized in and through meditative thinking, wherein the mind expands to its true form. Thus it is the meditative mind that experiences the holonymous structure of the Unified Field.

Something astounding happens in the quality of experience as mind expands from its egological form to holistic form. In its artificial existential state it experiences a world in which the "self" is an experiencing *subject* in the surrounding universal and unifying field of "reality." In some deep sense this "I" is a central point of reference around which its experience is centered and oriented. Its world shows itself as having a rational structure in which there are diverse kinds of things and a range of diverse qualities, properties, categories which comprise those things. The existential self names the basic categories like "space" and "time" and "relation" and "thing," etc., each of which appears to be a universal domain of reality. It is intrinsic to this existential self that it is in some important sense *individuated* and differentiated from other things, and that it is self-existent and independent of its surrounding reality. It accepts this structure of differentiated reality as an unquestioned (and perhaps unquestionable) given or absolute.

By contrast, the meditative mind centers itself in the Unified Field and works itself out of the artificial construction of the individuated or subjectified self. In this self-expansion and re-centering, experience goes through a profound revolutionary change as mind enters the gravitational field of the Continuum of Reality. So, for example, while the existential mind experiences the relative fixity of things, including itself, the meditative mind discerns the unfixability of things, names, concepts, categories, etc. In the phenomenology of the expanding mind what was disjointed and separated and disconnected and differentiated begins to show itself as vibrating with multiple meanings, fluid, mutually implicated and co-relative. As mind expands there is a simultaneous co-expansion of all names and forms as the Holistic Principle begins to emerge. In this confluence of Self and Reality the existential differentiation of experiencing subject and experienced object is dissolved and a deeper form of rational experience is reached.

It is important here to notice that holonomy does not dissolve or water down real differences in the Unified Field. For, as we have indicated earlier, the Unitive structure of the Continuum essentially and originally involves difference, differentiation and plurality. There is no tension between the Unitivity and Relationality of the Continuum and Difference. The Holonymous structure of Reality does not mean that everything is the "same" or "identical" according to the egological standards of naive "identity."   Rather, the Principle of Relativity is an original *Alterity* wherein sameness *and* difference are co-given and inseparable. It is the egological mind that insists on severing the forces of "unity" (identity, sameness) from the forces of "plurality" (difference, differentiation). Relativity understands that the relational structure of Reality is primitively in Alterity which is the original mutuality of identity and difference, unity and plurality— the Unitive structure of the Unified Field is originally *differential*. This means that it is Relativity that truly accounts for real difference and plurality and individuation in the Unitive context of the Continuum. So original *Unity* is always already in *Alterity*. This is its *Dialogical* nature.

As we now move more deeply into meditative speech and enter the logical space of the Continuum it would be helpful to employ a notational device to remind ourselves of the holistic use of terms: for any conventional term x let us indicate its conventional use as "x," and its holistic use as ((x)) (holistic quotes).

It is readily seen that in fact the holistic voice is always surrounded in holistic quotes, and not just the individuated terms it uses, for it becomes clear that there can be no separation between the Holistic Voice, Holistic Speech, and what it Speaks; all this is already situated in an unbroken Continuum.

So as we meditate on the logical form of Logos or the Unified Field we do not take terms one by one, as if they were separated, but take a range of fundamental terms together in their contiguity and mutual implication or univocation. Holistic Speech is an open-ended formula or original logical space wherein all terms already stand in Continuum. The holistic narrative over-flows any term, any predication, any sentence or paragraph. Its ((Text)) is un-ending, un-broken, un-interrupted like the Continuum which it expresses. So let us jump into the middle of this beginningless and endless Unified Field of Speech.

Let us begin by focusing our attention on the meeting point of Logos and ((Self)). It is at this dialogical meeting point that the meditative voice speaks the Continuum. This noumenal center indicated by ((I)) finds itself fully implicated in the Unified Field. Its very ((thinking)) is its ((being)); its ((speech)) is the ((activity)) of the Continuum; this ((I)) is self-constituted in its very thinking and speech.

As we meditate here we find that any term speaks for any other, and each is a self expression of the Continuum. The Holistic Formula reveals itself:

Logos is ((Being)), ((Self)), ((Mind)), ((Consciousness)), ((Thought)), ((Intelligence)), ((Idea)), ((Word)), ((Concept)), ((Meaning)), ((Language)), ((Sign)), ((Rationality)), ((Goodness)), ((Truth)), ((Life)), ((Knowledge)), ((Action)), ((Judgment)), ((Beauty)), ((Nature)), ((Time)), ((Space)), ((Matter)), ((Energy)), ((Speech)), ((History)), These are a few sample ((Names)) taken at random in any "order"; in Holistic Space they are well ((Ordered)), each immediately ((Implicated)) in the other and meeting at the same ((Point)).

These sample Holonyms are not "names" or "predicates" which refer to or describe the Continuum, they are rather self-expressions or ((Faces)) of the Unified Field, each reflecting the other. Perhaps it would be helpful in approaching the Universal ((Formula)) of the Continuum to contrast it with conventional "names" in conventional "reason." While conventional mind is two-dimensional— situated in a logical space which is divided between the "I" and the universal field which is both differentiated from and surrounds this "I," i. e., the "not-I," Holistic ((Space)) is ((N-Dimensional)) where "N" ranges to ((Infinity)). We could equally say that Holistic Rational Space is ((O))-dimensional, since all dimensions immediately meet and express one another.

The point is that in conventional discourse, any "name" indicates its own "field" and is differentiated and separated from the signification of other "names." Thus, if we take "word," it is taken to be some sort of linguistic item, which is existentially different from "I," or "mind" or "thought" or "idea" or "meaning" or "thing," etc. Each of these "names" indicates a separate realm or field which must not be confused. The "word" as a linguistic entity may be uttered or written, but it is not to be confused with the thinker who uses it, or the "idea" it purportedly represents, or the "meaning" that it allegedly has, or the "thing" it is taken to stand for, and so on. Conventional discourse would collapse and fail if these diverse fields were taken to meet at the same point.

Nevertheless, in the Logical ((Space)) of the Continuum it is impossible to separate off any Holonym into a distinct field of its own; to do so would be to destroy the texture of Holistic ((Speech)).

Accordingly, in meditating on the Holistic Formula we may say in the Holistic Voice: Logos is ((Word)). We may very well say, ((In the Beginning is the Word)), and mean by this that this Holistic ((Word)) is ((Being)), ((Speech)), ((Idea)), ((Consciousness)), ((Intelligence)), ((Meaning)), ((Truth))...and so on.

This original ((Word)) is the Continuum itself, the Universal Word of all other possible words. It is ((Speech)) itself, or the ((Breath)) of Logos. This Primordial ((Word)) is Pure Mind, Intelligence, Consciousness. Here it is impossible to separate off the realm of "word" from "mind" or "thought" or "speech" or "meaning" or "being." The Original ((Word)) is ((Being)) Itself, and so on.

We may of course perform the same meditative ((experiment)) with any Holonym: We could ((say)): Logos is ((Goodness)), and this summary of the Holistic Formula expresses the meditative insight that ((Good)) is the Holonym that *orients* all possible things. For Logos is the Universal Form of all possible Forms and as such must be the universal point of reference for all things. In this respect, all things are oriented to Logos as the Unifying Principle and this gives direction and orientation to the Unified Field. This ordering principle is the telic force which organizes all things into a Coherent ((Whole)), into a ((Universe)). In this respect we may say that ((Goodness)) is the original force that holds the Universe or Continuum together, and all things gravitate to Logos as its ((Center)). So ((Goodness)) is the ((Telic)) form of the Continuum of Reality.

Further meditation on this formula makes clear that the Holistic Principle is the Form of ((Unity)) itself: Logos is Absolute Unity and as the ((Form)) of all possible forms, it expresses the essence of any possible name or form. Here it may be said that any Holonym expresses the form of ((Unity)), and in their mutual entailment they conjointly stand in ((Unity)) and express ((Unity)); and this is the Continuum.

This means that any Holonym is a Unifying Principle which expresses ((Unity)) in some primordial sense: For example, ((Goodness)) unifies all things by being the Universal Telic Point of Reference; ((Being)) unifies all things by being the most comprehensive Universal Field of Reality— the ((Universe)); ((Self)) is the transcendental noumenal unifier which conditions all possible ((Experience)); ((Rationality)) is the Order of Implication wherein all things stand in ((Coherence)); ((Nature)) is the universal field of all possible ((Phenomena)) under Law, and so on. It might well be said here that the more Unity or Univocation that is realized, the more ((Truth)) is expressed, so that ((knowledge)) is the realization of Self ((Unification)).

Again, we may focus on the Formula of the Continuum as ((Nature)). Here we may see the creative ((Process)) of Nature as the Speech-Acts of the ((Word)), the Self-Expression of the ((Voice)) of the Continuum. In this context the Holistic Narrative speaks itself forth as the Natural ((History)) of ((Energy)). In this History or Evolution the Primordial "Stuff," ((Matter)) or ((Substance)) of the Continuum is seen to be the Evolution of ((Mind)) or ((Intelligence)), wherein we recognize the full Univocation of the Mind/Matter Continuum. This Holistic Evolution or Process of ((Nature)) may be seen as Primary ((Energy)) or ((Rational Force)) and the ultimate ((Substance)) of the Continuum shows itself to be a ((Psycho-Physical)) continuum. Similarly, meditation of the primary ((Matter)) or ((Energy)) reveals that the primary ((Stuff)) of Nature shows itself as the ((Space-Time)) Continuum, and so on.

Similarly, meditation on the inner Energy or Force of the Continuum discloses that ((Reality)) or Universe may be seen as the expression of ((Truth-force)) or the ((Rational Action)) of ((Meaning)). In this Holistic Context the Laws of ((Nature)) are synonymous with the Laws of ((Truth)), ((Meaning)), ((Thought)). No ultimate separation may be found between the Laws of ((Nature)) and the Laws of ((Logic)). The Continuum of ((Matter-Mind)) makes evident that ((Life)) is a Unifying Principle which expresses the Logos-as-Flesh. And this ((Life)) expresses itself as ((Intelligence)), ((Rational Energy)), the Force of ((Meaning)) or ((Truth)), and so on.

This is just a preliminary example of the meditative expansion of the Holistic Formula. It illustrates how the Holonyms mutually imply one another and form a Continuum, all expressive of Self Unity. This gives us the inner pattern of the ((Dialectics)) of the Holistic Principle. Here we see that no Holynym stands above any other, but each is at the same time an Holistic Center of the Continuum, mutually reflecting and entailing one another. The Holistic Thesis reveals that all categories, all names and forms, are immediately derived from the Continuum, which is the Universal Context of all discourse; the Continuum is the Unity and ((Unity)) of ((Discourse)); it is Universal ((Grammar)). The ((Unity)) of the Unified Field is so profound that it univocates the conventional polarity of "Unity" and "Plurality"; it is the meeting point or place of *all* conventional dualities, polarities, oppositions.

Our meditation on the Unified Field of ((Reality)) makes it apparent that the Holistic Mind is the noumenal ((Self)); the Holistic Voice is the Voice of the Continuum; the Holistic ((Self)) is one with the Continuum Itself. And this Insight encourages us to see that the conventional "self" indicated by "I," with all its fluctuations, vagaries of references, indeterminacy, equivocity, and with all its alleged uniqueness, particularity and determinacy, remains ever grounded in its Noumenal ((Self)), in the Continuum. The phenomenal "self" exists and lives within the Presence and Jurisdiction of the Noumenal ((Self)). And the activation or awakening of the meditative ((Voice)) is simply the ((Remembering)) of the intrinsic grounding of the "self" in the ((Self))— the Univocation of "self" with ((Self)).

This means of course that the Continuum, as the Noumenal or Holistic ((Self)) does not negate or destroy the uniqueness, particularity, individuality, specificity or alleged determinacy of the "self," or of any other conventional "thing;" on the contrary, the ((Unity)) of the Continuum which rules over all things is precisely what makes any uniqueness or particularity possible. Indeed, any trace of real or constructed "unity" found in conventional life is made possible by the Principle of ((Unity)), which is the Continuum.

Thus, it may be said that the Continuum is the Transcendental Condition of all life, experience, existence, discourse, etc. Any possible "name" or "thing" or "identity" or "speech," etc. is always ((Situated)) in the midst of the Continuum as its Noumenal Self. Any individuality, uniqueness or particularity I may have as a "self" must necessarily be an expression of Holistic ((Self)). And if I am able to negotiate this passage in meditative reason from my phenomenal or individuated "I" to Holistic ((I)), the general pattern for discerning the Noumenality of *any* phenomenon becomes evident.

So, for example, let us direct meditative attention to this "tree" which stands before us in the visual field. While the conventional "mind" sees it and speaks of it as a unique, individuated, relatively fixated and differentiated "thing," the Holistic Mind is able to fathom the deep structure of "this tree" and discern its ((Essence)) in the Presence of the Continuum. In the ((Phenomenology)) of meditative thinking this "tree" is implanted in the soil of the Continuum and is seen to be a specified showing or speaking of the Continuum. The Holistic Mind discerns in this "tree" the presence of a being, of matter, of a spacio-temporal something with color, figure, texture, motion, something living, engaged in activity, growing, becoming, etc. These diverse names, forms, qualities, categories, which constitute this "tree" supposedly find some univocating meeting point in the "tree"; otherwise, the tree would not be a true individuated being but just a collection of diverse attributes. For this "tree" to be an individual, a unity, it must univocate the diverse categories which it specifies.

But how are we to find the true meeting point of these diversified fields? The Holistic Mind traces the supposed unity of this "tree" right to its Noumenal roots in the Continuum where the diverse categories are found to truly meet; and it is here that we encounter the Noumenal ((Tree)) which speaks itself forth in this "tree." In the Holistic Narrative it is more correct to say that the Holistic Mind directly ((Meets)) the ((Tree)); encounters the Noumentality of this "tree." The ((Self)) of the ((knower)) finds itself directly implicated and mutually implicated with the ((Tree)) in the Implicature of the Unified Field. In this way it is seen that the pathway from "I" to ((I)) is precisely analogous to the pathway from "tree" to ((Tree)). And so for all things.

In this elaboration of the Holistic Thesis it becomes more apparent that all life, experience, discourse is necessarily situated in the Universal Context of the Continuum, which is ((Reality)). It should be clearer that any conventional form of life has no true independence or autonomy but is relative to the Unified Field. And in the ((Light)) of the Continuum it is proper to make such Holistic Remarks as: ((Life)) is ((Self Expression)); ((Life)) is ((Speech)), ((Intelligence)), ((Rational Energy)), ((Truth-Force)), ((Judgment)), ((Knowledge)), ((Interpretation)), and so on. These Holonyms for ((Life)) are reminders that true ((Life)) must be Holistic in Form, a life in which Self-Unity is realized. And such a Life is a ((Rational)) Life, one which achieves Self ((Realization)), which accomplishes ((Knowledge)), which is One with ((Truth)) and ((Meaning)), and so on. It is this blossoming of ((Life)) in the Continuum that sets the Universal Standards of a Life that is Real, True, Good, Free and Fulfilling.

2) Towards a Holistic Account of the Diverse Human Pathologies:

Fragmentation in the Human Condition.
In the light of the Holistic Mind and the Continuum of Reality we are in a better position accurately to account for pathology in the human condition. Our Holistic Narrative continues as we give a general and unified account of the diverse pathologies found in human existence. Here we see that it is not only the "universe" that is fragmented, but the conventional "self" is found to be profoundly fragmented together with its life, its world, its experience, its discourse. In this section we shall give a survey of the diverse pathologies and attempt to show that they are all symptoms of a common generic pathology which is intrinsic in the existential human

condition. In this section we focus on the holistic phenomenology of the diverse pathologies, and in the next section we explore the inner dynamics and dialectics of the pathologies in a more systematic way.

Let us focus our meditation on the human condition. If ((Reality)), ((Self)), ((Life)), ((Mind)) are a Continuum, if the ((Universe)) is a Unified Field, then how does it come about that the "self" and its "life" and its "universe" are in a fragmented form? Indeed, it needs to be *established* that the human condition is fragmented and pathological. For the conventional mind does not see itself to be fragmented and does not acknowledge that its existence is pathological. On the contrary, the normal "self" takes itself to be whole, healthy, integral, and living a relatively successful, rational, coherent life. And although it may readily admit that there are areas of conflict and tension in its life, it does not recognize the claim that its world is in a fragmented form.

Of course, the Holistic Narrative takes account of this self image of the conventional self and finds it to be a typical symptom of the problem. For the individuated mind is not in a position to discern or acknowledge its profound self-division and fragmentation. It is only with respect to the Holistic Principle that this pathology becomes apparent.

To see this it is necessary to examine how the conventional "self" comes to be. We have used several terms to designate this "self"— "existential," "conventional," "individual," and the like. It would be helpful here to collect these diverse terms under one name: let us call it the "ego" and understand this to specify the "self of identity" or the "mind of self-identity." The ego-self lives in a primordial faith in absolute self-identity. It takes itself to be a self-existent thing, individuated, differentiated, unique, particular, finite, definite. It comes to be in the light of this *Principle of Absolute Identity*. Though it may be dependent on other beings the ego-self sees itself at its core as being relatively independent and having a certain existential autonomy. And this feature of the ego-life was called "self-existence."

This ego takes its being and lives *within* the structure of Absolute Identity. This is its absolute ground or foundation, its original faith. Its very *existence* is constituted in Identity and apart from this principle, it could not be. To question this "absolute principle" would be to question its very possibility and actuality. However, we shall now see that this axiom or postulate of Self Identity breaks the self off from the Continuum and creates an artificial space in which it resides. The ego-mind in its self-existence cuts itself off from ((Self)) and ((Mind)), and this self-eclipse from the Unified Field brings a proliferation of fragmentation which permeates the life and world of this "self."

The ego-mind, then, is *born* in eclipse from ((Reality)) and brings profound fragmentation with it. And since it arises in and creates this fragmentation it is unable to detect it as such. It is only when this ego-self begins to awaken to its Holistic origins, to its ((Self)) which remains ever-present to it, that it begins to question Absolute Identity in the light of Universal Relativity. When the ego-mind begins to recognize that the principle of Self-Identity is a postulate of faith which is not only not "absolute" but a highly questionable hypothesis at that, it opens a new horizon in which it can step beyond Identity and see its devastating consequences. So the fragmentation and pathology that is generated by Absolute Identity cannot be detected while one is under the spell of this postulate. For Identity has ingenious ways of persuading itself that it is coherent and has integrity.

Nevertheless, let us examine the fragmentary condition of the ego-self. We said that in postulating itself as an absolute self-existence the ego-self gives birth to itself by eclipsing itself from the Continuum. In taking itself to be an individuated thing with self-identity this self places itself in a field of its own which is its universe. To exist as an individuated thing in this universal space is to take up its own space and to be *differentiated* from all other things. This differentiated state is accomplished by this ego being a logical subject possessing diverse attributes or properties which mark it off from all other things in its universal field. In this way this ego is already situated in a primordial division of space between the locus in which it exists and the rest of the universe which stands over against it. So the ego-self shows itself in an original division between itself (as one field) and the universe (as another). And in some sense this self takes itself to be a central point of reference in its universal space. Here we see that the self-identity of the ego inherently arises in the division and differentiation with everything else. Identity implies duality and differentiation or otherness.

Furthermore, this differentiated self-existence of the ego implies a certain determinateness and relative fixity. The existential identity of this ego can arise only in a universe which has determinate characteristics, certain ones of which constitute the ego and marks it off from all other things. This means that to exist, to have self-identity is to be situated in a world of determinate character. Let us call the determinate nature of a given world or universe of discourse a "grammar" of existence. To exist is to be already situated in a determinate grammar of existence which makes the ego self possible. We may see such a grammar as a rational structure of categories that gives the world in question its character, order, determinacy. And since this grammar is the place within which this ego lives with other selves, we may also see this grammar as an ontology or world-view that makes the experience of the ego possible. This grammar of experience defines the rationality and discourse of the ego and defines what makes sense and what does not; this is its universe of discourse.

It is important then to see what is inherently given with the postulation of self-identity: self-identity means self-existence; self-existence means determinacy and individuation; individuation means differentiation; and all of these mean being situated in a grammatical field which is an all-encompassing universe, a universal field. But it is also implied in individuated self-existence that it is a self-unity— that it is a definitive unified and univocal self; self-identity means *self-unity*.

The presence of this individuated self which takes itself to be a self-unity is problematic. For its presence eclipses the Unified Field and creates an artificial space wherein there is a recursive and reiterative self-division that can never find true self-unity. Within this problematic space there is a polarity between the ego-self on the one hand, and the universal field that surrounds it. This primal polarity is absolutely essential for the very self-existence of the ego. But this surrounding world field which shows itself in some determinate grammar is self divided in every direction into other fields— categories like space, time, matter, thing, property, action, motion, and so on. But without these self-existent fields, the very self-existence of the self could not be established— for we saw that the individuation of this ego essentially turned on its being differentiated and individuated through its attributes. Now we see, however, that each attribute is itself an identity, a self-existence. That is to say, it is not only the ego-self that has self-identity, but every possible name, form or thing in its universe of discourse likewise has self-identity. And this begins to portray a world in which there is a vast diversity of distinct fields, each being a self-identical field, having self-unity like the ego-self.

The Pathological Quest for "Self-Unity"
But this presumed "self-unity" turns out to be an empty postulate of the ego, for in the light of the Continuum no self-existent unity is ever found. Instead, the individuated self is found to be an artificial construction which is lodged in a profound flux and indeterminacy. In postulating its absolute self-existence the Unified Field which is the origin of all Unity is eclipsed and negated. The ego constitutes itself by its own faith or will and this creates a hypothetical space which becomes its universe. But this Original "self-assertion" places it in the predicament of denying its ((Self)) and thus precluding any real possibility of Unity and Autonomy.

In arrogating a space of its own which is its absolute dominion the ego self creates an artificial mind-space which nevertheless remains within the Presence of the Continuum. This space of the ego is artificial in the sense that it is self-constructed and its presumed independence and self-unity is imagined and has no validity apart from its own self-assertion. But this faith, insistence or belief in its independent self-unity is certainly not sufficient to establish any absolute unity in itself or its world. Indeed, the Holistic Voice which sees through the "myth" of self-unity finds the ego to be caught in a recursive and futile attempt to ground its unity in its hypothetical space. Despite its deepest conviction that it is an autonomous unity the ego lives in the midst of a radical indeterminacy and flux. Whatever stability, coherence, order, regularity and unity it finds in itself and its world is due to the Presence of the Continuum which sustains all things. It is the Holistic ((Self)) which is ever-present in the heart of the ego that though eclipsed or even negated sustains the possibility of artificial unity.

Let us scrutinize more closely the futile attempt of the ego to account for its self-unity. It was already suggested that the individuated self is a differentiated thing. As such it situates itself in its hypothesized universal space which purports to have determinacy and self-unity as well. And the determinacy of the universe shows itself in the specification of diverse categories, attributes, names and forms which arise in its grammar of existence. Each item of this universe of discourse allegedly has self-unity as well. In general, all things, all identities are postulated to be self-unities. So the faith in Absolute Identity immediately translates into all "things" having some degree of self-existence and self-unity; it is not just the ego that enjoys this privileged status. We may now say that whatever has identity has "atomic unity."

However, upon closer inspection we find that any purported atomic self unity is vacuous and points to some other alleged unity to sustain itself, and so on *ad infinitum*. For the self-unity of the ego can never be found in atomic isolation, no matter how deeply the ego voice probes into its inner space. On the contrary, its quest for its inner unity leads it into the foreign territory of the universal field within which it has situated itself. But this grammar-field, which is its world, itself has no unity apart from the specificity of the discrete fields or categories which gives it determinacy. So the ego seeks its unity in the attributes which supposedly constitutes it and gives its particularity, specificity, individuality. Apart from its attributes it would not be specified as an individuated and differentiated thing. But here again, the attempt to locate its unity in its constitutive attributes fails since instead of finding a unifying principle it encounters a multiplicity of fields each purporting atomic self-unity. So instead of finding its inner unity it discovers instead what appears to be a plurality of discrete unities. Ironically, each of these constitutive properties looks to its resident subject to ground it and give it self-unity; no attribute-field has its inner atomic unity within itself. And in any case, if there is not an ultimate substantial referent wherein these multiple attributes could inhere there would be only a bundle of discrete atomic attributes.

But no attribute has self-unity in atomic isolation, nor is there an encompassing unifying field which would collect them into a "bundle" even if they did have self-unity. So the ego cannot find its self-unity within itself, nor can it find it in the foreign field which surrounds it as its "world" and makes it possible. It is tempted to locate its absolute unity within the all-encompassing universal field which is its "universe." Clearly this must be a unified field which connects all things, all subjects and attributes, all names and forms, into a unified whole. But this move only repeats the same futile attempt to ground its self-unity. For we have seen that the self-unity of the "universe" cannot be found apart from the specificity of its constituent subjects and attributes which we have found to be vacuous of self-unity. Furthermore, we readily see that the alleged self-unity of the universal field that is the home of the ego can be determinate and individuated only in contra-distinction to an "Other" that stands in foreign territory beyond its imagined boundaries. The predicament of finding self-unity on the "micro" level within the ego is simply re-iterated on the "macro" or global level for the universe as a whole.

Nowhere, then, is *any* self-unity found within the artificial space of the ego field. On the contrary, what is found is a perpetual dynamic which defers self-unity in a recursive loop that re-iterates *ad infinitum*. This is a vicious circle which depicts the emptiness of self-unity and the death of the logical or ontological "atom."

This emptiness of the self-unity of the ego within the faith of Absolute Identity is the origin of the radical indeterminacy of ego life. For if the ego voice is without inherent self-unity then its identity is in flux and its existential status is likewise vacuous. But if the ego-mind is without determinacy, self-existence or self-unity, all its world reflects the same condition; nothing in the ego's universe has inherent determinacy or self-nature. If the ego's faith in Absolute Identity be taken in its own terms, it places the ego in an impossible and intolerable situation. The ego's intention is to establish its absolute self-unity and self-existence and to secure its foundation as a determinate and individuated entity. But the hypothesis of Absolute Identity leads to the opposite result of placing the ego mind in a profound existential indeterminacy. This is the original existential condition of the ego-self when it is eclipsed by its own will from the Unified Field of Reality.

Of course, the ego-mind is not directly in touch with its inherent flux and indeterminacy. Since it has an absolute commitment to its faith in Absolute Identity it asserts itself and insists on its self-unity and self-existence. It was suggested earlier that this priordial self-assertion is a denial and negation of the ((Self)) or the Continuum. In absolutizing its self and insisting on its inherent self-existence the ego voice constructs an identity and consents to a narrative which is designed to protect its existence, preserve and conserve its identity and self-unity, and make its form of life possible. Nevertheless, in all its self-constructive activity it trades on the Presence of the Continuum, taking its life from the Unified Field while all the time rejecting, denying, negating, refusing to acknowledge its true foundation.

The ego voice, then, originates in a primordial nihilism and bad faith. It is here that we find the original source of its pathological condition.

The Existential Condition

We are now in a better position to explore the human existential condition. The Holistic Narrative suggests that we cannot get an accurate reading of the existential condition *within* the narrative of the ego voice whose discourse is ruled by the principle of Absolute Identity. Rather, it is in the light of the Continuum that the general dynamics of human pathologies may be accurately seen. For the measure of pathology is a function of the degree to which the ego voice is closed off to its Holistic Self. The greater the degree of ((Self)) denial, the greater the degree of "self" fixity and closure, the greater the degree of pathology. Conversely, the greater the degree of openness to the Continuum, the greater the degree of readiness to critique, revise and expand the "self," the greater the degree of health. The deeper the openness to ((Reality)) and ((Self))' the more rationally healthy is the form of life. In short, human health is measured by the capacity of the self for ((Unity)); the greater the negation of ((Unity)) the deeper the pathology and suffering. In this context, then, human pathologies are all versions of dis unity, dis-integration, or self-division.

Let us reflect further on the pathological condition of the ego or individuated self. The fact that the ego is lodged in radical indeterminacy and existential flux is too threatening for it to face directly. The prospect that the ego has no atomic self unity, no independent self-existence, no determinate univocal voice, is too devastating for it to countenance. And with good reason. For the emptiness of self unity would mean the death of the ego: its very existence is constituted in its presumed self-unity and univocal determinacy. So the ego believes it has no choice but to invest all "its" life force to insist on its self-unity and self-existence. As a self-constructed entity it is born in the shadow of death and its life is perpetually haunted by the real threat of death and extinction. Thus, although the ego is too frightened to face its abysmal emptiness it cannot escape the terrifying presence of the primordial indeterminacy that surrounds and envelopes it.

The ego is conceived in negativity and born in nihilism. It subsists in a double-threat of extinction: its identity is threatened within its postulated space with the emptiness of indeterminacy and nihilism, on the one hand, and it is threatened by the overwhelming though eclipsed Presence of the Unified Field on the other. Its existential status is threatened by the emptiness of self-unity in its self-created indeterminacy, and its very identity and sense of absolute self-autonomy is threatened by the fullness of the Continuum. It "experiences" both as entailing its death. Its existence is threatened on one side by "dis-unity" and on the other by ((Unity)). So by its own will it invents a "unity" in an attempt to avoid both dangers; it constructs its "self" and strives to sustain its identity, unity and self-existence by its own will.

In Chapter 9 we focus on the teachings of the Buddhist dialectician Nagarjuna as one classical exemplar of the move to meditative psychotherapy. We could have taken alternative routes into the transformative therapy of meditative reason and universal grammar. But Nagarjuna is instrumental in performing an unprecedented breakthrough into the dialectics of relativity. It would be helpful in opening the foundations of meditative psychotherapy and psyche analysis to follow his teachings as a further avenue into the practice of meditative reason and universal grammar.

CHAPTER 9

MEDITATIVE DIALECTIC AND HOLISTIC PSYCHOLOGY

SYNOPSIS

This chapter attempts to develop a Universal diagnosis of human pathology and language of holistic or meditative psychotherapy. We focus upon the teachings of the Buddhist dialectician Nagarjuna, who founded the Madhyamika school. Nagarjuna formalized the essential teaching of the Buddha which concerned the termination of real human suffering which is generated by ego-identity. But it is not at all clear from Nagarjuna's apparently abstract teaching that a powerful psychotherapeutic language is at work. Nor is it clear that the powerful ontological dialectics taught by Nagarjuna can speak to the actual pathological conditions of contemporary Western life. So a primary aim of this essay is to develop and systematically recreate the meditative psychotherapy which is implied in Nagarjuna's teaching. Nagarjuna presents the essential teaching of the Buddha as being a critique of essential (absolute) identity and the positive teaching of the powerful principle of relativity (relative non-dual identity). But the real connection between the life of ego-identity and the actual condition of human suffering is not at first evident. Here we find a challenge to the development of meditative psychotherapy— to show the step by step real connection between the dynamics of identity (duality) and the condition of real human suffering and pathology.

The first step towards Meditative psychotherapy requires the recognition of the ontological or hermeneutical thesis: that all experience, all existence, all meaning, all mental phenomena arise with respect to some ontological life-world or grammar of existence. The chapter makes clear that ontology is the foundation of psychology, not to mention all forms of experience. This hermeneutical theme— that all experience is interpretation relative to a determinate ontology or grammar of reality— naturally includes the various languages of psychotherapy, for psychoanalysis and psychotherapy are essentially hermeneutical arts which attempt to interpret and make sense of human life and behavior. So the ontological thesis applies to psychotherapy as well.

In developing this hermeneutical theme it is shown that the principle of essential identity which structures life-worlds (whether cultural or inter-cultural) is the origin of ontological pathology. An ontological hermeneutic is presented in which the mental disorders, whether of so-called normal "sane" life or of abnormal "insane" life are common in origin— they are essentially hermeneutical (ontological) disorders arising, as the Buddha taught, from the pathology of identity. Various forms of mental disorders are analyzed in terms of the fragmentation of identity, and it is shown that this principle of life structurally requires the splitting of consciousness into the conscious and the unconscious. But this fragmentation of life generated by essential identity pervades all levels of existence and reveals the nature of ontological repression, impotence, bondage and self-alienation. The pathology of identity explains various forms of self-alienation such as, ontological schizophrenia, paranoia, forgetfulness and compulsions. It is found that the violation of the deep drive to ontological universality, freedom and power is the source of mental or hermeneutical disorders. The real force of the Buddha's teaching that existence is suffering is made explicit.

In developing the ontological theme for psychotherapy it becomes clear that onto-centric psychotherapy works with a relative concept of sanity and mental health and attempts to bring the mental patient into conformity with the ontological consensus. The politics of conventional psychotherapies is called into question and is challenged in the light of ontological relativity— the teaching that there are alternative actual life-worlds (languages of existence) or multiple realities. This challenge of relativity (which is not to be confused with relativism) raises the need for a language of psychotherapy which overcomes the limitations of onto-centrism. The

Madhyamika teaching of relativity opens the way for a truly universal holistic (non-dual) language of psychotherapy.

The Madhyamika's powerful principle of relativity heals the fragmentation of life generated by the pathology of identity (ego-identity and egocentric life) and overcomes the bad faith that gives dualized life worlds their distorted meaning. Non-dual life, which is achieved through the rigorous discipline of dialectical meditation, opens the way for the healthy psyche to enter an integrated, liberated, universalized life of well-being and peaceful sanity. Most important, the Madhyamika teaches that essential identity violates true worldly life but relativity (dependent co-arising) vindicates life in the world. The principle of sunya (emptiness) makes existence and experience work, while the pathology of identity makes it sick and incoherent. This principle of relativity points the way to the onto-dynamics of dialectical psychotherapy.

PREFACE

The Madhyamika *Karikas* of Nagarjuna provide a powerful model for psychotherapy. These aphorisms are highly condensed universal principles or formulas which must be meditated upon and systematically activated in particular contexts to unleash their inexhaustible meaning. By their very nature their meaning cannot be rigidly fixed in any interpretation. Instead these highly formal teachings of Nagarjuna must be reconstructed and articulated ever anew. This is particularly true in the context of psychology and psychoanalysis, for the essence of the Buddha's teaching concerned the therapeutic termination of real human suffering through the ontological analysis of the formation of the psyche (ego, self) which is seen as the source of mental disturbance. The Buddha was concerned with finding a pragmatic therapy to terminate this existential suffering which arose from the desires of a self-existent individual self. Nagarjuna, presenting the essential teaching of the Buddha, broke dramatically with the earlier established school of Buddhism. He noticed that this Buddhist orthodoxy— the Hinayana tradition— fell into the same metaphysical theorizing about the psyche which the Buddha sought to terminate. In his *Karikas* he presents a dialectical language of analysis which probes more deeply into the nature of human consciousness, the origin of mental phenomena, the formation of the self as an individual entity, the constructive activity of the mind in constituting objects and reality, and discloses the laws of transformation of consciousness which bring liberation and peace.

But the language of therapy which is contained in the *Karikas* needs to be drawn out, made explicit and systematically reconstructed, especially in the contemporary context of psychoanalysis. For several effective and sophisticated languages of psychotherapy have been developed in recent Western psychology since the innovative work of Freud. These languages give different accounts of the nature of the self, of the dynamics of the psyche, of the nature of sanity and insanity, and they present different therapeutic strategies for bringing about mental health. By contrast, the Madhyamika teaching focuses on a critique of the principle of essential identity (svabhava) which not only gives rise to self-identity (the constitution of the individual self) but to all other entities, concepts, categories, human experience, in short, the world. In this critique it is demonstrated that the principle of identity leads to incoherence and all experience (and the world), when based upon such identity, is incoherent and unintelligible. Furthermore, in explicating the Buddha's primary teaching in the four noble truths, Nagarjuna demonstrates that the principle of identity is the source of suffering and mental disturbance, and the way to freedom (nirvana) comes with the deeper ontological critique which overcomes the fatal error of essential identity. Nagarjuna introduces the powerful principle of relativity (relative identity— pratitya samutpada) or dependent co-origination as the principle which terminates suffering and brings peace and well-being.

However, for anyone seriously studying Nagarjuna's teaching it is not at all clear that the *Karikas* provide a psychotherapeutic language which can speak to the contemporary condition or rival the more successful current forms of psychotherapy. Is it not an ancient esoteric teaching which had validity in a foreign cultural reality? Can it really provide a relevant and effective psychotherapy for contemporary Western culture? What does the critique of essential identity have to do with the real existential suffering, despair, depression and various forms of mental and rational illness which so many people suffer in our contemporary society? Can the teaching of the Buddha concerning the termination of suffering be effective with the diverse forms of human anguish suffered by so many "mental patients" in contemporary society? Is it able to deal creatively with the real problems of sanity and insanity? Would it not entail that those of us "sane" ones who live a life of ego-identity and satisfaction of desire are also mentally disturbed? Does it not imply that the entire culture which takes the ego or self to be independently real must be out of touch with reality, must be "insane"? And would not the forms of psychotherapy which assumed the independent existence of the ego or psyche also be out of touch?

The focus of this essay is to attempt to address these and related questions. Because of the formal and abstract nature of the *Karikas* it will be necessary to *develop* the language of psychotherapy which is implicit in Nagarjuna's teaching. This difficult task will involve the introduction of a language of pure *ontological* analysis and the clarification of the *ontological theme.* "Ontology" refers to the science of reality, and it will be shown later that Nagarjuna was a master ontologist who saw through the restricted metaphysical thinking of previous thought and forms of life. While metaphysical thinking and living takes the principle of essential identity as being absolute, *ontological* analysis as developed by the Buddha and formalized by Nagarjuna demonstrates that such metaphysical ways necessarily lead to suffering, self-alienation, incoherence and ill-being.

Thus, in developing the Madhyamika language of psychotherapy it will be necessary to introduce the ontological thesis which teaches that all possible forms of experience— meaning, interpretation, values, judgment, explanation, understanding, human action, mental phenomena, etc. arise from some ontological foundation or world. Ontology reveals how reality is constituted in some particular grammar of existence which shapes experience in its totality. To live is to be in some world or ontology, to experience is to interpret and to interpret is to reside within an ontological grammar. For this reason the ontological thesis is also called the *hermeneutical* theme— all experience is hermeneutical, in the ontological sense of arising in some ontological grammar of existence.

One clear task, then, is to apply this theme to psychology and psychotherapy. The languages of psychology and psychotherapy necessarily arise within some ontological hermeneutic, and this *primacy of ontology* has not been properly appreciated in the past. We shall see that questions of sanity and insanity are *ontological* questions having to do with being in touch with reality, and they are *hermeneutical* questions having to do with the significance or *meaning* of life. The nature of the psyche (person, self) itself radically differs in different ontologies so naturally psychology too is ontologically relative. What constitutes mental health or well-being are primarily ontological concerns which likewise vary in different ontological grammars. If ontology is the foundation of psychology, then it will be crucial for us to make explicit this relation and explore the form, formation and transformation of ontologies. The Madhyamika teaches that any possible ontological grammar arises from the illusory construction of essential identity. This means, of course, that any language of psychotherapy which takes the principle of essential identity seriously (individual identity of the psyche) is suspect. The Madhyamika hermeneutic is a critique of the principle of essential identity. A life-world organized on this principle is necessarily incoherent, unintelligible, and out of touch with reality. The essay explicates the existential connection between the Buddhist truth— all existence is suffering— and the principle of essential identity.

First it is found that the principle of identity is a principle of opposition— identity arises in differentiation, so the principle of unity— individual identity, is at the same time the principle of differentiation or duality. The principle of identity splits consciousness into a polar opposition (a dualism) which recurs on all levels of experience and mental phenomena. This recurrent dualizing principle sets up an inner tension within a life-world which determines the agenda of a life. The deepest life-force of a life-world is its quest for meaning, integration, unity, wholeness, universality, freedom or autonomy, and power. But the life of dualism, the life structured by the principle of identity is necessarily a fractured and self-divided life that is born in incoherence and irresolvable opposition. Thus, the first task of this essay is to demonstrate that the principle of essential identity is the principle of suffering, the principle of divided consciousness, the principle of self-alienation, the principle of repression and forgetfulness, the principle which divides consciousness into the conscious and the unconscious, the oppositional principle which reveals the inherent polar opposition in experience and meaning, the principle of self-deception, sin, alienation, privation, desire, disintegration, fragmentation. For this reason the dualized life necessarily fails to achieve true integration and remains limited in particularity, in bondage to karma or existential determinacy, that remains trapped in existence, that fails to achieve authentic meaning, universality, freedom and power. It is in this explication of the principle of identity/duality that we begin to understand the Buddhist principle that existence is sorrow, that suffering is caused by desire. For existence is constituted in identity (ego-identity) and this principle is necessarily the principle of bad faith, inauthentic meaning and existence, ill-being and bondage. It is the principle of identity which gives rise to the life of desire and structures all psychological phenomena into incoherent and unintelligible meaning.

Any life-world (personal or communal) which is structured on this principle of ignorance (duality) remains existentially fractured. We begin to see that it is a *life-world* which is the unit of existence hence of health and well-being. It is just as possible for a *culture* (a shared life-world in an ontological consensus) to be sick as for any individuals in it. In the politics of reality we begin to see the relativity of health and sanity. Since a culture constitutes or defines what is real or meaningful, it inherently provides its norms or standards of reality, health, sanity— to be sane is to be normal, to be normal is to share in the political consensus of the shared life-world. In this relative sense, *internal* to a given life-world and with respect to its criteria of "normal," to be healthy is to conform to the consensus, and to be abnormal is to be outside the ontological consensus.

But any psychotherapy which arises in the principle of identity and its necessarily distorted form of meaning or logos must equally fail to achieve true health and well-being. Here we find that any psychotherapeutic language and praxis is on trial to defend itself against onto centrism— the mistake of taking itself to be definitive of reality and universal for humanity. Instead we find that what passes as norms of "health" and "sanity" are relative to the norms of a life-world, to a consensus, and psychotherapy consists in transforming the patient (the mentally ill) into some workable relation with the ontological consensus.

However, the meditative psychotherapy reminds us that any psychotherapy or form of life which arises on the principle of identity/duality must remain fractured and disintegrated. It attempts to develop a truly universal therapy which avoids the relativism of onto-centrism. Instead, it presents an alternative principle of meaning (logos) which heals the fracture and incoherence of dual identity and this discloses a model of holistic (integrated, unified) health and being. The meditative principle of relative identity or dependent co-arising reveals the incoherence of dual-essential identity and provides a new insight into mental disturbance and the workings of consciousness. It opens the way to a truly universal therapeutic language for human well-being which is not culture-bound or restricted by the determinacy, particularity and contingency of a divided life-world.

In this respect meditative psychotherapy provides a model for holistic health, sanity and well-being. In moving beyond the split of dualized consciousness it transforms sick life into integrated and holistic awareness which is finally in harmony with reality. The sanity of holistic life and meaning reveals the true nature of mental disturbance and illness. It becomes clear that certain mental disorders are *ontological* in origin— these arise in a false principle of meaning and existence (logos). Mental illness, disturbance, disease in many of its forms, are really distortions and varieties of disintegration of logos (meaning, experience, existence, life). All mental illnesses are *hermeneutical* disorders in which the *meaning* of a life-world is fractured, incoherent, self-alienated, repressed, self-forgetting, existentially in bondage, un-free, ontologically impotent and particularized in the contingency of ego-identity and mal-practice.

It is here that we see clearly that mental or existential illness derives, as the Buddha taught, from the principle of essential identity. For this principle of opposition and disintegration necessarily impedes the deepest drive of a life-world to achieve ontological freedom, autonomy, power and universal integrated being. The principle of absolute identity does this by creating recurrent dualisms within the life-world at all levels: it splits consciousness into oppositional poles such that one eclipses the other, it dualizes life into a rift of thought and action, it creates a chasm between the mental and the physical (mind and body), it creates a self-alienation in consciousness between the conscious and the unconscious, it leads to splits between the ego and the life-worlds of the other (other egos) which threatens true communication between persons, it also leads to pathological splits within which lead to fragmentation of the personality and the breakdown of inner dialogue and self-communion, it drives a wedge between the isolated ego and the rest of reality— the world, the universe, the infinite— and so creates the opposition between the existential feeling of complete independence or complete dependence, it creates the splintering of meaning (logos), which prevents the healing of unified meaning of a life, and with the loss of authentic meaning it leads to existential depression and despair, it provides false structures of meaning which pretend to be true and authentic so it creates a life of bad faith, it structures life into the division of ownership (possessiveness, ego-identity) and dis-ownership (projection, hostility, alienation) of the Other.

These are the dynamics of "normal" life— the life as part of the ontological consensus of a shared reality. We then see that those who are designated as "insane" with respect to the norms of a consensus are simply more progressive forms of hermeneutical disorders: the hermeneutical diseases of paranoia, depression, dis-related multiple selves, and the dynamics of existential repression, impotence, compulsions and forgetfulness, etc. are advanced forms of breakdown of meaning and communication. Mental breakdown in certain forms turns out to be the ontological breakdown that comes with a disintegrated world. In this light we begin to see the deep insight of the Buddha's teaching— that even those of the normal ontological consensus are just as much suffering and mentally disturbed as those in extreme hermeneutical chaos. It becomes clearer that a culture as a whole may well be pathological and out of touch with reality.

In contrast, the principle of relativity (of holistic identity) provides the ontological principle which can heal the deep fracture of consciousness and transform a life-world to integrated (holistic) being, authentic and true meaning (right-mindedness, right-speech, right-thoughts, right-deeds) to true ontological freedom and liberation, to true power and peace (nirvana). This principle provides a new hermeneutic or psychotherapeutic language which makes possible the self-transformation of a life-world from sickness and sin (duality) to integration and health (non-duality). Through the *meditative* science of logos it exorcises the compulsions of rigid identity and frees life for the spontaneous flow of freedom and transparency (sunya).

Holistic psychotherapy flows from the principle of non-duality— a principle of relative identity which melts the dualisms of consciousness/object, thought/deed, mind/body, theory/praxis, finite/infinite, particular/universal, I/Thou and the divisions between life-worlds which prevent true communication, dialogue and healthy relationality. The psycho-dynamics of holistic therapy emerge in the dialectics presented by Nagarjuna. The pure ontological analysis of the *Karikas* breaks the bounds of metaphysical thinking that arises with essential identity. The relation between the therapist and patient is reflected in the ongoing inner dialogue of the *Karikas* between the Madhyamika (the voice of the Buddha) and the skeptical disciple or opponent. The process of holistic therapy involves the deep self-transformation of rationality or logos from the split and incoherent dualized form to the healed integrated non-dualized identity. This self-transformation of logos or conscious life follows precise *meditative* patterns and principles which play themselves out in the dialectics of a progressive dialogue.

Thus, this essay has set for itself a most difficult task— to meditate upon the *Karikas* and develop and re-create, if only in an initial sketchy and crude form, the hermeneutic of holistic psychotherapy. This task is undertaken in the confident faith that the proper development and articulation of the language of therapy hidden in the *Karikas* will provide a truly universal language of therapy which is *not* culture-bound and which effectively addresses the condition of human ignorance and suffering. At the same time it naturally provides a powerful critique of the current languages of psychotherapy which begin with some form of the essential identity of the self or psyche, and proceed in the egological paradigm.

In carrying out this task I shall proceed as follows:

i)   review of some of the main teachings of Nagarjuna

ii)   begin the development of the hermeneutic of holistic therapy by sketching an ontological language implicit in the *Karikas*

    a)   sketch the ontological or hermeneutical theme which shows that psychology and psychotherapy derive from ontology

    b)   show that all psychological mental phenomena arise from the ontology of the self (person)

    c)   show that meaning of a life arises in the ontology of a life-world

    d)   show that a life-world constitutes reality and is at once personal and communal (culture)

iii)   demonstrate that a life-world arises in the principle of essential identity (the principle of duality/opposition)

    a)   show how rigid identity divides consciousness (the psyche) into polar opposites which creates the dualism of conscious/unconscious

    b)   make clear how identity is the principle of repression and self-alienation: the principle of sin and suffering

    c)   explicate the origin of pathology in the hermeneutical disorders arising from ego-identity (dualism)

    d)   make clear the politics of the ontological consensus which lead to the relative distinction of sane/insane

    e)   explain how essential identity leads to ontological bondage, ignorance, suffering and existential impotence.

    f)   critique of psycho-therapeutic languages which assume the principle of ego-identity

iv)   Develop the alternative hermeneutic based upon non-duality ontological relativity, relative identity and dependent co-arising

    a)   explain how non-duality heals the fractures of essential identity

    b)   make clear the transformation to holistic existence and holistic health

    c)   draw out the connections between holistic life, ontological liberation, peace, the cessation of mental disturbance, effective living in the world, and various aspects of the Buddhist eight-fold path

    d)   explain how the principle of relativity (dependent co-arising) breaks through the ignorance and fiction of self-existent objects and leads to true self-realization.

v)   Conclude by sketching and outlining the dynamics of holistic psychotherapy

    a)   what are the dynamics of self-transformation from dual consciousness to non-dual awareness?

    b)   what are the actual psycho-dynamics between the effective therapist and the patient

c) how practical is this psycho-therapy for those of us who are ego-centric and mentally disturbed in contemporary society?

d) in what way is holistic psychotherapy a truly universal inter-cultural language?

i) Summary Review of Some Main Teachings of Nagarjuna

The following summary review is abstracted from several earlier essays which develop these themes in systematic detail. Nagarjuna, in his *Karikas,* introduced a radically new way to understand the nature of consciousness and thought, the workings of natural language and experience, the construction of mental phenomena and the origin of self, objects and the world. This instruction, presented as the essential teaching of the Buddha, revealed that experience and all objects of experience are *sunya* (empty, void, devoid of essence, self-identity or substance), that the self and all entities arise co-dependently *(pratitya-samutpada),* and that the liberation of consciousness emerges with the silence of the middle way *(madhyam-pratipad)* between *all* opposites or contraries.

His treatise focuses in consecutive chapters on a range of the basic categories and features of experience— causality, process, becoming, elements, time, space, self, self-realization, and so on. In each case Nagarjuna demonstrates in dialogue with the skeptical opponent that experience which is based upon the formal principle of self-identity *(svabhava)* collapses *on its own terms* in incoherence and unintelligibility. He demonstrates that if any object or concept is constituted in independent self-existence (absolute identity) then on this very principle such an object or concept becomes unintelligible and meaning breaks down.

Nagarjuna presents a formal ontological analysis of experience, self and world which reveals that the principle of identity is at the same time the principle of radical opposition and duality, and it emerges that there is a deep formal opposition in the heart of consciousness. This principle of opposition is the principle which governs the formation of thought and judgment as well— it is focused on the opposition between *is/isn't*. This primary opposition leads to two complementary and incompatible formal languages of existence— the language of being (is), on the one hand, and the language of non-being (isn't), on the other. In the Indian metaphysical tradition these two languages of existence were developed in the Hindu tradition of (the Atma-language) as well as in the Early Buddhist tradition (the *Anatma-language).* Nagarjuna saw that both languages were often interpreted as metaphysical in that they arose from the common principle of essential identity *(svabhava).* His dialectical analysis showed that these complementary polar languages of consciousness and experience exhausted the range of possible "views" and that each mutually excluded the other. On the one hand the Atma language of being took substance to be the ultimate metaphysical subject and this led to some form of ontological monism. On the other hand the Anatma language of radical becoming (the Buddhist Abhidharmic theory of existence) stressed a pluralism and atomism of experience and existence. The former language took the logical subject to be absolute and independent while the latter focused on the predicate or attributes (dharmas) to be the elements of existence. But Nagarjuna made clear that neither language alone could account independently for existence or objects of experience. The ontological subject can never be postulated independently of the attributes or properties, but equally the attributes could never be postulated independently of the primary subject. Nevertheless, each polar language of experience took itself to be complete and self-existent.

Thus, Nagarjuna uncovers a formal incoherence in the structure of consciousness when it takes itself to conform to the principle of essential (absolute) identity. He teaches that identity necessarily involves difference or opposition and he shows that identity is the principle of dual opposition or *either/or*. But Nagarjuna does not naively *deny* this principle, for he sees the deeper trap of all thought or judgment which arises from this principle— the oppositional principle of *affirming or denying,* of being or not-being, of is and isn't. That is, he sees that *language itself* as it is constituted by the principle of identity must be therapeutically dissipated— to move between the extremes of is and isn't, to move beyond *all* dual oppositions that structure the life of identity. This means that his own therapeutic language cannot flow from the principle of identity which defines the enterprise of description, propositions, facts, reference, and judgment. His own language must function in a non-propositional or non-descriptive way. It is this feature of Nagarjuna's language that leads to the *middle way* beyond all dual opposites and pathological objectification.

However, Nagarjuna wishes not only to speak a therapeutic language which transforms consciousness beyond the entrapment of essential identity, but more importantly to *save natural language* and experience from the irrationality and incoherence of either/or identity. He wishes to demonstrate meditatively that language works, the world works, thought works and experience flows only in the principle of dependent-co-arising or the relativity of identity. A term used for this principle is *sunya* and that *nirvana* (sunya-consciousness which is peaceful and tranquil and liberated from the bondage of fixed identity) is non-different from *samsara* the perpetual cycle of natural existence). So Nagarjuna's therapy at once breaks down the ignorance that constitutes the samsara of dualistic identity (the world of sin and suffering) and goes full circle to vindicate worldly existence and language as making sense and flowing only on the principle of relativity. It is this principle of relativity (relative identity or dependent-co-arising) which opens the way to liberated existence— of right action, right speech, right thoughts, right mindedness. It emerges that the true worldly life (of the eight-fold path of virtue) flows in non-duality and is liberated from the bondage of rigid independent identity.

In effect the therapeutic language of Nagarjuna shows that essential identity is a construction or fabrication from primary or original consciousness which is *sunya*. The ontological imagination in constructing essentialistic reality— with ego-identity— loses and forgets itself and falls into the eclipse of original awareness. The two polar languages of consciousness themselves co-dependently arise in sunya then fall into the inevitable dualistic ignorance of taking themselves to be independent and absolute. The therapy which brings liberation and wisdom from this illusion finds the way back to original pure or natural consciousness which is the practice of the middle way— Nirvana.

ii) Meditations on the Karikas: Developing a Language of Meditative Psychotherapy

But all of this appears to be highly formal and abstract and far removed from the concerns of existential suffering and mental disturbance. We need to make this teaching more tangible and specific in order to see how it would naturally lead to a psychotherapy. There seems to be a great leap from the formal problems of essential identity and the real practical concerns of mental disorder. There is at first no obvious relation between the duality and opposition which is obviously in everyday experience and the felt suffering of disturbed people. The silence of the middle way seems too mute and distant to speak effectively to the noisy lives we live. We must now extend and develop the Madhyamika teaching to show how it speaks to our condition.

a) The Hermeneutical Theme: Psychology Derives From Ontology

One of the first themes that would help to build a bridge to meditative psychotherapy is what I shall call the *hermeneutical theme*. This will help us to make sense of the Madhyamika's instruction that *all views are empty*. Some terminology might help in the explication of this theme. Three terms in particular need to be introduced— *ontology, hermeneutics and logos*. First, *ontology* is the science of being or reality. But this most general science of all sciences naturally includes the science of meaning, thought and language, for there is no meaning apart from the structure of reality, and thought and language must reflect and constitute the form of reality. Similarly, experience as an intelligible enterprise gets its form and significance from the order of existence. The point is that ontology necessarily investigates simultaneously the inter-related realms of existence, experience, thought, language and rationality. It is not so much a matter of whether one is more primary than the other— rather, these realms are necessarily so mutually inter-related that they must be taken together. So it would be helpful to introduce a term which holds these domains together in one concept— let *logos* be a term which connotes reality/experience/thought/language/meaning. It may be said, then, that *ontology is the science of logos.*[1]

It is here that we may introduce the term *hermeneutics:* for ontology reveals that logos takes the form of a *world*. A world is a universal structure which gives from to reality and manifests itself as a language of experience. As such it determines what makes sense and what does not, what is possible and what is not possible. That is, a world defines meaning and makes experience possible. As a universal grammar it constitutes a language in virtue of which the universe in its totality may be comprehended. In this respect a world *is* reality and it makes all forms of experience possible— understanding, judgment, interpretation, theory, praxis, not to mention all other cultural forms. A world is *lived* and for this reason it is called a *life-world*. A life-world may be personal and communal, and a shared life-world constitutes a community or culture. So another way to present a life-world or ontology is to say that it defines a culture or grammar of experience. A life-world makes experience as a whole possible, it makes viewing possible, so it cannot be reduced to a mere view. With this in mind we can easily discern the hermeneutical theme: to experience is to reside in some world, and the term *hermeneutics* indicates this fact that intelligible experience arises in some ontology— to *experience is to be in a life-world;* to be meaningful is to arise in a life-world; to exist is to be constituted in a life-world. I use the term *hermeneutics,* then, to indicate the realm of experience, and the hermeneutical theme makes clear that experience and meaning is ontological or grammatical.

This theme is critical for our purposes, for it requires us to see that all mental phenomena arise with respect to some life-world or other. This, of course, includes the activities of interpretation (making sense of phenomena) theorizing, explaining, and any meaningful form of human activity— like psychotherapy. That is, it is important to recognize the primacy of ontological hermeneutics in approaching psychology or psychotherapy. If psychology is the science of the psyche or self then it is critical to acknowledge that *psychology arises within ontology.* Likewise, psychotherapy, as an attempt to make sense of human thought, mental phenomena, human behavior, as well as to transform the person (psyche) into a healthy state— attuned to reality, then *must equally be conditioned by ontology.*

This obvious point has often been overlooked for various reasons. Freud, for example, wished to get away from metaphysical speculation and ground the science of the psyche on empirical science. But this anti-metaphysical theme in no way escapes the range of ontology, and Freud naturally proceeded to develop a hermeneutic or language which arose out of an ontology. In any case it should be clear that the science of psychology, in order to be truly scientific and self-critical, must rise to the level of making clear its ontological grammar in virtue of which it makes sense of mental phenomena. This is particularly critical because different ontologies or life-worlds make sense differently of reality. What is intelligible or possible in one life-world fails to make sense in another— for life-worlds or ontologies constitute or define what makes sense and what does not. For example, what counts as psychology in the Hindu life-world may not be recognizable as such in the Christian life-world. What makes sense in a materialistic language of empirical science may not be intelligible in an idealist ontological grammar. The behaviorist school of psychology treats mental phenomena in terms of the observable behavior of bodies. But the mentalistic schools of psychology take phenomena of the mind to be *mental* and not reducible to bodily concepts. We may say that they arise from different ontological grammars. Thus, in articulating the hermeneutical theme it is found that all experience arises in some life-world or other, and more specifically, that psychology and psychotherapy must arise from *ontological* foundations.

This theme of ontological hermeneutics reminds us that a primary concern for psychology and psychotherapy is to make explicit the ontology of the psyche (person or self). The ontology of the self or person in the Hindu life-world is very different from the ontology of the self in the life-world of Freud's hermeneutic, and so on. If a given psychology is relative to the ontology of the person of a particular life-world, then this makes urgent the question of the onto-centrism of any language of psychology. That is, to what extent is a given language of psychology or psychotherapy universal for humanity or bound by the limits of its ontological grammar.

Of course, this question is at the heart of our specific concern about the nature of sanity and insanity. For if sanity or mental health has to do with being in touch with reality, then it appears that sanity and insanity are relative to the particular grammar of reality (life-world) under consideration. But can there be a concept of the human being— the person of psyche— which is not bound by any particular ontological grammar? Can there be a concept of sanity which is trans-world in its universality—

valid for any possible world? Is it possible to have a psychology or psychotherapy which is likewise universally valid for any possible world? These questions will be addressed in the sequal.

b) The Life-Force of Life-Worlds: The Quest for Universality, Autonomy and Ontological Power

As we attempt to make sense of the Madhyamika's teaching that *all life-worlds are empty,* it is natural to follow up the hermeneutical theme by exploring the inner form and structure of life-worlds. It was suggested that a shared life-world is a culture and that all forms of cultural experience arise within the universal cultural grammar. For example, the ethics, religion, politics, esthetics, science, rituals, everyday behavior, etc., of a given culture all arise and take their significance from the cultural grammar in question. Another way to understand this is to appreciate that a life-world is *universal*— it purports to be all-encompassing of reality. A life-world constitutes the universe and is all-inclusive of reality. This is why it is a mistake to reduce worlds to mere world*views,* for a world makes viewing itself possible. It is important to stress this point because it is highly problematic to postulate alternative possible or actual life-worlds. For worlds, being universal universes, are not to be differentiated on a par with the sort of difference that holds between objects *within* a given world. In some sense different worlds are incommensurable.[2]

The universality of a life-world may be put in another way. Every life-world is structured between the limits of fully differentiated objects on the one hand, and a unifying ultimate point of reference which unifies the universe, on the other. One limit of the world is plurality and diversity and the other limit is unity. (We shall see shortly that this inner structure of a life-world reflects the principle of identity which the Madhyamika brings under critique.) The limit of differentiated objects is the limit of finitude while the limit of unity is the transcendent infinite point of reference. A life-world, then, arises within the duality of finitude and infinitude. There is a natural striving within life-worlds to universalize itself in the direction of infinitude. In this respect a life-world is organic and grows or expands its horizons as new foreign objects come into view. This drive to *ontological universality* leads a life-world to transform any new and foreign Other into its own terms of reference. For example, any universal grammar of a given culture will naturally attempt to translate a newly encountered cultural world into its own terms to make sense of it. Or any hermeneutic of psychology will naturally attempt to appropriate any new phenomena it encounters into its own grammar.[3]

This quest for ontological universality of a life-world or universal grammar may be called the *will to be.* It is experienced in the form of ontological freedom or self-definition or autonomy. The deepest offense to the being of an Other is to impose upon its ontological self-determination or to limit its ontological power. The notions of ontological universality, freedom and power are synonymous. We shall see in what follows that the violation of the healthy will to be is a source of mental disturbance and hermeneutical disorders.

c) The Politics of Reality: Consensus, Communication and Sanity

In preparing to explore (in the next section) precisely how life-worlds arise in the principle of essential identity/duality it is timely to introduce another theme which will help in the development of meditative psychotherapy. The theme of the *politics of reality* is central to ontological hermeneutics. For we have left it an open question whether a life-world is personal or communal. A life-world is always *lived*, whether by an individual person or in the shared life of a community. The dialectics between individual and community— the possible *ontological* harmony and disharmony between them— raises questions about the *relativity of reality* itself.

We have seen that reality is *constituted* in a life-world and the possibility of a plurality of *actual* life-worlds entails the possibility of multiple realities. This possibility, of course, is of the utmost importance for our discussion since it is *prima facie* given that to be sane is to be in touch with reality. But if the possibility of multiple realities has validity, then this places the *ontology of sanity* in a new light.

The field of comparative ontology recognizes that there is, indeed, a plurality of alternative possible and actual life-worlds. This is most easily seen in the case of inter-cultural investigation. For example, the shared or communal life-worlds of world cultures— Hindus, Christians, Buddhists, Confucians, and so on— indicate that empirically there exists radically different cultural worlds. Earlier research in comparative ontology has shown that we cannot reduce these alternative life-worlds to mere "world-views" of a common, neutral, "objective" reality. The hypothesis of a neutral noumenal reality independent of life-worlds is very much in question, especially in the context of meditative critique of absolute essential identity.

If we take the possibility of an *actual plurality* of life-worlds seriously, then, of course, this immediately raises urgent questions about validity, authenticity, truth and objectivity. It is natural to ask whether amongst alternative possible worlds one is more valid or true than others. This interest in truth and validity is one expression of the deep ontological urge to universality, freedom and power we have just discussed.

More immediately, however, the case of inter-cultural alternative life-worlds (realities) serves as a reminder that the very same possibility arises *within* the context of any given conventional or historical culture. It always remains a real possibility *intra-culturally* that on the level of individual persons different life-worlds are present. That is, the thesis of alternative possible worlds arises for *individual person* within any given culture. If this is not obvious we can see in cases of conversion or ontological revolutions or transformations how outstanding persons have opened the way to new forms of life. For example, Socrates stood outside of the communal consensus, Jesus taught the way to a new life, the Buddha was an ontological revolutionary and opened the possibility of a new form of life, and so on. In other less dramatic ways individuals like Spinoza, Freud, Einstein have challenged the ontological consensus and succeeded in bringing about cultural or hermeneutical revolutions.

But we need not take these more dramatic cases. The point is that for each individual person it remains a real possibility that his or her form of life may or may not conform to the ontological consensus. It remains a possibility that any conventional culture may in fact consist of a range of multiple forms of life (grammars of reality) existing simultaneously. For example, what is called contemporary "American culture" consists of a range of life-worlds, ontologies or cultural grammars juxtaposed within the context of "common sense": the various religious cultural grammars, the grammars of natural and social sciences, the languages of psychotherapy, etc. It is clear that anyone in this "culture" lives in the midst of a plurality of life-worlds which constitute reality in different ways. The implication of this, of course, is that it is always a real question whether there is real communication between the individual persons *within* a shared conventional "culture." For comparative ontology has demonstrated that there is *systematic ambiguity* of meaning between different life-world language. If two different individuals reside in different life-worlds or realities and speak different ontological languages, how can they communicate and share common meaning? We now begin to uncover the critical concern of sanity and insanity— who is really (legitimately, authentically) in "touch" with reality? Is the ontological consensus necessarily more sane than any individual person who lives outside of this consensus? This question opens the theme of the politics of reality and sanity.4

Until the question whether one life-world is inherently more valid or legitimate than another is settled the issue of sanity and insanity must remain open. Meanwhile, conventional psychotherapy proceeds with the criterion of the *ontological consensus:* true "reality" is what the ontological majority agree it is, and has adopted. Any ontological grammar outside of this consensus is deviant and *abnormal*. Insanity is determined by ontological tests as to whether the patient can coherently speak the ontological grammar of the current consensus.5 But of course the conventional criterion of sanity according to the norm of the ontological consensus is now on trial on the charge of being *onto-centric*. By its own ontologically subjective criteria it makes a relative distinction between true reality and false reality, true meaning and false meaning, legitimate life and illegitimate life. However, comparative ontology shows that there is no reason why any person outside of the ontological consensus may not be more sane than the majority, and there is no reason why a culture as a whole cannot be eclipsed from reality. Onto-centric psychotherapy attempts to get the patient to conform to the ontological consensus and proceeds to convert the ontological deviant to the norm of "true reality." Onto-centric mental health attempts to get the patient to become "well adjusted."6 Thus, the ontological theme has introduced the following concerns:

a) the ontological unit of meaning/existence is the life-world

b) there is a plurality of alternative actual life-worlds

c) life-worlds may be both personal and communal

d) a conventional "culture" may in fact consist of a plurality of ontological sub-cultures or life-worlds

e) there is no necessity that the ontological consensus conforms to the truth or to true reality

f) there is always the real possibility of miscommunication between the languages of different life-worlds

g) the ontological consensus may well be out of touch with reality

h) the politics of the ontological consensus *defines* by its own criteria what is to count as sanity and mental health

i) onto-centric psychotherapy must be called into question

The paradigm of meditative therapy would insist that true psychotherapy must overcome onto-centrism and master the relativity of reality. We shall now see just how the suspect principle of essential identity structures any life-world and leads to fragmentation. This next exploration will help us to appreciate the meditative teaching that all life-worlds are empty.

iii)   Essential Identity: the Origin of Suffering and
Hermeneutical Disorders

In this section we shall take the next natural step in the development of Madhyamika holistic psychotherapy and explore precisely how the principle of essential identity is the formal principle which generates life-worlds and which fragments existence, life, experience, meaning and consciousness (i.e., fragments *logos*) into incompatible dualisms. We shall then be in a better position to see why this principle is the principle of suffering and leads to ontological disorders.

a) Identity and the Inherent Duality of Life-Worlds

Now we need to appreciate how the principle of identity (ego identity) is at the same time the formal principle of duality. This synonym is usually overlooked and the critical connection between identity and the life of suffering becomes eclipsed. In what follows I shall review some of the main points which are developed in systematic detail in earlier chapters.[7] The structure of a life-world arises within the polar extremes of differentiated objects (individual entities) on the one hand, and a unifying point of reference which makes the life-world a unified whole, a universe. These two limits of any life-world structurally arise from the form of essential identity. This principle of being and thought (logos) is often expressed in the statement— *A is A* or *A is* identical with A. But the same meaning is expressed in the principle of *different— A is not B*. It is important to see that in identity (individual univocal determinacy) there is difference; in the identity of A is implied otherness or difference from what is *not-A* (call it B). Thus, inherent in identity is negation, difference and otherness: to be a given thing is precisely to stand in opposition to what it is not. If there is nothing over against which it stands in contrast and distinction, then it would fail to have any determinate identity.

This version of the principle of identity yields the formal *principle of essence:* to be something, to have determinate identity, is to be differentiated from what is other. When it is clear that the formal principle of identity or essence inherently involves difference and opposition and negation, it is then easily seen that this principle is the principle of all other principles; as Aristotle puts it, the first principle of thought and being (of rationality)— the principle of non-contradiction. This version of identity states that: A given thing S cannot be both P and not-P at the same time and in the same respect. The converse version of this principle of identity is known as the law of excluded middle: A given thing S must be either P or not-P. So to be committed to individual identity is to be committed to the opposition of either/or.

The meditative paradigm uses this oppositional structure of essential identity to demonstrate that any possible world must live between the dual oppositions. Inherent in the structure of life-worlds is the existential tension and polarity between the limit of unity (identity) and the limit of differentiation: the inner space of a life-world arises within the polar tension of the transcendent point of unity (infinity) and the immanent limit of complete individuation, particularization, determinacy and atomicity (i.e. finitude).

This primary polarity inherent in the principle of identity spawns and reiterates dualities in every sphere of the logos of a life-world. It is easy enough to find pervasive dualisms throughout the structure of existence— between mental and physical (mind/body), between consciousness and object, between self and other (not self), between thought and world, between appearance and reality, between word and object, between essence and existence, between being and becoming, between rest and motion, between universal and particular, between theory and practice, between substance and attribute, between subject and predicate, and so on. But it is more difficult to *understand* the formal origin of these dualities, more difficult to see how they arise inevitably from the principle of essential identity.

The dynamics and dialectics of identity/difference helps us to see how dualisms necessarily arise in the structure of a life-world. First, it must be remembered that the principle of identity is a principle of opposition, for to have identity is to be differentiated or discriminated: the principle of *contrariety* is implicit in the principle of identity: *Every item P has a contrary un-P.* The point is that contrary opposition formally requires a unifying point of reference in virtue of which they may be in the relation of opposition. This may be illustrated with any attribute in a life-world: Take any attribute P, to be P (identity) is to be differentiated from un-P (what fails to be P) but the contrariety of P and un-P must be referred to some unifying point of reference to stand in that contrary relation— let /P/ indicate that unity. The /P/ is a unifying condition of the relation P and un-P. For example, if "wise" is a property with determinate identity, then "unwise" is its contrary. But this opposition is held in contrary relation by implicit reference to the more primitive unity /wise/, which indicates all those things in the world which can be wise or un-wise. This formal dynamic of contrariety/identity is the source of dualism in any life-world.

Perhaps an illustration of contrary opposition may be helpful. If we focus on *becoming* (process, change, motion, etc.) as the Madhyamika does, we immediately see that *contrariety is the condition of becoming.* In order for anything X to become P entails that it must be un-P as a formal condition of its becoming P, that is, *duality and privation* is a *necessary condition* of all becoming; becoming takes place between contrary opposites. Of course, these very dynamics take place in the identity formation of any *entity* as well. To be an entity X is to be differentiated in contrariety, from what fails to be that entity.

This brief review of the duality of identity should now help us to appreciate how in the identity of the psyche or self (ego) the principle of duality is at work. The formation of ego identity involves (for any life-world) the particularization or individuation of an entity through certain properties— to be an individual entity is to have determinate attributes which distinguishes that entity from all others. Individual identity consists in having discriminating properties. So in the very formation of ego identity is differentiation from other entities through unique properties, and this process of individuation results in determinacy and particularization of that entity. The more determinate the entity in identity, the more the differentiation from other entities in its life-world. If a person *identifies* with the individuated ego then he takes on the full determinacy and finitization of that ego identity. Here we see the seeds of ontological bondage.

The *Karikas* demonstrate over and over how the principle of identity/duality recurs on all levels of experience, but most of all it points to a deep polarity in consciousness— it reveals two polar languages of consciousness (of logos) which are mutually exclusive and incompatible. It demonstrates how one polar language is the language of unity (monism, substance)— the Atma language of the Hindu life-world, while the other is the language of diversity (atomism, no-substance) the Buddhist Anatma language of radical becoming. This bi-polarity in the structure of logos reflects the two structural limits of any life-world, between the unifying infinite and the diversifying finite.

But because these two formal languages are oppositional and mutually incompatible they force a deep split in logos which the principle of identity cannot possibly overcome. Another way to state this is that the principle of identity structurally splits consciousness into the realm of the conscious and the unconscious— logos is bifurcated into two realms each of which eclipses the other. For the principle of identity makes it impossible (on pain of contradiction) to bring the two polar languages together. Thus, the coming forth of one necessarily leads to the eclipse of the other, and here we find the formal ontological necessity of the duality between the conscious and un-conscious. This means that any life-world based upon identity must be self-alienated, self-eclipsed or ontologically alienated from itself. Identity creates a deep split in a life-world which alienates it from reality, and this is the ontological source of mental disturbance.

h) *Ego Identity; The Origin of Suffering, Bondage and Sin*

It is precisely the formal ontological analysis of ego-identity that makes clear the Buddha's teaching that the life of ego desire is the life of sorrow.

In *any* possible life-world, when consciousness (logos, psyche) takes an ego-centric identity it is ontologically separated not only from other egos of that world, but from the world as a whole and its very self. But egocentric life of individual identity not only identifies consciousness with the ego, but it also identifies its life-world with reality. In its separation from its world it experiences its existence as finite, particular, determinate, contingent and dependent. On the one hand, ego-identity presents itself as ontologically self-existent (svabhava), but in its inherent separation and delimitation or finitization it also experiences existential contingency or dependency (the threat of death). Already we find an existential incoherence in the life of ego-identity.

Ego-centric life takes itself to be unlimited and complete (independent) but its very identity shows it to be particularized, localized and dependent. This existential tension is precisely the tensions referred to earlier between the polar limits of logos— between being and becoming. The inherent incompleteness of an ego generates the condition of *ontological privation,* lacking complete being, and this is the origin of *desire;* desire is an inherent ontological condition of an ego. Thus, the condition of becoming and the condition of desire are synonymous ontologically. But we have seen (the principle of contrariety) that for something to *become* P presupposes that it must be *un-P,* so becoming arises with *existential privation.* Here we find the ontological connection between ego-identity, contingency, becoming and desire. The Buddha's ontological insight that existence is suffering and that suffering is caused by desire can perhaps be better appreciated in this light. It would also help to see that existential privation is the condition of *sin.* Ontological sin is the condition of suffering privation in being, and desire is the force of becoming which generates human action. But the ontological drive for universality, freedom and ontological power which is the life force of a life-world cannot possibly be satisfied in any object of desire or any action of becoming. The egocentric psyche can never achieve ontological completeness or independence through any action born of desire. It is this ontological condition of sin (separation from being) and desire (privation and incompleteness) which is often discussed in the Indian tradition in terms of *karma.* Karma indicates the individuating attributes which gives a given psyche its discriminated ego: karma involves the ontological attributes which gives an ego its unique identity, so it is existentially connected with finitude, bondage to particularity and entrapment in samsara (the cycle of becoming and egological existence).

But the ontological disturbance inherent in ego-centric life becomes more manifest when we see the *dualized* life that comes with ego-identity. For not only is the individuated psyche alienated from being in its finitized form, and traumatized by its contingency and impending death, but it also suffers the inner split into conscious/ unconscious, the split into mind/body, the split between consciousness and object, between thought and action, between I and Thou, and so on. Logos becomes fragmented on all sides into irreconcilable dualisms. This disintegration of psyche's logos arises *structurally* from ego identity. Again, this is the force of the Buddha's ontological insight into the nature of mental disturbance and the sorrow of ego-centric existence.

The logos of a life-world strives for universality, freedom and ontological power, but the pull of individual identity traps it in particularity, finitude, limitation, alienation, incompleteness and ontological impotence. This is a formal condition of any individuated ego in any possible lifeworld. Examples of this disturbed ontological condition abound in the history of life-worlds. For example, in the Christian life-world it is explicit that the finite individual person is born in sin (separation from God) and is condemned to a life of disturbance unless that person enters a new life of salvation, a life which overcomes the alienation from God and triumphs over death. Similarly, in the Hindu life-world, the individuated ego lives in bondage to karma in the cycle of samsara. This life of individuated ego is the life of alienation from true Self (Atman), an inauthentic life of vanity and illusion and ignorance. Here, too this sick condition may be overcome only with the saving wisdom which comes with the recognition of the true nature of Self which is infinite, universal (cosmic) and liberated from the bounds of existence (samsara, birth and death). The early Buddhist life-world, too, moves in a similar pattern of rejecting a *substantial* ego identity and instead turning to a radically different ontological grammar in which the ego identity is fabricated from more elementary atomic dharmas (qualities). With the dissolution of ego identity comes liberation from desire and the suffering that attends it. By coming to understand its universality and freedom in Buddha-nature the finitized ego is liberated from suffering. And so on.

c) Ontological Pathology: Hermeneutical Disorders and Existential Illness
The meditative dialectic, in exposing the common source of disturbance for any essentialistic life-world, opens the way to true *holistic* logos: true integrated life, authentic meaning, coherent experience, effective action,

the liberation of psyche, and the peace and well-being of the person. The dissipation of essential identity clears the way for the principle of holistic life— the principle of relativity (dependent co-arising, relative identity). It is with respect to this non-dual principle of identity that we may now examine various *ontological* disorders of dualized life.

We saw earlier that the unit of meaning is the life-world, and the source of mental disturbance, in all its forms, is to be found in the *form of life* or structure of life-worlds. This means that the unit of ontological pathology is not only the person but the shared life-world, the *culture* or community as a whole. An ontological consensus which defines the norm (normal) may well be pathological, live in bad faith. The meditative paradigm suggests that any life of essential identity is a life of illusion, hence of inauthentic meaning (logos) and bad faith. Thus, the inner life force of life-worlds which strives for the authenticity of universality, freedom and power necessarily defeats itself when it lives by the principle of disintegrated meaning (identity).

In taking the next important step towards meditative psychotherapy we must now explore how ontological pathology arises, especially within the shared illusion and bad faith of a false consensus. If we can recognize the mental diseases of "normal" life, we shall be in a better position to recognize that the more extreme forms of mental illness which onto-centric psychotherapies claim to treat are only differences of *degrees* of hermeneutical illness from the *normalized disorders* of the ontological majority. Thus, let us first attempt to get a general understanding of the normalized disturbances and then see how it also accounts for the perhaps more extreme "abnormal" disorders.

Perhaps the most generic form of hermeneutical illness is *onto-centrism*. The *pathology of identity* leads to the hermeneutical breakdown in the true communication and communion with other life-worlds. A given life-world, *in affirming* its own identity necessarily *denies* the identity of the Other. In dealing with a plurality of life-worlds (realities) a given life-world (my own) universalizes itself as a universal language of existence and thereby violates the integrity of the Other. The deepest form of violence is not physical, but ontological— the violation of the logos of Other. This ontological violation denies of the Other (life-world) his or her right to self-definition and self-determination— that is, it violates the essential ontological freedom of the Other. The aggressive life-world expands its grammar to appropriate and translate (reduce) the presence of the Other to its *own* grammar. Ontological chauvinism and imperialism is unable to open to the alien grammar of the Other. In missionary self-justification it proceeds to take over the space of the other and is therefore incapable of entering into the mutuality of dialogue (love). In effect, then, the alienation and violence of onto-centrism takes the form of the hermeneutical disorder to solipsism— the self-affirmation of a life-world as the absolute independent center of the universe (reality) and be-all of reality.

This fundamental disease of identity (on the macroscopic level of a life-world) naturally leads to two extreme forms in adjusting to the presence of Others (ontological plurality): it either *asserts* itself to be absolute (Absolutism), or else it *denies* itself to be Absolute (Relativism). But both extremes are really the attempt to re-affirm essential identity and preserve its false sense of coherence. The primary target of meditative critique is absolutism (the limit of svabhava) and its contrary, relativism. We saw earlier that every life-world has its ultimate unifying point of reference, its transcendent, absolute ground of meaning. This ultimate point of reference is required by the structure of identity (duality). The *quality of life* of a life-world is determined in part by the nature of the ultimate point of unity/identity for that world— that which lights up a given world with whatever meaning it has. In its religious dimension this point of reference (source of meaning) is often taken to be Divine (Infinite) nature or God. Religious life-worlds orient themselves towards Infinite Being as a way of transcending the bondage of ego-centric finitized life. But *every* life-world has its "religious" point of reference— its absolute. For some life-worlds it is money or symbols of fortune and material wealth, for others it is egocentric power or political power, for others it is the power of fame, and so on. But equally, various ontologies of empirical science (physics, for example) have their religious absolutes which structure the meaning of their worlds. This is why it is proper to measure the health of a life-world in terms of the quality of its logos (meaning) and its *faith*. Every life-world lives in faith and faith is a clear index of its state of health and well-being. The Buddha teaches that the conduct of mind in the ways of identity and objectification is the life of bad faith.

The disorder of onto-centrism reaffirms its absolute as being absolute for *all* Others. It is this religious zeal which generates the malady of solipsism or egocentrism. In this hermeneutical strategy a given grammar of existence universalizes itself as the legitimate and authentic language for itself and for all Others. Thus, absolutism and onto-centrism are synonymous. In religious form (that is, in terms of historical, conventional religion) it takes the form of affirming that the God of my world is the one and only true God for all being— there is but one Absolute!

But it is interesting to see, at the same time, that the *opposite* hermeneutical strategy for dealing with a plurality of Others (ontological pluralism) is to deny that there is one absolute and affirm that there are many absolutes, as many absolutes as there are life-worlds. It is easy to see through this ploy of identity— it re-affirms identity by multiplying and atomizing identity, leaving no possible absolute unifying point of reference for the plurality of absolutes. This atomizing of solipsism and absolutism equally fails to overcome the malady of ontocentrism. For relativism leads logos into a deeper chaos, confusion, irrationality, incoherence and bad faith. The Buddha teaches the way beyond the extremes of absolutism and relativism.

Likewise, the meditative/critique sees through another more "secular" form of absolutism which comes from *scientism*. This "secular" hermeneutic postulates an absolute, objective, neutral and noumenal reality "out there," a reality of brute facts and objective referents which are pre-hermeneutical and independent of any human interpretation or conceptual framework. The Madhyamika easily sees the emptiness of this fanciful construction of absolute identity which stops at no limits to assert itself. It is willing to defy all reason and intelligence and project empty, unknowable, metaphysical identities to support the threatened life-world. *Any* form of absolutism and foundationalism (essentialism) leads to hermeneutical disorder or incoherence.

We have been examining the most generic form of illness on the macroscopic level of identity— the ontocentrism of a life-world. Now we may shift focus to the microscopic level of identity— the ego-centrism of self-identity. It should be clear that the index of hermeneutical health is the mode of relating to Others; it is equally clear that the *internal* index is the mode of relating to the Self. In both the external and internal cases (Inter-Personal and Intra-Personal) the critical concern is the ability to encounter the other in its integrity, to be in dialogue, communication and healthy open relations.

But we have seen that essential identity violates the integrity (integration) and inner life of a life world. The pathology of identity fragments a life-world into the splits of dualism. In this respect we come to see that the principle of identity (dualism) is the principle of Self-alienation, Self-deception, and leads to various forms of ontological fragmentation. For the unconscious is eclipsed from the conscious and this divides the Self against itself— one domain of psyche is out of touch (alienated) from the other complementary domain, and there results a breakdown of inner communication and dialogue. This dualizing of the psyche leads to the interior creation of different identities (personalities, voices) which often enter into war for control and domination. It is here that we witness the impotence of the conscious will— despite all good intentions and good will, the unconscious takes control and eclipses the realm of the conscious and asserts its identity and will.[8]

This bifurcation of the psyche into consicous and unconscious (notice again the principle of contrariety opposition at work) is the source of *ontological repression* in all its forms. The very same mechanism of identity which leads to ontological alienation from Others turns upon itself and leads to Self-alienation, Self-repression, Self-violation and inner violence (ontological destruction). The principle of Possessiveness— the formation I-consciousness— as Nagarjuna teaches, carries with it the dynamic of *dis-owning* (not-I). The inner dynamic of *owning and dis-owning* gives rise to ontological repression and suppression which in turn generates the dynamic of *ontological projection*. What is identified as not-I becomes the object of projection, the enemy or estranged other. Naturally, this inner enemy is usually externalized and projected outward and identified with the external Other who becomes the identified enemy. This outward projection of the inner self-violation manifests itself in the hatred, fear, suspicion of the Other. This dynamic of identity projection leads to the various pathologies of *ontological paranoia*.

The dynamics of owning and dis-owning which generates ontological fragmentation also creates hermeneutical splintering and internal incommensurability in different ways. One dynamic is the creation of multiple personalities— multiple identities of the "I" which remain juxtaposed in incoherence. It is not difficult to see that this is the *normal* condition of contemporary life. Any given person in American life, for example, lives in the ontological pluralism of what is called *common sense*. We know from common sense (communal ontological consensus that the various languages of science are valid— the language of physics of physiology or biology teach one truth about the person, the religious grammars have their place, and they teach us different truths about the identity of the self, and the languages of psychology and psychotherapy teach us still different truths about true personality, and so on. The normal person resides in a plurality of life-worlds or ontological grammars which lead to different identities of "I." *Normal fragmentation* with multiple fragmented identities is content to remain in its ontological chaos and incoherence. Normal self-eclipsed ones are quite content with this hermeneutical condition because it takes ontological relativism to be the norm. Thus, the Self is not only fractured into the dualism of conscious/unconscious, but multiplies identities and inner voices which cannot recognize each other, cannot speak to each other and cannot enter into true inner communion. So the logos of psyche remains splintered, impotent and incoherent.

The Pathology of Identity, we have seen, impedes and stifles the deep ontological drive to Self-realization, liberation, universalization, integration, and expression of ontological power in self-determination.

When this healthy life-force is blocked and violated ontological repression results. This repression naturally goes with the self deception which comes with normal self-alienation. The self-violation of identity must go negative and further pathological symptoms emerge. The familiar forms of *depression* are hermeneutical breakdowns in which even the impaired meaning of a life of bad faith falters. This ontological stifling of the life-force to holistic meaning leads to varying degrees of the degeneration of meaning, and the patient enters into the anxiety and despair of emptiness— of absurdity and meaninglessness of existence. The patient loses focus on the source of light of the life-world and life becomes eclipsed in darkness. This extreme form of ontological impotence and loss of meaning and freedom often leads to the ultimate self-violation of suicide. We have already touched on the "normal" forms of onto-centrism and inner fragmentation. The same onto-dynamics apply to the more extreme forms that are encountered in conventional psychotherapy. Extreme onto-centrism comes with the exaggerated form of projected self-alienation in which the Other is perceived as existentially threatening. Such a patient retreats into a degenerate "abnormal" form of closure and loses touch with the ontological consensus. Similarly, the "abnormal" fragmented self splits away from the life-world of the norm and degenerates into extreme forms of multiple selves and the chaos of identity and meaning. It should be noted that extreme ontological fragmentation results from ontological repression— when the healthy expression of the drive to ontological freedom (the drive to be) is violated in an extreme form either by the self or by others, this results in the inner expansion of psychic space in the creation of multiple voice-fields. The onto-dynamics of extreme fragmentation is a perverse expression of the will to be, to express power and freedom.

But there are other familiar forms of hermeneutical disorders which arise from self-deception and self-forgetfulness— the various forms of neurotic compulsions. Hermeneutical compulsions are also perverse and impotent attempts to preserve and maintain a sick life-world. Such ritual behavior attempts to maintain the semblance of ontological order, balance and coherence — that is, to re-affirm identity. Compulsive behavior or life is an attempt to express ontological power and control over the structure of one's life-world. Often this takes the form of self-alienation which willfully forgets and attempts to drown out the noise and chaos of meaning through various forms of hermeneutical addiction. A typical form of self-deception is the strategy of hermeneutical amnesia.

Of course, we need not focus too much on extreme (abnormal) forms of ontological repression, for the hermeneutical disorders are quite evident in more normal forms. For example, in normal sexual repression the pathology of identity shows itself. The sexual drive, ontologically understood, is a perfect example of the drive to liberation, universalization, and power. When this is impeded or repressed by identity, it takes a false turn. Ego-centric dualized sexuality objectifies the sexual partner because it objectifies itself. Both the self and other of dualized sexuality remain within the bondage of particularized identity, and sexual desire (arising from ego-identity) becomes eclipsed from holistic union and communion. Those who are familiar with Tantric Buddhism— the yoga of sexuality— have a good model of the dynamics of universalized holistic sexuality. It is not the finitized male ego that joins with the finitized female ego, for in any case such an attempted union is precluded by identity/duality. Rather the love partners, through rigorous meditative techniques of self-unification, lose dual identity in the unitive consciousness of the universal male and female which come into true ontological communion. In liberated sexuality true love (communion, communication, dialogue) spontaneously emerges. Needless to say, the same dynamics of self-alienation arise in normal (dualized) love. The love partners objectify (essential identity) each other and the love is doomed to bad faith and failure of true relationality. It does not take much ontological imagination to see the innumerable forms of hermeneutical disorders which are routine in normal ("sane") life. These range from racism, sexism, national chauvinism, imperialism, religious fanaticism, dogmatism, classicism, and other forms of closure. In all of these varieties of hermeneutical ossification and fixation the pathology of identity rules. Hermeneutical liberation is the remedy for these disorders of self-alienation.

In preparing now to make the explicit move to holistic psychotherapy we may leave this theme of ontological pathology in noticing the fine ambiguous line between "madness" and holistic sanity. We have seen that conventional (onto-centric) psychotherapy takes the ontological consensus to be definitive of reality and strives to convert and transform the ontological deviant (patient) to re-enter the consensus in some way. The creative therapist labors in good will and good intentions to repair and reconstruct the life-world of the patient by helping him or her to conform and become adjusted to the norm of reality and hopefully to be functional and productive. But we have also seen that there is a powerful incentive to live outside of the conventional consensus— for to conform to the consensus can mean giving up or impeding one's ontological freedom. Conventional psychotherapy which attempts to transform the patient to the norm may unwittingly violate the ontological rights of the patient. For it is one thing to be able willingly to negotiate the rules of the game of the consensus, quite another to enter into an onto-centric form of life.

The person who chooses to live outside of the ontological consensus of a community has one thing in common with the person who approaches holistic sanity and well-being— they both see that naive (uncritical) conformity to the ontological majority is a loss of ontological freedom and power. But this common interest in being outside of the consensus ends here. For the fragmented person who lives the dualized existence of absolutims and relativism is a long way from the integrated holistic of life of relativity and non-dual holistic sanity.9

iv) Holistic Psychotherapy: Onto-Dynamics of Relativity and Non-Dual Holistic Life

At last we are ready to make the next explicit move to the dynamics of holistic (non-dual) life. The meditative principle of relativity: of relative identity and dependent co-arising, offers a remedy for the fragmentation and pathology of essential identity.

a) The Principle of Relativity: Non-Dual Identity

While the principle of essential identity splits and fragments logos in every possible way, the meditative principle of ontological relativity, of relative (non-dual, holistic) identity, *unifies,* integrates and heals the dualism of logos in every possible way. The principle of *dependent co-arising* is a *formal* ontological principle which teaches that essential identity is mistaken, a fictional construction of the ontological imagination, which postulates the independent self-existence (identity) of entities. This is why the principle of relativity is the principle of *sunya* (emptiness of essential identity); once we question and give up the fiction of ontologically independent, individual, identity, the way is clear for the radical transformation to non-dual logos and holistic life.

This radical transformation to holistic logos, of course, cannot be approached in the mentality of essential identity. We have seen that the hermeneutic or mentality of dualistic identity leads to absolutism and relativism, and when pressed to its limits, breaks down in dualisms. So a different mentality or form of understanding must be induced in order to approach ontological relativity. It is the radical transformative power of meditation— of meditative reason— that can break the barrier of essential identity and transform reason and understanding (logos) to relativity. Thus, the disciplined science and art of meditation is fundamental for holistic life and psychotherapy.

We may approach the *logos of meditation* by exploring how it reverses the degeneracy and pathology of essential identity. We have seen that essential identity must dualize and split in order to preserve coherence and avoid contradiction and inconsistency— this is why it is the principle of opposition and division. If incompatibles, contraries, or opposites were to be united and identified, then contradiction would result. So whenever a possible alleged unity of opposites arises, the principle of essential identity detects "contradiction" and either rules it to be impossible or else splits it in two and disarms the purported contradiction. This is the ontological dynamic which produces dualisms.

By contrast, meditative logos transforms reason to a more primitive and primary consciousness (sunya) in which *opposites are identified and unified* in non-dual unity. Thus, what appears to be contradiction to the logos of essential identity manifests itself as primitive unity and literal truth to the logos of relativity. An example would be helpful here, so let us now sketch the process of transformation of logos from the phenomenology of duality to the phenomenology of non-duality.10

First, we have seen that essential identity individuates and particularizes the ego and leads to a *plurality* of irreducibly distinct (self-existent) egos. Similarly, this principle individuates and particularizes life-worlds and therefore discriminates a *plurality* of irreducibly distinct realities. So essential identity gives identity to individual egos as well as to life-worlds. But we have seen that different life-worlds (distinct universal grammars of reality) are different systems of meaning, different languages of existence, which shape meaning itself in different ways. So just as individuated egos within a shared reality cannot be identified or unified without falling into the incoherence of contradiction, the same form of incoherence will result if different life-worlds (realities) were unified or identified. For example, the identity of "I" across different languages of reality must be *systematically* ambiguous— the sense of "I" in one world is incommensurably different from the sense of "I" in another: the *sense and reference* of "I" in the life-world of Christianity is different from the *sense and reference* of "I" in the Hindu, or Buddhist, or Confucian life-worlds.

In general, the existential identity of "I" is *radically* different in different life-worlds and there can be no primary unity or point of unifying reference for all of these senses within the logos of essential identity. It would be a contradiction to postulate a unity of "I" for all of the distinct possible identities of "I" in different languages of reality. So the logos of essential identity must be content with a *plurality* of meanings of "I"— it cannot succeed in the postulate of absolutism (the postulation of a transcendent noumenal unifying "I") or of relativism (the postulation of a plurality of absolutely distinct realities of "I"). But the inevitable pluralism of meanings of "I" across different worlds leads to a form of ontological fragmentation, for natural logos or psyche remains open to all possible life-worlds at any given time. There is no reason (other than essential identity itself) to suppose that psyche cannot be open to a plurality of realities at the same time, and if this is so, then we are back to the fractured situation of a psyche ("I") having multiple identities (existential and experienced senses and references) at any given time. So life in essential identity leads to the splintering of identity across life-worlds.

This splintering of "I" in multiple identities is integrated and healed in the meditative logos of relativity— the principle of relativity formally and actually unites radical difference into primitive unity; not the naive (dual) unity of essential identity but the holistic non-dual unity of sunya. Essential identity takes the concept "one" as the paradigm of unity, but relativity takes "zero" (sunya) as the model of unity. The concept "one" is a concept of dual unity; for like any other case of essential identity, it must be differentiated from an Other (e.g., "two"). But "zero" involves a more primitive form of unity which is prior to essential identity. It is in meditation that the critical transformation from dual unity to non-dual unity (identity) can be approached.11

The awakening of original non-dual logos, of undifferentiated (collective) consciousness, in meditation may be seen in the dynamic transformation of meaning often found in *metaphor* and *symbolic* meaning. The logos of metaphor works precisely in defying essential identity and unifying into a primitive identity opposite or incompatible meanings. For example, while the color blue and the thing we call "love" cannot literally (really) be combined or unified, we nevertheless combine these incompatibles in the metaphor— "love is blue." But metaphor is only one common example of dynamic meaning which points to non-dual identification. What appears metaphoric to dual logos is disclosed as primary truth to non-dual reason.

Thus, in meditating on the non-dual unity of "I" it is found that the true *relative identity* of psyche resonates with inexhaustible (infinite) possibilities of "multiple" (essential) identities. But relative identity (non-dual unity) recovers primary logos which does not require systematic ambiguity or splintering of identity. The principle of relativity must not be confused with the pluralism of relativism; it does not lead to the mere postulation of multiple differentiated identities or life-worlds but is a more radical transformation of logos to primitive form (prior to one and many) of zero-unity. It is precisely because the *meditative "I"* has zero essential identity that it can *unify primitively* all possible identities without falling into the incoherence of contradiction.

The recovery of original logos in meditation is effected by a similar reversal of the splintering of life at *all* levels by essential identity. We saw earlier that the splits between differentiated life-worlds— the split between "me" and "you," self and other, I and Thou— presents a pathological barrier to the individuated ego. This split too must be addressed by meditative logos. But this is true of *all* of the splits in the sickness of identity: consciousness/object, word/object, consciousness/unconsciousness, mind/body, psyche/non-psyche, thought/deed, thought/feeling, universal/particular, finite/infinite, male/female, etc., etc. The principle of relativity *necessitates* the full organic healing of logos into holistic life. The zero-unity of *holistic identity* reveals that the identity of everything— anything ontologically pervades everything, and everything pervades anything. It is in the meditative disclosure of reality that ontological dependent co-arising of *universal* identity is revealed. When the fetters of essential identity are removed from I-consciousness, the way is ontologically cleared for psyche to associate anew with diverse possible forms of existence in all possible life-worlds. Thus, once the bondage of particular identity is dissipated in meditation, the psyche is liberated to true *holistic universality:* meditative identity is ecological and realized in the unitive field of Universal Grammar.

Of course, all of this *must* appear to be vain speculation and vacuous mystification to the essentialized individuated psyche. Bounded self-eclipsed psyche must remain skeptical to the suggestion of meditative transformation. This is why holistic or rational psychotherapy becomes necessary to awaken and transform the ossified and alienated ego. Precisely due to the diseased state it is inherently incapable of hearing or understanding the principle of relativity. The paradox of psychotherapy is that the bounded psyche cannot understand relativity, but only relativity can transform and save the fractured psyche. The middle way through this impasse must be the self-transforming power of meditative logos. Here we find the first principle of holistic psychotherapy.

In this spirit the student-patient must willingly suspend initial skepticism and disbelief and enter into the therapeutic transformation to non-dual logos. There is, of course, a deep ontological incentive for this; namely, the relief from the existential suffering and pathology and frustration that must attend ego-identity. The deep ontological drive of psyche to universalization, liberation, power, self-realization and well-being (happiness) is ever present and relentless. Non-dual logos— original holistic life— is precisely where psyche realizes its full freedom and power.

It takes ontological or *meditative imagination* to approach original Logos. For essentialistic imagination is impotent when it attempts to approach true non-duality: imagine universal psyche which is not split into mind and body, not split into consciousness and object, not dualized into thought and action, not alienated into the specism of person and non-person, which is not separated into the polarity of individual and community, which associates freely with all possible names and forms. Universal or *holistic identity* breaks the barrier between universal and particular, finite and infinite. It is *neither* differentiated nor undifferentiated, neither finite nor infinite, neither particular nor universal, neither one nor many, neither person nor non-person, neither individual nor community, neither mind nor body, neither conscious nor unconscious, beyond all pairs of opposites. Thus, it would be a mistake of the essentialistic mind to imagine that non-dual Logos-Psyche is any kind of *object,* or has any specific or generalized *properties,* or can be referred to or described, or is transcendent or immanent, phenomenal or nominal. The Logos of sunya is neither immanent nor transcendent and takes the middle way between Being and Becoming— it neither is nor is not, as the Madhyamika teaches over and over. This means that non-dual Psyche *neither affirms nor denies* particularity and identity: it would be a mistake to infer that relative identity *denies* differentiation and particularity and identity. On the contrary, it opens the way to truly honoring particularity and identity. Meditative identity is true identity and particularity. Psyche gives up the pathological identity and particularity and celebrates non-dual identity and particularity.

b) Bi-Polar Consciousness and Holistic Psyche

But this talk about relativity and non-dual Logos is still formal and abstract and remains distant from the lived experience of everyday life. If meditative psychotherapy is to be effective with the inherent illness of ego-centric life, we must show in more tangible detail just how it accounts for hermeneutical disorders and how it can transform the fragmented psyche into holistic life.

First, it should be explicitly seen that *non-dual Logos is Psyche.* The concepts of ego or self or psyche of conventional psychology and psychotherapy often arise from essential identity and hence must be particularized and differentiated from non-ego. Conventional concepts of self, we have seen, are systematically ambiguous across different life-worlds or grammars of existence: the concept of self in a materialist language (which takes matter and body as ontologically primary) is radically different from the self in an idealist language (which takes *mind* and consciousness to be primary or independent of body). Similarly, a concept of self as a substantial entity, or a dual entity (mind and body), or as in the grammar of Hume or the early Buddhists, a bundle of phenomena, and so on, necessarily involve different languages of psychology. From the point of view of comparative ontology it is clear that there must be different (incommensurable) languages of psychology (and psychotherapy) in different life-worlds. Each such language is onto-centric and relative to its grammar or reality. But *holistic* psychology is a science of *holistic psyche* (non-dual Logos), and it alone can be a truly *universal* psychology. Since each language of reality constitutes the phenomena of the psyche anew, here, too, we should expect and find a new disclosure of the phenomenology of psychic experience.[12]

1) Relativity and Altered States of Logos (Psyche). This may be seen in the *ontological* analysis of so-called "altered states" of consciousness. Thus far we have directed attention to altered *being* of logos in the transformation to different life-worlds— reality is constituted anew in different life-worlds. Ontological relativity supports the multiple validity of alternative *actual* worlds. It recognizes a *plurality* of realities having ontological legitimacy. But now we may approach this theme from the point of view of "altered states" of psyche, even *within* a given life-world.

Whatever may be the shape (ontological grammar) of a life-world in its "waking" state, natural psyche flows back and forth into altered states— waking, dream, deep sleep. While essential identity is prejudiced in favor of the primacy of *waking* psyche in its determinate form, relative (holistic) identity sees the primacy of the *full range* of ontological transformations of consciousness. The hermeneutic of dream consciousness differs from that of waking life, and the meditative traditions, be it Hindu or Buddhist, etc., recognize that the life of dream can be closer to holistic reality than the fragmented, dualized and ossified waking world. So meditative logos takes dream reality as being just as valid or sometimes more valid than "waking" life. This is primarily because the logos of dream is less shackled by the domination of essential identity than waking consciousness. Waking consciousness is one extreme of logos— in its fully determinate, particularized, dualized, fixated from. So it is natural for the ego-centric mentality to gravitate to the waking world. But relativity is open to dream reality because identity begins to lose its grip on the inner freedom and spontaneity of natural logos. It even goes further to teach that deep sleep— the fully indeterminate world— is ontologically higher consciousness than sleep or waking reality. The reality of dreamless sleep is as close as ego-centric life can come to holistic logos and sunya.

Thus, relativity calls the prejudice of essential identity into question by legitimizing (provisionally) the reality of the dream world and the world of deep sleep. It teaches that natural logos is essentially free and ontologically fluid. It explains this ontological spontaneity in terms of the ontological relativity of logos, in terms of the holistic identity of psyche. The Madhyamika teaches that holistic consciousness— Buddha nature, sunya— is ever present in all ontological states of logos— whether of alternative life-worlds or alternative "states," but can never be captured or identified with any possible form or state of egological psyche.

2) Relativity and Bi-polarity of Psyche. The natural ebb and flow of oceanic psyche between the limits of full determinacy (determinate identity) of *waking* reality to the full indeterminacy (indeterminate identity) of dreamless sleep proscribes the range of all possible states of reality. The Madhyamika teaches that there are two limiting polar languages of psyche— the language of Being (Atma) and the language of Becoming (Anatma). We saw earlier that these two polar limits of logos were explicitly articulated in the Indian ontological tradition before Nagarjuna. One of Nagarjuna's great contributions was to have seen that all possible forms of reality must arise within these polar limits. This means that the life of essential identity is *continually* structured at all times by the bi-polar structure of logos. Even if (specifically if) psyche takes a form of life— a life-world— that is at one polar extreme, the presence of the other pole remains efficacious and determines the onto-dynamics of psychic life.

Thus, just as natural psyche flows into altered forms of consciousness where the reality of experience and meaning takes altered forms, so, too, essential identity in its lived pathology remains under the continued influence of the bi-polar structure.

3) Bi-Polar Psychology and Pathology of Identity. We are now in a better position to return to the fluid onto-dynamics of the psychology of ego-identity. Earlier we looked at the pathology of ego-centric life prior to the introduction of the theme of bi-polarity and holistic relativity. At this point we are ready to take a further step towards holistic psychotherapy by examining the pathology of ego-identity in bi-polar logos. Holistic psychotherapy *begins* with the recognition that holistic psyche is ever-present to the natural psychological life of ego-centric psyche, and that this life is continually shaped and determined by the bi-polar or holistic structure of psyche. So let us see how this starting point can interpret and make sense of the psycho-dynamics of everyday life.

First, it must be remembered that the life of ego-identity is a life of inherently self-divided consciousness. The onto-dynamics of identity structurally *requires* that the formation of ego-identity necessitates the eclipse of consciousness and the creation of the un-conscious or pre-conscious. This ontological split is beyond any volition or intentions or willful effort on the part of the ego. Indeed, the more the ego tries to remember or recall the unconscious the more it remains eclipsed. Insofar as ego life is able to move into the territory of the pre-conscious, it thereby eclipses the conscious and makes it into the unconscious. The one way out of the double-bind of ego-identity is to cure psyche of identity itself.

Second, this inherent split in ego life is experienced as ontological sin, guilt, anxiety and insecurity. The guilt arises from the primitive awareness of the self alienation of the ego. In the presence of holistic psyche, the ego already knows in a primeval way that it is split and disintegrated. The silent trans-temporal presence of the holistic psyche is the *ontological conscience* of the alienated ego. It is a constant reminder that the ego is in a state of sin and spiritual death. This is the source of the free-floating existential anxiety and insecurity which the Buddha spoke of as the inherent suffering of existence. The ultimate double-bind of ego-life is that it must choose its form of spiritual death and suicide. For ego-centric life (onto-centric existence) is spiritual death. The existentialist philosophers, like Camus, were right about the question of suicide, but possibly wrong in their response to it. For to choose one's essence-identity is precisely to choose *ontological suicide* and loss of holistic freedom. The self destructive ego strives in every way to escape the pain and disturbance of existential identity, but despite its best (self-asserting) efforts it remains in the state of ontological guilt, anxiety and death. While holistic psyche appears to be a contradiction to ego-centric psyche, the latter is revealed as being in the ultimate self contradiction and double-bind: the ego experiences loss of identity as existential death, but holistic psyche experiences ego-centric existence as living death. The ego must die if holistic psyche is to be born.

But let us look more closely at the vain efforts of the normally sick psyche to deal with its sin and death. We have seen that every psyche operates under the influence of the bi-polar *ontological archetypes* of consciousness. Most normally sick egos live somewhere within the midst of both poles, but it would be instructive to take the more extreme cases where the given ego lives at the extreme poles.

One pole is the language of monism and unity (Atma), while the other pole is the language of atomism and diversity (Anatma). Life in the former is an identity of Being, while in the latter it is an identity of Becoming. A life of Being is removed from the flux and contingency of ongoing change and process, but a life of Becoming is momentary and ever-changing without continuity of identity. *Monistic identity* is permanent and continuous and necessary and substantial, but *atomic identity* is discontinuous, associational, contingent, non-substantial and ever-changing. Monistic identity remains continuous with the flow of time, while atomic identity is as discontinuous as the fleeting moments of time.

The life of identity at either extreme leads to particular pathological disorders. The life of atomic identity leads to the incoherence of *temporal incommensurability and fragmentation*— the disorder in which ontological memory is fragmented in the flux of time. This psyche experiences a lack of continuity through time, ontological amnesia. Reality is ever-changing and relative to the present moment. The past is no longer real or relevant and the future is unreal and beyond experience. This ego is highly volatile and moody— (modal) and unpredictable from moment to moment. There is an inherent incorrigibility in the structure of this form of life— no continuing growth, habit formation, learning from past experience. There is lack of a mediating principle which gives ontological perspective, and this life degenerates into momentary relativism.

On the other hand, the life of monistic identity is cut off from the experience of spontaneous change and process and falls into an extreme form of absolutism. There is an obsession with fixity and continuity and order. This psyche is unable to deal with the reality of change and is existentially threatened by changing identity and creative spontaneity. The passage of time is either denied or causes existential melancholy. Existential insecurity is dealt with by fixating on the eternal, the necessary, the absolute. This form of life attempts to deal with the anxiety of death by seeing identity as eternal. While the life of Being is in a way affirmative and has perspective, it thereby lacks perspective on Becoming and is negative in this respect.

Each polar life eclipses the other, each is the "unconscious" of the other. Each excludes the other, but each desperately needs the other to survive. Bi-polar psychology explains why "opposites attract" in ontological terms. Each polar life experiences reality in radically different ways— they speak different languages. The life of becoming reaches out to the "love" partner who is centered in being. The latter provides the needed principle of continuity through time which the former lacks. The life of becoming experiences an existential need (confused with love) of its opposite. This need is insatiable and neurotic since its identity is found in the partner. The atomic psyche needs the other *to live,* and this need necessarily turns into existential resentment and hate.

By contrast, the monistic psyche desperately needs the momentary psyche in order to be in touch with the pulse of time and what is happening now. This is an existential virtue of the atomic identity— it is free to take on new identity in time precisely because of its associational and discontinuous structure. It is not bounded by continuity and substance. Here, too, the need of the other is compulsive and neurotic and is experienced in the typical love/hate double-bind.

It becomes clear that these polar ontological archetypes existentially depend upon the other for identity. Atomic psyche lives the pathology of relativism and monistic psyche suffers the disorder of absolutism. But the common source of illness is essential identity which is manifested in a form of alienation from self and other. For the atomic psyche who finds its identity in the permanent other, the threat of separation from its identity-partner is death (separation anxiety). But for the monistic psyche who is self-contained and independent the threat of dependency on its partner for identity is death (intimacy anxiety). The former polar archetype is ontologically extroverted, the latter is introverted.

This has been quite sketchy, but it should provide enough detail to help us to draw a contrast with the psychology of Jung. His polar principles— anima and anumus— were presented as female and male psyche, and the path to well-being was taken to be the process of individuation in which both polar principles are "integrated." Jung has been criticized for being sexist in his feminine psychology. The Madhyamika would suggest that he is onto-centric as well. His psychology of individuation is precisely the formation of the *identity* of the psyche. But the ontological polar archetypes of the Madhyamika are formal principles which are not necessarily tied with male/female identity, and not bound in any particular life-world. What Jung referred to as the collective unconscious takes a different form in holistic psychology: holistic consciousness is the collective *pre-conscious* of ego-centric psyche. Bi-polar psychology presents ontological archetypes of identity which must be unified in the non-dual unity of holistic psyche. We could read Jung in this holistic way.

4) Dynamics of Holistic Psychotherapy. If essential identity in its bi-polar form is the source of existential suffering, then the primary focus of holistic therapy is to overcome the fixation of identity. We have seen that meditation is the essential mode of detachment from identity. The techniques of Madhyamika meditation are designed to detach psyche from the illusion of identity and to transform dualized psyche into its holistic integrated form. We have seen that holistic consciousness heals the inherent split in individualized psyche and gives rise to the awakening of full awareness which is *neither* conscious nor un-conscious. Holistic awareness (sunya) is original logos out of which bi-polar identity arises.

The question of well-being and pathology is a matter of communication: inter-personal and intra-personal. The Madhyamika makes it clear that communication (true dialogue) breaks down in the self-alienation of essential identity and is possible only in relativity and holistic awareness. True well-being arises when true communication and dialogue can take place, and this can come forth only when the dualism between ego/Self and ego/Other have been therapeutically dissipated. When the split between ego and inner Self, and ego and outer Other-self is removed, the way is open for true communication in the form of communion or dialogical co-relation.

The ontological meditations of the Madhyamika teach the student-patient to awaken to an awareness of relativity and non-dual logos. The patient is taught that non-dual logos manifests itself in all forms. For example, language and meaning is expressed not only verbally but physically in "body language." More importantly meditations of relativity teach that Logos (the Word) may live and be flesh, as the dualisms of mind and body, word and object, evaporate. It teaches that true reason, intelligence and understanding must be holistic, and it becomes clear that the dynamics of holistic therapy are the dynamics of faith, salvation, and liberation.

c) Holistic Religion and Psychotherapy

Finally, it should now be clear that mental pathology is a religious disorder, and the question of sanity, well-being and happiness must be essentially religious concerns. But just as we have seen that conventional psychotherapy (based upon essential identity) necessarily mis-diagnoses the origin of existential illness, conventional religious life likewise fails to address the true origin of sin and the concern of liberation. Any form of religious life which is based upon essential identity must lead the psyche into deeper alienation and delusion. The Madhyamika teaches that any onto-centric psychotherapy or religious life-world remains in bondage to identity and ignorance— all views or ideologies are empty. Mental disturbance arises in bad faith— the faith of essential identity and true sanity and well-being arises in relativity and holistic life-holistic faith or the practice of relativity.

Perhaps the most daring teaching of the Madhyamika is that Nirvana is non-different from Samsara. Meditation on this non-difference (not to be confused with essential identity) reveals that Logos goes full circle and that meditative psychotherapy cannot be especially "Buddhist," rather than "Christian" or "Hindu." We would miss the primary instruction if we were in the end to fall back into the essentialistic trap of taking the Madhyamika therapy to be especially "Buddhist," unless we were clear that "Buddhism" is not just another view or life-world amongst others. Holistic Buddhism must be a universal therapy which permits the patient to honor and celebrate the true particularity of his or her life-world tradition. It would require the Christian to become an holistic (non-dual) Christian, require the Hindu to be an holistic Hindu, and teach the Buddhist to be an holistic Buddhist. The Madhyamika Christian, for example, learns that Jesus is precisely the Living Logos, the Logos become flesh, and is the living paradigm of the true therapist— the therapist who is able to heal the split of ontological sin in the non-dual unity of finite and infinite being. Jesus taught that the ego must die if one is to be spiritually born again, and ego-less Christian love is a good example of *holistic* love. The being of Jesus Christ is a living example of non-dual holistic life. This self-transformation to Christ consciousness is a universal way to meditative psychotherapy. This would be equally true of the Madhyamika Hindu— where Krishna-consciousness brings the patient to holistic consciousness in communion with the true non-dual Self. It would be true, too, of the Madhyamika Buddhist who finds in the sunya of Buddha-nature the holistic being of true liberation and self-realization. Understood in this way, we may take Jesus Christ, Lord Krishna and Lord Buddha as paradigms of holistic life and exemplars of the true holistic therapist.

Notes

1 For a systematic discussion of ontological grammars see especially "Formal Ontology and Movement Between Worlds" and "Comparative Ontology and the Interpretation of Karma.

2 The incommensurability of different worlds is discussed in the essays just referred to.

3 The dynamics of universalization of a life-world are discussed in detail in chapter 7.

4 R.D. Laing is one of the few psychotherapists who comes close to explicitly discussing the politics of reality and sanity. In his own way he approaches the real *ontological* issues. See his *The Politics of Experience*.

5 Comparative ontology makes it clear that psychotherapy must master the transformative rules of translation between different ontological grammars. For example, if the patient lives in some strange and "incoherent" life-world, the psychotherapist must be able to communicate with that patient in his or her own ontological grammar in order to be effective in therapy.

6 It becomes clear that questions of meaning and communication are essentially ontological concerns. Communication between persons within a conventional culture or between cultures is a matter of understanding the transformational rules between life-worlds or ontological grammars. See "Meditation, Metaphor and Communication" (chapter 9) for a development of this point.

7 See especially "Nagarjuna, Aristotle and Frege on the Nature of Thought," (chapter 7) and more recently "A Hermeneutic for Inter-Cultural Religious Life."

8 It should be clear that despite conscious good will and good intentions the deep power of onto-centrism and ontological fragmentation render the will of the ego impotent.

9 Nietzsche's philosophy of the true human rising above the herd mentality in the will to power could easily be adapted to the present analysis if he were taken in the ontological sense.

10 For a more detailed and systematic development of this radical transformation see "The Relevance of Indian Thought to the Evolution of World Philosophy."

11 The transformation of meaning from the principle of essential identity to the principle of relativity (non-dual identity) is discussed in detail in "Meditation, Metaphor and Communication." (chapter 9) " Here it is shown that from the ontological point of view, the principle of relativity is the principle of metaphor— the principle which unifies opposites into a non-dual unity. But "metaphor" as it is commonly understood in the logos of essential identity is not the same as *metaphor* as understood in meditative logos.

12 In general, the principle of relativity is the principle of holistic science. The non-difference of non-dual Logos and Psyche opens the way to a non-dual original Energy which is the "Object" of investigation in holistic science. Holistic physics or medicine or psychotherapy must be non-different, must lead to the same laws of transformation of Energy. Holistic medicine must recognize this Original Logos (Energy) which takes the form of both mental and physical phenomena. This non-dual energy (psyche) which is neither "mind" nor "body" opens the way to discover of the transformative laws of energy from mind to body and vice versa. This allows a true understanding of the nature of psychosomatic illnesses and symptoms. (For a systematic discussion of holistic physics and relativity see "A Metaphysical Critique of Einstein's Thought.")

CHAPTER 10

MEDITATION, METAPHOR AND MEANING

SYNOPSIS

This chapter is an attempt to understand the nature and origin of meaning. The focus is on metaphor because meaning cannot be understood until metaphoric meaning is adequately explained. In ordinary language meaning is taken to be primarily literal and metaphor is measured against the literal. The essay suggests that this prejudice of the literal mind distorts meaning and makes metaphor impotent and unintelligible. The literal mind is incapable of understanding metaphor or meaning for that matter. Thus a primary aim of the essay is to show that literalism leads to absurdity and fails to account for meaning. It is only when the prejudices of literalism are overcome that mind is truly open and capable of appreciating the rational power of metaphoric meaning, indeed of rationality itself.

The essay attempts analytically to describe the nature of the literal mentality in its general form. It is shown that literalism is a faith which pervades ordinary life and ordinary language. The inner workings (logic) of literalism are presented and it is suggested that the vast range of language games which comprise ordinary language are dominated by the prejudices of egocentric literalism. It is seen that literalism is grounded in a view of reality which upon critical reflection turns out to be highly problematic. The first part attempts to explicate the logical dynamics of the literal mind and finds that there are two competing voices in the speech of literalism. Literalism grounds itself in the principle of absolute identity and it takes this principle to be the foundation of meaning. And analysis of the dynamics of identity makes clear that the polar voices of identity when exposed are mutually alienated, unmediated and incoherent. The discussion attempts to clarify the dynamics of identity and shows that there is a general pattern of self-splitting, dualising, and incommensurability that is generated by the objectification of meaning by the literal mind.

Earlier discussions attempt to critique literalism and make clear the pathology of meaning that is inherent in the literalist faith. Specifically, it is shown that literalism cannot truly cope with metaphoric meaning which is essentially meditational and unifying. Instead, metaphor must be judged to be an aberrant form of meaning when measured by the standards of literalist discourse. Since literal meaning is the measure of egological rationality and reality itself, the extra-literal, like metaphor, is taken to be extra-rational and hence removed from reality. Ironically it turns out that the foundation of literalism is incoherent, fragmented and irrational. And when the unintelligibility of clarified literalism is brought to light the logic of metaphoric meaning comes to the fore. What the literal mind fragments and renders incommensurable the metaphoric intelligence renders coherent and rational. Thus it is shown that the principle of identity violates metaphor just as literalism insists that metaphor, literally speaking, violates the logic of identity.

Chapter six in particular attempts to begin anew reflection on metaphoric meaning without the prejudices and pathology of literalism. It suggests that common sense (reason) has two dispositions which have not usually been mediated and reconciled. Common sense has been dominated by literalism which has eclipsed and repressed the trans-literalist or metaphoric disposition. This discussion suggests that the metaphoric disposition of common reason is the primary origin of meaning and the essence of rationality.

First it is shown that metaphoric meaning reflects the principle of relativity which is found to be the origin of meaning; but relativity is not the ground of meaning and reason in the sense of the foundationalism and fundamentalism typically found in the literalist form of life. What identity leaves incoherent fragmented and incommensurable, relativity renders coherent, united and mediated. Indeed, metaphoric intelligence is relativity at work— the voice of reason which places all things in relationality and co-dependence (dependent co-arising).

The generic form of metaphoric meaning is explicated in terms of the principle of relativity which is the essence of rationality. This ironic turn of events— that metaphoric meaning reveals the nature of rationality and reality— is not surprising to meditative reason. For the long and noble tradition of meditative understanding has insisted all along that the fixation of meaning in the life of identity is pathological and in breach of everyday understanding. And it has taught that true understanding and meaning arise when identity and literalism are defeated. Thus we find that meditative reason which has always been implicit in common sense makes discourse work and enables us to see that metaphoric meaning is the origin of rationality.

PREFACE

The Primacy of Metaphoric Meaning

There has always been something mysterious about metaphors, and common sense has usually been ambivalent about it. One voice of common sense remains in awe of metaphoric meaning regarding it as the highest flight of poetic imagination and the deepest reaches of insight. But the predominant voice of common meaning takes metaphor to be frivolous, decorative, and secondary. This ambivalence in ordinary language persists and the two dispositions of common sense remain split and unmediated. The result is that metaphor has not been properly understood, and with the eclipse of metaphor all aspects of meaning become shrouded in darkness.

Perhaps the main reason for the mystification and deprecation of metaphoric meaning is that the literalist voice of common sense has dominated consciousness and repressed the other intuitive non-literalist voice. One task in this study is to explore the workings of the literalist mind and show how it systematically reverses the order of meaning and leads to a pathological condition in everyday life and language. The literalist voice believes that literal meaning is autonomous and primary and that all other forms of meaning are derivative and based upon the foundation of the literal. It teaches that all modes of meaning have central reference to primary reality which is disclosed in the literal vision of the world and experience. It moves in the faith that literal meaning is the absolute standard of fact and truth, and that other modes of meaning must be measured against this standard. Indeed, the literalist voice is taken to be the voice of rationality and understanding itself, hence the ultimate judge of what makes sense and what does not.

This study will attempt to show that the literalist mind has gotten priorities reversed and has forgotten the primacy of metaphoric speech. From its prejudiced point of view the literalist mentality is incapable of appreciating the true liberating power of metaphor and in fact only leads to absurdity and irrationality. By contrast, the repressed alter-voice of common sense— is brought to the fore and an attempt is made to mediate the two voices of common sense. While the literalist voice leads to absurdity and irrationality, the other voice makes clear that common sense essentially trades on metaphoric meaning in its every breath. It is disclosed that metaphoric meaning is primary discourse— the noble but repressed voice of common sense which can liberate the mind from the bondage and fixation of literal meaning.

Thus, it is only with the true appreciation of metaphor that meaning and understanding come into focus. But to come to this appreciation the mind must first transform itself beyond the artificial limitations of literalism. So another objective of this study is to attempt to understand the dynamics of transformation of consciousness from literalism to metaphoric meaning. When the repressed and pre-conscious metaphoric voice of common sense comes to consciousness it then comes to light how common sense meaning can work. We then see that metaphoric meaning essentially calls for a transformed consciousness to be understood, but at the same time they are the primary vehicles of such transformation.

Literalism and Primary Meaning: The Faith of the Literal Mind
To understand literal meaning we must approach it in the context of the form of life from which it arises. Literal meaning is an expression of a mentality which I shall call "literalism", so let us approach literal meaning by analyzing the features of the literalist mind. Literalism is an *ontological* disposition— a way of being in the world, an attitude towards reality, an understanding about thought and language and meaning as these reflect that reality.

Meaning is primarily an ontological affair, and this is no less true of the forms of meaning which comprise "common sense" as expressed in ordinary language. So let us explore the ontological attitude of common sense.

The Fixation of Meaning
Common sense teaches that the conscious, rational thinker lives in a world that surrounds her, a world that is external to and independent of her. The world is changing, but with relative fixity of things. Things "out there" have a certain fixity and continuity in change so that we can identify them fairly easily. In ordinary language, which reflects common sense, names are given to things and these names stand for the things they name. We can

use names to refer to things and pick them out in the environment. Things are identifiable and have properties for which we also give names. These attribute names stand for properties or qualities of things, and we can pick things out by naming them and describe things by using the property words. One important function of thinking and using language is to pick out things and describe them, and in this way we represent or picture the world out there. Despite ongoing process and change both in the world as well as in ourselves the names and terms of our language and thought have a relative fixity of meaning. A given name means the thing it refers to. So there is an ongoing one-to-one correspondence between words and things. The stability of meaning is grounded in the relative stability and fixity of things. This fixity of things gives a certain order to thought and the world and allows language to work.

The first point of interest in this simple common sense picture is that there is logical space between the thinker and the world— there is a structural distinction between the locus of thought and the locus of world. This original dual structure is a primary ontological feature of the literal mind: it sets the stage for the nature of meaning as representational— where meaning is a correspondence between the two realms.

The second point to notice of ontological interest is that meaning is grounded in things... the way the world is. And things have inner stability which allows us to identify them and which differentiates them from other things. To state this in ontological jargon— things have essence and continued identity . Again, things are differentiated from one another by their unique properties— to be a thing is to comprise unique properties.

Since thought as expressed in ordinary language replicates the world we find that on the side of thought the structure of things is reproduced. Thought consists of names standing for things, and property words which stand for the qualities of things. In logic this is called "predication"— thought consists in combining logical subject and predicate. The main point is that thought copies the world and meaning consists in a primary relation between the two. Later we shall face the question of the nature of this supposed relation— what do the two realms have in common to allow thought to replicate the world? What is the unity between thought and world that allows signification or meaning to take place?

In the above relatively simple common sense picture of meaning we find the ontological origins of literalism. It is so simple and powerful and intuitively clear that it seems to be beyond question to the literalist mind. Common sense has been carefully cultivated over centuries. And centuries of the best philosophical reflection has attempted to articulate and formalize this intuition of literalism. In logic from Aristotle to Wittgenstein the logic of literalism has been explored and formalized. Here the central concern has been with understanding logical form— the form of thought. Likewise in ontology the history of the tradition has been an attempt to articulate and formalize the nature of things with special emphasis on identity. Let us draw out briefly some of the main points of the tradition which has attempted to articulate and explain the literalism mentality— the philosophy of common sense and ordinary language.I shall suggest that when the more complete picture of literalism is articulated it will be exposed as being incomplete, highly problematic, incoherent. To facilitate a brief sketch of the features of literalism I shall review some themes discussed in more detail in earlier chapters.

The Ontological Explication of Common Sense

Ontology is the science of common sense, the science which gives an account of meaning as it arises in relation to reality and thought. We have seen that common sense (the shared meaning of a community of speakers) situates itself in a structure which makes reference to the world, to thought and to things. But common sense is not something that stands on its own apart from the speaker or thinker who entertains the sense, it is essentially an expression of the form of life of the speaker. The texture, quality and being of this sense is essentially a function of the state and quality of life of the speaker-thinker. The presence and identity of the speaker is implied in common sense, it usually remains implicit and in the background and is taken for granted. Yet it is of the utmost importance in ontological analysis to query the identity of the speaker-thinker, for the origin of sense is not just to be found in the words that are uttered, nor in the form of language spoken, but in the very voice or consciousness of the speaker-thinker. Common sense is a form of human life and literalism is an ontological mentality which expresses a certain quality of life of the speaker-thinker. Thus, in exploring the ontological structure of literalism we must constantly remember the central reference to the *identity of the speaker* in literalist thought, speech and meaning.

We tend to think of common sense as though it were an object having independent existence, analogous to how we think of the world, or language or thought. It seems that sense or meaning is an objective relation between these three things having no essential dependence on the identity of the thinker. Indeed, the identity of the speaker-thinker is taken to be just another entity in the world; it is an entity which thinks and apprehends sense. But we shall see that in the ontological analysis of common sense this naive view must be corrected.

Literalism is the predominant way in which common sense has articulated itself. It has evolved over centuries in different cultural traditions; it is in effect an ontological theory or self-interpretation of sense— thought interpreting itself. There are numerous alternative ways in which we may approach the *ontology of literalism*.

One place to begin is to notice that sense is essentially some sort of relation which arises in a dual structure in which thought stands over against the world. We may say that reality is a comprehensive unity which encompasses any possible thing including thinker, thought and world. While the thinker is in the world and part of it, thought stands over against the world and attempts to think or apprehend the sense of things. Thus, sense appears to arise in a dual structure.

Another starting point is to notice that common sense begins with dual intuitions both of which appear to be primitive— one is the intuition of unity, the other of diversity or plurality. That is, reality must be all encompassing, a totality of existence spanning all possible things. While the world consists of innumerable diverse things, reality is a universal ontological space which "contains" it all— a unifying whole. We shall see that this intuition of an absolute unity is a formal condition of the rationality of common sense. And this unity is not just the unity of reality, but a recurrent requirement throughout common sense— the speaker-thinker must have a unity, language must have a unity, there must be unifying condition of meaning, objects have their unity, and so on. At the same time, common sense teaches that there is diversity, difference, plurality, multiplicity. An essential part of the particularity and identity of things is that they are *differentiated* from one another and irreducibly distinct. It will be crucial for us to determine how the dual requirements or conditions of common sense reason (of unity and diversity) are to be reconciled. The central problem of this study is to understand how common sense accounts for unity in the presence of duality and diversity.

Sense, Grammar & Logos: Ontological Space

In preparation for the articulation of literalism we need to see how this *dual structure* of sense arises and it is necessary first to explicate some fundamental terms and themes which set the context for the literalist mind. First, I shall use the term "Logos" to indicate that space which makes possible and holds together in mutual relationality the realms of thinker, thought, world and language. The term "Ontology" specifies the science which accounts for Logos— the science of reality. Thus, "Reality" is synonymous with Logos and indicates the all encompassing space that includes all being. I shall use the word "sense" to indicate the essential relatedness of thinker ("I"), thought, language and world— all of which are incorporated in Reality, or Logos. It may then be said that Ontology is the science of Logos/Reality/Sense. I use the term "Ontological Space" to indicate that universal domain in which thinker, thought, world and language co-exist in mutual dependence and relatedness. And the term "Grammar" is the form of Logos or Ontological Space.

It is crucial for our purposes to understand the pervasiveness and depth of *ontological grammar:* all aspects of common sense are grammatical, all forms of experience reflect grammar, the world as such is constituted in grammar, language and its diverse forms of meaning arise in grammar, the very identity and existentiality of the thinker and thought are possible only in the context of grammar, and so on. To live, to interpret, to think, to speak, to understand, to be rational, is to be grammatical. Let us call this the "hermeneutical theme": any form of sense or meaning is the expression of grammar— any form of interpretation must be relative to grammar.

Literalism is a certain attitude towards grammar and sense, and it is appropriate here to elaborate on the origin of sense in ontological grammar. A grammar is a structure or system which defines a language of reality, and historically diverse grammars have been developed. For example, the traditional Hindu language-world is the expression of a certain grammar. This grammar differs in fundamental ways from, say, the traditional Christian grammar or world. Human history has articulated a diverse range of ontological grammars which have emerged in the form of world cultures. And it is evident that what makes sense in one cultural grammar does not make sense in another. The particular shape of ontological space in the Hindu world differs remarkably from the grammatical form of the Christian grammar. Thus, from the ontological point of view reality, experience, rationality, and meaning are differently constituted in diverse grammars. What is taken to be common sense facts of existence in one world are not even intelligible in another world; common sense itself differs dramatically in diverse cultural grammars. So the first fundamental point about meaning is that sense is relative to a grammar of reality, and what literally makes sense in one grammar differs from what literally makes sense in another.

Grammar and Voice: Ontological Univocity
First we need to explore the origin of the literalist *voice.* In developing the hermeneutical theme it would be helpful to introduce the concept of "voice". It was just stated that the very existence of the thinker is already situated in grammar. Here the "thinker" includes any possible form of experience and human life— to be human is to be grammatical. So whether "thinker" includes thinking, willing, judging, speaking, acting, etc,. these are all activities situated in grammar. Let us use the term "voice" to indicate any possible mode of "I" as the speaker in grammatical space. Now

we may say that the primary condition of speech and meaning is that voice be *univocal*. "Univocity" means having a Primal Unity, Uniformity or Universality. The primary transcendental condition of discourse is that grammar and voice *be univocal*.

The Univocity Condition may be explained as follows:

If Grammatical space were not Unified and a unifying Force, discourse would not cohere. So Univocity means primal unity, consistency, uniformity and universality.

Ontological Universality needs to be explained: To be universal is to be all encompassing, and this means to be a unifying point of reference for all possible things. An ontological universal cannot have its unity be external to itself. This is another way of saying that an ontological universal must constitute the Universe.

It has long been recognized that rationality in some sense depends upon there being ontological univocity. If grammatical space were not univocal then meaning would not cohere and would be *incommensurable*. Furthermore, the Univocity Condition requires that *voice* be ontologically univocal with grammatical space as well. If voice were not univocal with grammar, then speech would not cohere. There must be a primal unity (non-difference) between voice and grammar.

This means of course that the features of grammar are the features of voice: and the univocity condition holds for voice as well— voice must be univocal for speech to be coherent.

It has been taken for granted throughout the history of thought that voice is ontologically univocal. Usually this point is not even brought up for discussion, it is simply assumed. Even in voices like Hume's where it is seen that there is no existential univocity for the "I" from moment to moment, (for Hume questioned existential univocity) he nevertheless assumed ontological univocity in his own speech (in his own voice) otherwise his treatise would not hold together in self unity.

If we carry Hume's point to the ontological level it would be readily apparent that ontological univocity of voice is a condition of intelligible speech:

Imagine (if it is possible) that voice were discontinuous from moment to moment and not univocal. (And we should question as well the univocity of time itself in this respect) If voice were not ontologically univocal— a continuity, unity, uniformity and a universal condition— thought, speech, meaning would disintegrate into chaos or indeterminacy. It must be stressed that ontological univocity (universality) is not the ordinary form of univocity or unity that we find in experience. For we shall see shortly that conventional univocity already eclipses the primal univocity of grammar. Primal Univocity is in some sense non-dual and prior to there being any possible determinate identity or differentiation. The mere presence of the differentiated "I" or voice has already disturbed the original univocity of grammar and voice.

The Holistic character of primal univocity of grammar/voice has already been explored in earlier chapters. But it is essential that we begin with a preliminary sense of the univocity condition, if only by contrast to the artificial univocity of the literalist voice.

The literalist mentality or voice has already divided (equivocated) grammatical space and cannot in its own terms recover or apprehend the primal univocity of grammar. Holistic Univocity is prior to identity/difference, internal/external. There is no separation, duality, diversity, multiplicity, and unity, polarization, opposition, differentiation, individuation, particularization. In short, it has none of the features which arise with the duality of identity or literalism. Thus, in primal univocity grammar is a unity and unifying condition unto itself, there being no external or internal unifying point of reference.

Features of Artificial Univocity of Literalism
With the particularization or individuation of voice grammatical space is divided against itself and there is a fault between voice and grammar, often experienced as the dual structure of "consciousness" standing over against the world (object). When grammatical space is thus divided the primal univocity of grammar/voice is lost, and a self-polarization of voice takes place.
But (the literalist) voice recognizes the need for univocity and creates an artificial univocity in an attempt to replicate the original univocity condition.

The presence of the individuated voice structurally divides grammatical space and sets a recursive divisiveness or polarization in perpetual motion. Let us see how this polarization of artificial univocity works.

The polarized grammatical space of literalism is committed to there being individuated identity— and this means a differentiated self existence or existential independence and determinacy. But any locus of grammatical space inherits the univocal feature of grammar. The individuated voice sets itself up as the univocity condition within its domain.

Any individuated locus of grammatical space replicates (inherits) the features and dynamics of grammatical space as a whole. This means that any sub-divided portion of grammatical space will require the univocity condition in that domain.

So each domain will universalize itself and attempt to be a universe unto itself— having its unifying condition within itself— self referential univocity. This is the ontological meaning of self-existence— not being dependent upon an external thing for unity and integrity. Thus, any domain of divided grammatical space will universalize itself and have absolute dominion over its space. It will fill its space and be a universe unto itself. Notice that this individuated univocity is set within a deep structural duality in which it stands over against *what is other than itself*. There exists a division between internal and external when grammatical space is divided.

Grammatical Cosmology: The Origin of Grammars

The literalist voice is one that takes itself to be one which exists, which has determinacy and identity, which is (distinctive) unique and differentiated. It takes its own features to be an absolute necessary condition of the way things are. When we *begin* with this individuated voice grammatical space takes on a particular appearance, and we need to pause to inquire into the grammatical background that makes the individuated voice possible.

Identity divides grammatical space, and to exist is to occupy a domain of grammatical space. The division of holistic grammar of course interferes with primal univocity and a divisive polarization is introduced. Let us do some grammatical cosmology and attempt to recover the dynamics which were set in motion with the dividing of Logos. This is not a temporal (historical, evolutionary) process.

With the division of grammatical space a self-polarization arises which recurs throughout any domain, for the primal univocity condition is eclipsed.

With division comes polarization and with polarization identity and difference emerges. Now it is possible to differentiate regions of grammar and this implies a univocal point of reference with respect to which differences are held together.

Any region universalizes itself and stakes a claim over its territory This is the law of existence— to exist is to occupy grammatical space and the force of existence is to create its own univocity— to be ontologically autonomous, independent, and self-identical. In effect this means that the differentiated voice strives to take up its space universally (universally being precisely fully occupying one's space). This dynamic of self-universalization inherent in divided space expresses itself in the form of *self-existence*— the self reference (reflexivity) in which it provides its own inner univocity.

But self-existence finds itself in a deep predicament in attempting to provide its own univocity— for in defining its territory (domain, field) it finds itself in opposition to *otherness* (other univocities), the presence of that over which it stands in having its boundaries. The presence of otherness is ontologically threatening to the universality and univocity of the individuated voice. In declaring itself universal and a universe, hence independent, it finds itself delimited and limited by the presence of the other. It thus finds itself in an inner tension of taking itself to be univocal, but at the same time realizing that its very existence reveals it to be delimited, particularized, differentiated and not univocal.

Another prefatory note would be timely. In a grammatical excursion such as this it is important for the author to flag his own voice as a reminder for himself and the reader of the locus of his voice at any given time. We shall see that an essential feature of voice is its ability to occupy diverse regions of grammatical space simultaneously and thus speak in multivocity.

Let us begin with the inner dynamics of the individuated voice in its own self- referential grammaticality.

The Literalist Voice
The individuated voice finds itself thrown in a deep tension and predicament.

On the one hand it sees itself as independent and self-existent and having its own inner integrity and univocity. In this respect it universalizes itself and claims universal dominion over its space. It takes itself to be the universal point of reference and the univocal condition of discourse. However, in so doing it comes to see that its own inner self existence places it in polar opposition to external others and otherness in general which borders its space and delimits it. The mere presence of the *Other* ontologically threatens its self image of being the universal point of reference and univocity— and a dual inner tension arises.

On the one hand it sees itself as being unique and universal and independent, but in that very image it realizes that it is dependent, delimited, particularized and challenged in its purported univocity. Its response to this predicament is to assert itself in its self-universality and expand its territory and dominion to be all encompassing. It sees that two distinct voices cannot occupy the same space so it expands space, i.e.. its *univocity,* to find a higher point of univocity which would encompass the diversity of otherness. But this polarized dynamic and triangular strategy only finds itself in the same dilemma of univocity of the higher locus, for it too is individuated and differentiated, and the polarization continues, without beginning or end.

The above grammatical cosmological myth of "origins" needs to be drawn out more fully.

Now the author will step outside the internalized self-image of polarization and take a more distant external and neutral locus and perspective to discern the larger polar dynamics of space.

The self universalizing (univocating) forces of divided grammatical space place any individuated voice within the polarized dynamics.

The drive to univocity of any voice expresses itself in polar ways: The internal inertia to universality operates on the individuated voice to become a universe onto itself, to fully encompass all of its space and be fully self existent and independent. This gives rise to the atomic tendency to be its own univocal condition and hence to be grammatically unique and incommensurable, a totality unto itself.

When the individuated voice takes this polar voice, it finds itself polarized by an external force beyond itself which reminds it that it is delimited, not universal and stands in opposition to something beyond itself. This polar force is an *anatomic* tendency which calls for a higher point of unity and univocity. The anatomic voice of universalization is a self transcending force which recognizes that the way to univocity must be a higher more encompassing point of reference. Since the universe is an all encompassing, all inclusive totality and unity the anatomic voice addresses itself to a higher point of unity to encompass polarized opposites.But this voice must remain open ended and recursive since, as we have seen, any purported transcendent point of univocity in divided space will always fall short of the primal univocity of holistic grammar, and polarization and triangulation goes on without end.

It is not just for individuated voice that the polar dynamics holds, for polarization is the inner feature of divided grammatical space itself, and whatever appears in localized space will show within itself the oppositional dynamics of identity— the simultaneous pull of the atomic and anatomic poles.

Let us elaborate on the polarization of voice and univocity in divided space.

It was just suggested that divided space strives for a univocity which it cannot achieve since voice becomes divided against itself in polar opposition. The atomic voice strives for self-universalization in one direction while the anatomic voice pulls in the opposite direction to reach its univocity, but the polar voices remain self-divided and the irony is that in each striving for univocity equi-vocity is produced, and the necessary condition of rational coherence is violated at the deepest level.

The atomic strategy is to achieve absolute univocity by *excluding* anything else from its space— it moves to the limit of complete exclusion of any other and complete self-inclusion and simplicity. This form of self universalization moves towards full determinacy and specificity and finitude and it carries finitization to its infinite limit. It expands its *interior* space to the infinite limit which gives rise to an internal self-transcendence and indeterminacy.

By contrast, the anatomic voice makes the external self-transcending move to find a higher univocal point of reference which would be all-inclusive and encompass all possible space, all possible objects. This voice strives to the limit of infinitude as the universal point of univocity thus achieving universality on the cosmic level. Here it presses external self-transcendence to its infinite limit of complete indeterminacy.

The net result of this polarization is that any discriminated thing— any identity in grammar— will "speak" these two voices at the same time and thus be fundamentally equivocal.

We are in a better position now to resume the direct presentation of the general hermeneutical theme.

It was suggested earlier that grammar makes the world, thought, experience, language, meaning and thinker— "I" possible. And although we began this presentation taking the literalist voice as the starting point, we then found it necessary to back up and inquire into the grammatical origins of the literalist voice and of the literalist grammatical space. We may now proceed to see how divided grammatical space conditions and makes all things possible.

With the division of grammar into voice and field a dual univocity is initiated. And the attempt of voice to recover or recreate univocity only deepens the problem and leads to a pernicious multi-vocity.

Our aim now is to try to understand the general dynamic of the separated voice to achieve univocity in grammar.

The irrepressible drive to univocity takes the form of a fixation of voice—a tendency for voice to fixate itself in grammatical space— to take a determinate point or locus as the univocal point of reference. Univocity becomes a fixity of voice/locus in grammar.But the most striking feature of the separated voice is the division of grammatical space into voice on the one hand and the *field* (field of consciousness) on the other.

It is within this division (duality) of voice and field that the dynamics of univocity is to be discerned.

What makes this task complicated is the ability of voice to take diverse univocal points of reference in the field as well as to stand back from the field and witness the field. (In the present meditative phenomenology, we are rehearsing how the egological voice arises in the division of logical or grammatical space. It should be remembered that the life of the egological voice is always situated in the voice of relativity— the voice of natural reason— and it is this power of natural reason that allows the ego-voice to have multivocity.)

There is, in effect, an initial multi-vocity of voice in this dual context, one which can be seen in grammatical ambiguity in the meaning of "I". The self-referential term "I" becomes equated with the voice-locus in grammar.In one breath the "I" may be identified with "ego" as the univocal point of reference. The ego is an object in the field, like any other object; to be an object of any sort is to be located in univocity in the field. The field of grammar takes on one reality when voice is identified with "I = ego". But voice may identify itself at any other univocal locus outside the ego in the field, and this gives a different phenomenology of grammar. Or the voice may take a generalized univocal position in the field transcending any given object in the field, including the ego-self. Here again grammatical space is disclosed in a different voice with this center of reference. Again, the voice has the power to disassociate itself from the field as a whole and the "I" becomes the witness of the field as a whole. In this contemplative posture the dynamics of univocity discloses itself in a different voice, and so on. Thus, the variability of voice in its univocity-locus requires that we remain mindful of multi-vocity of speech in this exploration of univocity. We shall see that literalism includes this variability in voice in grammatical space. It is a strategy and habit of univocity within the context of the multi-vocity of voice. So all the life of the ego voice essentially trades on Relativity, Natural Reason, Meditative Voice for all its moves in grammatical space.

The Self and "I" in the Grammatical Field

It is natural to begin with the locus of the Self and "I"— the self referential voice in the grammatical field. For this becomes the universal conditioning univocity of voice in any further thought or experience. The first person univocating voice conditions all further thought, experience, meaning, world. It is a transcendental condition of speech and life, and certainly in the conversational structure of the present inquiry and author's voice. So we must begin with the recognition of the ever-present *self-referential univocity* of voice in the grammatical field of any speech. This transcendental point of self reference of "I" is also noticed by Kant in his transcendental deduction. And in effect, Descartes reconfirms this finding of the univocity requirement in his meditative experiment in the voice of the Cogito. (The pronoun "I" is a *variable of univocity* of voice in grammatical space which can take different univocity positions. There is inherent multi-vocity in the univocity of "I")

With this as a transcendental preface we may now proceed to discern the general dynamics of univocity in the grammatical field: We want to understand the fixation and fixity of voice and meaning that is found in common sense in its literalist voice. As we explore the field of common sense we find discernible things— the self (referred to in the first person voice "I"), the world, or cosmos, objects, events, relations, thought, language, meaning, speech, and so on. There is a typical dynamic of univocity that conditions anything in the grammatical field. Let us begin with "I":

That the self (I) is a univocal point of reference in grammar is readily seen. Indeed, the "self" is a postulated transcendental univocity, which univocated all diverse utterances of "I" at different grammatical loci (space) and at different grammatical "times". Common sense assumes an on-going, continuous, ever-present univocal point of reference in the grammatical field which is the very existence of the self. This univocal self conditions all discourse.

With the univocity of the self comes the dynamics of polarization spoken of earlier. With the self-referential univocity of "I" comes the polar voices, each of which strives for primary univocity: First, the postulated univocity of "I" immediately in its specification and differentiation discerns the *not-I* (that which is *other than I)* as immediately given with the presence of the univocal I; with the I arises the not-I as an alien univocity. But the need for universal univocity in the field calls the "I" to a higher univocity, a higher encompassing point of univocity which can encompass both the I and the not-I; and this need for univocity calls for an equivocity in the I both in itself and beyond itself at the same time. It should be remembered here that the "univocity" we speak of here is the *presumed* self-unity of the egological voice. The point is that true univocity is possible only in the meditative voice of Relativity. In this context we may make an interesting comparison with Buber, In the egological voice that "not-I" is an "it"— the "I...It— relation; whereas in the meditative voice we have the "I...Thou". This produces a self-transcending univocity in the postulated univocity of the I and thus we find the *anatomic voice* as a univocity requirement of I. On the other hand, the polar opposite voice— the atomic voice feels the threat of complete existential dependency on the internal univocal point of reference and asserts its independence. It moves to its inner autonomy or univocity and takes its inner (self-existent univocity) to be its absolute center of reference. In this voice the self-referential univocity takes the position of the cosmological universal for all discourse.

Thus in the very attempt to find its self-referential univocity the voice of the self finds itself split in a polar equi-vocity which appears to be beyond reconciliation or univocity.

For each of the polar voices, the move to its cosmological universal is a recursive process— a self transcending postulated univocity that recurs *ad infinitum*— there is something of the infinite in this process of self-univocation.

One polar limit leads to the transcendent infinite univocity— sometimes called "God" in certain religious grammars. The other polar limit leads to the immanent infinite univocity of absolute self-existence— the substantial self which underlies all attributes of the self, and is itself without attributes.

But this very dynamic of univocity recurs in any item which may be discerned in the grammatical field. Let's look at the "world"... the cosmos...which is the grammatical field itself taken as a whole. the all inclusive grammatical space of reality.

As we proceed with the grammatical cosmology we may now focus on the field of grammar which stands over against voice, which surrounds voice and envelops it as well. Holding the positioned univocated voice in the background for now, we may inspect the presence of grammatical field as a whole.

Here too we find the expected univocity condition which makes a unified field possible; indeed, the univocity condition of the field is precisely the cosmic universal (univocity) mentioned earlier. The cosmic univocity is that transcendent and ever-transcending cosmic point of reference which encompasses all possible reality. But despite this infinite recursivity of the cosmic univocity we nevertheless find the polarization of multi-vocity at this global level as well.

For the field as a univocal whole stands over against the univocity condition of voice and these compete for being the one and true univocity of grammar. The alleged cosmic univocity of the field cannot tolerate the independent univocity of the voice which necessarily conditions it and makes it possible: there would be no discernible cosmic field without the otherness of voice nor with the otherness of at least the *possibility* of an alternative field. So here again the drive to univocity finds itself in a self-divided situation of equi-vocity which cannot be resolved or mediated. To negate or defer the univocity of voice to the cosmic field is not the answer. And the strategy of postulating a higher mediating neutral univocity would be self defeating as well.

The background hermeneutical context is now prepared so that we may get closer to the literalist voice and the literalist specification of the grammatical field. We are trying to trace step by step the determinants of the literalist voice in the full determinacy of common sense. We must remember that when we began our reflection centered in the voice of common sense we were *already* located in a highly determinate voice and grammatical field. We are ready now to examine the ontological dynamics in which the literalist voice is positioned in a determinate grammar of reality— a life world.

Let us begin with the internalized voice centered in a grammatical world. This voice lives in a cosmos which has determinate texture and specificity. *The cosmos* (reality) is taken to be identical with the life-world in which it is centered. The grammatical field has universal specificity and the (voice/self)— locates itself in this field and takes on specificity of the field as well.

The first point to notice in this internalized voice is that the world or cosmos in which it finds itself— its life-world— has a cosmic univocity or universality which encompasses all reality. Viewed from within (positioned within this univocity) no external independent reality or world can be conceived or imagined or exist. The question of alternative independent worlds or grammatical fields cannot arise for this internalized voice.

We have seen that with the separation of holistic grammatical space into voice and grammatical field the dynamic of polarization and the problem of primary univocity arises. And we have seen that all subsequent speech-life is conditioned by the self-referential postulate of univocity of voice— that the voice of the speaker-thinker is indeed univocal and determinate in the speech situation. But we have suggested that this alleged postulate of univocity of voice is problematic and cannot be granted from the start. On the contrary, it is more appropriate to assume the *indeterminacy* of voice in ordinary language. That is, despite the required postulate of univocity of voice the dynamics of polarization in fact lead to multi-vocity of voice and it cannot be assumed that there is a true univocity of voice in conventional speech. This original indeterminacy of voice should emerge more clearly as we excavate the hermeneutical layers of the ordinary speech situation. So the question which prefaces this inquiry is: If the self-referential voice of the speaker-thinker is not univocal, not operating under a true univocal point of reference, then how can ordinary speech be coherent or rational?

Within the primary polarity of voice and field we may now witness how the basic hermeneutical categories of world, thinker, thought, language, meaning mutually interrelate and replicate the same dynamics of polarization (univocity) just sketched. First, a world in general in the hermeneutical sense is an all encompassing univocity. The field as a whole which stands over against voice and even encompasses voice is the form of the world. Anything that does, or may or could appear in the world-field is postulated to be encompassed under a cosmic or global univocity condition. The form or substance of the world is precisely the universal univocity of the field. This formal univocity condition of the world necessitates that there could be nothing that is not encompassed within the world. The world is thus a self universalizing univocity for any possible thing.

The world, of course, ambiguously encompasses voice and yet must be witnessed by it as its "other". And this original ambiguity is part of the indeterminacy of voice we just spoke of. Voice apparently has the capacity to fixate at different univocal points of reference in grammar. If voice takes the global univocity as its point of reference the voice too must include itself within the world-field. And voice may equally fixate on any thing *in the world*, taking it as its provisional point of univocal reference. So there is a sort of univocal transparency in voice— it is able to focus on a given object and take its univocity as its own point of reference and in a way *becomes* joined with that object. In this way, the polar dynamics of univocity reiterates itself for any given univocal point of reference in grammar.

Conclusion

In concluding this meditative exploration, therefore, we have found that all meaning in natural language is conditioned by the presence of voice/grammar. We further found that the presumed univocity of meaning (literal meaning) traces directly to the presumed univocity of voice of thinker/speaker. But our experiment found that within the literalist mentality no real univocity of voice can be achieved. Instead, we found that the presence of voice in natural language always turns out to be inherently equivocal, multi-vocal and inherently indeterminate. The voice-field that conditions all natural language is found to be lodged in primordial indeterminacy *if* we begin from the postulate of literalism. And of course this discovery of the indeterminacy of voice is devastating for the literalist faith since it implies that all meaning in natural language would be infected with original indeterminacy of sense/reference. In recent discussions in logical theory we have become more used to the possibility of radical indeterminacy of meaning in ordinary discourse. For example, in Quine's discussions of radical translation we are now familiar with the idea of ontological indeterminacy of the referent. Our meditative experiment has followed the lead of Nagarjuna and expands this limited indeterminancy of Quine's to its full form in the radical indeterminacy of voice (speaker/thinker). But with Nagarjuna we find that this pervasive indeterminacy in natural language is really a radical critique of the literalist mentality with its deep compulsion to reify self, voice, mind, meaning, discourse and world. Our meditative critique has shown that it is the reifying mentality that is reduced to absurdity and incoherence, and cannot adequately account for the workings of meaning in natural language. And this clarified result brings us to the horizon of a more powerful hypothesis that has been explored in earlier chapters.

We have suggested that the vital univocity condition for natural language and natural reason cannot be achieved in the egological paradigm of naive dualistic identity. Instead, we find that it is the holistic principle of Universal Relativity that truly accounts for unities and relationalities that make everyday discourse and common sense work. But we have seen that once the prejudices of the literalist paradigm are set aside the way is opened to see that all natural language and natural reason lives and thrives on metaphoric meaning. And Universal Relativity, the logic of natural language, discloses the true holistic nature and power of metaphoric meaning. It is in the meditative voice which is ever present to everyday language and natural reason that the full force of metaphoric meaning is released.

POSTSCRIPT

UNIVERSAL GRAMMAR, NATURAL REASON
AND
RELIGIOUS DISCOURSE

PREFACE

The Paradigm of Universal Grammar

Religious life is the recognition, articulation and celebration of the Infinite Word. And there is no discourse or form of life that is not already constitutively situated in the Space of this Infinite Word and ever under its Presiding Presence and Jurisdiction. This means of course that all the diverse attempts in the evolution of global history to approach, approximate and express the Absolute Word are all essentially encompassed within the universal scope and expressive power of its hermeneutical force. The very Idea of the Infinite, Absolute Word implies a Universal Grammar that surrounds and situates all possible grammatical modes or hermeneutical forms of life. And this is not only a result of the hermeneutical experiments of history, but also a constitutive requirement inherent in the idea of Universal Grammar itself.

No matter how variant, divergent and apparently incommensurable the diverse cultural forms of life that have emerged in the evolution of history may be, they are nevertheless essentially situated in the scope of Universal Grammar— the Grammar of the Infinite Word. So the Infinite Word and

its Hermeneutic of Universal Grammar must be the presiding Paradigm—
the Paradigm of Paradigms— in all hermeneutical life. Whatever Meaning
or Truth may be found in any grammatical form, it must be traceable to
the Presence of Universal Grammar and the forces of its logic or
Hermeneutic. In this respect, all proposed models, paradigms, criteria of
religious or inter-religious life are situated in the space of Universal
Grammar and under the influence of its universal paradigmatic life. Thus,
the Infinite Word and its Universal Grammar, its Logic and Hermeneutic,
is the Universal Paradigm of paradigms, the Living Form of all forms of
life.

There is no getting around the Infinite Presence and Jurisdiction of the
Infinite Word. For in its self revelation it shows its Infinite logical and
grammatical powers to be all pervasive and universal in scope. This Power
is expressed in its infinitely Unitive force which extends in all directions
and constitutively situates all possible forms of life. So infinitely rich is
this Universal Logic that it both situates and overflows all historical
experiments in hermeneutical or cultural praxis. For this reason, the wide
variations in hermeneutical forms that have emerged in global history are
already situated in the Common Ground of the History of the Word and
inherently, one way or another, to varying degrees of adequacy, express
this Universal Logos.

Those hermeneutical forms which speak of a transcendent divine being, a
Personal God, when rightly situated in Universal grammar, are expressions
of the Infinite Word. Those hermeneutical experiments which disclose that
the Word is infinitely empty and beyond name and form likewise proceed
under the sway of its Universal Grammar and to varying degrees express
its Truth. Similarly, the most skeptical or nihilistic denial or alleged
disproof that there is anything "absolutely first", any "infinite word" or
"absolute grammar" is constitutively ill-formed and self-deconstructive of
its own voice, and begs all the fundamental issues. For it is the Infinite
Word that constitutes and makes all thought, discourse, reason, and
hermeneutical praxis possible. There can be no hermeneutical activity,
narrative, or form of life that is not constitutive confirmation of the
Presence of Universal Grammar.

The Logos or Logic of the Infinite Word presides over our deepest conduct
of mind and prescribes our hermeneutical praxis. The very Infinition of
Logos reveals itself and constrains our thought to conform to its Unitive
Force which can encompass the most widely variant narrative forms of
life. For it is this Infinite Unitive Force of Logos that makes all diversity,
differentiations, plurality, opposition and apparent incommensurability
possible. The depth of this Infinite Unity when rigorously and coherently

thought, reveals a more potent logic that at once constitutes and overflows any historical narrative form that has emerged in global history. This Unitive Force of Universal Grammar implies a Universal Domain or Unified Field which is the extension and intension of the Word. And this is the Primal Space-Time of Reality which informs and encompasses all possible narrative forms of life.

As the Universal Common Ground of all hermeneutical forms the Paradigm of Universal Grammar is the generative principle of all narrative forms and places them in co-constitutive mutuality. It is the ground of discourse between worlds, the origin of dialogue and ongoing mutual revision and growth. No narrative form, no matter how divergent, diverse, or deviant can stand outside the relational space of Universal Grammar. All hermeneutical forms of life are constitutively in a co-relationality that opens an horizon for ongoing evolution, expansion, self-revision in the dialogical space of the Word.

As the Origin of all forms of life the Principle of Universal Grammar must be a Living Principle— the Principle of Life itself. And as the Infinite Living Center of all life forms this First Principle can never be reduced to any narrative content, ideology, doctrine, categories, names or forms. In this way Universal Grammar is Living Form which, while always being to some degree of adequacy expressed in historical grammars and cultural narratives, is nevertheless irreducible to any predicative content and is deconstructive of any fixity of meaning. And of course this means that any historical narrative, to the degree that it is faithful in expressing the Infinition of Living Form, the Living Word, must rise to that higher Logic wherein the essence of what is expressed is never any inert content but the Form of Life itself. And so the Hermeneutic of Logos is such that the Meaning of what is expressed may never be reduced to any fixated predicative content nor severed from the living voice that expresses it.

Accordingly, a powerful hermeneutical inversion or transvaluation takes place when any evolving historical narrative tradition explicitly situates its discourse in the space of Universal Grammar. To the degree that its grounding in the Unitive Field of the Living Word has been eclipsed or suppressed by its own "historical" self understanding, it undergoes significant self revision and amendment when more explicitly situated in the presiding History and Evolution of Logos. For there is always constitutive Alterity between a given self-understanding of a narrative form of life and the corrective Hermeneutic of the Living Tradition of Logos. This means that any narrative expression of the Word is under ongoing self-expansion, self-revision and transvaluation in the Presence of Universal Grammar. This is another way of understanding how the Living

Infinite Word at once constitutes the particularity of any narrative form, but also overflows its bounds, stands ever higher and constitutively Other and perpetually calls for its self-revision and hermeneutical openness.

Furthermore, the Infinite Living Presence of the Universal Word is so infinitely rich in its Unitive Force that it expresses itself in irreducible *Alterity*. We have suggested that this Unitive Power of Universal Grammar is the very origin of differentiation, multiplicity, plurality and radical diversity of narrative forms of life. And far from competing with or being threatened by plurality and even opposition, this Primal Unitivity spawns and encourages irreducible plurality of forms of life as *evidence* of its depth and power. Indeed, this is its very Infinition— the power to embrace radically diverse narrative forms of life in its Relational and Dialogical Form. And so the Paradigm of Universal Grammar would insist on the irreducible Alterity of narratives of the Infinite Word which speaks of a Personal Transcendent God, and those which gesture to an Ultimate Reality which is non-personal, non-transcendent, radically empty of name and form, etc. Nevertheless, in this irreducible Alterity of the Universal Word, the Living Principle, manifests itself in a profound Univocity.

In this context it is important to see that the Life of the Universal Word in *not* "transcendent" in the sense that it is some distant, "neutral" "trans-historical" Absolute which is beyond the ongoing historicity and particularity and plurality of the forms of life that constitutes the human conversation. Rather, the Infinite Unitive Field expresses its Life in the ongoing conversational inter-play of living grammars and forms of life. We humans are always situated in some modality of grammar, in some form of life and hermeneutical praxis which in turn is situated in Universal Grammar. We have no "independent" or "neutral" non-perspective in which to access "Universal Grammar in itself" apart from the evolution of grammar in the human conversation. It is in the very inter-play of living grammatical forms that the Infinite Word is self-revealed. So there is and always has been a Living Presiding Historical Tradition of Universal Grammar— the Divine Creative Process of the Living Infinite Word which, though always in process, is nevertheless always fulfilled and accomplished. This Universal History and Unitive Perspective of Universal Grammar makes itself manifest in all forms of life, in all cultural forms, in all hermeneutical activity. So it may be said that the Noumenality of the Word reveals itself in the Phenomenal play and inter-play of grammar. In this way the Infinite Presence of Universal Grammar places all historically situated grammatical life under ongoing constitutive self-revision, self-critique, self-expansion, and self-alterity.

The Paradigm of Universal Grammar as the Hermeneutic of the Infinite Word is the Living Form of the community of forms of life and hence must be a living hermeneutical praxis. This Infinition of the Living Word is the very conversational or dialogical space that both situates and perpetually amends all historical grammatical forms. For this reason the hermeneutic of Universal Grammar calls for a *living* hermeneutical praxis that is self-reflexive and self-critical and self-transformative in its deepest conduct of mind. In this respect Universal Grammar is a heurestic with normative and regulative powers which governs our hermeneutical activity. And this gives us the clue to Truth and Integrity in the right conduct of mind— the disposition to be ever open to deeper instruction in the presence of the Infinite Word, to resist the tendencies to reductive objectification of meaning in our hermeneutical activity, to recognize that Meaning and Truth can never be fixated and reduced to any "finite" objectified interpretation or predicative content. For any attempt to capture, reduce or fixate Truth, to nail down meaning in reducing it to some predicative content is another form of crucifixion of the Living Word which becomes deconstructed and resurrected in the Living Hermeneutic of Universal Grammar. Thus, Truth is the very process of self-revision, the virtue of open ongoing inquiry in the Alterity of dialogical praxis, for this is the life pulse of the Living Word. And it is through this ethic in the life of the mind, in our hermeneutical conduct, that we enter into deeper unitivity and communion with the Infinite Word.

When grammatical traditions or forms of life conceive themselves as arising in relative isolation and independence from the Living History of Universal Grammar, certain misconceptions and distortions in self-understanding inevitably result. But when it is recognized that the Living Presence of the Infinite Word has always been presiding in the grammatical life of any cultural form, a new horizon opens within its very center. As long as we look to objectifiable meaning or predicative content as the essence of what a grammatical form of life expresses, we will inevitably see deep incommensurability between diverse grammatical narratives. Thus, in attempting to get at the essence of the teaching of Jesus, if his Meaning is objectified in predicative content, it appears to be incommensurable with the teaching of the Buddha. When we look to predicative content and objectifiable meaning this tends to abstract and sever significance from the Living Presence of the Teacher, from his or her living grammatical performance in the Space of Universal Grammar. But when the living speech-acts and performative life-acts of a teaching are rightly situated in the living historicity of Universal Grammar new possibilities reveal themselves.

When, for example, Jesus says "I am the way, the truth and the life", this living utterance of the Living Word cannot be severed from the Living Presence whence it is spoken. The living performative force of this utterance, like the Cartesian "I am, I exist", must be rendered in its First Person living voice. In this context the utterance of Jesus is a living performance of the Universal Law which is made manifest in his living presence, and this is one enactment of Universal Grammar. Similarly, when we enter into the teaching of Buddha, and resist, as he himself instructs , the fixation or reduction of his meaning to any dogma, ideology or predicative content, we find another powerful enactment of the Universal Law or Dharma which can not be severed from the living voice whence it is spoken. Thus, when placed in the context of the historical tradition of Universal Grammar we discover deeper affinities which this living dialogical space opens up. And this is a key to discerning Truth in alternative grammatical enactments of Universal Grammar.

In a sense, then, everything depends on our hermeneutical starting point and our hermeneutical conduct. If we begin with a hermeneutical faith which posits a pluralism of worlds or universes of discourse individually constituted beyond the Presiding Jurisdiction of Universal Grammar, the living center of a given grammatical form of life may be severed from its roots in the living history of the Infinite Word, and its grounding in Universal Grammar may be severed. Such a hermeneutical praxis may itself create barriers in the dialogical process of discerning deeper affinities and Common Ground that are already found to obtain when situated in the origins of Universal Grammar. For the Common Ground is not any predicative content, but the form of life, the conduct of mind, the living praxis of open dialogical conduct which signals *how* one stands in grammar.

In this connection, the inevitability and virtue of there being irreducibly diverse narrative forms of life is precisely the ongoing challenge and reminder that the Infinite Word in its Infinite Unitivity can never be reduced or captured in any one narrative performance. But it is also the challenge to be open to see that despite irreducibly diverse narrative content, the form of life in being open to the Infinite Presence is nevertheless expressive of the same Univocal Universal Law in the conduct of mind. It is here that the most radical "non-dual" narrative of the Absolute as being beyond all predication and content, and the speech-acts of a Jesus can exhibit the same Universal Law and be genuinely expressive of Universal Grammar. This is the criterion of Truth in diverse religious forms of life, and indeed of diverse forms of grammatical praxis. It is the form of life which is performative of the Living Word that is well-formed, true to Form, and expresses Truth. Veracity in hermeneutical conduct is a function of the spirit in which the grammatical form is lived and performed; and the conduct of mind which remains ever open to the Living ever deepening Presence of the Infinite Word, authentically expresses and honors in fidelity the Universal Law. In this context the teaching of Buddha can help to deepen the understanding of the teaching of Jesus, for example, and the teaching of Jesus, in its unique historicity, can deepen the self-understanding of Buddha's teaching. And of course the community of teachings in the context of Universal Grammar remain mutually open to ever deeper performative readings in the Light of the Infinite Word.

Universal Grammar, then, is not *another* grammar among the plurality of grammars, but focuses on the *conduct* of our grammatical life. What one expresses in a grammatical form of life— its Meaning and Truth— is always constitutively a function of the hermeneutical conduct of mind in which the grammar is lived. It may be considered a Universal Hermeneutical Law issuing from the Living Presence of the Infinite Word, a Moral Law governing our conduct of mind. We suggest that this is a Law which has been formulated, reiterated, and verified in diverse ways in the rich array of grammatical experiments that have emerged in the history of Universal Grammar. It is an infinitely deep Universal Law which, in its Univocity, remains open to ever deeper formulations and enactments in our ongoing corporate dialogical life. Indeed, the direction of Truth in our hermeneutical conduct is measured by the Unitive and Univocal Force of the Infinite Word which is performatively enacted in the enterprise of Universal Grammar.

Of course this opens the case as to what is to count as a genuinely religious form of life, both within the more conventional ways of parsing "sacred" and "secular" praxis. For if religious life is measured in relation to the Infinite Word, the Absolute, Ultimate Reality, then it is *prima facie* open as to what is to count as genuinely religious or sacred. Presumably, any and every aspect of our hermeneutical or grammatical praxis may be conducted in a truly religious or sacred mode, be it common sense, daily life, political or moral practice, scientific or artistic conduct, etc. Indeed, the presiding presence of the Infinite Word governs all aspects of our hermeneutical existence and in this respect every moment of our being is under its jurisdiction. Thus, a scientist, in an open and genuinely experimental conduct of grammatical life, in a living dialogical relation with the Word in its disclosure as Nature, may be genuinely religious. Similarly, a creative Artist, in her genuinely open and creative expression and celebration of some mode of Grammar may live a truly sacred life, and so on.

In this respect it becomes apparent that religious discourse must be constitutively inter-religious in its ultimate concerns as it comes to terms with the profound alterity of grammatical disclosures of the Infinite Word. And our very enterprise of dialogical inquiry into the appropriate paradigms and criteria of inter-religious discourse is itself a religious inquiry which continues the living tradition of Universal Grammar. What is needed at this time is the performative articulation of a more potent paradigm of Universal Grammar and a deeper understanding of its Natural Reason. Such a paradigm would have to move us closer to discerning the dialogical common ground between the most extreme and apparently incommensurable narrative forms of life regarding What is First. And it is increasingly evident that such a Paradigm would have to recognize that there is a primordial alterity at the heart of Natural Reason which invites the mutually irreducible flourishing of divergent narrative forms of life which nevertheless remain faithful to the Infinite Word. In the following essay we attempt to further open this exploration.

PROLOGUE

Perhaps the deepest lesson of global history is that we humans are situated and implicated in the space of Unity. This is the presiding truth of our existential condition, the most obvious, simplest and clearest, but also the most difficult to see. For our existence is so immediately and thoroughly implicated in the forces of Unity which condition our life in every way, and in every moment, that our very act of seeing and thinking can eclipse our unitivity and alienate us from our very Selves.

Our Unitive condition extends in every direction and pervades every conceivable aspect of existence. It makes it possible to exist, to be a living human being, to be a Self. It makes it possible to be in a living space, a world, a context, an environment. It makes it possible to be in relation, to have relationality with Self, and others, to have an inner and outer space, to be in space and time, to be conscious, to think, to experience, to feel. The Unitive space and force we inhabit and which inhabits us, makes it possible to participate in relationality and thus makes identity and difference possible. This primordial relationality makes it possible to be in a polis, a shared public space of co-existence, wherein intercourse, discourse, communion and disunion can transpire. This original political and ecological condition of human life is the source of sense, shared meaning, common life, common sense, human reason. And so it may be said that the very possibility of being in discourse, in having a perspective, in inhabiting a world, in sharing in language, common sense, meaning, in being rational, arises from our Unitive condition.

In this way, every moment of existence, every pulse of life, experience, thought, discourse, already confirms the presiding presence of our Unitivity. Our very capacity to think at all, of any topic whatsoever, already confesses the primordial Unitive condition that is implicit in all thought. All thinking, all forms of life, all forms of discourse, whatever the topic or subject matter, is evidence of the presence and workings of the force of Unity. For this reason, any and every narrative is directly expressive of Unity and participates in meaning and truth to the degree that it is faithful to the presiding forces of Unity.

In this respect the very texture of existence, of nature, of life and experience, of thought and language, of discourse and reason, of common sense and action, are all originally implicated in one another and thus constitutes an unbroken primitive Unitive Field. So powerful is this Unitive Force Field that no concept, name, being or thing can exist beyond its sphere of influence. Indeed, this pervasive Unitive condition makes difference, diversity, plurality, opposition and strife possible. And the most radical denial or rejection of the rule and Law of Unity can only have the effect of affirming and confirming Unitivity.

Global history has taught us that there is a deep drive in the human condition, in cultural life, to achieve liberation and fulfillment or self realization. This relentless and perennial quest has taken many forms and has been expressed with such diversity and variety that it is difficult, if not impossible to discern any consensus or common ground. In the varieties of religious forms of life we see a certain gravitation towards an ultimate concern with an Absolute, Infinite Divine Presence. But the diversity of approaches to what is Absolutely First appears so varied, even opposed, that no consensus is evident. Certain religious forms of expression focus on an alleged Divine Infinite Being; while other approaches to What is first, denies that there is any "Being" at all and opts to speak in a different voice.

Again, in the vast array of philosophical narratives, we find a deep quest for the ground of meaning and truth; philosophical and religious investigations reveal such a diversity of options and opinion that there appears to be not only a lack of consensus or common ground, but even a glaring incommensurability amongst philosophical narratives and religious forms of life. This is true not only within a given "philosophical tradition" but perhaps even more so between diverse traditions in the context of global discourse. And this trend toward irreducible variety of narratives concerning What is First (The Absolute, Being, Existence, the human condition, Discourse, Meaning, Truth, Value, etc.) is evident within and between human cultures in general. So it appears that we are left with a plurality of human narratives about the human condition, about what is truly meaningful, and meaningfully true, about what is possible for us humans, about the deepest issues of self realization, liberation, and human fulfillment. However, the very question of our human condition, and of the alleged common ground of What is First has been controversial, and continues to be more controversial today than ever before.

There is a certain orientation to the conduct of mind that centers itself in the space of discourse, indeed, creates and constructs a certain space, in which the self is taken to be an entity of a certain sort amongst others. From this orientation and perspective, the environment is determined as a world of entities, objects, events, facts— a world or universe which encompasses and surrounds the individuated self. In this orientation of mind and thought, any approach to What is First, or any alleged Absolute Being or Principle of Universal Form or Law, Divine Being, is taken to stand in some transcendent relation to the thinking self, and this space both separating and holding together self and the Absolute, is the space which organizes and orders the world. This space between self and Not-self, is the space of reality or existence which is the world. When mind and discourse are oriented in this way it has been found over and over in philosophical and religious experiments over the centuries that What is First, The Unitive Condition, is constitutively breached and all attempts to think Universal Law in this context only eclipses What is First and proceeds in an alienation that leads to deep pathologies in the conduct of life.

Certain diverse traditions have seen through this dis-orientation of mind and thought in different ways and strategies have been developed to reorient life in alternative ways that overcome the pathological condition and finds more authentic ways to encounter and live in the presence of What is First. Thus, in the global context, traditions in eastern and western thought have designated the orientation of mind just described as ego-centric, egological— centered around and structured by the presence of the individuated self, taking itself to be an entity in the world. Such an orientation is committed to a faith in the identity of things, including itself. It proceeds with the presumption that it is an object or entity or being of a certain sort, situated in a world of specified and individuated objects, events, facts, things with determinate characteristics.

In this way the faith in identity structures the self, thinker, mind, thought, experience and the general environment or world that surrounds the self. In this practice of identity-thinking, whatever exists is some kind of being or entity, and this applies even to any alleged First Being or Absolute Unity, Universal Law or Presiding First Principle. All thinking proceeds in the space of identity-practice, hence takes on the form of things with identity. And if this ego-centric practice of identity names the ultimate Universal Being or What is First— Logos— the Absolute Word— then the logical space or universe of discourse of this ego-self may be said to be "logo-centric": for its universe is organized and ordered in the presence of this Absolutely presiding First Being which is the existential condition or ground and cause of all that exists, including of course the ego-self. So all the Universe exists in the presence of this Absolute Logos, and the ego-self too exists and "revolves" around this Absolute Center of the Universe.

So this Presiding Logos-principle is present to all things, and the ego-self lives in the presence of this logos. It becomes apparent that the so-called logo-centric orientation is a direct expression of the faith in identity-practice and a direct result of this conduct of mind. We begin to see a certain mutual equivalence between the ego-centric, the logo-centric and the conduct of life which is a faith in identity, and it makes all the difference how we critique and deal with this ego-centric orientation to life. Certain meditative traditions have developed strategies to diagnose the ego-centric condition and practice and to separate and distance intelligence from this orientation, and go through a profound reorientation in the conduct of mind and experience. What typically happens in such strategies is that the entire ego-centric structure of discourse and space of thought is dismantled, dissolved, deconstructed, surrendered, in order for a very different orientation of mind to emerge.

Typically, in these meditative strategies, it is found that the ego-centric condition is the very source of human alienation, suffering and pathologies. And so the overcoming of this dis-orientation of mind which is due to illusion and ignorance, is found to be essential in true self realization, liberation, achievement of knowledge and right conduct and rational health. These transformative narratives typically suggest that both the Self and the Absolute are violated and eclipsed in the egological conduct of mind and life. It is stressed in these traditions, that the true Self cannot be objectified, is not an entity and cannot be processed in the artificial space of ego-centric mind. Equally vital is that the Absolute, What is First, cannot be objectified, and cannot be processed in egological mind. Meditative traditions develop alternative forms of conducting mind and thought as more suitable for approaching What is First— and hence for the conduct of life and for human fulfillment.

But other approaches than "meditative" practices have likewise seen that everyday conventional understanding is lodged in ignorance and alienation, and have developed tools and strategies for overcoming the state of ego ignorance and logo-centric thought, to conduct a life in which self violation and violation of Logos is overcome.

The crucial issue seems to be whether thought proceeds in the ways of Identity and ego-logical practice, or whether this alleged pathological conduct of mind can be truly and authentically overcome.

One alternative to the ego-logical orientation which proceeds with its habits of objectification, subjectification, and patterns of individuating entities, itself included is to proceed with a radical re-orientation to the space of experience: in this re-orientation is found that nothing can stand apart or exist independently with separable identity. In this re-orientation, it is found that all things are primitively co-related, co-existential and in co-identity. This orientation to the conduct of mind recognizes that all existence— the environment of the universe— must be in immediate co-relationality, and that all things, all being, events, facts, concepts, somehow so implicate one another as to be in a deep continuum of co-existence. This vision of a unitive field of inter-relationality of things, which implies a continuum where no breaches of duality can obtain, may be called the orientation of *Relativity (Relationality)*. Here it may be said that all things are in immediate relationality, and to inquire into the identity of any thing inherently opens it up to relationality with all else in its environment. In this way the naive objectification of egological practice is avoided, and human thought and experience itself proceeds in a form of thinking which is itself implicated in the unitive relational order of things.

In this orientation of Relativity, which is a practice and conduct of mind and experience, What is First, cannot be objectified or distanced, and so the logo-centric malpractice of ego-logical mind, is avoided. The polarities and dualism that are spawned in ego-centric and logo-centric practice cannot arise in the space of Relativity. And so it is found that there is a viable alternative to logocentric thought that can still countenance Absolute Logos, and proceed in immediate relationality with Logos. The practice of Relativity teaches that Original Unity or the Absolute or Universal Law, cannot be objectified or distanced, but must be immediately encountered and lived in the practice of Relativity. And so this opens up an alternative form of life and conduct to the egological orientation.

One troubling problem that has persisted through the centuries, and is alive in contemporary discourse, is the failure to see that between these two basic orientations and practices of mind, all the terms, concepts, names, of one form of life are dramatically and systematically transformed in the other orientation. Thus, Fact, Identity, Thing, etc. take on a new meaning when we move from the egological practice of identity to the unitive practice of

Relativity. The problem is that certain critiques of the egological are captured by the forces of Identity and identify the primary terms associated with Logos, with the egological or logo-centric: and so the terms Logos, Absolute, Foundation, Law, Truth Form, Reason, etc., are taken to be the offspring of the logo-centric hence produced and belonging to the logo-centric domain. In this way these important terms, vital of course for the conduct of Relativity, are rejected as intrinsically contaminated with logo-centric pathology.

We see this danger in certain forms of contemporary thought which are called "post-modern discourse". Here a common theme is to see that logo-centrism is wrongful and must be overcome. And post-modern practice attempts to develop powerful tools of critique and deconstruction of the artificial constructions of logo-centric mind. But if all we have is the space of Identity, then this can lead to a pernicious rejection of Reason, Law, Truth, Principle, Logos. And this can be devastating to the best interests of the Human Condition.

We suggest that this would be a fatal mistake. For it would attempt within the space of Identity to deny, eclipse and reject Logos, Reason, What is First, Law, Truth, which of course makes its discourse possible in the first place. The mistake is in not seeing that there is an alternative conduct of mind to the logo-centric orientation, namely the orientation of Relativity. Thus, the post-modern temperament would immediately balk at and reject any discourse of Logos, Reason, Law, Form, as being inherently tainted with logo-centrism. And so the crucial challenge is to see from the start that the orientation called logo-centric is not the only choice in the conduct of mind, and that its talk of "logos" and "rationality" and "truth" and "law" must not be *identified* with the discourse of identity. We must leave open the possibility for alternative orientations in the conduct of mind, especially in the light of centuries of deep and tested enduring traditions which have rejected logo-centric habits of mind and continue to countenance Absolute Law, Logos, first Principle and What is first, without falling into objectification and pernicious dualism.

The present postscript focuses on such an alternative. We shall here attempt to develop the orientation of Relativity and demonstrate that human reason essentially works on the principle of Relativity, that there is Universal Reason in the human condition. Approaching what is First in the discourse of Relativity discloses Universal Grammar and common ground between human narratives. We suggest in this exploration that the Presence of Original Logos does preside over all existence, and that in our open rational inquiry we are directly led to the recognition of a profound primordial Continuum or Unitive Field in which all human thought and life is directly implicated.

We invite the reader to attempt to suspend any habits and prejudices of logo-centric practice, and experiment with us in the discourse of Relativity to see whether and how this approach to What is First, and to Reason and experience would unfold. We will try to show that the orientation and practice of Relativity will open the way to Universal Grammar and support, confirm and fulfill the highest and best objectives and aspirations of diverse traditions which have emerged in global discourse.

Let us begin with reflection on the Absolute, the Universal Original Word, and let us provisionally and experimentally pronounce this Infinite Word: *Logos*. In this experimental opening we situate our inquiry with the Greek origins of philosophical discourse and recognize that the term "Logos" has a certain situated history and particularity, and is laden with connotations. But this is good, and can and will work to our advantage in our present exploration into What is First. For as our reflections unfold it will become clearer that the apparent contingencies associated with the candidacy of Logos for the Universal Word shall expand into universal import when situated in the discourse of Relativity. And so it shall become apparent that we can begin with the Universal Word in its ever open universal power only in the very passage and process of our inquiry into its deeper resolution. For it is in the praxis of inquiry that the ever expanding universal beginning can be realized.

This Universal Absolute Word, Logos, expresses itself in a most potent logic which commands our thought and directs our inquiry. For as the Absolute it comes First in every possible sense, is Universal and all encompassing, and is the central presiding reality in the universe of discourse. In this way we see that the Absolute is limitless and infinite in its presence, scope, jurisdiction and power. Thus, as we reflect on What is First it discloses itself as Absolute and opens itself up to our reflection and expands our reflection under its power. We see that our very presence and power to reflect directly originates in this presiding Power. We see at once that all possible names, forms, things, phenomena must directly arise out of this Absolute Center. And so the inner Logic of Logos shows immediately that the Absolute is the space of discourse itself, the space and time of existence, the locus and scene of history and process. Wherever we glance we see a reflection and expression of this Universal Presence in whose presence these reflections are situated and proceeding. And so we see this Presence that opens up space-time for all possible names and forms, for all existence and phenomena, for all events and processes, discloses itself in a powerful series and continuum of Original Names.

The Absolute is First, The Universal Origin, Original Source. As such it is Universal and Unitive. It is Universal because of its infinite scope and jurisdiction, and Unitive because as the Universal Origin of all possible names, forms, things, it is a Unifying Field and Principle placing all things in a domain of order with direction and orientation. This Presence immediately discloses itself as Absolute Unity, but for this very reason, it is the power of diversity, plurality and differentiation: all differentiation is the expression of the infinite Unitive force itself, explicating itself, expressing itself in the very Space-Time that it opens up. So Space and Time are immediately given Original names together with Universal, Unity, Difference, Power, Presence. And as the Origin of all Names, Words, Language, Thought, Discourse, it is the Original Word. As Original Word it is the full power of Speech, Thought, Expression, Articulation in all the Language Art-forms. And in this Absolute power of the Original Word it is Universal Form, Essence, Meaning and Truth: Universal Grammar.

This reveals that all life and thought and consciousness come from and expresses Absolute Presence, so it is the highest form of Universal Life, the Living Word. As such this Word, as Absolute Living Truth is absolute Consciousness, Intelligence, Pure Thought and Universal Reason. All possible forms and states of mind arise from this Origin, which is the power of all discourse. Equally, all of Nature, all phenomena, are a direct expression of the Absolute Word— the entire unfolding Universal Field of all Existence is the direct Extension and Expression of this Presence. So it becomes apparent that the universal range of all existence is the immediate discourse and self expression of the Absolute.

Thus far, our opening reflection instantaneously and spontaneously opens up into a universal deployment of the revelatory power of the Absolute: we see there is not a name, form, category, word, idea, phenomenon or field that we can turn to or think that is not immediately implicated in Absolute Presence. This shows that the Absolute is Infinite Unity and expresses Unitive Powers in self deployment into the Universal Field of Reality. We are constrained by the Logic of Logos to discern Reality, which situates our own presence and reflections, as an Absolutely Unitive Universal Field wherein all that is given is immediately implicated. We may call this Existential Field of Logos— the *Universal Continuum*. This Continuum of Logos is the Unified Field of Reality, and this is the Universal Domain or Context which situates all possible discourse and phenomena— Universal Grammar.

This is the Field of inter-relationality and co-implicature. It is apparent that nothing in this Logos Field can constitute itself apart from Logos and that all possible names and things are directly co-implicated existentially in the space-time of Logos. And so it becomes clear that the Unitive Force of Logos expresses itself as *Universal Relationality*— all things are in mutual relationality within the Unitive Power of the Continuum. This means that the meaning, identity, being of any thing is precisely its situated locus within this Relational Field: all things are thus governed by the Logos Power of Unity or Relationality: and we shall call this the *Law of Relativity*. Here we see a face of Logos as Universal Law, and this is the Law governing all existence, nature, life, thought, discourse. It should be possible to explicate this Law of Logos to show how all possible phenomena proceed under the Universal Law of Unitivity or Relativity.

Logos is Universal Law; this is another face of the Continuum of Reality, which is the Self Expression of Logos— Universal Grammar. By virtue of this Continuum of Logos we see that all original Names form a co-implicated Continuum, and thus to focus on any one primitive Name or Form immediately co-implicates its peers in a communion or community of names and forms.

Logos as Universal Law is at once the Law of Nature, the Moral Law, the Law of Thought and Hermeneutical Praxis. In the Hermeneutic of Logos religious life is expressed in every aspect of human existence— in our common sense daily life, in our artistic expression, in our scientific inquiry, in our economic and political praxis, and of course in our more formalized religious praxis. The Law of Logos governs all aspects of the conduct of mind that issues in human experience. And here we find the Universal Principle that univocates the diverse expressions of law in the human condition. This Law of Reason equally presides over our scientific, moral, religious and philosophical forms of life. Thus, when the conduct of mind conforms to Law the essence of religious life is shown in daily common sense, in scientific inquiry, in "religious" expression.

Let us focus our attention, then, on the further articulation of Universal Grammar or Natural Reason.

IMPLICATIONS OF UNIVERSAL GRAMMAR FOR INTER-RELIGIOUS DISCOURSE

The Paradigm of Universal Grammar poses a transcendental challenge for inter-religious discourse. It suggests that the first order of business is to come to terms with the preliminary question of how inter-religious discourse is possible: are there diverse religious worlds or are the diverse narrative forms of life that we call "religions" *already* mutually constitutive and expressive of a Univocal Principle?; if there is a plurality of religious forms or worlds does this mean that they are independently constituted and thus a pluralism of forms, or is the diversity or plurality itself *evidence* of a Universal and Univocal Principle?; if there is a pluralism of religious worlds then how is Univocity, relationality, comparative judgments, common ground between such forms possible? etc.

In this context, these issues become the essence of the matter and everything turns on assumptions, presumptions, presuppositions about original Univocity or Equivocity in inter-religious discourse. If we *posit* some "transcendent" univocal common ground between religious worlds or forms of life, then this calls for intense critical scrutiny— on what grounds is *any* Univocity postulated to hold between diverse religious narratives? If we *posit* a pluralism of religious worlds, forms, narratives, then how is this pluralism or "diversity" to be established? If we make comparative judgments of identity or difference between religious worlds, then how are these to be grounded or accounted for? If we are not to beg fundamental issues, we must at the outset come to terms with the question of the hermeneutical praxis we *begin* with in inter-religious discourse, for everything turns on our conduct of mind— our interpretation, judgment, grammatical conduct. If we speak, for example, of there being some "Transcendent Reality" or Ultimate Absolute, which all religious forms of life "refer or respond to" then on what grounds is such a postulate presented? Is this to be taken as self evident? Is it a transcendental condition of inter-religious discourse? If so, why should we or must we accept such a bold hypothesis?

The Paradigm of Universal Grammar attempts to confront these issues at the start and suggests that inherent in discourse itself, wherever we may be situated in thinking, interpretation, experience, there must be a Universal Principle or Unitive Form which makes thinking work. Irrespective of the "content" of the thinking, any thinking itself already presupposes Unitivity as its absolute condition. And so an Absolute condition is found already in the heart of thinking which when rigorously and consistently thought opens up a Unitive logic which is found to be constitutive of thought. This Unitive Principle commands a certain conduct of mind and discloses a profound Universal Logic which governs all possible thinking. It is in this context that Universal Grammar opens up the Logic of the Infinite Word, Universal Form, Absolute Principle, Ultimate Reality. And it is here that there is a "transcendental deduction" of Absolute Unity, Univocity, Common Ground and original relationality between diverse forms of life. Thus, the praxis of Universal Grammar attempts to elucidate and disclose the Absolute Presence of Original Infinite Unitivity and not simply assume, posit, stipulate or postulate "Absolute or Ultimate Reality."

This method of Universal Grammar— which attempts to give a meditative or transcendental disclosure of What is First or Absolute— makes all the difference in the world. For it inexorably enters into the space of the Universal Logos or Logic of the Absolute Principle which is found to preside in all possible discourse. And the Universal Logic of Infinite Unitivity that reveals itself is found to regulate and govern our hermeneutical activity and options. In this respect this Logic of the Infinite Word prescribes certain universal conditions of discourse and hence for inter-religious discourse. And here it is found that any narrative, model or proposed criteria are initially open and subject to interpretation and elucidation in the Hermeneutic of the Universal Word. Thus, if we speak of a "transcendent Absolute Reality," the very meaning of "transcendent" cannot be cashed out as we choose, as for example, in a dualistic logic that makes it some distant or independent field, but must play out in a sense that is consistent with the Principle of Unitivity itself. Again, if we posit a plurality of religious forms of life, the very meaning of this "plurality" is under the immediate hermeneutical force of Universal Grammar and cannot be assumed to indicate some "atomic" form of pluralism that is in breach of the Law of Unity and Diversity, and so on.

More specifically, the Hermeneutic of Universal Grammar suggests certain generic features which would be constitutive of any religious form of life, and thus discloses certain conditions for a "global" interpretation of religions. Here are some main implications of Universal Grammar for religious life:

1)   If *any* religion is True, then Universal Grammar is immediately implied. For any opening to sacred truth is an opening to Universal Law or the Infinite Word or Divine Form or Presence and this entails Universal Grammar.

2)   Sacred Truth, whether this is expressed in the form of a Divine Being or Infinite Form or some other Ultimate Expression or Absolute Silence, is constitutively an opening to the Infinite which plays out into some version of the Universal or Absolute First Principle having universal infinite jurisdiction. In this respect Sacred Form is Holistic and cannot be rendered partial or limited in any way.

3)   We have proposed the name *Logos* as this Absolute, Infinite, Universal First Principle or Law which is the name for Universal Grammar. Logos is the Absolute and Infinite Universal Name or Form or Word or Living Presence which constitutively presides in all possible forms of life, all possible worlds, all possible forms of discourse or narratives or fields.

4)   Logos, as the Absolute Infinite Name-Form-Law is absolutely Universal and has absolute scope and jurisdiction over all reality and existence. For this Reason, Logos is the presiding First Cause, Origin, Foundation,and Moving principle for all that exists or may exist. Logos is the Origin and Genetic Principle for all possible forms of life, for all religious or cultural worlds.

5)   Accordingly, Logos is the Infinitely Universal Principle hence Infinitely Unitive in its Power and Scope. As such Logos is the Unifying Point of Reference for all existence— for all names and forms, for all events and things, for all language, experience, cultural forms of life. Indeed, Logos is the infinitely Unifying and Unified Force or Field of Reality itself in which all things co-exist and co-arise. Universal Grammar is the Universal Domain or Unified Field of Reality which existentially incorporates all that exists.

6)   And of course it follows that Logos or Universal Grammar as Infinitely Unitive— as the Universal Law or Form or Force of Unity— must be non-dual in every way and hence cannot be objectified or distanced as an *object* of thought.   This means that all intelligence, reason, consciousness, life, thought must immediately arise in and from Logos— in the Living existential unified field of inter-relationality. Thus, Universal Law or Universal Grammar is the Living Unitive Field or inter-relationality and co-arising— the living infinite process of Historical Evolution, the Universal History of the Infinite Word.

7)   Logos is the Universal and Univocal Reality for all possible worlds or forms of life. There is no culture, field, discipline, religion, ideology that is not made possible by Universal Grammar so Logos is the Universal Field of all fields— the inter-cultural, inter-religious, inter-disciplinary and inter-personal Common Ground. As such the Field of Universal Grammar is the Common Reality for all possible worlds— the Universal Historical Process or Evolution in all cultural worlds, in all texts, narratives, scriptures, fields of inquiry and research, etc.

This means that all religious narratives, scriptures, teachings, forms of life are alternative renderings of Logos or Universal Law. For example, the life of Moses, the life of Jesus, the Life of Buddha are all alternative renderings of the Universal Life of Logos— the Living Universal Law or Word.

Similarly, all historical cultures, all ideologies, philosophies, religions, sciences, are renderings of the Infinite Process of the Living Word. So a science, such as physics or biology, in its attempt to interpret and represent

Reality under the name of Nature or Life Process is constitutively an attempt to express the Universal Field under some name, rubric, category, conceptual framework and so on.

Thus, it is not only alternative religions that constitutively have Logos as their central reference, presiding concern, universal topos, and common ground, but all other cultural forms like the arts and sciences. This is inherent in the nature of Universal Grammar.

8)   Logos, as the Living Unified Field of Reality is the creative, dynamic process of Universal History— the creative Evolution of Universal Form or Law. And as the Law of Relativity, holding all things in constitutive inter-relationality— it is neither "transcendent" nor "immanent": Logos cannot be rendered as a "transcendent Being" beyond Space-Time and Historical Process, nor can it be reduced to the local particularities— local cultural practices or hermeneutical activities of particular life worlds as they experimentally evolve and self-transform. Rather, the Universal Principle of Relativity is inherently Dialogical, Dialectical and involves Otherness and Alterity and Differentiation in its creative play or Self-evolution.

This means that the Universal History or Evolution of Logos or Universal Law is the universal context of interpretation for all cultural forms of life and for all processes of Nature. There is no Natural or Cultural event that is not essentially situated in the domain of Universal Grammar and the Presiding Story of the Evolution of Universal Law.

In this context it is apparent that all human experience, all life-worlds essentially involve interpretation and are renderings or narratives of the dynamic Historical Process of Logos. So all cultural praxis may be seen as experimental conjectures or hermeneutical hypotheses of "Reality," hence always provisional, open to ever deeper self-development, self-revision, in its Dialogical encounter with Logos.

This is why it is a grave mistake to reduce or identify the Living Infinite Creative Dialogical Process of Reality with any "human cultural interpretation" in its local historical contingency. Rather, any human narrative or shared tradition of interpretation, from the Point of View of the Living History of Logos, is always a better or worse hypothesis playing a dramatic part in the ongoing incarnation and formulation of Universal Law, and hence always perpetually open to ever deeper Dialogical self-revision in the higher inter-play of alternative narrative forms of Life.

It is in this respect that the Universal Historical Dialectic of the Living Word remains ever higher and transcendentally Other to the more localized contingent histories of cultural religious traditions. But at the same time this Universal Dialectic of Universal Law is immanent in the dialogical interplay of diverse forms of life and constituted in the creative interrelations of ongoing formulations of Law in the evolution of Nature and Culture. And it is when a cultural form of life rises in critical self-awareness to the praxis of the Universal Grammar that it moves in unison with this creative process of Truth.

9)   Logos, the Creative Expression and Evolution of Universal Law is the Universal and Univocal Reality for all cultural forms. As the Universal Unitive Domain of Universal Grammar this Unitive and Unifying Field is the Universal expression of all possible worlds— the common ground or foundation of all worlds. So all cultural forms of life are readings or conjectures or grammatical hypotheses of this Universal Domain. Diverse cultural traditions, diverse religious forms of life, diverse sciences are all alternative renderings of this Universal Common World. And this means that there are universal concepts, phenomena, facts for diverse renderings of the World. For example, there are common universal and univocal concepts and phenomena for diverse religious narratives: sin, death, law, ethics, justice, love, salvation, liberation, sacrifice, prayer, communion, worship, violence, peace, meeting, and of course being human, the self or person.

10)   Logos, as Infinitive Unitive Form is the Universal Form of all formulations of law. We have suggested that all cultural forms of life are expressions of Law and this means that all "local" formulations— the laws of thought or reason, the laws of language or discourse, the laws of nature— physics, biology, psychology, sociology, economics, etc.— the laws of ethics, and of course religious laws are all variations on the Universal proto-type or paradigm of all law. In this respect the formulations of laws in the sciences (human and natural) are systematically connected with formulations of laws in moral, political and religious life. Universal Grammar brings out these constitutive relations between formulations of law.

11)   In any form of life what is all important is how that life-form stands in Grammar, in the Universal Historical Process of the formulation of Law. We have suggested that every life, every form of life, is constitutively or existentially situated in the Unified Field and its quality of life is a function of how it negotiates the Law.

And here it is apparent that it is the conduct of mind— the manner and mode in which discourse is conducted— that is decisive in measuring the authenticity and truth of a life. For it is not in any alleged "content" or "doctrine" or "propositional beliefs" that the truth of a life is measured, but by the manner and method in which one conducts his voice, mind, thinking, discourse, reason, and all aspects of hermeneutical life. Indeed, we have suggested that the Meaning and Value of any "content" is a function of the conduct of mind and discourse— the hermeneutical conduct of grammar. And of course there is no form of life that is not the direct expression of some hermeneutical faith, some praxis of mind.

12) This is what is all decisive in determining what is to count as *religious life*— every form of life, since it is an expression of a hermeneutical faith and praxis of mind that shapes its world, meaning, values and grammar, is in some religious mode, is a religious form of life. So in the generic context of Universal Grammar— all hermeneutical life expresses some faith which governs its conduct of mind, its hermeneutical life and is a religious mode. This means that the scientist, in choosing to conduct his or her mind in a certain ultimate commitment is making a religious choice; the so-called "secular life" is directly a faith expression— a religious commitment in the conduct of mind and life, and so on. There is no getting around being in some religious mode or faith or ultimate grammatical commitment in the conduct of mind.

13) The crucial question thus becomes, what is to count as Good religious faith or True religious praxis— in the conduct of mind and discourse. And the Paradigm of Universal Grammar suggests that it is the form of life, form of mind, that conforms to Law that is right, and good and true and preferable, and the form of life that is in breach of Universal Law that is ill-formed, inauthentic, inadequate or wrongful. How a form of life stands in its grammatical conduct— in Universal Grammar— is all important in determining whether it is a well-formed life. It is in the right conduct of mind that all hermeneutical forms are well conducted, be it worship, scientific inquiry, political praxis, artistic expression or moral life. The Universal Law as a direct living expression of Logos Presence is a Universal Ethics that governs all forms of life focused in the right conduct of mind.

14) Logos as the Universal Domain of all Reality incorporates all forms of life under its jurisdiction. For the Unified Field is the existential Continuum and in all that exists co-arises in mutual determination. This Universal Continuum teaches that there is a decisive difference between Good and evil, Truth and falsity, Right conduct of mind and mal praxis of mind. But it also entails that there must be a Continuum between Good and

evil, Truth and falsity, and other polar opposites. For evil and falsity arise in the field of Universal Grammar and essentially trade on the workings of Universal Law even while in direct breach of this Law. Indeed, this is the signature of evil, falsity, and all forms of mal praxis of mind— that it is internally incoherent, existentially self-divisive, self-contradictory and self-destructive. The evil conduct of mind is in a direct denial of the very Law which makes it possible; the mal-praxis of mind is divided against itself in being grounded in the Universal Law which it nevertheless directly denies or rejects in its form of life. Even ill-formed language or discourse shares in Grammar and must be "well-formed" to some degree to be ill-formed or bad grammar. This is why all evil acts, while constitutively breaking the Law thereby confirms and in some ways conforms to Law.

15)   Still, there is a clear and objective difference in the conduct of mind between thinking and hermeneutical conduct that conforms to and advances Unitivity and the Historical Dialectic of Universal Law, and conduct of mind that opposes, eclipses, denies, fixates, objectifies and reduces the Living Evolution of Law. In all such cases there is breach in self-unity, self-coherence and existential integrity; in all forms of falsity or evil the opposite of Unity, Dialogical Due Process, Living Form is expressed— strife, incoherence, incommensurability, violence, irrationality, ignorance, self-destruction, fragmentation, death. The difference between Good and evil is clear: any conduct of mind which conforms to Law and affirms and advances Unitivity and Dialogical Alterity is Good, and any act of mind which while trading on Law nevertheless produces the opposite of Unity and violates Alterity in itself and others is evil.

16)   It is because of this very difference *and* Continuum common ground between Good and evil, Truth and falsity that there is always the possibility of existential transformations such as conversion, awakening, salvation, liberation, dialogue, communication, growth, experimental self revision and development, etc. It is the presence of the Universal Law that makes possible comparative judgments, evaluations, interpretations between cultural worlds or diverse religions or disciplinary forms. Universal Grammar is the objective universal standard in virtue of which a given culture may be judged to be better or worse in its own self-evolution, or that one cultural form of life may be judged to be better or more preferable to another form. A form of Life, in its conduct of mind that more effectively conforms to Law is preferable to one that is in breach of Law. Alternatively, diverse forms of life, as in diverse religious worlds, may be judged to be equally adequate formulations of Universal Law— each offering creative openings for the authentic expression and growth in the Law. For example, the formulation of the Law in the life of Jesus (as one exemplar of the Living Word) may be judged authentic and truthful,

just as the formulation of the Law in the teachings of Buddha (as another exemplar of the Living Dharma) may be found to be authentic and truthful according to the Universal Standard and Criterion of Universal Grammar.

17)   The Unified Field of Logos is the Living Process of Dialogue in the ongoing living performance of Law.   Reality itself is constitutively dialogical in structure and all names and forms, all signs and things have this universal dialogical structure of the Life Form.   This is revealed in the fact that Absolute and Infinite Unity (the living form of Logos) expresses itself in Diversity, Difference, Multiplicity— in Alterity.   All that exists constitutively co-arise in the dialogical inter-play of the Unified Field of relationality: This is the Universal Law of Relativity.   And this original Alterity implies the dynamic living Historical or Evolutionary process which is the drama and creative evolution of Law.   In this context all forms of life are originally constituted in this Alterity— they inherently co-arise in alter-forms, in their significant Others.   Thus, a given religious form of life or tradition, can never be taken "in itself" as "self-existent" apart from its ongoing dialogical interactions with Other forms of life, for example other religions to which it is existentially bound.   Again, the very Self is constitutively dialogical and has this structure of Unitive Alterity— it is inherently bound in the Other— in other lives, in the culture, in the polis, in the universe of discourse, in the Historical Evolution of Law.

18)   Universal Grammar, as the topos or living field in which the conversational or dialogical evolution of Law is played out entails that all forms of life are inherently under dynamic ongoing review, critical self revision and revision by History.   Indeed, since the essential factor in authentic religious life is not any fixated "conceptual content" or "doctrine" or "propositional beliefs" but rather the praxis of mind in conformity to Law, it is apparent that it is the Open Dialogical Mind that is the universal signature of the authentic religious way of Life.   Here we see that the truthful religious life— conformity to Universal Law— is the open self-critical and ongoing dialogical process in the ever deeper formulation and expression of Law.   And of course this ever deepening dialectic of self revision in living dialogue with the Other, with Logos, is the very form of Life itself.

19)   The Dialogical Nature of Logos holds all forms of life in constitutive relationality or co-arising.   This Unified Field of creative evolution of the Infinite Word implies a Continuum in which diverse religious lives, teachings, scriptures, traditions of interpretation, are inherently in dialogical co-arising.   Here it is important to see that the Life, Teachings, Revelations of Universal Law in the life of Jesus or Buddha, for example, are always infinitely deep— as deep as Universal Law itself— and can

never be fixated or reduced to any final historically contingent tradition of interpretation. The Historical Jesus— the Universal Christ Voice and enactment of Law— can never be fixated or finally captured in any "historical narrative" or tradition of interpretation of an ego-logical historicity. The same may be said for the revelations of Law in the life of Moses or Buddha and so on. It is well known in a certain tradition of Buddhist praxis that the living presence of the Buddha-teachings— the Dharma for the right conduct of mind— can never be fixated in any content, objectified formulations or fixated narrative. Rather, authentic formulations of Law— as Living Form— call for ongoing first-person performative enactments in the creative Historical dialogue of the Law. And it is the Continuum of Alterity between and amongst the religions that makes it possible for the Christ Voice to have universal jurisdiction for all religious worlds, or for the Buddha Field to be the Universal existential field for all beings. Thus, in the Dialogical space of Universal Grammar the Buddha-Christ Voice Field reveals itself as a Universal Office of Logos.

20)   In this Living Continuum of Universal Grammar the Universal Scripture plays out. Here we find the common ground and universal source of all Scriptures and religious forms of life. This Universal Drama of the Dialogical Evolution of Law is the Ground of all religious worlds, the topos and telos of all Scriptures and religious performances. And it is not surprising to see that diverse scriptures and religious revelations and teaching have a common Universal Origin and telos: the transformative, performative and liberative enactment of Law in the conduct of voice, life, mind, discourse.

There may be no "religion in general", but each religious form of life constitutively expresses the Absolute, Universal law, and so "generality" or "global features" are already constitutive of Religious Life.

A "global interpretation" of religions is not a meta-narrative that generalizes from the diversity of religious narratives. Rather, Universal Grammar is the constitutive Universal or "global" hermeneutic that is *already* alive and presiding at the heart of diverse religious worlds.

All religious meaning conforms to the Universal Law of Unitivity, hence has living import, metaphoric or symbolic meaning, and so all intentional content or predicative utterances are constitutively subject to the Semantic Field of Universal Grammar.

The deepest particularity and specificity and intentional content of a religious world or narrative form *already expresses* the "global semantic" of Universal Grammar. Thus, the Universal Word or Absolute Principle is already constitutive of religious particularity and historicity, and not alien and foreign and external to it.

Diverse religious forms of life, as narrative or grammatical forms, *express* Universal Grammar and do not have to *refer* beyond themselves and their living narrative practice to some external "transcendent reality". Rather, a religious form of life formulates, articulates, shows, performs and expresses the Absolute Form or Ultimate Reality in its inner narrative life. This is what makes it a religious form of life.

Thus, Universal Grammar as the living expression of Universal Law is the articulation of Natural Reason, Universal Ethics and Religious Life.

Revisioning Philosophy

The series seeks innovative and explorative thought in the foundation, aim, and objectives of philosophy. Preference will be given to approaches to world philosophy and to the repositioning of traditional viewpoints. New understandings of knowledge and being in the history of philosophy will be considered. Works may take the form of monographs, collected essays, and translations which demonstrate the imaginative flair of examining foundational questions.

The series editor is:

David Appelbaum
Department of Philosophy
The College at New Paltz
New Paltz, NY 12561